THE CHURCHES SPEAK ON:

Pornography

Sources for Additional Research

For further information on the religious groups covered in this publication, consult J. Gordon Melton's *Encyclopedia of American Religions,* which contains information on approximately 1,600 churches, sects, cults, temples, societies, missions, and other North American religious organizations.

For additional information on the beliefs held by the religious groups covered in this publication consult the *Encyclopedia of American Religions: Religious Creeds,* a companion volume to the *Encyclopedia of American Religions,* which provides the creeds, confessions, statements of faith, and articles of religion of the groups covered.

To locate organizations concerned with the topics covered in this publication, consult the following terms in the Name and Keyword Index to Gale's *Encyclopedia of Associations:*

- Censorship

- Civil Rights and Liberties

- Communications

- Decency

- Obscenity

- Pornographic

- Pornography

- Women

ISSN 1043-9609

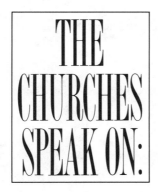

THE CHURCHES SPEAK ON:

Pornography

Official Statements from Religious Bodies and Ecumenical Organizations

J. Gordon Melton
Gary L. Ward, Contributing Editor

Gale Research Inc.

DETROIT • NEW YORK • FORT LAUDERDALE • LONDON

J. Gordon Melton

Gary L. Ward, *Contributing Editor*

Amy Lucas and Bradley J. Morgan, *Project Coordinators*

Aided by:
Susan L. Dessner, Julia C. Furtaw, Jeanne A. Gough, Frances C. Locher,
Archana Maheshwari, Annette Novallo,
Christine Tomassini, and Gwen E. Turecki

Donald G. Dillaman, *Programming Consultant*

Mary Beth Trimper, *Production Manager*
Marilyn Jackman, *External Production Assistant*

Arthur Chartow, *Art Director*
Cynthia D. Baldwin and Bernadette Gornie, *Graphic Designers*
C. J. Jonik, *Keyliner*

Laura Bryant, *Production Supervisor*
Louise Gagné, *Internal Production Associate*
Kelly Krust and Sharana Wier, *Internal Production Assistants*

Copyright © 1989 by Gale Research Inc.
835 Penobscot Bldg.
Detroit, MI 48226-4094

ISBN 0-8103-7221-5
ISSN 1043-9609

Printed in the United States of America

Contents

Statements

Roman Catholic Church

Statements in this section are arranged chronologically by issuing date.

Protestant and Eastern Orthodox Churches

This section is arranged alphabetically by individual church, religious
body, or ecumenical organization; the statements issued by each organization are presented chronologically within that organization.

Jewish Groups

This section is arranged alphabetically by individual religious organization; the statements issued by each organization are arranged chronologically within that organization.

Other Religious Bodies

This section is arranged alphabetically by individual church, religious body, or ecumenical organization; the statements issued by each organization are presented chronologically within that organization.

Preface

The Churches Speak is a quarterly series of monographs which systematically brings together the major official pronouncements of North American religious bodies and ecumenical organizations on the issues dominating today's headlines. Each monograph is devoted to a single topic and provides an overview of the topic itself, its historical background, and the full range of opinions found in the individual church statements. The statements themselves provide a unique and conveniently arranged survey of opinion on important contemporary issues, cutting across theological and denominational boundaries to influence the climate of social and political thought in our culture.

The formal statements issued by churches and other religious bodies are intended primarily to inform and guide their members, adherents, and supporters on the issue in question. These statements often attain additional importance, however, since they also exert influence on the actions of the religious agencies, clergy, and church administrators who initiate, direct, and regulate organizational programs. Church statements are also indirectly aimed at nonchurch members in an attempt to alter public policy, mobilize public opinion, or advocate changes in legislation. And they can also become the focal point of intense controversy, functioning as the bulwark against which many people direct their dissent on a given issue. This controversy can become magnified within the issuing organization itself when a significant minority of its members dissent from the positions taken by its hierarchies, judicatories, and boards of social concerns.

Focus is on Contemporary Topics From Major Religious Bodies

Each issue of *The Churches Speak* focuses on a single topic or a few closely related topics chosen for their high current public interest. Topics covered represent a wide range of vital social and political issues, such as AIDS, abortion, racism, the Middle East, euthanasia, capital punishment, and the ordination of women. Statements of major North American churches and religious organizations are included for each topic, providing comprehensive representation of the full range of opinions held on each topic.

The documents included in *The Churches Speak* were obtained through a mailing to all of the religious bodies in North America with more than 100,000 members. On any given issue, additional churches and religious organizations (including some outside of North America), and even some secular organizations known to have a special interest in the topic under consideration, were also solicited for their statements. Other statements have been identified in the files of the Institute for the Study of American Religion in Santa Barbara, California.

While most large churches and religious bodies make formal statements on important issues, it should be noted that many of the more than 1,500 denominations and religious organizations located in North America will not formulate any official statement or speak out on such issues. A number of religious bodies, including some of the largest denominations, do not make such statements as a matter of principle. Rather, they choose to leave actions and beliefs concerning social issues strictly up to individual effort and opinion.

Authentic Texts Used for All Statements

The statements presented in this series are in their authentic form, although obvious typographical errors have been corrected. The original wording, grammar, and punctuation of each statement remains intact. No attempt has been made to introduce foreign material or explanatory notes into the body of the statement's text.

Arrangement and Content

Each issue of *The Churches Speak* begins with an introductory essay which provides an overview of the topic itself and traces its recent historical manifestations. This essay also summarizes, compares, and contrasts the opinions found in the individual statements, allowing the user to place each one in the appropriate context. Each essay concludes with bibliographic citations to sources for further reading on the topic.

The statements presented in each monograph are arranged into four main sections based on broad religious families or traditions: The Roman Catholic Church (which represents the single largest religious body in the United States); Protestant and Eastern Orthodox Churches; Jewish Groups; and Other Religious Bodies.

Within the Roman Catholic Church section, statements are arranged chronologically by issuing date. The remaining sections are subarranged alphabetically by individual churches, religious bodies, or ecumenical organizations; the statements issued by each organization are presented chronologically within that organization.

Each of the four religious family sections is preceded by a note which provides background information on the family and analysis of its perspective on the issue in question. Individual statements contain the following elements:

Issuing organization. The name of the religious body or ecumenical organization issuing the statement.

Statement name. The actual or formal title of the statement. When no formal title is given, a descriptive title has been assigned.

Text of statement. The text of the statement is presented in its original form.

Notes. These appear in italic type following the text of each statement. When applicable, these remarks provide background information on the issuing organization's membership size and geographic distribution, and details about the circumstances under which the statement was made—including when it was passed, why it was passed, and whether or not it is binding on church members.

Index to Organizations, Statements, and Subjects Provided

To facilitate access to the material presented, each issue of *The Churches Speak* contains an Index to Organizations, Statements, and Subjects included in that issue. The index lists, in a single alphabetical sequence, the full titles of all the statements, the names of all religious bodies and ecumenical organizations mentioned in the statements' texts and notes, specifically named individuals, and specific subjects covered within the statements. Statement titles and organization names are also listed by important keywords that appear in their titles/names. Citations in the index refer to page numbers; page numbers rendered in boldface after an organization name indicate the location of that organization's statement(s) within the main text.

Sources of Additional Information

Additional information on many of the religious bodies covered in *The Churches Speak* can be found in the *Encyclopedia of American Religions*. The *Encyclopedia* provides details on approximately 1600 religious and spiritual groups in the United

States and Canada, and is divided into two parts. The first part contains an essay covering the development of American religion, an essay providing a historical survey of religion in Canada, and historical essays grouped by general religious family. The second part contains directory sections listing individual churches and groups constituting the religious families discussed in the historical essays.

A companion volume, the *Encyclopedia of American Religions: Religious Creeds,* provides a comprehensive compilation of 464 religious creeds, confessions, statements of faith, summaries of belief, and articles of religion currently acknowledged by many of the churches or religious groups described in the *Encyclopedia of American Religions.* It also includes extensive notes on the history and textual variations of creeds, reflecting changing social, political, and doctrinal climates throughout the centuries. The material is arranged by major religious families, following, with minor variations, the approach used in the *Encyclopedia.*

Institute for the Study of American Religion

The Institute for the Study of American Religion was founded in 1969 for the purpose of researching and disseminating information about the numerous religious groups in the United States. More recently, the Institute's scope has been expanded to include religious groups in Canada, making it the only research facility of its kind to cover so broad a range of activity. After being located for many years in Evanston, Illinois, the Institute moved to Santa Barbara, California, in 1985. At that time, its collection of more than 25,000 books and its extensive files covering individual religious groups were donated to the Special Collections department of the library of the University of California—Santa Barbara. *The Churches Speak* has been compiled in part from the Institute's collection.

Suggestions Are Welcome

Users with particular questions about a religious group, suggested topics for coverage in or changes to *The Churches Speak,* or other information are invited to write to the Institute in care of its Director:

> Dr. J. Gordon Melton
> Institute for the Study of American Religion
> Box 90709
> Santa Barbara, CA 93190-0709

Introductory Essay:

A Survey of the Pornography Issue
by Gary L. Ward

Introduction

Americans are troubled by pornography. A poll for *Time* magazine reported on July 21, 1986, that almost two-thirds of the respondents were "very" or "fairly concerned" about the pervasiveness of pornography in the United States. Sixty-five percent of those polled believed that it led people to be more sexually promiscuous and 61 percent believed that it encouraged people to consider women as sex objects.[1] Pornography is, however, no longer something hidden in dark alleys or confined to "undesirable" or "shady" people. In the general American population, 85 percent of men and 70 percent of women report some experience with sexually explicit materials.[2] These figures also indicate that it is not the exclusively male domain commonly pictured. A 1985 Gallup poll found that of people aged 18-20 who bought or rented X-rated videocassettes, males outdistanced females by only five percentage points.[3] It is unknown to what degree women obtain the cassettes for their own enjoyment or merely at the request of a man. It is also unknown how many of those who report misgivings about pornography nevertheless enjoy it themselves. Even among those who agree that at least some kinds of pornography are harmful, there is great disagreement on how to identify that harm, how to isolate the harmful aspects, and how to regulate it. This essay examines some of the ways in which the issue of pornography has occupied the energies of courts, police, politicians, sociologists, feminists, and, of course, the religious communities.

Definition

Part of the problem with pornography is that there is no universally accepted, authoritative definition of the term. *Webster's New Universal Unabridged Dictionary* offers this definition: "1. originally, a description of prostitutes and their trade. 2. writings, pictures, etc. intended to arouse sexual desire. 3. the production of such writings, pictures, etc."[4] But this definition is too vague to be useful in court cases on pornography, where "intention" to produce pornography is difficult to prove. Advertisers often intentionally use sexual desire to sell their product, yet this is rarely termed pornography. Even as culturally acceptable a product as *Reader's Digest,* with headlines such as "Five Sex Secrets Men Wish Wives Knew" (February 1986), clearly uses sexual attraction as a selling point. Is *Reader's Digest* pornographic? Jon Huer, author of *Art, Beauty and Pornography*, suggests that this kind of cultural context means that "anyone who ever attempts to exorcise or isolate pornography from the community is overwhelmed by ambiguous definitions and the ubiquity of this cultural phenomenon."[5] Noting that a definition of pornography needs to be sensitive enough to exclude both the explicit sexual depictions of a medical book and the sensual paintings of a Renoir, Huer asserts that a full definition of pornography includes 1) a sexual subject; 2) the intent to arouse prurient interest; 3) mass production; and 4) for the purpose of profit.[6] This still could be broad enough to include the use of sex to sell a product, but that may serve to substantiate Huer's point about the conflict between the amoral marketplace and moral social relationships.

Other definitions of pornography typically are more pejorative, indicating that pornography does more than just arouse sexual desire, but arouses it in a manner contrary to acceptable social standards. Thus pornography becomes connected to the term "obscene," which is synonymous with words like "repulsive," "offensive," "filthy," etc. David Copp, in *Pornography and Censorship,* believes that pornography should be considered as a subcategory of obscene. Whereas a portrayal of violence may be obscene without being sexual, pornography is both obscene (offensive) and specifically sexual in content.[7] The courts have produced definitions as well. A landmark definition was offered by the Supreme Court in the 1957 case of *Roth v. United States,* in which pornography was deemed to have three characteristics: 1) the dominant theme appeals to prurient interest; 2) it is offensive in affronting contemporary community standards; and 3) it is utterly without redeeming social value.[8] This definition, of course, raises further questions about how one determines the "contemporary community standards" and what is of "redeeming social value." The nature of the dilemma led Supreme Court justice Potter Stewart to remark in the *Jacobellis v. Ohio* case of 1964, "I don't know how to define it, but I know it when I see it."

Early Social Reactions

The ancient Greeks did not attempt to censor pornography and generally were not upset by it, although both Plato and Socrates mentioned concern about its effects on children.[9] The invention of the printing press elevated the concern for censorship; England had an obscenity law as early as the sixteenth century, but it was aimed not so much at sexual material as at writings or plays that attacked either the church or the state. (In fact, a common complaint was that "bawdy" books were quickly licensed, while books of a more serious nature were held up.[10]) The first attempt to prohibit pornography in the American colonies was a 1712 Massachusetts statute outlawing obscene pictures or books.[11] In England in 1727, the Edmund Curll case established obscenity as a common law crime for the first time. Curll's book, *Venus in the Cloister or the Nun in Her Smock,* was outlawed, using the new notion of "obscene libel."[12] This case coincided with a general change of taste that we now call Victorianism. Prosecutions in England were generally pursued by private parties or organizations, like the Proclamation Society for the Discouragement of Vice, begun about 1788, which was succeeded in 1802 by the Society for the Suppression of Vice. By the early 1800s, several books had been banned in both England and the United States. The first obscenity case to be tried in the United States was in 1821 over the book *Fanny Hill,* which was condemned as obscene.

The principle that later led to the condemnation of books similar to *Fanny Hill* was authoritatively formulated in the British case of *Regina v. Hicklin* (sometimes called *Queen v. Hicklin*) in 1868. In his judgment Lord Cockburn said, "I think the test of obscenity is this, whether the tendency of the matter charged as obscenity is to deprave and corrupt those whose minds are open to such immoral influences, and into whose hands a publication of this sort may fall."[13] This understanding was used in American courts until the *Ulysses* case in 1933 and was based on the idea that both youth and adults need to be protected from moral harm, which presumably would follow from exposure to explicit sexual materials. In 1821, Vermont passed the first state law against obscenity, while the first federal law was the Tariff Act of 1842, which prohibited the importation of "all indecent and obscene prints, paintings, lithographs, engravings and transparencies."[14]

In 1865, Congress banned pornography from transmission through the postal service, due to complaints about such material being sent to soldiers during the Civil War. This law was not heavily enforced, and in 1868, grocery store clerk Anthony Comstock became upset at the unchecked proliferation of pornography. Using a recent New York law on obscenity, he began his own crusade against pornography, eventually forming an alliance with the YMCA and creating the Committee for the Suppression of Vice. In 1873, this coalition successfully forced Congress to enact a tougher law against obscenity in the mails, and Comstock was appointed special agent in charge of enforcement. Its first test case, interestingly, was an 1873 ruling that upheld the conviction of two men who sent through the mails a powder intended to produce abortions.[15]

By 1900, 30 states had laws against the distribution of obscene materials. By the 1920s, the literary works of Balzac, Voltaire, Rabelais, Aristophenes, Rousseau, and others were being seized by United States Customs. This trend was halted in 1933 when the U.S. Court of Appeals considered the case of *U.S. v. One Book Called "Ulysses."* This novel by James Joyce was ruled not obscene, and that ruling established new grounds for testing obscenity. Instead of the material having to be considered corruptive of those minds "open to such immoral influences," obscenity now had to be judged by its "effect on the average person."[16] The court also ruled that the work had to be considered as a whole and not on the basis of isolated passages. For some time after this verdict, legislation tended to grow progressively more permissive. Anti-obscenity forces were temporarily discredited as a result of being, in the words of one commentator, "unable to distinguish between pornography and literature."[17]

The years since that 1933 decision have seen a large increase in the availability, visibility, and acceptability of sexually oriented material. *Playboy* magazine was first published in 1953 by Hugh Hefner, and by 1957, it had reached a circulation of nearly five million, mostly from newsstands.[18] It was the first magazine of its kind, combining nude pictures with an overall atmosphere of sophistication, making it acceptable in many middle-class and "upwardly mobile" American homes. Concern over the increasing impact of such sexual materials has led to continued examination of the government's proper role and assessment of the meaning of pornography.

Supreme Court Decisions

The first U.S. Supreme Court ruling on pornography came in the landmark case of *Roth v. United States* in 1957. Samuel Roth was a New York author and publisher who was prosecuted for selling the magazines *American Aphrodite, Photo and Body,* and *Good Times.* Justice Brennan wrote the majority opinion that cleared Roth of his conviction, finding the former *Hicklin* case formula, customarily applied in pornography cases, to be objectionable for several reasons: 1) it permitted isolated passages to be read out of context; 2) it allowed obscenity to be judged by effects on unusually susceptible persons; and 3) it presumed fixed standards of appropriateness, regardless of time, place or circumstance.[19] The Court upheld much of the *Ulysses* decision as it came from lower courts, agreeing that obscenity is not protected by the First Amendment, its effects on the "average person" had to be judged, and that the work as a whole had to be considered according to its appeal to "prurient interests." The two major additions to the obscenity test were whether the work was "without redeeming social importance," and the application of "contemporary community standards."[20]

In the 1961 case of *Manual Enterprises v. Day,* the Court added the concept of "patent offensiveness." In *Jacobellis v. Ohio* (1964), the Court ruled against the idea of local standards in favor of a national standard for obscenity. In the 1966 case of *Mishkin v. New York,* the "average person" test was modified such that "when the material in question is designed and primarily disseminated to a clearly defined group, it is to be judged by the standards of that group."[21] This did not mean a liberalization, but rather provided a means to uphold the conviction of Mishkin, who was charged with selling materials depicting such things as sadomasochistic sexual acts. These materials would repel, rather than appeal, to the prurient interests of the average person, but they did appeal to the prurient interests of the special audience to which they were directed.

Ginzburg v. United States was decided on the same day as *Mishkin* and also resulted in a conviction being upheld. Ginzburg was accused of violating the federal statute against obscenity by publishing the magazine *Eros* and the book *The Housewife's Handbook on Selective Promiscuity.* Ginzburg's lawyers argued that a mixture of literary and journalistic materials gave the matter a redeeming social importance, but Justice Brennan decided that Ginzburg's own advertising indicated that only prurient interests were involved. He also objected to the fact that such publications were "available to exploitation by those who would make a business of pandering to 'the widespread weakness for titillation by pornography.'"[22] The court thereby returned to the *Hicklin* sense of protecting the public from their weaknesses. Still another case decided on the same day as *Ginzburg* and *Mishkin* was *A Book Named "John Cleland's Memoir's of a Woman of Pleasure" v. Attorney General of Massachusetts.* The more popular name of that book is *Fanny Hill,* which had previously been banned from the United States in 1821. It was published again in the United States in 1963, and charges were immediately brought against it. The Supreme Court ruled that it was not obscene by the *Roth* case standards.

In the 1969 case of *Stanley v. Georgia* the Court decided that private possession of pornography was not a crime. On June 21, 1973, the Court decided both *Miller v. California* and *Paris Adult Theatre I v. Slaton.* In the former case the Court eliminated the attempt at a nationwide standard in favor of local community standards. This seems to allow a cosmopolitan place like New York City a more liberal guideline, but it also tends to restrict nationally distributed films and literature to the standards of less liberal communities. When Larry Flynt, publisher of *Hustler* magazine, received an order for a copy of his magazine from a town in Ohio and mailed one, he was tried for violation of Ohio obscenity laws and received a 7-25 year prison sentence.[23] The *Miller* decision also replaced the "utterly without redeeming social value" test with a standard requiring only that the work lack "serious" literary, artistic, political, or scientific value. This change was intended to allow more aggressive prosecution of pornographers.[24] Smaller jurisdictions overall, however, have been just as unable to deal consistently with obscenity as the Supreme Court, with the result that local authorities are often reluctant to take action against pornographic merchants.[25] In the *Paris Adult Theatre* case Chief Justice Burger stated that the government has a right to suppress pornography if it feels that such material tends "to injure the community as a whole."[26]

In the 1974 case of *Jenkins v. Georgia,* the Court moved away from the community standard position when it overturned a finding that the movie *Carnal Knowledge* was obscene. The court maintained that local juries did not "have unbridled discretion" to determine what was offensive. Nudity alone was deemed not to be patently offensive sexual conduct and could not be banned.[27] In the July 1982 *New York v. Ferber* case (which involved a review of Paul Ira Ferber's films), the Court handed down a unanimous decision that encouraged sweeping curbs on child pornography, an aspect of pornography that has typically provoked little opposition to attempts at repression.[28] The Court held that states could prohibit the distribution of child pornography even if the material was not otherwise legally obscene under *Miller* or *Roth* tests. The interest of the state in protecting children from sexual exploitation was deemed sufficient to overcome First Amendment interests.

Special Commissions on Pornography

There have been several influential commissions on the issue of pornography in the last 25 years. The first one in the United States was the U.S. Commission on Obscenity and Pornography (also called the Johnson Commission), which was established in 1967 and issued its final report in 1970. This report became famous for its liberal response to pornography. The commission was charged with four tasks: 1) analyze current laws and evaluate and recommend definitions of obscenity; 2) assess the volume and means of distribution of pornography; 3) study the relationship of pornography to antisocial behavior; and 4) recommend actions necessary to regulate pornography without crossing constitutional bounds.[29] It concluded that 1) no significant relationship exists between antisocial behavior and the use of pornographic materials; 2) most Americans did not favor censorship laws for adults (unless harmful effects could be proven); 3) repeal of current restrictions would not increase availability of materials; and 4) no linkage was found between pornography and the breakdown of moral attitudes.[30] Pornography was found to have some positive effects relating to education, recreation, and catharsis. Twenty-one percent of the women polled reported improved sexual relations in themselves or someone they personally knew as a result of the use of sexually explicit material. The producers of pornography were portrayed as otherwise average businessmen who made modest profits. The commission found "insufficient data" with regard to the involvement of organized crime.[31] Twelve of the 18 members recommended the repeal of all obscenity statutes, except for sales to minors. The commission noted that advisory commissions in Denmark, Israel, and the United Kingdom had arrived at similar conclusions. The report was both widely hailed as enlightened and criticized as slanted, with inadequate attention to child pornography, violent pornography, and the exploitation of women, among other things. The Senate rejected the commission report by a 60-5 vote, and President Nixon denounced its conclusions, calling them "morally bankrupt."[32]

In England, the Home Office Departmental Committee on Obscenity and Film Censorship (also called the Williams Committee) was established in 1977 as the culmination of two decades of similar, smaller working groups. Its conclusions were much the same as the Johnson Commission. In 1983 Canada established the Special Commission on Pornography and Prostitution, which made its final report in 1985 in two large volumes. It endorsed classification instead of censorship, which on the one hand seemed liberal, but on the other hand generally cast a negative view of pornography as something the law should restrict. The Canadian commission proposed increased barriers to the importation of certain materials and increasing from 16 to 18 the age at which persons could purchase such material.[33]

In 1985, President Ronald Reagan established the Attorney General's Commission on Pornography (also called the Meese Commission), which issued its final report in 1986. This commission was widely understood to be designed to counter the liberal findings of the Johnson Commission, as six of its 11 members had previously supported government action against sexually-oriented books and films.[34] The new commission noted that violent types of pornography were largely outside the circle of the old commission's inquiry, which primarily examined more innocuous styles of pornography, and that study of the two kinds of pornography might lead to two substantially different conclusions as to harmful effects.[35] The Meese Commission found that violent forms of pornography caused harmful effects and were becoming more prevalent. It paid particular attention to a study which found that exposure to nonviolent forms of pornography created an appetite for stronger, more violent forms. It recommended an expansion of existing obscenity statutes, for instance, prohibiting the transmission of obscene material by telephone and eliminating the "utterly without redeeming social value" clause still found in some state statutes.[36]

The Meese Commission was both hailed as realistic and criticized as biased, a reception similar to the one received by the Johnson Commission report. The Meese Commission was criticized, for example, for ignoring contrary sociological findings about the effects of different kinds of pornography. It was also criticized for finding that organized crime was substantially involved in pornography, even though the U.S. Federal Bureau of Investigation, presumably the most knowledgeable source, did not completely substantiate this claim.[37] One problem for the commission was the letter it sent to 23 large bookstore chains, booksellers, and convenience stores, saying that it had "received testimony that your company is involved in the sale or distribution of pornography" and that their final report would list "identified distributors." As a result of the letter, Southland Corporation, owner of the 7-Eleven chain of convenience stores, decided to remove *Playboy* and *Penthouse* from its racks. The two magazines and the American Booksellers Association filed suit, and on July 3, 1986, federal district judge John Garrett Penn ruled against the commission. He ordered the Justice Department to send another letter explaining that the original letter was not meant to imply that the publications they sold were obscene or that a blacklist would be created.[38]

Other Activists and Continuing Issues

The pornography battle is fought not only in the courts and in high-powered commissions, but also by citizens who band together for their cause or by independent researchers in educational institutions. For those who are against pornography, that subject tends to be symbolic of broader concerns centered around the problems of social change. One major study suggested that antipornography activists, compared with the majority of citizens, 1) have had a more punitive family history toward pornography; 2) more often associate pornography with various kinds of crime, psychological pathology, and communism; 3) more often perceive differences between themselves and users of pornography; 4) are overrepresented in fraternal/service, civic/political, and youth-serving voluntary organizations, and underrepresented in job-related and recreational voluntary associations; 5) are more religiously active; 6) are more often reared in smaller communities; 7) are less often employed in professional or technical occupations; 8) are less often previously married; 9) are less powerless; 10) are less normless; 11) are less alienated; and 12) are less politically tolerant. They will additionally differ from their opponents in being, among other things, 1) older; 2) less educated; 3) parents of more children; 4) less interested in politics; 5) more Republican; 6) more politically conservative; 7) more authoritarian; and 8) more inclined to traditional attitudes toward sex and the family.[39]

A major antipornography interest group that differs from the above description consists of feminists. This is one of the few issues on which feminists will side with conservatives, though the reasons tend to be different. Feminists tend not to be concerned with nudity or depictions of sex per se, but with the depersonalized depictions of women. One cannot overestimate the importance of the feminist argument in the contemporary pornography debate, as all parties involved in the debate now have to take that argument into account when formulating their own policy. The whole tenor of the debate has shifted from a focus on indecent sexual exposure to an equal concern about the depiction of women as "playthings" and as objects for sexual aggression.

Feminists, however, are not in agreement on pornography. The "hardliners" often mention the motto "porn is the theory, rape is the practice," and direct much of their energy to combat pornography. Other feminists might be too anchored in the sexual revolution to condemn anything connected with sexuality, or wonder if efforts against pornography represent a mistake similar to that made by nineteenth century feminists who went to battle against alcohol, or have a number of other hesitations about taking a hard line against pornography.[40] The hard-line group is represented by such authors as Andrea Dworkin, Catharine A. MacKinnon, and Susan Brownmiller, who define pornography basically as a specifically male vehicle for depicting the sexual subordination of women, their dehumanization as sexual objects, and/or their physical abuse in the context of sexual arousal.[41] Pornography is portrayed by them as something that reinforces women's position as second-class citizens who can be physically abused with impunity. Author Susan Griffin agrees, commenting that "the pornographer reduces a woman to a mere thing, to an entirely material object without a soul, who can only be 'loved' physically."[42]

The other feminist group is represented by such authors as Kate Ellis, Barbara O'Dair, and Abby Talmer, who argue that if pornography itself is defined as the enemy, it may serve to bolster sexual shame for women who are then afraid to be honest about their sexual desires. They suggest that pornography "carries many messages other than woman-hating: it advocates sexual adventure, sex outside of marriage, sex for no reason other than pleasure, casual sex, anonymous sex, group sex, voyeuristic sex, illegal sex, public sex."[43] Some aspects of pornography, then, are pictured as liberating for those women who want to break away from traditional sexual mores. Some women are asking how pornography (or sexually explicit erotic films and literature) might look if produced by women for an audience that would include women.

The issue of violence or other kinds of harm is obviously key to the discussion of pornography. There does seem to be some amount of organized crime involved, though it is still not clear to what extent. The possibility of wide profit margins offered by such films as *Deep Throat,* which reportedly cost $25,000 to make and brought in worldwide receipts of over $50 million, would be attractive to both organized crime and legitimate business people.[44] In 1976, two detectives from the sheriff's office in Dade County, Florida, opened a retail pornography store and found that they were then involved with organized crime contacts throughout the country. The FBI was brought in, and on February 14, 1980, the investigation, now code-named MIPORN (Miami Pornography), culminated with the indictment of 55 persons in ten states.[45]

The issue of child pornography is the least controversial aspect of pornography because it is condemned by almost all quarters as a practice that destroys proper personal development and exploits persons who do not have the means to protect themselves. The Federal Child Abuse Prevention and Treatment Act of 1974 includes provisions against obscene depiction of children for commercial purposes. The child pornographer often exploits the belonging needs of those who have a troubled family life, and it is difficult to estimate the frequency with which child pornography occurs. It has been suggested that less than 50 percent of child molestation and abuse is reported, and generally that figure does not include victims of pornography. One estimate is that approximately seven percent of the total pornographic market involves children, with between 40,000 and 120,000 children involved each year, many of them becoming involved in street prostitution. More than 260 different child pornography magazines have been identified.[46] Other estimates state that, each year, 1.2 million children under sixteen are involved in commercial sex—either prostitution or pornography or both—and that of the $2.5 billion industry, $1 billion is from "kiddy porn."[47] A more typical estimate of the total pornography industry is that of the Meese Commission, which believes it to be an approximately $8 billion dollar a year enterprise.

When it comes to other kinds of social harm, such as pornography leading men to act aggressively toward women, the evidence is more sketchy and controversial. For some, though, hard evidence is not necessary. James Kilpatrick has written: "Common sense is a better guide than laboratory experiments; and common sense tells us pornography is bound to contribute to sexual crime.... It seems ludicrous to argue 'bad' books do not promote bad behavior."[48] Social science research specifically addressing this topic is relatively new, and the differences between the Johnson and Meese commission reports illustrate the lack of consensus in the field. On the pro, or "innocuous," side, one study found that convicted sex offenders and rapists actually had less exposure to pornography than the control group. Another study found a superficial connection between sex offenses and pornography, but when social factors were mathematically controlled, that connection disappeared. Joseph Scott at Ohio State University found no relationship in each of the 50 states between rape rates and the number of adult theaters and adult bookstores. Other studies on the con, or "harmful," side, especially by Fishbach, Malamuth, and Donnerstein, have suggested that exposure to violent erotic films may encourage aggressiveness. Baron and Straus at the University of New Hampshire found a statistically significant relationship in each of the 50 states between sex magazine circulation and rape rates.[49]

One famous example that has been used by those who argue that pornography is "innocuous" is the experience of Denmark since liberalization of its pornography laws in 1967. Since that time, sex crimes have reportedly measurably decreased, thereby giving credence to the notion that pornography may act as a "safety valve" or catharsis measure for potential sex offenders, giving them an alternative to acts of violence. Others have countered that in 1967, Denmark simultaneously decriminalized many offenses, and "therefore the actual increase in rape was hidden."[50] This criticism has itself been countered by noting that rape was not decriminalized and clearly increased after the liberalized laws, but that this was due to an increased willingness to report rape, rather than to an actual increase in its occurrence. It is pointed out further that West Germany liberalized its laws in 1973, and since then, the incidence of reported rape has remained steady while other violent crimes have increased.[51] These West German figures suggest that liberal pornography laws need not lead to an increase in rape, but they also seem to discount the theory of pornography as a "safety valve," since the rape rates did not decrease.

Donnerstein, Linz, and Penrod have found that under certain conditions "there can be positive attitudinal effects from the viewing of certain sexually explicit materials."[52] Their main finding is that sexually explicit material, in itself, does not foster antisocial attitudes or behavior, but sex combined with aggression, or aggression alone, does. This is congruent with studies that have shown that rape is not primarily a sexual act, but an act of power and aggression. The negative impact of media portrayals of aggression against women, these authors say, should be of great concern to the public and to policymakers, but the bulk of the concern should not be directed toward pornography, where the amount of violence in triple-X films has remained steady or decreased. Major concern, they suggest, should instead be directed at the R-rated slasher films and the like, which have a much larger and younger audience and which have heavily increased in volume since the early 1970s. These films often explicitly connect scenes of violence against women with soft-core erotic presentations of women. Although such portrayals cannot themselves turn someone into a rapist, they could enhance already present feelings of aggression, lead persons to feel that they could "get away" with such a crime, or desensitize viewers to real victim distress.[53] Sexual aggression, they point out, is portrayed everywhere in our culture, including television. There were some well-known episodes of the daytime soap opera "General Hospital" which were devoted to the rape of one popular character by another popular character; the two characters eventually married.[54]

Religious Responses

It is not uncommon for the church to be connected, in the popular mind, with the attempt to control or suppress pornography. Purity of morals is, after all, often considered to be the particular concern of religion. For some, however, pornography would not be a problem if the church had not helped make it so. As one author put it, "The problem really began when society, in league with the church, decided that sex was one of the undesirable attributes of mankind."[55] The same author, however, notes that medieval Christianity allowed a great deal of bawdy literature, being far more concerned with doctrinal heresy, and did not take significant active steps against pornography until the Victorian era, when the church's ability to control doctrinal issues had proportionately declined.[56]

In the United States, the Catholic Church established the Legion of Decency in 1934 to review motion pictures and bring pressure to bear upon Hollywood to remove objectionable scenes or plots. Catholic pledges to the legion amounted to about seven million of the estimated total Catholic population of 20 million. Protestants also joined in pledging by the hundreds of thousands.[57] This pledge has fallen into disuse in the last 20 years, but Bishop Leroy T. Matthiesen of Amarillo, Texas, has recently called for a revival of the pledge. Protestants, Catholics, and Jews were also represented through the Department of Public Relations of the Motion Picture Producers and Distributors of America, a watchdog industry organization led by Presbyterian Will H. Hays. In 1938 the Catholic bishops established the National Office for Decent Literature to coordinate efforts to ban literature deemed threatening to the moral and social life of the nation. The list was sent to 20,000 subscribers and included books by Erskine Caldwell, John Dos Passos, William Faulkner, Ernest Hemingway, Aldous Huxley, D.H. Lawrence, John O'Hara, J.D. Salinger, and Emile Zola.[58]

In more recent times, the churches have exerted pressure to establish (or now reform) the current motion picture rating system and the prime time "family viewing" slot on television. In addition, various local church groups have often picketed adult bookstores or theaters and used their political power in an attempt to get them removed. The religious bodies are practically unanimous in their condemnation of pornography, especially child pornography. Although the Bible does not have the word "pornography" in it, there are a number of passages which are drawn upon for ammunition in the fight against pornography. Galatians 5:17-21a is a good example:

> For the desires of the flesh are against the Spirit, and the desires of the Spirit are against the flesh; for these are opposed to each other, to prevent you from doing what you would. But if you are led by the Spirit you are not under the law. Now the works of the flesh are plain: fornication, impurity, licentiousness, idolatry, sorcery, enmity, strife, jealousy, anger, selfishness, dissension, party spirit, envy, drunkenness, carousing, and the like (Revised Standard Version).

Other examples include Matthew 5:27-30, Leviticus 18:22,23, Ephesians 5:3, Romans 1:24, Exodus 20:14, and I Peter 2:2. The Old Testament book The Song of Solomon, however, is filled with erotic imagery. It provides an interesting counterpoint for those who wish to make a case for an approved eroticism and a means of appropriately reveling in "the desires of the flesh." This is one place where the conservative and liberal religious groups tend to diverge, the liberal groups being more apt to make distinctions between harmful pornography, described as violent or degrading to women, and acceptable adult eroticism, which may also be sexually explicit but which does not have the negative factors of the harmful pornography. Many conservative groups focus on hard-core or child pornography, fully aware of the nearly universal disdain the public has expressed for such material. This emphasis, however, does not mean that they are accepting of other kinds of media pornography or eroticism.

Another place where conservative and liberal approaches differ is in the understanding of the nature of that which is agreed upon as harmful pornography. Conservative churches (such as the Wesleyan Church) are likely to see pornography as primarily an issue of personal "holiness-style" morality and connect it with a general phenomenon of "lower standards" in society, standards which they think lead to teenage pregnancy, rape, breakup of families, etc. Pornography, then, is thought of as similar to other morality issues like gambling and alcoholism, which the Southern Baptists group together. The liberal approach, on the other hand, echoes the position taken by the Reformed Church in America, which believes that "if we understand it to be simply sin, perversion, decadence, filth and moral decay, then we will arrive at limited solutions. We will end up affirming human decency, sexual wholeness and ethical purity, which is all well and good—but not sufficient." Liberals tend to look for the role of societal structures and, particularly in the light of feminist critique, see pornography as an issue more related to the role of women in society than sex per se. The major study done by the Presbyterian Church (U.S.A.) sees sexism as a fundamental cause of pornography and suggests that one positive response to this is to work towards passage of the Equal Rights Amendment. This kind of linkage is foreign to most conservative churches and highlights how a common condemnation of pornography may mask very real differences in approach and perspective. Both liberal and conservative churches try to avoid heavy "repression" or "censorship" language.

These liberal/conservative approaches in Christianity are similar to the liberal/conservative split in other traditions, including Judaism. More liberal Jews, however, voice concern about pornography (especially child pornography), but are very sensitive to the issue of government censorship and thus do not give the issue of adult pornography a high priority. The Islamic approach emphasizes the sacredness of the family and the importance of modesty of dress and high-mindedness of recreation.

The Future

It is difficult to predict the degree of regulation of pornography in the future and whether the issue will rise or fall in the churches' agenda. Some degree of soft-core pornography (such as *Playboy*) seems entrenched in the culture and not likely to decrease. There does seem to be increasing consensus on the necessity for eliminating child pornography and great concern about the violent tendencies of some types of pornography. The technologies behind videocassettes and home publishing, however, are making it increasingly difficult to put effective controls in place. As long as parents are concerned about the material confronting their children, and especially insofar as the feminist critique of male/female relations maintains a presence, pornography will remain a topic of widespread concern.

Endnotes

[1] Donnerstein et al., ix.

[2] Potter, 1.

[3] Hawkins and Zimring, 55.

[4] *Webster's New Universal Unabridged Dictionary,* 2nd ed. (New York: Simon and Schuster, 1979), 1402.

[5] Huer, 11, 12.

[6] Ibid., 188-193.

[7] David Copp, "Pornography and Censorship: An Introductory Essay," in Copp and Wendall.

[8] Potter, 5.

[9] Donnerstein, 145.

[10] Potter, 2, and Barber, 23.

[11] Potter, 2.

[12] Donnerstein, 146. According to Potter (p. 3), even in the Curll case the main issue was the attack against organized religion, rather than explicit sexuality.

[13] Joel Feinberg, "Pornography and the Criminal Law," in Copp and Wendall, eds., 116.

[14] Potter, 3.

[15] Kilpatrick, 43.

[16] Potter, 4.

[17] Ibid., 4.

[18] Murphy, 84.

[19] Feinberg in Copp and Wendall, 117.

[20] Potter, 5, and Feinberg in Copp and Wendall, 120.

[21] Potter, 5, 6.

[22] Feinberg in Copp and Wendall, 127.

[23] Ibid., 130.

[24] Donnerstein, 150.

[25] Potter, 7.

[26] Donnerstein, 151.

[27] O'Brien, 60.

[28] Ibid., 62.

[29] Ibid., 57.

[30] Ibid., 58.

[31] *The Report of the Commission on Obscenity and Pornography,* 23, 47.

[32] Hawkins and Zimring, x.

[33] Lacombe.

[34] Hawkins and Zimring, x, 15.

[35] Donnerstein, 87.

[36] Ibid., 84, 172.

[37] Hawkins and Zimring, 65.

[38] Ibid., 16.

[39] Zurcher and Kirkpatrick, 318, 321.

[40] Kappeler, 35.

[41] See Dworkin, MacKinnon, and Brownmiller books.

[42] Griffin, 3.

[43] Ellis et al. in Hawkins and Zimring, 168.

[44] Potter, 8.

[45] Ibid., 21-33.

[46] O'Brien, 19, 20.

[47] Florence Rush, "Pornography: Who Is Hurt?," in Lederer, 77, 80.

[48] Donnerstein, 1.

[49] See Potter, 10, 11, for a review of these studies. See also Donnerstein, 66-69, for a discussion of the Baron, Straus, and Scott studies.

[50] Griffin, 93.

[51] Donnerstein, 61, 62.

[52] Ibid., 84.

[53] Ibid., 92, 136.

[54] Ibid., especially 91, 109, 113, 129-136, and 177.

[55] Barber, 173.

[56] Ibid., 21-32.

[57] Facey, 58-61.

[58] O'Brien, 54.

Selected Sources

Barber, D.F. *Pornography and Society.* London: Charles Skilton, Ltd., 1972.

Brownmiller, Susan. *Against Our Will: Men, Women and Rape.* New York: Simon and Schuster, 1975.

A Survey of the Pornography Issue

Copp, David and Susan Wendall, eds. *Pornography and Censorship.* Buffalo, NY: Prometheus Books, 1983.

Donnerstein, Edward, Daniel Linz, and Steven Penrod. *The Question of Pornography: Research Findings and Policy Implications.* New York: The Free Press, 1987.

Dworkin, Andrea. *Pornography: Men Possessing Women.* New York: Putnam, 1985.

Ellis, Kate, Barbara O'Dair, and Abby Talmer. *Caught Looking.* New York: Caught Looking, Inc., 1986.

Facey, Paul W. *The Legion of Decency.* New York: Arno Press, 1974.

Final Report of the Attorney General's Commission on Pornography. Rutledge Hill Press, 1986.

Griffin, Susan. *Pornography and Silence.* New York: Harper and Row, 1981.

Hawkins, Gordon and Franklin E. Zimring. *Pornography in a Free Society.* Cambridge: Cambridge University Press, 1988.

Huer, Jon. *Art, Beauty and Pornography.* Buffalo, NY: Prometheus Books, 1987.

Kappeler, Susanne. *The Pornography of Representation.* Minneapolis, MN: University of Minnesota Press, 1986.

Kilpatrick, James Jackson. *The Smut Peddlers.* New York: Avon Books, 1960.

Lacombe, Dany. *Ideology and Public Policy: The Case Against Pornography.* Toronto, ON: Garamond Press, 1988.

Lederer, Laura, ed. *Take Back the Night.* New York: William Morrow and Co., 1980.

MacKinnon, Catharine A. *Feminism Unmodified: Discourses on Life and Law.* Cambridge, MA: Harvard University Press, 1987.

Murphy, Terrence J. *Censorship: Government and Obscenity.* Baltimore, MD: Helicon Press, 1963.

O'Brien, Shirley. *Child Pornography.* Dubuque, IA: Kendall/Hunt Publishing Co., 1983.

Potter, Gary W. *The Porn Merchants.* Dubuque, IA: Kendall/Hunt Publishing Co., 1986.

The Report of the Commission on Obscenity and Pornography. New York: Random House, 1970.

Zurcher, Louis A., Jr., and R. George Kirkpatrick. *Citizens for Decency: Antipornography Crusades as Status Defense.* Austin, TX: University of Texas Press, 1976.

Pornography

Roman Catholic Church

The Roman Catholic Church, which is the largest Christian church in the world, is headquartered in Vatican City. With more than 50,000,000 members in the United States and an additional 10,000,000 in Canada, it is also the largest religious body in North America. Its tremendous size, influence, and resources have both required and enabled it to make statements offering guidance on many of the pressing issues of the world, including pornography. In the United States, the National Conference of Catholic Bishops is charged with setting official policy; it follows guidelines established by the Pope and other officials in the Vatican. Statements from other committees or from individual bishops may often serve as guidelines for discussion, even if they are not fully authoritative.

The church has a long history in the United States of activism against pornography, indicated by the 1932 Resolution on Indecent Literature. It has consistently been an opponent of media portrayals of immorality and has used both persuasive and legal means to limit such material. Unlike the issue of abortion, the church has not experienced significant internal dissension on this issue. This section also includes statements from the Canadian Conference of Catholic Bishops and the Catholic Daughters of the Americas. This latter statement indicates the attention the church is paying to the views of Catholic women on this issue.

ROMAN CATHOLIC CHURCH—U.S. CATHOLIC CONFERENCE

RESOLUTION ON INDECENT LITERATURE (1932)

Issued by the Administrative Committee of
the National Catholic Welfare Conference

1. Much has been said and written on the causes of the present depression. Undoubtedly those causes are in the main economic, but it would be blindness not to recognize the looseness and laxity of morals which both hastened the economic chaos of the world and now plays its part in extending laxity in public morals, loss of public decency, and consequently, a lowering of the standards of citizenship.

2. One of the most potent factors in this debasing of the individual and the public conscience is the increasing flood of immoral and unmoral books, periodicals, pamphlets, which are widely advertised throughout the country. Great metropolitan dailies, literary journals, carry laudatory advertisements of books that have always been known as obscene. Publishers repeatedly issue new books outdoing the old ones in obscenity. Public opinion has influenced the courts of the nation to such an extent that it is now

almost impossible to have the most obscene of books debarred from the customs or from the mails.

3. Literature has its uplifting, human mission. Wholesome, healthy reading promotes both entertainment and education. Talented men and women are today producing worthy literature, devoting themselves to it as one of the greatest of the arts. A practical guide to such literature may be found in the lists of the Cardinal Hayes Literature Committee, published in our Catholic press.

4. It is further undeniable that many writers, beggared of talent and of true literary gifts, are playing up the sexual, the sensational, and the superficial, and that these books are exploited by many reviewers as literary productions. They speak of the flesh rather than of the mind.

5. We call upon our own Catholic people, young and old, to maintain valiantly the standards of worthy, clean literature. We ask them to make it part of that crusade of Catholic Action, of which the Holy Father speaks. Catholic organizations can and should express publicly to daily newspapers, to magazines, their protest against this corrupt and corrupting reading and picture matter. Cooperation by committees of Catholic organizations with the local public library would be conducive of much good. Our people should not be misled by books written under the cloak of medical advice, instruction on matters of sex many of which are indecent beyond expression.

6. The corruption of private and public morals wears away more surely than any other agency the foundations of a nation. The publication and unobstructed distribution of indecent books and periodicals is, at the present time, one of the greatest menaces to our national well-being.

Notes: *This 1932 statement, issued by the Administrative Committee of the National Catholic Welfare Conference and presented as a pastoral letter on behalf of the U.S. Catholic Conference, lays partial blame for the Great Depression on moral laxity, a condition that was enhanced by obscene literature. It suggests a reading list of appropriate literature compiled by the church.*

ROMAN CATHOLIC CHURCH—U.S. CATHOLIC CONFERENCE

A STATEMENT ON CENSORSHIP (1957)

*A Statement Issued by the Catholic Bishops of
the United States*

1. Censorship is today a provocative and sometimes misleading word. It generates controversy by provoking those who would deny in fact any restrictions, legal or moral, upon freedom of expression. It misleads, since few approach the problems of censorship without emotion.

2. Obviously the state does have some power of censorship. In times of war or great national danger, few will deny it a preventive power. In normal circumstances, however, the state exercises only a punitive function, placing restraint on those who misuse liberty to deny equal or greater rights to others. The state's power of censorship is not unlimited.

Teacher of Morals

3. Morally, the Church can and does exercise what is called censorship. This right is hers from her office as teacher of morals and guardian of divine truth. Her decisions bind her people but her sanctions upon them are only spiritual and moral. She does, neverthe-

less, express her judgments to all men of good will, soliciting their reasoned understanding and their freely given acceptance and support.

4. Most commonly in civil affairs the particular freedom that is involved in discussions of the subject is freedom of the press, not only in newspapers and other publications, but also such dramatic expression as is represented in the theater, motion pictures, radio, and television.

5. Because in modern times the press has been a major instrument in the development of knowledge and the chief means of its diffusion, freedom of the press is closely bound up with man's right to knowledge. Man's patient plodding ascent to the heights of truth evidences the spiritual powers given him by God and at the same time their wounding by sin. His search for truth is an enriching and ennobling experience, uniquely proper to man.

6. The right to know the truth is evidently broad and sweeping. Is the right to express this knowledge, whether through speech or press, equally broad? That man has a right to communicate his ideas through the spoken or written word is beyond challenge. And yet it can be recognized at the outset that expression adds a new element to knowledge. Directed as it is to others, it is an act that has social implications. Society itself must take cognizance of it. Although man must claim and hold to freedom of expression, he must also recognize his duty to exercise it with a sense of responsibility.

7. This is a freedom that is intimately bound up with other freedoms that man prizes. Freedom of the press is patently a key safeguard of civil liberty. Democracy does not exist without it. The day free expression of opinion is extinguished and all are constrained to fall into a single pattern of political thought and action, democracy has died.

8. As indispensable as is freedom of expression to us as citizens, it is no less indispensable to the Church in carrying out her mission to preach the Gospel. The content of man's knowledge of God derived through the use of his native powers has been immeasurably enriched and perfected and has been given certainty by the revelation made by God to man through Jesus Christ. This knowledge has been attained not through man's effort, but through the goodness and mercy of God. It is accepted by an act of faith made with the help of divine grace. Of this deposit of revealed truth the Church is the divinely appointed custodian.

9. Without an unfettered means of communication, the teaching office of the Church is sorely hampered. She counts among her special blessings in our own country the important and fruitful Catholic press.

10. Because freedom of the press is a basic right to be respected and safeguarded, it must be understood and defended not as license, but as true rational freedom. The kind of uncritical claims for and defense of liberty which so often have been made in our day actually places that liberty in jeopardy. For this reason we feel that light must be thrown not only on its meaning but also on its limits.

Serve the Common Good

11. To speak of limits is to indicate that freedom of expression is not an absolute freedom. Not infrequently it is so presented. It is alleged that this freedom can suffer no curtailment or limitation without being destroyed. The traditional and sounder understanding of freedom, and specifically freedom of the press, is more temperate. It recognizes that liberty has a moral dimension. Man is true to himself as a free being when he acts in accord with the laws of right reason. As a member of society his liberty is exercised within bounds fixed by the multiple demands of social living. In the concrete this means that the common good is to be served. It will entail, among other things, a respect for the rights of others, a regard for public order, and a positive

deference to those human, moral, and social values which are our common Christian heritage. it is within this context that freedom of expression is rightly understood.

12. This recognition of limitations has been given statement in recent decisions of the Supreme Court of the United States: "We hold that obscenity is not within the area of constitutionally protected speech or press." (Roth v. United States, 77 S. Ct. 1304, Alberts v. California, 77 S. Ct. 1304—June 24, 1957.) The decisions touching on this subject are encouraging to those who have been deeply concerned over trends that threatened to destroy the traditional authority exercised by the state over expressions and displays of obscenity.

Obscenity Demands Restraint

13. Contrary to this trend, the court has held that there is such a thing as obscenity susceptible of legal determination and demanding legal restraint; that laws forbidding the circulation of obscene literature are not as such in violation of the Constitution; that the federal government may ban such publications from the mail; that a state may act against obscene literature and punish those who sell or advertise it. The decisions reasserted the traditional conviction that freedom of expression is exercised within the defined limits of law. Obscenity cannot be permitted as a proper exercise of a basic human freedom. Civil enactments as well as the moral law both indicate that the exercise of this freedom cannot be unrestrained.

14. Ideally, we could wish that no man-made legal restraints were ever necessary. Thus, restraint on any human freedom would be imposed rather by one's own reason than by external authority. In any case, restraint's best justification is that it is imposed for the sake of a greater freedom. Since, however, individuals do act in an irresponsible way and do threaten social and moral harm, society must face its responsibility and exercise its authority. The exigencies of social living demand it.

15. In his recent encyclical of September 8, 1957, Our Holy Father has spoken not only of the competence of public administrators, but also of their strict duty to exercise supervision over the more modern media of communication and entertainment—radio and television. He warns public officials that they must look on this matter not from a merely political standpoint—but also from that of public morals, the sure foundation of which rests on the natural law. What he has said applies with even greater force to the older media—the press and motion pictures—since they have been and continue to be subject to even greater abuse and supply so much of the material used in the programs presented through the more modern media. Pope Pius XII writes:

> Nor can it be asserted that this watchful care of the state's officials is an unfair limitation on the liberty of individual citizens, for it is concerned not with the private citizens as such but rather with the whole of human society with whom these arts are being shared.

16. Although civil authority has the right and duty to exercise such control over the various media of communications as is necessary to safeguard public morals, yet civil law, especially in those areas which are constitutionally protected, will define as narrowly as possible the limitations placed on freedom. The one purpose which will guide legislators in establishing necessary restraints to freedom is the securing of the general welfare through the prevention of grave and harmful abuse. Our juridical system has been dedicated from the beginning to the principle of minimal restraint. Those who may become impatient with the reluctance of the state through its laws to curb and curtail human freedom should bear in mind that this is a principle which serves to safeguard all our vital freedoms—to curb less rather than more; to hold for liberty rather than for restraint. .

4

Discretion and Prudence

17. In practice the exercise of any such curbs by the state calls for the highest discretion and prudence. This is particularly true in the area of the press. For here an unbridled power to curb and repress can make a tyrant of government, and can wrest from the people one by one their most cherished liberties.

18. Prudence will always demand, as is true under our governmental system, that the courts be in a position to protect the people against arbitrary repressive action. While they uphold the authority of government to suppress that which not only has no social value, but is actually harmful, as is the case with the obscene, the courts will be the traditional bulwark of the people's liberties.

Legislation Not Enough

19. Within the bounds essential to the preservation of a free press, human action and human expression may fall short of what is legally punishable and may still defy the moral standards of a notable number in the community. Between the legally punishable and the morally good there exists a wide gap. If we are content to accept as morally inoffensive all that is legally unpunishable, we have lowered greatly our moral standards. It must be recognized that civil legislation by itself does not constitute an adequate standard of morality.

20. An understanding of this truth together with the knowledge that offensive materials on the stage and screen and in publications have a harmful effect moved the bishops of the United States to set up agencies to work in the field—for motion pictures, the National Legion of Decency; for printed publications, the National Office for Decent Literature.

21. The function of these agencies is related in character. Each evaluates and offers the evaluation to those interested. Each seeks to enlist in a proper and lawful manner the cooperation of those who can curb the evil. Each invites the help of all people in the support of its objectives. Each endeavors through positive action to form habits of artistic taste which will move people to seek out and patronize the good. In their work they reflect the moral teaching of the Church. Neither agency exercises censorship in any true sense of the word.

22. The competence of the Church in this field comes from her divine commission as teacher of morals. Moral values are here clearly involved. Her standards of evaluation are drawn from revelation, reason, and Christian tradition and from the basic norms of the moral law. These are the standards on which our nation was founded and their preservation will be a safeguard to national integrity. A judgment of moral values in these areas is of prime importance to the whole nation.

23. Although the Church is primarily concerned with morals and not aesthetics, the two are clearly related. Art that is false to morality is not true art. While good taste cannot supply the norm for moral judgment on literature or art, yet it must be admitted that good taste will inevitably narrow the field of what is morally objectionable.

24. Who can deny that in modern American life there are many grave moral problems? This is not the judgment solely of the Catholic Church. When the Select Committee of the U.S. House of Representatives calls pornography big business, a national disgrace, and a menace to our civic welfare; when the National Council of Juvenile Court Judges attacks vicious and evil publications as a major cause of the change of juvenile delinquency from the thoughtless and mischievous acts of children into crimes of violence, armed robbery, rape, torture, and even homicide; when the New York State Joint Legislative Committee at the end of its five-year survey assures us that by actual count trash and smut on the newsstands have the advantage of numbers and that those same stands reflect an acceptance of and growing concentration on lewdness—in the face of all this we can only say that we are confronted with conditions which are fraught with peril.

Legion of Decency and NODL

25. Through the National Legion of Decency and the National Office for Decent Literature, we Catholics give public expression to our opinion on this subject. Through these agencies we voice our concern over conditions which, tolerated, merit expression of public indignation. But we assert that our activities as carried out by these organizations cannot justly be termed an attempt to exercise censorship.

26. The right to speak out in favor of good morals can hardly be challenged in a democracy such as ours. It is a long-standing tradition of this country that groups large and small have given expression of their concern over injustice: political, social, and economic. Their efforts, put forth within the framework of the law, have been directed toward dislodging evils against which the law itself is powerless. In many instances such efforts have made a valuable contribution to the community.

The Right of Children

27. It is in full accord with this tradition that the work of the Legion of Decency and the National Office for Decent Literature is carried on. The rights these agencies seek to protect are among the most important and sacred—the right of parents to bring up their children in an atmosphere reasonably free from defilement, the right of children to be protected from grave and insidious moral danger, the right of all not to be assailed at every turn by a display of indecency. Through the work of these agencies, the Church is able to give concrete expression of her concern.

28. The evaluations of these agencies have been a guide to our Catholic people. At the same time, they have enlisted the support of many others who share our concern. No one can fail to be stirred by the evident desire of so many people to remedy an unwholesome situation. And surely all those who are conscious of the gravity of the problem will applaud the efforts of the Church to safeguard the moral standards of the society in which we live.

Agencies Must Continue

29. It would be most gratifying to find it unnecessary to carry on this work. One could wish that the sense of responsibility of those who write and those who produce motion pictures would make superfluous action of this nature. Past experience, however, does not permit us to look forward to a day when this sort of evaluation will no longer be called for. Far from curtailing the work of these agencies, we must have them continue. Nor can we fail to be watchful over the fields of radio and television. Meanwhile, our existing agencies must be prepared to meet a continuing evil with an unremitting effort.

30. As a nation, we are intensely jealous of our freedoms. We are filled with pride that they have been so fully assured to us in our democracy. The reverence in which we hold our Constitution is due in great part to the care with which it has set down for all to know basic human freedoms that are inviolable. From childhood, these truths are taught us; they become the support of our adult life.

31. A freedom perceived in its true essence, in its exact limits, in its context of responsibility, is a freedom doubly secure; a freedom misunderstood risks becoming a freedom lost.

Signed in the name of the bishops of the United States by members of the Administrative Board, National Catholic Welfare Conference

Edward Cardinal Mooney,
Archbishop of Detroit

Samuel Cardinal Stritch,
Archbishop of Chicago

Francis Cardinal Spellman,
Archbishop of New York

James Francis Cardinal McIntyre,
Archbishop of Los Angeles

Francis P. Keough,
Archbishop of Baltimore

Joseph E. Ritter,
Archbishop of St. Louis

Patrick A. O'Boyle,
Archbishop of Washington

Leo Binz,
Archbishop of Dubuque

Karl J. Alter,
Archbishop of Cincinnati

John F. O'Hara, C.S.C.,
Archbishop of Philadelphia

Albert G. Meyer,
Archbishop of Milwaukee

Emmet M. Walsh,
Bishop of Youngstown

Thomas K. Gorman,
Bishop of Dallas-Fort Worth

Joseph M. Gilmore,
Bishop of Helena

Notes: *This 1957 statement issued by the U.S. Catholic Conference presents a defense of the church's active attempts to curb indecent literature (through the National Office for Decent Literature) and films (through the Legion of Decency). At the time the statement was issued, the Catholic Church was acutely aware of the fact that many people were suspicious of the church and thought it was an undemocratic institution. Thus, many people who otherwise agreed with the church's position on decency in the media were critical of the church because they feared it was trying to impose an authoritarian uniformity of belief on the American people. To combat that, this statement took great care to recognize the values of freedom of speech and the free press while at the same time calling for higher decency standards that would benefit the community.*

ROMAN CATHOLIC CHURCH—POPE PAUL VI

EXCERPT FROM "HUMANAE VITAE" (1968)

Promotion of Chastity

22. We take this opportunity to address those who are engaged in education and all those whose right and duty it is to provide for the common good of human society. We would call their attention to the need to create an atmosphere favorable to the growth of chastity so that true liberty may prevail over license and the norms of the moral law may be fully safeguarded.

Everything therefore in the modern means of social communication which arouses men's baser passions and encourages low moral standards, as well as every obscenity in the written word and every form of indecency on the stage and screen, should be condemned publicly and unanimously by all those who have at heart the advance of civilization and the safeguarding of the outstanding values of the human spirit. It is quite absurd to defend this kind of depravity in the name of art or culture or by pleading the liberty which may be allowed in this field by the public authorities.

Appeal to Public Authorities

23. And now We wish to speak to rulers of nations. To you most of all is committed the responsibility of safeguarding the common good. You can contribute so much to the preservation of morals. We beg of you, never allow the morals of your peoples to be undermined. The family is the primary unit in the state; do not tolerate any legislation which would introduce into the family those practices which are opposed to the natural law of God. For there are other ways by which a government can and should solve the population problem—that is to say by enacting laws which will assist families and by educating the people wisely so that the moral law and the freedom of the citizens are both safeguarded.

Notes: Humanae Vitae *(meaning "human life")*, *one of the most important statements issued from the papacy in the twentieth century, is particularly well-known for addressing the issue of contraception. This excerpt, however, relates to pornography, asking for stricter control of obscenity as a means of defending the "values of the human spirit."*

ROMAN CATHOLIC CHURCH—BISHOP ERNEST PRIMEAU

DISTINCTIONS: SEXUALITY, OBSCENITY AND PORNOGRAPHY (1972)

There is no easy solution to the problem of obscenity and pornography in films, printed matter and other media. The recent controversy over the findings of the President's Commission on Obscenity and Pornography, and much nearer to us the current litigation in Rockingham County, clearly demonstrate that the problem is compounded by a lack of unanimity both in assessing the gravity of sexual exploitation and in suggesting practical means of dealing with it. Part of the difficulty stems from the fact that, within the context of a free and pluralistic society, there is no general agreement in understanding human sexuality and in defining its correct use. The problem is still further aggravated by the wide divergence of views concerning the regulation of mass media.

Positive Starting Point

To avoid possible misunderstanding, it should be clear that as Catholics we start from the positive premise that sexuality is an intimate and sacred area of human life. It is basically good but separated from the context of love or isolated from the responsibilities of procreation it is subject to misunderstanding and distortion. It is also, as we are all sadly aware, subject of exploitation.

In our reaction to the dangers of obscenity and pornography we must be careful, therefore, to distinguish between the legitimate and healthy progress being made in understanding sexuality and the deviations which depersonalize and cheapen sex. We must not, for example, indiscriminately condemn all forms of sex education as we endeavor to protect our community from the debasing influence of sexual exploitation.

In making this necessary distinction, however, we do not intend to minimize the dangers that threaten our community. Although we in New Hampshire have been spared much of the systematic commercialized exploitation which plagues large urban centers, recent events in our state community have opened our eyes to the fact that we are far from being unaffected by the subtle and not so subtle forms of pornography and obscenity that can be purchased at your newsstands and bookstores, brought to our mailbox, or seen on our own television sets and local movie screens.

Film Industry Unable to Regulate Itself

The film industry—and to a lesser extent the television industry—is a special object of our concern. Parents who are endeavoring to guide their children in arriving at personal maturity are at a loss to protect them from the debasing influence of lowered moral standards so prevalent in today's films. In 1968 it was hoped that the voluntary rating system devised by the Motion Picture Association of America would be a positive contribution in this regard. It was described by Catholic film agencies as "consistent with the rights and obligation of free speech and artistic expression, as well as with the duty of parents and society to safeguard the young in their growth to responsible adulthood."[1]

Unfortunately these hopes have not been fulfilled. In a statement of May 1971 the National Catholic Office for Motion Pictures, in conjunction with the Broadcasting and Film Commission of the National Council of Churches, pointed out that the rating system did not fulfill the basic requirement of protecting the young from material with which they were unable to cope. The report went on to say that "the ratings at present do not take into account sufficiently the total context of a given film, that they place too much weight on overt visual sex, and not enough on the implicit exploitation of sex and the overall impact of violence and other anti-social aspects of the film on the child.

"In addition, overt visual sex is now finding its way into the 'GP' (All Ages Admitted, Parental Guidance Suggested) films. This pivotal rating thus has become worse than useless because, a parent, having once been mislead, has no way of knowing whether other 'GP' rated films contain similar material." The church agencies concluded that they were obliged to withdraw their support from the MPAA Rating Program as presently administered.

They further explained: "It is our judgment that the public's confidence in the plan has already been seriously eroded, and that its confidence will not be restored until the ratings become more reliable, more local theaters seriously enforce the ratings, and advertising reflects more concern with informing the public and less with exploiting sex and violence."

Self-Regulation Preferable

The question that immediately arises is the one of censorship. If the motion picture industry is unable to regulate itself, must someone else assume that responsibility? In this matter the above-mentioned agencies offer guidelines that can be helpful to us in our efforts to arrive at effective local controls. They state: "We are committed to the principle that motion pictures remain free of censorship through effective self-regulation. We believe that by expressing our lack of confidence in the present implementation of the rating system, the best interest of the movie-going public, and of the industry as a whole are served. It is essential that the motion picture industry itself realizes that it must develop a workable dependable and credible system if self-regulation is an alternative to governmental censorship."[3]

Public Opinion

In keeping with these guidelines our responsibility as citizens will be directed toward the development of informed and articulate public opinion. Rather than use civil authority to create difficulties or to suppress (though in extreme cases this might be a last resort)[4] our task is one of promoting effective self-regulation through the formation of voluntary associations, and through the use of the media itself to disseminate information and express opinion.

More practically, all of us, priests, religious and laity of the Diocese of Manchester should cooperate in providing our statewide community with high-quality movie reviews produced by proven experts in the field of ethics and cinematography. Existing organizations and publications should be used for this purpose whenever possible but we should not hesitate to create new agencies whenever existing structures are not adequate to our new needs. In this regard the new film and television service provided by the National Catholic Office for Motion Pictures should be most useful. It is a weekly service and is precisely a response to the need of Catholics for reliable and critical information about the media and about films in particular.

To restate the problem, there is no lack of reliable motion picture critique. The difficulty we face is to make this information easily available to all the members of our community—especially to parents. In trying to arrive at this objective, it is essential that we respect the principal of subsidiarity—which encourages civil or religious authority to refrain from doing themselves what can be done just as well, or often better, by individuals, private groups or official agencies at a lower level of organization.

Accordingly, along with individual concern all diocesan agencies, from the Department of Community Affairs to individual parish councils, must assume responsibility in this matter. In doing so, however, it should be kept in mind that different local situations will require different responses. Neither should it be forgotten that the requirements of religious, ethical and political pluralism should also be a major consideration whenever we deal with problems that are shared by the community at large.

Printed Pornographic Material

What we have said about motion pictures can also be said of the printed word. Reluctance to resort to censorship along with a concerted program of informing our citizenry also applies to the problem of printed pornographic material. In this area, however, society has an equally serious but perhaps more difficult task of protecting the young from permanent psychological harm.

Here the complexity of the problem will more often require that society protect itself from moral and cultural pollution through the use of legal measures. In the words of the recent Pastoral Instruction on Communications, "it is the task of legislation in this field to give the necessary support to the family and the school in educating the young."[5]

We again insist that, in keeping with our American heritage of free speech, the action of legislators should not be used as a substitute for programs of information which form public opinion. We fully admit that free speech is a precious American tradition and must not be infringed upon. But as Cardinal Dearden recently pointed out, "it needs to be borne in mind that the Supreme Court itself has said that obscenity is not entitled to First Amendment protections."[6] While the question of legislation in this area will remain difficult and delicate, it still remains, within a specific constitutional framework, an option that is open to us as we seek effective means of controlling the commercial exploitation of sex within our community.

Positive Reaction

Because we are undergoing the stress of rapid growth and development in all areas of our lives, it is especially difficult today to consolidate and further develop a healthy moral climate in our society. It is precisely at such times of accelerated change that the possibility of regression and deviation becomes more menacing.

The debasing influence of obscenity and pornography represent just such a deviation from Christian values and the generally accepted moral standards of our community. Our response to this danger, however, requires more than a negative reaction. While we recognize our right to protection from the pernicious influence of sexual exploitation, we must also recognize our obligation to combat evil with good. As St. Paul would put it: Where sin increases, grace must far surpass it.[7] To put it in still other terms, we must become more convinced that our obligation, as a community witnessing to the mystery of God's love through Jesus Christ, is to spread Christian values though the example of our lives.

We must conclude that obscenity and pornography can only thrive in an atmosphere that is hospitable to them. No amount of containment will be successful until the atmosphere itself is changed. Our task, therefore, will be ultimately to educate, to motivate, to inspire. It will be to uplift the society we live in through the power of the Word we preach and the example we show. Our task is not an easy one but it is the only one that is compatible with our Christian calling and the only one that offers any hope of success.

With every good wish, I am

Cordially in Christ

Ernest J. Primeau
Bishop of Manchester

Footnotes

[1] *Statement of National Catholic Office for Motion Pictures and the Broadcasting and Film Commission, National Council of Churches, May 19, 1971.*

[2] *Ibid.*

[3] *Ibid.*

[4] *Pastoral Instruction on Communications. Issued June 3, 1971, by the Pontifical Commission for Social Communications, No. 86.*

[5] *Ibid., No. 89.*

[6] *Statement of John Cardinal Dearden, President, United States Catholic Conference, October 1, 1970.*

[7] *Romans 5:20.*

Notes: *This is a pastoral letter to the Manchester, New Hampshire, diocese from Bishop Ernest Primeau. It specifically reacts to the 1970 report of the Commission on Obscenity and Pornography (the Johnson Commission), which was very liberal and recommended elimination of many of the laws restricting pornography. Recognizing the problems in a plural society of relying solely on legal solutions, but recognizing also the need to curb exploitive sex and violence, Bishop Primeau concludes that the church's task "will be ultimately to educate, to motivate, to inspire."*

ROMAN CATHOLIC CHURCH—BISHOPS OF CALIFORNIA

PORNOGRAPHY/SATURATION IMPACT (1972)

We Californians, in recent months have witnessed a shocking increase in outlets for pornographic materials and lewd entertainment. We have seen an alarming growth in the production, distribution, sale and exhibition of material exploiting human sexuality, often to a perverse and depraved degree.

The intrusion of these corrupting influences—not only into the lives of those who seek them out, but to all segments of society—young and old alike—is a matter of grave concern. The sensibilities of the entire community are assaulted by blatantly obscene marquees and store fronts and by advertisements for pornographic outlets in many daily newspapers.

The saturation of communities by this depravity has led to a "toleration" and an "acceptance" of immoral sexual content in even so-called legitimate channels of entertainment and information—TV, radio, magazines, newspapers and major studio motion pictures. The result is a deplorable lack of morally uplifting entertainment suitable for family viewing or attendance.

Promiscuous sex is being glamorized, exploited and encouraged at every opportunity by the media to which young people are constantly attuned. This is reflected in pandemic venereal disease among that age group, which social agencies seem at a loss to curb. A solution is not likely as long as traditional concepts of sexual morality are ridiculed and held up to scorn in debased "sex education" materials provided by pornographers, lyric writers and other elements of the entertainment industry.

Promiscuity as promoted by pornography is also reflected in soaring illegitimacy, scandalous fashions and—most threatening of all—the potential destruction of the basic unit of society—the family. Truly the golden calf of modern man is sexual obsessiveness which—as Paul VI pointed out—is causing man to "walk in the mud."

Conscious of our role as teachers of morality, we, the Roman Catholic Bishops of the State of California, therefore urge all Catholics—and indeed all right-minded citizens—to reaffirm Judeo-Christian moral principles and to refrain voluntarily from supporting pornography—either directly by not purchasing, attending or viewing obscene material—or indirectly by withdrawing support of sponsors, advertisers, exhibitors or retailers of pornographic wares.

Strengthened laws controlling pornography and vigorous enforcement of them are vital if the pollution of the moral atmosphere of our country is to be eliminated.

Joseph T. McGucken, Archbishop of San Francisco; Timothy Manning, Archbishop of Los Angeles; Floyd L. Begin, Bishop of Oakland; Hugh A. Donohoe, Bishop of Fresno; Merlin J. Guilfoyle, Bishop of Stockton; Alden J. Bell, Bishop of Sacramento; Harry A. Clinch, Bishop of Monterey; Leo T. Maher, Bishop of San Diego; John J. Ward, Auxiliary Bishop of Los Angeles; William J. McDonald, Auxiliary Bishop of San Francisco; Mark J. Hurley, Bishop of Santa Rosa; Norman F. McFarland, Auxiliary Bishop of San Francisco; Juan A. Arzube, Auxiliary of Los Angeles; William R. Johnson, Auxiliary of Los Angeles.

Notes: *This 1972 statement is from the California bishops, who make connections between pornography and promiscuity, the spread of venereal disease, and the breakdown of the family unit. The bishops urge people not to purchase pornographic products and to withdraw support from businesses that support those products.*

ROMAN CATHOLIC CHURCH—U.S. CATHOLIC CONFERENCE

STATEMENT ON THE INTRODUCTION OF THE FAMILY VIEWING PERIOD DURING PRIME TIME BY THE TELEVISION NETWORKS (1975)

A Statement of the Administrative Board of the United States Catholic Conference

I. Introduction

1. With the 1975 fall season, the three television networks have introduced their new policy of a "Family Viewing" period during prime time programming hours.

2. In summary, the following guidelines will be observed by the networks. The first hour of network entertainment programming in prime time and the immediately preceding hour are to be set aside as a "Family Viewing" period. Secondly, in the occasional case when an entertainment program broadcast during the "Family Viewing" period contains material which may be unsuitable for viewing by younger family members, a "viewer advisory" will be broadcast in audio and video form. Moreover, viewer advisories will also be employed during the later evening hours for any program containing material that might be disturbing to significant portions of the viewing audience. Finally, broadcasters will endeavor to inform publishers of television program listings of these programs that will contain "advisories." A responsible use of "advisories" in promotional material is also urged upon broadcasters.

3. This new network policy on family viewing is the result of conversations that the chairman of the Federal Communications Commission had with network leaders in the early part of this year. The results of those negotiations were made public by the

Commission in its "Report on the Broadcast of Violent, Indecent and Obscene Material" on February 19, 1975 (FCC 75-202, 30159). The report, which was in response to congressional directives on the subject, addresses the "specific positive action taken and planned by the Commission to protect children from excessive programming of violence and obscenity." The acceptance by the Commission of the "Family Viewing" concept constitutes the major element of this plan.

II. Presuppositions

4. Before evaluating this "Family Viewing" policy, we wish to outline certain presuppositions which the United States Catholic Conference views as important and relevant to the question at hand.

5. (1) In our society today, television is the single most formative influence in shaping people's attitudes and values. It is not only the power the medium itself possesses that supports this proposition. Of even greater significance is the cumulative effect upon an individual of his daily television experiences, frequently passive and uncritical, from early childhood until the evening of life. By the time they have completed high school, most children have spent more hours before a television set than they have in the classroom. The average adult also spends considerable time each day viewing television.

6. (2) Unquestionably, therefore, the *experience* of television is both an *ordinary* and *integral* part of American *home life* today. Hence it follows that any evaluation of the role that television plays in the American experience must focus on the actualities, first, of substantial daily viewing by the average American, and second, of the home environment in which the viewing is experienced. We are not dealing then with the occasional entertainment experience that a child or adult may have by going out of the home to see a movie. Much less are we dealing with the even rarer entertainment experience of a nightclub show.

7. (3) The Church respects the enormous potential that television has: for education; for providing full and accurate information so essential to enlightened public opinion; for building understanding and community among men and nations; for preserving and, indeed, creating art; for providing entertainment and relaxation that recreate the human spirit and emotions.

8. In the face of this enormous potential, broadcasters cannot view themselves as merely entertainers or technicians. Because social communications are so central to modern life, the vocation of a broadcaster is a calling of high honor—and of heavy responsibility. The broadcaster, more than others, helps to shape the very ethos of the world in which we live.

9. (4) It should be noted as well that American broadcasters' responsibilities go far beyond the frontiers reached by their signals. They have a global responsibility because they belong to an industry that has established American international leadership in the technology, the content, and the style of contemporary mass communications. One example is enlightening: during 1974, of 1,707 film entertainment programs shown on Brazilian television, 1,267 programs were of American origin; only ten were Brazilian productions. American broadcasters cannot therefore take a parochial or narrowly nationalistic view of their responsibilities. They must be increasingly sensitive to the cultural and moral imperatives of societies other than our own. The American people, sharing as they do a collective responsibility in our interdependent world, have every right and duty to protest whenever broadcasters may manifest indifference or insensitivity to the needs of their sisters and brothers across the world. In a word, the question of the broadcast of violent, indecent, and obscene material has to be viewed from an international as well as a domestic perspective.

III. USCC Evaluation of the "Family Viewing" Policy

10. At the very outset of our evaluation of the FCC acceptance of the "Family Viewing" policy, it seems important to state that if our opinion of the Commission's recommendations must be largely negative, it is not because we have failed to appreciate the most difficult task of the commissioners.

11. The FCC report (p. 3) quite rightly observes that "administrative actions regulating violent and sexual material must be reconciled with constitutional and statutory limitations on the Commission's authority to regulate program content." Not only do we support this observation but we would oppose any recommendation that would call for the direct involvement by government in the content area of programming. Section 326 of the Communications Act specifically prohibits the Commission from exercising the power of censorship. This prohibition must be maintained.

12. Opposition to *direct* governmental involvement in program content, however, does not call in question the role required of the Commission by the same Communications Act, namely, that it ensure that broadcast licensees operate in a manner consistent with the public interest. The *Red Lion* decision of the Supreme Court explicitly reminded broadcasters that they are "public trustees" with fiduciary responsibilities to their communities. We strongly support the Commission's policy that program service in the public interest is an essential part of every licensee's obligation.

13. Nor again, by opposing *direct* involvement by government, do we intend to cast any doubt on the obligation that Congress has to legislate effectively against the broadcast of violent, obscene, or indecent material. Specifically, we support the Commission's legislative proposal that Congress amend Section 1464 of Title 18, United States Code, in order to remove the present uncertainty of the Commission as to whether it has statutory authority to proceed against the video depiction of obscene or indecent material (*Report*, p. 9).

14. In the light of the constraints placed on it by the Constitution and Section 326 of the Communications Act, the Commission understandably notes that it "walks a tightrope between saying too much and saying too little" when applying the public interest standard to programming. In the present instance, the Commission decided that "regulatory action to limit violent and sexually-oriented programming which is neither obscene nor indecent is less desirable than effective self-regulation" (*Report*, p. 3). Hence, the chairman of the Commission met with broadcast industry leadership in the hope that he might "serve as a catalyst for the achievement of meaningful self-regulatory reform."

15. Although the effort of the chairman is commendable, our judgment is that the results are unacceptable. Our reasons are as follows:

16. *(1) Self-regulation must be open, accountable, and cooperative.* The United States Catholic Conference has been, is, and will continue to be firmly committed to the principle of voluntary self-regulation for all the communications media. We therefore share the Commission's conviction that broadcast self-regulation is the basic solution to the problems at hand. However, we strongly disagree with the Commission's apparent conviction that a few modifications in the status quo will enable the networks to achieve "meaningful self-regulatory reform" in the area of broadcast entertainment.

17. Self-regulation is not a unilateral activity performed behind closed doors by a few powerful individuals at the top. Self-regulation, to deserve the name, is an *open, accountable,* and *cooperative* process, involving both broadcasters and the public they serve.

18. We are far from convinced that broadcast management is genuinely *open* to dialogue with the public or accountable to it. The very corporate structure of the networks, for example, is such a forbidding and complicated maze that it appears designed to

guarantee that, insulated from public scrutiny, top management may, without fear of challenge or other encumbrance, pursue the uniquely important goal of maximizing profits. And yet, of all the communications media, broadcasting should be the one most open to dialogue with the public, precisely because the airwaves belong to the public and broadcasters are public trustees with fiduciary responsibilities to their communities. The polished rhetoric of industry public relations releases is not dialogue but self-serving monologue. In spite of good intentions, the series of closed meetings which the chairman of the Commission held with the inner circle of network top management strikes us as having little to do with openness to public dialogue or public accountability. Even worse, it can only serve in effect to strengthen the claims currently being made by some broadcasters that the public does not really own the airwaves.

19. Neither will the quality of openness and accountability characterize industry self-regulation as long as the public is without ready access to reliable advance information about broadcast entertainment programming. This need for information is not satisfied by industry-generated publicity releases or advisories. Books, plays, records, movies, circuses, exhibits of all manner are also the object of publicity and promotion, but before buying, the interested consumer has critical evaluations of the product available to guide his or her choice. Since, apart from summer repeats, broadcast entertainment is essentially a one-time presentation, reliable advance program information would only be possible were networks and local stations to adopt and implement a policy of prescreening *all* entertainment programs for critical review. We are aware, of course, that the "rating-game" approach to television entertainment effectively precludes even the consideration of any prescreening policy that might, in effect, serve to restrict potential audiences. Without it the broadcast industry cannot justify claim to be open and accountable to the public it claims to serve. One might have expected that the chairman of the Commission would have seen this as an important question to have posed to network top management.

20. Self-regulation is also a *cooperative* activity that should involve every local broadcaster. A frequent complaint of the local broadcaster is that he is rarely consulted or otherwise actively involved by the networks in the decision-making process with regard to network entertainment programming. To the best of our knowledge, top network management did not invite the *prior* counsel of their affiliate stations on the subject of whether there ought to be a family viewing period during prime time. Neither are we aware that the Commission sought the opinion of the affiliates in the matter. If the decision has been unilaterally taken by the networks and accepted by the Commission, it may be because, were it left to local affiliate management, who alone must bear the ultimate responsibility to the public, many of them might have rejected the idea on the grounds that their prime time audience is a family audience. At the very least, they might have demanded stricter and more precise standards.

21. Self-regulation also involves *cooperation* on the part of the *viewing public*. No system will succeed unless it enjoys public confidence and support. Part of our complaint is that neither the networks nor the Commission made any effort to consult the public on whether it was indeed prepared to accept the introduction of a distinction between family-type and adult programming and, if so, under what conditions. We seriously doubt that the average parent would or should find it reasonable to insist the older children be excluded from watching television in their own home after certain time periods. By what mandate or legal title, parents might rightfully demand, can the Commission and the networks unilaterally decide that henceforth minor children are entitled to enjoy only a limited access to evening television entertainment? A more than lurking suspicion remains that the audience for prime time television is after all not the general American public but older teenagers, young adults, and the affluent who have the money to spend on the products advertised. In short, children, the poor, and the

aged are to be disenfranchised. How all of this relates to high-sounding network appeals to creativity and First Amendment guarantees or is to be reconciled with serving the public interest is difficult to perceive.

22. *(2) Commercialism—Core Problem.* And so we come to what must be acknowledged as the *core* obstacle to effective self-regulation in the broadcast industry—its complete domination by commercial interests. What American commercial television is all about is not primarily either information or entertainment, neither news nor culture. Its primary objective is to create a meeting place for consumers and advertisers. American television is essentially concerned with the sale of consumers to advertisers.

23. As long as this equation controls programming decisions, especially during prime time when network competition is keenest, the central concern of broadcast management has to be to air that type of program which will deliver the greatest possible audience. And what kind of programming is this? Look at the record. Do we find serious dramatic works or programs that might challenge viewers to confront disturbing social issues or documentaries that might open American minds and hearts to understanding and compassion for the powerless at home and abroad? What has the average American viewer of prime time entertainment programming learned about the global village, the interdependent world in which we are said to live—about Africa, Latin America, Asia, Oceania? The record will reveal that network management programming decisions have much more to do with appealing to the alleged lowest common denominator of audience interest: smart comedy, crime, violence, and sex. Were the record otherwise, the Commission would never have been mandated by Congress to undertake its study.

24. *(3) Lessons Learned From Motion Picture Code and Rating Program.* On page five of the Commission's report, it is stated that "the Chairman raised the possibility of the adoption of a rating system similar to that used in the motion picture industry." We believe that some sobering conclusions might have emerged for the members of the Commission had they reflected on what has happened to American motion pictures since October 7, 1968, when the Motion Picture Association of America (MPAA) first announced the details of its new and expanded plan of movie industry self-regulation.

25. The MPAA plan bore the title "The Motion Picture Code and Rating Program." We wish to emphasize that it was a *code* as well as a rating program. At the top of the document appears a section entitled "Declaration of Principles of the Code of Self-Regulation of the Motion Picture Association." A few excerpts from this section are of interest:

> This Code is designed to keep in close harmony with the mores, culture, the moral sense and change in our society.

> The objectives of the Code are:

> 1. To encourage artistic expression by expanding creative freedom; and

> 2. To assure that the freedom which encourages the artist remains responsible and sensitive to the standards of the larger society.

> We believe self-restraint, self-regulation, to be in the American tradition. The results of self-discipline are always imperfect because that is the nature of all things mortal. But this Code, and its administration, will make clear that freedom of expression does not mean toleration of license.

> The test of self-restraint—the rule of reason—lies in the treatment of a subject for the screen.

26. Under the second section of the MPAA document which is entitled "Standards for Production" there are eleven standards enunciated which will determine whether a motion picture will qualify for a Code Seal of Approval. Those standards read as follows:

a. The basic dignity and value of human life shall be respected and upheld. Restraint shall be exercised in portraying the taking of life.

b. Evil, sin, crime, and wrong-doing shall not be justified.

c. Special restraint shall be exercised in portraying criminal or anti-social activities in which minors participate or are involved.

d. Detailed and protracted acts of brutality, cruelty, physical violence, torture, and abuse shall not be presented.

e. Indecent or undue exposure of the human body shall not be presented.

f. Illicit sex relationships shall not be justified. Intimate sex scenes violating common standards of decency shall not be portrayed.

g. Restraint and care shall be exercised in presentations dealing with sex aberrations.

h. Obscene speech, gestures, or movements shall not be presented.

i. Undue profanity shall not be permitted.

j. Religion shall not be demeaned.

k. Words or symbols contemptuous of racial, religious, or national groups shall not be used so as to incite bigotry or hatred.

l. Excessive cruelty to animals shall not be portrayed and animals shall not be treated inhumanely.

27. The Motion Picture Code and Rating Program envisioned two distinct questions for its administration. The first question pertained to these Standards for Production; if the submitted motion picture conformed to the standards, it would be issued a Code Seal of Approval. If it did not qualify for a Code seal, it could only be rated (X). For a Code-approved film, a second question was then to be applied, namely, which of the first three ratings (G, M, or R) were to be applied.

28. The United States Catholic Conference and the National Council of Churches endorsed in principle this MPAA program "as being consistent with the rights and obligations of free speech and artistic expression, as well as with the duty of parents and society to safeguard the young in their growth to responsible adulthood." The churches, "relying on the good faith of the industry," gave "genuine and full support to this plan" and urged "its conscientious implementation on every level of production, distribution, and exhibition."

29. The churches maintained their support of the MPAA plan for over two and a half years. Finally, on May 18, 1971, after a detailed statement of concern published a year previously, the churches, because they could no longer in good conscience be party to a charade, withdrew their support.

30. How could a plan which had been welcomed with genuine enthusiasm only two and a half years previously have failed so miserably? The best of motivation and the highest good faith could not stand up to the pressures of commercial competition. Within a few short weeks of the introduction of the Code and Rating Plan, there began to emerge an attitude on the part of some film producers that "now that the kids are protected, anything goes." And in no short order, almost everything did go—including the standards for production, which, as noted previously, were to determine whether films qualified for the Code Seal of Approval. Although the MPAA has not formally advised the public, the Code is officially dead. All that remains is the rating aspect of the original plan.

31. One result of all this is that the theatrical motion picture as such has become a lost experience for the majority of Americans. For the industry, in spite of the occasional box-office successes that keep some of the Hollywood glitter going, the loss of the

general audience has resulted in serious financial reverses for many producers and exhibitors across the industry. Perhaps the worst consequence of all for American society is that too many of the creative community of producers, writers, directors, and actors have been replaced by hacks whose artistic perception is limited to ''exploit-the-audience-with-sex-and-violence.''

32. Our purpose in this review is not to focus on the problem of the motion picture industry but to raise the question of why a reasonable person would be expected to accord greater confidence to effective self-regulation by the television networks than to the MPAA. To the credit of the MPAA, it has involved itself in broad consultation with representatives of the public before introducing its Code and Rating Program and continued to collaborate with them in an effort to make the program work. Again, the film industry prescreens its product for public review and takes its chances at the box office. As already noted, the broadcast industry's self-regulation is a closed shop and, short of the risk of challenge at license renewal time, is not otherwise accountable to the public. In fact, the networks do not even have to face that risk—except in the narrow area of their owned and operated stations.

33. We have no confidence that once the commercial broadcast industry as presently constituted is permitted without challenge to introduce what is in effect a rating system for programming, the identical excesses that have occurred in the motion picture medium will not be visited upon the American public—but this time not at the local theater but in the American home. In making this judgment we are not limiting our concern to the pressures of commercial competition presently experienced by the networks. We are also looking down the road when the networks will have to face the added competition from pay-television, video-cassettes, video-discs, and whatever else technological genius may develop.

34. *(4) Greater Handicaps for Parents and Family Life.* We have placed great emphasis upon television's role in American family life. We do not think that it is possible to exaggerate the centrality and importance of this role, especially at a time in our history when the very structure of family life is seriously threatened. We therefore commend the Commission when it states *(Report,* pp. 7-8):

> Parents in our view, have—and should retain—the primary responsibility for their children's well-being. This traditional and revered principle . . . has been adversely affected by the corrosive processes of technological and social change in twentieth-century American life. Nevertheless, we believe that it deserves continuing affirmation.

> Television . . . also has some responsibilities in this area. . . . The Commission has sought to remind broadcasters of their responsibility to provide some measure of support to concerned parents.

35. However, we must also seriously fault the Commission for then making recommendations which, in the light of our foregoing observations, will only serve to create even greater handicaps for parents as they struggle not only to assure the well-being of their children, but also to preserve family life which is so essential to the well-being of this or any nation.

36. *(5) Specific Criticism of ''Family Viewing'' Plan.* Although it may seem unnecessary to comment on the specific recommendations that the FCC report has proposed for the fall 1975 television season, we will do so anyway with the understanding, however, that these criticisms are secondary to our already stated core concerns.

37. (a) Inspection of the report reveals that the 7:00-9:00 p.m. ''Family Viewing'' period, which appears to have been the initial FCC objective, will hold only in fact for the Eastern and Western time zones. For the Midwest it will mean a 6:00-8:00 p.m. period and for the Rocky Mountain time zone 5:00-7:00 p.m. Why? The Commission lamely acknowledges that the networks had informed it that ''a standard based on a 9:00 p.m.

local time would require prohibitively expensive separate program transmissions to each time zone." This concession to commercial considerations is incredible. It hardly demonstrates an honest commitment by the networks to American parents.

38. (b) The use of the so-called "advisory warnings," the second point in the FCC proposals, is an equally incredible concession. "Viewer advisories," the report states, "will be broadcast in audio and video form *in the occasional case* when an entertainment program broadcast during the *Family Viewing* period contains material which may be unsuitable for viewing by younger family members" (emphasis added). Not only does this "advisory warning" concession open the door to abuse in order to attract larger audiences; there is something far more disturbing about it. It leads to the obvious conclusion that neither the Commission nor the networks are single-minded about keeping the "Family Viewing" period inviolate.

39. (c) The combination of "viewer advisories" and the "advance notice" to be given about such advisories clearly implies that a television *rating system,* almost as developed as that of the motion picture industry, is about to be foisted upon the American public without, however, it being candidly identified as a rating system and, of course, without any previous public debate as to the merits of same.

40. (d) Granted the advisory or rating system proposal, who is going to make the necessary judgments as to material "which may be unsuitable for viewing by younger family members" or concerning programs, "in the later evening hours," which "contain material that might be disturbing to significant portions of the viewing audience?" The Commission report makes much of the "subjectivity" of these matters. But even if artistic and moral considerations were actually as subjective as the approach of the Commission would imply, there is no reason to conclude, as the Commission does in fact conclude, that such decisions must be left to the networks. This, of course, touches on the basic issue: despite the fervent rhetoric of the FCC report, the networks continue to be answerable to no one but themselves. In some respects, the report of the Commission is an insult to the public's intelligence and inescapably lends credence to the suspicion that the main function of the FCC is, after all, to act as a buffer between the networks and public accountability.

41. (e) An integral part of the Commission's plan involves the incorporation of the "Family Viewing" period concept and the advisory warnings into the Television Code of the National Association of Broadcasters. It appears unnecessary to observe that the NAB as presently constituted has been neither organized for, nor is it capable of, taking on any serious representation role for the public interest. The NAB is a trade organization whose function is to argue for the interests of its members before the government and the public. Moreover, since no more than sixty percent of all stations belong to this voluntary organization, NAB cannot even speak for the entire industry. Nor, in fact, can it effectively discipline its members who choose not to abide by its Standards and Practices rules. Finally, the FCC has not yet secured agreement of the independent television stations to support the NAB TV Code's incorporation of "Family Viewing," despite the fact that the NAB voted to give independents a waiver on restrictions against sex and violence until September 1977, for any programs under contract since last April.

IV. Conclusions

42. For all the reasons set forth in this Statement, the United States Catholic Conference finds the proposals contained in the FCC's report to be unacceptable. Our principal reason is that those proposals stand or fail upon effective self-regulation by the broadcast industry.

43. Effective self-regulation has to be an open, accountable, and cooperative process. Our judgment is that to date the networks have not demonstrated a commitment to such a process. Moreover, we seriously question whether such a commitment is even possible

for the networks as long as no industry effort is undertaken to reduce the impact of commercial pressures upon their program decision making. In this connection, the "rating game" must be addressed specifically. A basic weakness of commercial broadcasting is that management is incapable of exercising responsible freedom in the program decision-making process because they are trapped in a rating thralldom.

44. If ratings objectively identified the needs of the public, they would be a true service both to broadcasters and the public they are to serve. We doubt anyone can make a case in favor of the rating organizations that would prove them to be providing a constructive service to the medium or the public. We therefore recommend that Congress investigate the program rating services which appear to exercise an inordinate influence upon television programming and which have thus far successfully resisted public scrutiny.

45. As for the broadcast industry, we strongly urge all broadcast licensees, whether network affiliates or independents, whether members of the NAB or not, to reflect anew upon their responsibilities to the public they are licensed to serve and to examine how well they are meeting those responsibilities. We fully appreciate that service to the community by commercial broadcasters cannot be delivered without a profitable operation. Yet the profit motive can never justify programming that debases rather than builds community.

46. As for the viewing public, it must respond and demonstrate to local station management that it cares and is ready to work with management for the achievement of a program schedule that serves the community's needs. In particular, we encourage our Catholic people, under the leadership of their bishops and pastors, to take an active and affirmative role in working with their fellow citizens, especially on an interfaith basis, in pursuit of the same objectives. Neither networks nor advertisers, neither Hollywood nor government can influence station managers who have their communities strongly behind them.

47. For its part, the Federal Communications Commission must demonstrate that it is more concerned about how well the public interest is served by commercial broadcasters than how well it serves the interests of commercial broadcasters. In particular, a scrupulous enforcement of the spirit as well as the letter of the community ascertainment requirement is essential.

48. Moreover, recent efforts either to exempt certain broadcasters from the requirement to ascertain community problems or to reduce the requirements for others must be resisted by the Commission. The Commission must also fully support the right of the public to challenge license renewals. This requires that communities have access to all necessary information and be afforded adequate time to exercise the right to challenge.

49. Finally, the business community has a special responsibility for the quality of commercial broadcasting. It is their advertising dollars that either enhance or debase the medium. If all advertisers had been as sensitive to the broadcast needs of the American public, especially of the family, as some have been, this Statement might not be necessary.

Notes: *This 1975 statement by the U.S. Catholic Conference examines the "Family Viewing Period" introduced by the three major U.S. television networks for the 1975 viewing season. Because the church believed that self-regulation had failed once before in the case of the Motion Picture Code and Rating Program, it was skeptical that this new attempt at self-regulation would work. Instead, it urged greater public accountability of the broadcast industry. It is interesting to note that section 31 of this statement bears some resemblance to section 4 of the 1932 statement* Resolution on Indecent Literature *(see index). The two sections are similar in that both portray the media as an institution in which untalented people who exploited sex and violence were taking over.*

ROMAN CATHOLIC CHURCH—CANADIAN CONFERENCE OF CATHOLIC BISHOPS

STATEMENT ON PORNOGRAPHY (1984)

Introduction

The hallmark of public statements by the Canadian Conference of Catholic Bishops has always been a deep concern for the dignity of each human being and for the well-being of society in general.[1] This same profound respect for life in all its manifold forms urges us as spiritual leaders of a major segment of Canadian society to appear before your timely committee to highlight once again the inherent beauty but also the vulnerability of human nature and to encourage the Federal Government through your efforts to effectively protect and promote the dignity of all people.

Knowing full well the government's responsibility to legislate for believers and non-believers alike we will submit, for the most part, considerations and arguments of universal validity. Indeed, experience tells us that most Canadians share in these views. We will begin by highlighting the meaning and inner dynamic of human sexuality as seen by many philosophers, scientists and theologians today. Such a vision of sexuality is in fact central to dealing successfully with the complex legal and social problems of pornography and prostitution.

1. The Meaning of Human Sexuality

Each human being is marked profoundly by his or her sexuality. However, the direction of this influence is shaped for the most part by the way each of us responds to this precious gift. The multi-faceted reality of sexuality can be the central force for existential and lasting relationships. But at the same time, it can also be the occasion for shameless exploitation and degradation of others, especially of women.

The Ambivalence of Sexuality

Sexuality is sometimes seen as a simple biological function, such as eating or drinking. No doubt, biology plays its part. However, more importantly, sexuality is a social reality that places us in relationship and possible communication with other people.

And yet, this relationship can also be abused and perverted into its opposite. Thus, the original goodness of sexuality (''In the image of God He created him, male and female He created them . . . and it was very good'' Gen 1, 27-31), often enough brings about domination rather than true encounter between people (Gen 3, 16). Because of this inherent ambiguity, human sexuality needs the guiding and humanizing power of culture and civilization. Culture, human history, and Jesus Christ Himself, invite us to move beyond the biological reality of male and female to a truly human relationship of man and woman.

Sexuality as the Experience of Otherness

As men and women we are different from each other. Thus, there is at first the threat of separation and division between people because of this otherness. However, inasmuch as we accept and appreciate this fundamental and seminal difference, the power of sexuality leads us to accept others in their newness and more radical still, enables us to create new life. In this way, sexuality is the basic force that makes encounter, communion, and new life among people possible. Thus, in human sexuality we find at once the threat of radical division and the promise of true encounter. Failing to recognize and appreciate this ambivalence, would mean failing to live our sexuality as human beings. Whenever we close in on our own desires, whenever we treat others as means for our own pleasure or profit, we deny their personhood and their fundamental right guaranteed by numerous charters of rights and freedoms to be different from us.

Sexuality does include the physical and pleasureful desire of the other person, even though it cannot be reduced to instinct alone. However, sexual pleasure which in itself signifies joy in life and the grateful acceptance of the gift of life, can also bring about harm and violence. This threat of violence arises from the inherent agressivity in sexuality. But even more so, it stems from the fact that others can threaten our very existence if they fail to welcome us as persons and to accept us in our otherness. Defensiveness, withdrawal from others and even violence towards others can have their origin in this ambivalence of human sexuality.

Pornography and prostitution must be seen in this broad context. Pornography separates our body into different segments and is therefore contrary to real enjoyment and acceptance of life. Prostitution, among other things, prevents its participants from accepting the creative risk of sexuality in its deepest sense. Both realities are marked by the rejection of true otherness so that anyone can be the partner in this relationship as long as they pay or participate in the play acting.

Sexuality and Pleasure

Pleasure can mean many things. It can mean affirming the other person in his or her dignity but it can also mean the denial of their personhood. Pleasure can mean withdrawal from others and from openness to society. It can signify the fear of the other person in his or her difference rather than his or her acceptance and enjoyment. The other person thus becomes an instrument of pleasure or profit to be handled at will.

Once praised as the liberation from social and personal constraints, sexual pleasure can become itself repressive and weaken rather than strengthen our freedom. Pornography and prostitution become in this way "opium of the people". They become the means for new enslavement creating a false world of fantasy, unreality and progressive intoxication with sexual desires and play.

The Unity of Body and Mind

Finally, against a false dualism that has long been the bane of Christian tradition, we cannot forget that *we are our bodies* (1 Co 6, 12-20). Thus, we would be seriously mistaken if we were to believe that we can use our bodies or those of others as simple means without involving at the same time our very personhood or that of others. Physical pleasure as well as pain have an influence on and are influenced by the totality of the person. Sexual activity in all its forms involves our whole person and the very depth of our personality. For Christians, the body takes on even added importance and value as the icon and sacrament of the Spirit of Jesus Christ living in us (cf. 1 Co 6, 19-20). Such a belief further strengthens our respect and concern for the integrity and value of our physical body.

Sexual language expresses and determines the totality of our being. Sexuality in its ambivalent potential of openness or separation is at the core of human interaction and communion without which we cannot exist, neither in our childhood nor as adult men or women. True sexuality is meant to be an experience of creative growth. This experience is found above all in the procreation of new life which can become the privileged moment of transforming otherness into communion and therefore of humanizing history.

In our view, the radical evil of pornography and prostitution and hence the urgent need for action against its pernicious influence arises from the very fact that both realities go radically counter to the true meaning of sexuality by decreasing rather than augmenting the humanizing powers in our personal and social history. This central point in the debate was already made by Archbishop Pocock in his 1976 statement against pornography when he said:

> "It is through our God-given sexuality that we as human beings can reach out to one another in love. It is in sexual union that a couple can express to one another tenderness, intimacy and permanent fidelity. The public and profitable exploitation of the sexual, so common around us, is a direct betrayal of the basic values of

sexuality itself. . . What was intended to be most precious becomes almost trivial. What was created to be most deeply personal is dehumanized''.

2. Pornography

The term ''pornography'' comes from the Greek word ''pernemi'' meaning ''selling a slave'' and its derivative ''pornos'' meaning ''prostitute''. Graphè'', on the other hand, relates to written material. Hence pornography has to do with depiction of slavery and, especially in our days, a depiction that derives pleasure from enslavement and thereby promotes it.

Pornography can thus be defined as any representation for the purpose of pleasure or profit of degrading or violent sexual behaviour whether it be real or simulated. Another way of making the same point would be to define pornography as that which exploits and dehumanizes sex so that human beings are treated as things and as sex objects.

The Perversion of Pornography

In a recent letter to the CRTC Chairman, our Episcopal Commission for Social Communications summarized the harm of pornography in this way: ''Pornography perverts human sexuality. The marvelous world of interpersonal relationships, human communication and love is reduced to a means by which one human being is exploited by another. This is not an innocent distraction, it is an offence against the dignity and rights of human persons.''[2] Pornography is therefore not only a *personal* moral evil but also a *social* evil. It promotes a vision of sexuality that is harmful for life in society.

As we mentioned earlier, our sexuality and its manifold expressions play a major part in the way we become responsible members of society and achieve mature adulthood. Pornography seriously impedes or even blocks this development. ''Pornography in all its forms contributes to a philosophy, a life-style, an attitude towards sexuality, in which another person is seen as an object, a means of fulfilling an urge or desire. It is a selfish sexuality devoid of love. When one human being is sold as pornography all are diminished and offended''.[2]

Moreover, pornography often suggests violence as a source of satisfaction and pleasure both for the victim and/or the aggressor. Any serious critic will agree that it is impossible for society to function well and at the same time to condone the presentation of violence as an acceptable and pleasurable means of achieving one's goals. Life in society is predicated on the stringent control of the latent tendency in us to use violent means for the achievement of our desires.

It is sometimes said that pornography helps to diminish violence by providing an imaginary outlet for the aggressive tendencies of its consumers. However, available evidence points increasingly in the opposite direction. Pornographic material of necessity makes us inclined to accept violence, to downgrade and even deny the dignity of other people, and to unleash our tendencies to dominate others, tendencies that are often the effect of affective and sexual deprivation or of economic, political and social powerlessness.

Pornography is pernicious for society because it leads us to accept and even promote attitudes of submission or domination. Such attitudes are indeed latent in all of us, but in our view and in the view of most Canadians they should not be encouraged. They need effective social control just as any hidden tendencies that might lead to theft or murder.

Pornography and Social Progress

The recent growth of pornography in our country highlights a disturbing social trend towards greater violence and disregard for people. As a society we can hardly let this development go unchecked, especially in view of the fact that it glorifies the domination of women and children. At a time when society recognizes that the status of women should be acknowledged and their image enhanced, it seems particularly contradictory that pornography should perpetuate a denigrating and especially offensive stereotype of women.

Moreover, pornography not only reflects social development but also actively influences the evolution of society. Thus we can rightfully ask whether governments can tolerate the risk of giving free reign to an industry which goes directly counter to the perhaps still imperfect but nevertheless significant humanization of the man-woman relationship, an improvement that has been achieved through the efforts of many centuries. To yield to the power of this industry would be an especially crass example of putting profits before people.

Pornography and Freedom of Expression

Freedom of expression is a fundamental right inasmuch as it permits critical comment. It is not meant to serve financial profit, but to prevent governments and other institutions from reducing or denying other people opportunities for critical questioning. Freedom of expression is a right inasmuch as it serves true progress and humanization. It is not an abstract right without limits. Individual rights such as the right to pleasure or to free expression are limited by the more fundamental right to be different from others. It is revealing in itself that the right to freedom of expression is often claimed for individual benefits, especially by those who have the financial means to dominate others.

An important function of the state is to protect the rights of the underprivileged. Freedom of expression must be placed in this basic perspective. The use of censorship may be unfortunate but it is surely a lesser evil than the exploitation or encouragement of hate and dehumanization. All expressions must consider and respect the human dignity of the people to whom they are addressed. Freedom of expression is subject to the more fundamental rights of respect for persons, justice and the need to grow in humanity. Limiting freedom of expression can be a sign of respect for these rights.

The Nihilism of Pornography

In sum, then, pornography can only be considered as *anti-life,* harmful to the dignity of people and to the development of sane and lasting personal relationships as the basis of healthy family life. Because it fails to accept sexuality as a unique gift for understanding and of creating new life in the image of the other person, pornography is *anti-sex.* Because it impedes or even prevents true personality growth and encourages violence and hate, pornography is *anti-social.* And finally, pornography is *anti-culture* because it degrades and destroys rather than ennobles and enriches as does true art and literature.

3. Prostitution

Prostitution cannot be defined simply "as the provision of sexual services for financial reward".[3] Such a limited definition overlooks the fact that at least two people are involved, not to mention the surrounding milieu and the involvement of the police and judicial system. It is rather revealing of the way we perceive the problem that our language has no special name for the other partner of this relationship.

The Twofold Focus of Prostitution

Prostitution should be defined as a momentary relationship where people exchange money for sexual relations. Such a definition recognizes the implication of both the client and the prostitute without denying, of course, the unreal and impersonal nature of this contact. No doubt, other factors are at play also such as one's self-image and one's place in society. However, the specifying characteristic of prostitution is the exchange of money on the one hand and sexual availability on the other.

Often enough prostitution is explained and excused as a response to physical need. However, the phenomenon of prostitution goes much deeper. The client asks for the play acting of another person who offers sexual availability but without the demands and the risks of encounter and mutual self-giving which characterize human sexuality. Thus prostitution, especially legalized prostitution—which we feel would be totally unaccept-able—"institutionalizes the concept that access to a woman's body is a right given to men by money, if not by God, and that sexuality is a service women ought not to refuse to civilized men''.[4] It may have been possible at one time to claim certain church authorities for such a position. However, this is no longer possible today if we consider the teaching of the Second Vatican Council.[5] As the Economic and Social Council of the United Nations has stated in almost the very words of Vatican II: ''Prostitution as the slavery of women and children is incompatible with the dignity of human persons and their fundamental rights.''[6]

The Personal and Social Harm of Prostitution

Predicated on illusion, play acting and withdrawal from true communication with others, prostitution harms both the client and the prostitute. It undermines the equal dignity of men, women and children. It goes counter to the vision of sexuality as described earlier where each person is enriched and grows through communion with others. Prostitution fails to use sexual relationships as an opportunity for greater humanization and especially denies the highest expression of this humanization which is the bringing into life of a new person.

Prostitution is a form of consumerism where personal inter-action is reduced to the fulfillment of egoistic needs and fantasies. Like pornography, prostitution disregards the other person in his or her otherness and uses ''it'' as a thing. The client is reduced to monetary value and the prostitute reduced to a sexual fantasy.

Finally, prostitution is also a form of institutionalized violence whereby some are given up to protect others. It is not without reason that prostitutes are often victims of contempt and extortion, of physical violence and even murder. They become the outlet for personal, economic, political and social problems. However, we seriously delude ourselves were we to believe that sexual satisfaction or even aggression could be the answer to our unfilled desires in life and to our need for personal recognition.

4. Law and Morality

Governments recognize their responsibility for the conditions of community life in a society. These conditions, however, and therefore the responsibilities of government, extend to the conditions of physical life. If we are our bodies and if our integration into society takes place above all through our bodies, our physical activities and their presentation in public have an impact on the way we become members of society and therefore on the future of society itself. This reality holds true even more so for sexual activities as sexual relationships ensure the continued survival of a society and have a major impact on the well-being of its members.

In this regard, governments must do more than simply adjusting laws to social realities, especially in areas of public disagreement. Such a withdrawal from responsibility would go counter to their very mandate. Governments have a responsibility to encourage all citizens to work for the common good. Of course, such encouragement will not be done by force but rely on persuasion in full respect for the freedom of each individual.

As legislators, governments should not impose on pluralistic society the moral views of a particular group. Nevertheless, they remain responsible for governing in such a way that the well-being of society and its progress in humanity is served, as defined by the duly-elected government of the day. In this sense then, the role of law and government is helping us do better. Thus, law does in fact depend on ethics or morality. It tries to protect and advance specific values, usually codified today as human rights. It helps us enjoy our freedoms in an increasingly complex world where the protection of the weakest remains a central responsibility of legislators. Hence, the purpose and goal of government remains the protection of the common good, i.e., of those social conditions that help each person, families, and other groups of people to achieve their own fulfillment inasmuch as possible.

This understanding of the role of government underlies the purpose of criminal law as defined in a recent publication of the Federal Department of Justice itself, namely "to contribute to the maintenance of a just, peaceful and safe society . . . ".[7] In other words, three basic values are identified as central to the well-being of Canadian Society and proposed as guiding principles for our legislators and laws. Criminal laws as all other laws receive their justification not from within themselves but from the basic options and goals we have chosen as a society.

This basic question of what are our common goals as a society, arises for example when we try to define the limits of the right to Freedom of Expression. Is this an absolute freedom or is it meant to protect other rights or realities, such as the right to political dissidence, respect for others, protection of the under-privileged, social progress, justice, and others? Freedom of Expression is meant to protect our rights from the unjustified needs for security or profit of a small group. And yet, we cannot fail to recognize that unrestricted freedom would eliminate all possibility of achieving the goals we have chosen as a society. Government is responsible for defining the rules for our social life and setting the limits of personal and social action that are still compatible with the well-being of individuals and of society. This intervention, especially in the area of criminal law, will be held to the necessary minimum. Nevertheless, legislators may be forced to choose between, e.g., the needs of Freedom of Expression and the survival of society, or between the economic needs of the market and the demands of improving the relationship between men, women, and children.

These considerations lead us back to the responsibilities of governments with regard to pornography and prostitution. Both of these realities are in conflict with profound human values. As we have seen, they can deform the development of the human person and threaten those human relationships on which society is based. Thus, while religious views reinforce and defend these values, they can in no way be identified and therefore disclaimed as the religious preferences of a certain minority. Recognizing these values and working to protect them remains a central task of government.

5. Specific Proposals and Comments

Regarding Pornography

From the preceding reflections, it becomes obvious that there can be no such thing as a claim of Freedom of Expression for the industry of pornography. Pecuniary interests are legitimate as long as they respect the totality of the human person. But they are not meant to be safeguarded by the right to Freedom of Expression. The right to be free from government interference does not include freedom to attack others. Freedom of Expression does not mean being free to depict, whether real or simulated, degradation, aggression or domination in sexual relations.

No doubt, it is sometimes difficult to clearly limit the rightful place of art, critical comment or scientific study. But these disciplines, too, are subject to the overriding limits and requirements of our common goal of growth in humanity.

Taking into account these multiple considerations we wish to make the following concrete suggestions for criminal law reform:

1. Any presentation by whatever means should be considered pornographic or obscene which, for a financial motive, depicts violent or degrading sexual behaviour whether real or simulated. As a definition for "degrading" one might think of enumerating certain actions such as enslavement, bestiality, and others.

2. The production, presentation, distribution, and exhibition of pornographic material should be considered an offense. In this regard, we request that urgent steps be taken whether by the Minister of Justice or the CRTC to curb the use of pornographic material on cable or satellite.

3. Pornography involving children, whether real or simulated, should be considered an especially serious offense subject to very severe penalties.

4. The words "or sex" should be added to the section of the Criminal Code dealing with hate literature (Section 281, 2).

5. If it should prove impossible to further criminalize pornography, as an absolute minimum there should be severe restrictions on the production and distribution of such material so as to make access as difficult as possible. Pornography must not be allowed to spread its heinous message of sexual aggression, torture, and disregard for the other person and his or her body.

Regarding Prostitution

The discussion paper of your committee proposes three legal options in this regard: criminalization, legalization, and decriminalization. In our view, legalization, i.e., the official recognition and control of prostitution, would be the least acceptable of these options, especially if we consider today's understanding of the body as described earlier as well as the increased recognition for the dignity and equality of women.

In line with a now outdated anthropology the Church at one point did support the control of prostitution by the State. However, this anthropology and understanding of the human body has seen development over the centuries, so that it is not longer possible to invoke previous statements without reference to their historical and cultural context, and the evolution of Christian thought.

We do support a strengthening of the law against procuring and living off the avails of prostitution, especially if it is joined with intimidation or violence. If we continue to prosecute prostitutes, either for soliciting or upkeep of bawdy houses, it seems obvious that their clients should be subject to similar prosecution. Otherwise, we would only maintain an unjust situation, especially with regard to the ordinary street prostitutes who have fewer financial means to defend themselves.

Finally, there is a strong consensus in our country to prosecute as criminals people who solicit minors or who engage them in prostitution. Once again, we encounter the State's primordial responsibility for protecting those who are weakest, be that in their emotional development or in relationship to other adults.

The Need for Education and Other Actions

Legal decisions are important but not the only measures to counteract pornography and prostitution. Educational, economic and cultural actions are required to respond to our sexual and affective needs in full respect for the dignity of each person and the requirements of true personal encounters. In its May 19, 1983 Resolution, the Economic and Social Council of the United Nations makes the following concrete suggestions to which we subscribe fully:

a. preventing prostitution through education in ethics (and sex education) and through social formation at school and outside school;

b. increasing the number of women who enter, on behalf of the State, into direct contact with the people concerned;

c. Eliminating whatever discrimination exists that marginalizes prostitutes and impedes their reintegration into society;

d. limiting the industry and commerce of pornography and applying especially severe punishment whenever minors are involved;

e. discouraging effectively the procuring and living off the avails of prostitution, especially if it involves minors;

f. helping with the retraining of former prostitutes and assisting their integration into society.

Above all, however, what is needed in all institutions that serve humanity, and what must be expected from the leaders of these institutions, is the stirring rediscovery of the dignity of men and women, a determined commitment to authentic human values and true human progress. Concern about pornography and prostitution is concern about the broader issues of which these two evils are a part. It is a deep and lasting concern to change the growing disregard and even unawareness of what constitutes true humanness.

6. The Special Task of Christians

In addition to the foregoing considerations based on universal human values, Christians have specific faith reasons for opposing pornography and prostitution. Thus, on the occasion of this brief, we wish to remind the members of our own Church that pornography and prostitution go counter to our adoption as children of God and brothers and sisters of Christ. This faith knowledge will strengthen our personal and community decisions in this regard as Catholic people whether these decisions involve:

1. the refusal to produce, present, distribute or consume pornographic material;

2. participation in a study or action group on these questions;

3. family and sex education of children and adolescents;

4. support for people with emotional or sexual difficulties;

5. personal and financial assistance for centres that support victims of sexual or emotional violence;

6. or support for women in their struggle to achieve economic, social, and cultural equality.

There are many possibilities for successful action. Above all, however, we need to recognize the nefarious consequences of pornography and prostitution and at the same time realize in humility that all of us can be tempted to degrade others and to soil the image of God in ourselves.

In the end, then, what really counts is our willingness to welcome people and to build together a more just and humane society where women, men, and children can live in decency and dignity without fear of being exploited or harmed. What is at stake is our humanity and our common dignity as children of God.

Endnotes

[1] Cf. the many CCCB Messages on issues of economic development and peace, especially the 1983 New Year's Statement by our Social Affairs Commission on Unemployment. Other examples are the recently published *"Ethical Reflections on Respect for Life"* and the *1983 Pastoral Message on Sickness and Healing.*

[2] *Letter of CCCB Episcopal Commission for Social Communications* to CRTC Chairman, January 31, 1983.

[3] Special Committee on Pornography and Prostitution, *Pornography and Prostitution,* Issues Paper, Ottawa, 1983, p. 48

[4] Suzan Brownmiller, *Le viol,* Montréal, L'Etincelle, 1976, p. 475

[5] *Pastoral Constitution on the Church in the Modern World,* 27

[6] Resolution of May 19, 1983.

[7] *The Criminal Law in Canadian Society,* Quotation taken from *Pornography and Prostitution,* Issues Paper, 9.

Notes: *This 1984 statement from the Canadian Conference of Catholic Bishops highlights* *the contributions of the Roman Catholic Church to the deliberations of the Canadian Committee on Pornography and Prostitution. It suggests that censorship is a lesser evil than permitting the continued message of "hate and dehumanization" present in pornography. It supports making all aspects of the pornography business criminal offenses.*

ROMAN CATHOLIC CHURCH—CATHOLIC DAUGHTERS OF THE AMERICAS

REPORT OF THE CATHOLIC DAUGHTERS OF THE AMERICAS (1985)

As national regent of the Catholic Daughters of the Americas, I am extremely pleased to have this opportunity to meet with your committee. In our judgement, it is vital to our organization and to your committee on women that we have close contact. We are personally grateful to you, Bishop Imesch, as chairperson for the bishops' committee for the pastoral letter on women, and to the entire committee for this invitation.

Let me briefly review the structure of our order. It is above all an organization for women, headed by a board of 14 officers. This board sets policy and meets twice each year. Our total membership is 164,894 women and is divided into 1,568 local courts in 43 states, Puerto Rico, Dominican Republic and Mexico.

Our membership consists of wives, mothers and grandmothers, as well as single women, who are dedicated to family life, our church and our order. Many of our members are business and professional women who have worked or are now working in a wide variety of careers.

We are women loyal to the tenets of the church and accept the judgments and decrees of the Holy Father.

Our national board held its semiannual meeting last week, and since each member represents a different region of the country, we invited their comments to be included in our presentation.

Reconciliation of Women in Society

Women in American society today are much better off than they were a mere generation or two ago. We have had the right to vote quite awhile now but, for instance, I was an adult before women in my home state could serve on juries. Now there is a woman in the Supreme Court and great numbers of women throughout the judicial system. This, of course, is true in practically all jobs and professions.

This acceptance of women as having equal capabilities is warmly welcomed by all of us, whether we are career-minded or chiefly homemakers. Women are now realizing a growing sense of their own self-worth and dignity as persons and appreciate being taken seriously in their particular roles. We grow spiritually by society's acceptance of some women's choice to remain single, realizing that married life and motherhood are not the vocations of all women and certainly not necessary to lead a normal, productive life.

Changing situations and today's economy have thrust a large number of women, including mothers, into the working world. For the most part, these women struggle daily with the fear and pain of adjusting to their lives and do not seek to compete with men. They yearn to be accepted as equal or simply as complementary to their male co-workers. Their role in bringing home additional income allows the father more time with his children and in the absence of a father, becomes the only income.

Reconciliation of Women in the Church

The members of the board were unanimous in their feeling that they were happy to be women and that one of the most important roles for women is the role of wife and mother. In this capacity she is the custodian of life. She is the center of the family circle. The love, understanding and education of her children are extremely important, as she is, in fact, the molder of future generations.

We recognize the fact that women in the Christian world are much better off than their sisters in other societies. We are saddened when we read that women are still traded for dowries, that they are mistreated by their in-laws and that some even allow girl babies to die for the reason that they would not contribute as much to the wealth of a family. A reading of the Gospels shows us that Christ recognized women as human beings, which was at that time a startling new attitude.

We appreciate our growing role in the life of the church. We feel that we have gifts which can be brought to the ministry and pastoral needs of the church. The new Code of Canon Law allows women to be named as eucharistic ministers, lectors, judges on diocesan courts, professors at seminaries and many other important positions. However, we still believe that prayerful pursuit of personal holiness is the first and most important responsibility of the Catholic woman.

Alienation of Women in Society

Sad to say, it seems that today's society has more absent fathers than ever before, and the media tell us that poverty is mainly female. Our laws should not allow these absent fathers to evade their responsibility of caring for and rearing of their children, whether married to the children's mother or not.

Even with some child support, a mother without a husband must look to support herself and family with some kind of job. How disheartening it is to read that, even with a comparable education, a woman will earn only about 59 percent of what a man would earn. This is an injustice. Equal pay for equal work by equally qualified workers should be standard business practice.

As caring and intelligent women, we can no longer tolerate pornography and immorality in the media. We feel that this degrades humanity and women in particular. More and more it is also being directed toward the debasement of children, and this no civilization can tolerate. We must press constantly for more regulations and laws, because while we may not be attracted to it or support it, pornography is a menace that destroys souls.

Further, we urge society to study the physical and mental abuse of wives and children. Battered women and children must be sheltered and supported by the community. Rape victims need supportive systems, and in particular, the community needs to be educated about this violent act.

Alienation of Women in the Church

More women than men today participate in adult education classes, the charitable works in the parish and take on the job of teaching religious education classes. Yet some women feel that they are not recognized for their capabilities, but simply tolerated as necessary workers. Too many times on a parish committee or parish council, if women are included, they will automatically be named as the secretary but seldom the president. Women do not want to feel inferior nor do they need to feel superior. They do, however, want recognition of their talents and capabilities as do men.

The community needs to recognize that women who remain at home to care for their families are doing an important and worthwhile job. By the same token, the community needs to acknowledge that women who work do so mainly to help support or entirely support their families. There is no changing the facts of rising divorce rates and increasingly more single-parent families. In this situation women often have no choice, but so much of the time they are made to feel guilty about leaving their children for some part of the day.

These working women are no less motherly than anyone else and would appreciate moral support instead of criticism.

Single women likewise merit respect and admiration for their values and their real contribution to the parish family.

Issues and Themes for Development

The most important theme for development as voiced by the national board was that of the importance of family life. We affirm the actions of Engaged Encounter, Marriage Encounter, Couple to Couple League and others who are doing such a tremendous job of reinforcing family life.

We also see the importance of continuing the cause of pro-life. Every effort must be made for all to acknowledge the beginning of life at conception. If left unchecked, the drive for the abortion of unborn children could lead to the termination of the lives of imperfect babies and the incapacitated.

As a further reinforcement of family life, we would like to see an emphasis on the extended family, stressing the importance of the contributions to the family from uncles, aunts, grandparents and godparents. We believe that by encouraging the veneration of family by children would lead to respect for all adults and people in authority.

Besides support groups or organizations for the single people in the parish, we see a tremendous need for a social environment for our senior citizens. So often their families have moved away and they are left alone, lonely and feel no part of the parish family. Every effort should be made to find a place, even a job or responsibility, in routine of the parish.

Notes: *This 1985 statement by the Catholic Daughters of the Americas was prepared for the U.S. Catholic Conference as it began work on a pastoral letter on women, the first draft of which was released in 1988 as* Partners in the Mystery of Redemption: A Pastoral Response to Women's Concerns for Church and Society. *One paragraph of the statement by the Daughters explicitly treats pornography as a "menace" that is degrading to women, which indicates the special concern for the topic by women in the church. The statement urges "more regulations and laws" against pornography.*

Protestant and
Eastern Orthodox Churches

While the Roman Catholic Church is the single largest religious body in North America, the Protestant and Eastern Orthodox churches together number more than 800 distinct church bodies and contain more than half of the religiously affiliated individuals in North America. The statements from this group, like those of the Roman Catholic Church, show a remarkable unanimity—virtually all of them condemn pornography as a blight which should be curtailed or eliminated. In another trait shared with the Catholics, Protestants have long been associated with the fight against what they view as "public indecency." In that framework, "conservative" and "liberal" attacks on pornography differ very little. The only real difference is that liberals may separate harmful pornography from erotic material that may have a place in society, and, at the same time, may view harmful pornography as one part of a larger issue (such as sexism) instead of one example of deteriorating morality.

Where possible, a number of different statements from the same group are included in order to show how a group may adopt different approaches to an issue at different points in time. A lengthy discussion of the issue by the Presbyterian Church (U.S.A.) is included, as are longer statements from the Reformed Church in America. None of the conservative churches appear to have issued longer statements, which is not surprising when one considers that conservatives view pornography as primarily an issue of self-control, whereas liberals view it as a more complex issue with underlying systemic problems.

AMERICAN BAPTIST CHURCHES IN THE U.S.A.

PORNOGRAPHIC ABUSE OF CHILDREN (1977)

We deplore the recent development of the pornographic use of children in explicit sexual acts and urge American Baptists to become informed about this problem and the dangers that it brings to our society. We call upon clergy, laity, and public officials to take the necessary steps to bring an end to this abuse of children. We urge the American Baptist Churches to make available materials that will provide information and guidance to our constituency on this concern.

Notes: *This 1977 statement by the American Baptist Churches in the U.S.A. (approximately 1,576,500 members) focuses on the dangers of child pornography.*

AMERICAN BAPTIST CHURCHES IN THE U.S.A.

A CHRISTIAN PERSPECTIVE ON SEX AND VIOLENCE IN THE MEDIA (1987)

The need to examine the issues of exploitive sex and excessive violence grows as the amount of both continues to increase on television and in films and as the program availability to our homes and families expands. A special threat is posed for children and youth.

While recognizing that media portrayals of sex and violence are often valid representations of life, there is the concern of their being interpreted as the norm. While being aware of the dangers of censorship, we affirm the importance of parameters of evaluation for the film and television industries and its viewers. We need to challenge the industries regarding the quantity and quality of this kind of programming.

Individuals and families need to be helped to develop criteria concerning TV and theater viewing habits in the light of Christian insights and convictions. It is difficult in our society to control the media bombardment; however, it is possible to sharpen the ability to develop discerning standards.

The following are recommended for areas of study and action:

1. Vigilance in monitoring and challenging the media is a responsibility of our churches in order to assess the danger levels of violence and sex exploitation leading to the expression of convictions. Based on this, we can raise questions of writers, producers, and advertisers concerning choices, standards, and selections of materials produced and promoted. We need to respect First Amendment rights as we exercise our responsibility.

2. The creation of church and media discussion groups is encouraged where parents, children, and youth can share ideas and issues in an attempt to develop personal and family guidelines.

3. The denomination is urged to produce curriculum for study groups and to include the development of standards and values as part of ongoing curriculum resources.

4. Churches are encouraged to develop resource centers which contain journals, magazines, and books pertaining to this issue.

5. Church groups and individuals should be encouraged to express their informed opinions to media officials and to congressional and Federal Communications Commission representatives.

Notes: *This 1987 statement encourages American Baptist members to lobby elected representatives and the broadcast industry to challenge the industry's portrayal of exploitive sex and violence, especially as it affects the way young people view the world.*

AMERICAN BAPTIST CHURCHES IN THE U.S.A.

A RESOLUTION AGAINST PORNOGRAPHY (1988)

The Bible is our record of God's creation of human beings, of the Creator's establishment of a moral code of conduct for men and women, and of God's covenant with the faithful. The Bible is also a record of the failure of humankind to abide by God's law, and Scripture is abundantly full of accounts of sin, including the sins of sexual perversion and sexual violence. There can be no greater evidence than the Bible itself that humanity has distorted and demeaned God's intentions for the relationships between men and women. The Bible writers were quick to condemn those who use sex for lustful or perverted purposes. Fortunately, the Bible is not just a Book of condemnation, but the story of how God redeemed men and women from their sins through Jesus Christ.

The topic of pornography is a distasteful and difficult one for American Baptists, and we seek to approach it in the spirit of our Biblical forebears: mindful of God's law, fearful of God's judgment, and hopeful of God's redemption through our Lord and Savior, Jesus Christ.

1. American Baptists join with their sisters and brothers in many other faith groups to condemn the presence of pornography in our society, and to call upon the institutions of society to work toward its elimination.

2. We define pornography as the portrayal of explicit sexual encounters which highlight violence and coercion. Pornography portrays women and men as demeaned sexual objects, and it victimizes and abuses children by enlisting them to act out roles as if they were willing sexual partners with each other or with adults. This kind of "hard core" pornography takes many forms, and is readily available to the public in video cassettes, films, books, magazines, newspapers, phonograph records, "dial-a-porn" telephone networks, and other media, as well as adult sexual "toys." Recent court decisions have taken strong stands against this type of pornography, and the U.S. Department of Justice characterizes it as "illegal obscenity," the existence of which is not protected by the First Amendment to the United States Constitution (1)

3. As Christians, American Baptists are concerned with the adverse spiritual, social, psychological, and public health effects of pornography.

   a. The sexual disinformation that is prevalent in pornography prevents many person from understanding that sex is a gift from God to enable God's children to procreate, and to be enjoyed in mutual expressions of Love between husband and wife. Any portrayal of sex as an unloving, violent, coercive act is clearly a defamation of God's gift. Any portrayal of sex as gratifying only in the context of domination, humiliation, or pain, is an outrageous corruption of our understanding of the relationship of women and men in the church, in the family, and in society.

   American Baptists believe that women and men are created in the image of God, and that the human body is the temple of God's Holy Spirit. God wants us to care for our bodies, to treat them with respect, and to use them to deepen our understanding of the spiritual side of our nature. We believe that although few of us escape physical suffering in this life, the human body was intended by God as a means of experiencing the joys of God's creation. Sexual intercourse is a joy to be cherished between husband and wife.

   Any medium which seeks to provide crude satisfactions which do not gratify the spirit, or which portrays the body in demeaning ways, or which portrays sexual intercourse as a spiritually sterile or violent act, is abhorrent to us.

   Pornography which victimizes children is especially abominable. In many ways, "child pornography" is the ultimate affront to God's intentions for the family, and for the spiritual development of human beings from earliest childhood. Jesus used children to illustrate the sort of simple faith He wanted His followers to have. Those who corrupt the innocence of childhood are singled out for special condemnation.

   b. Pornography harms the body as well as the spirit. The production, distribution and consumption of this pornography harms both those who produce it and those who consume it. Local outlets which distribute pornography, which often provide private viewing booths in which male masturbation may take place, become potential breeding grounds for venereal disease. Sexual "toys" and implements which penetrate body orifices have a potential for doing physical and mental harm to persons who use them.

   Most importantly, the inaccurate information about sex which spread by pornography causes some persons to conclude that sex is pleasurable when it is coercive, when it is engaged in with an anonymous partner, and when physical violence and sometimes torture is employed in the act. Moreover, studies lead researchers to believe that in some cases, there is a casual relationship between hard core pornography and violent sexual acts. (2)

4. Pornography has significant law enforcement implications. Local outlets which distribute pornography tend to attract prostitutes, drug dealers, and criminals. Hard core pornography is an $8-billion industry in the United States, (2) and elements of organized crime are intimately involved in its production and distribution.

5. The form of pornography which the U.S. Justice Department describes as "illegal obscenity" is particularly virulent in that it often portrays women, men, and children as engaging in explicit and often violent sexual acts. Some of the actors in these illicit media are injured or killed in the process of producing films, video tapes, or photographs. The injurious effects of illegal obscenity on its consumers and on innocent persons are numerous and profoundly disturbing.

Yet apathy toward the existence of illegal obscenity is widespread, and the public has not encouraged public officials and law enforcement officers to take action against it.

In many cases, this apathy is caused by a misunderstanding of what "illegal obscenity", or hard core pornography, is, and what it is not. Some persons hesitate to call for action against this hard core pornography because they are unaware of the differences between it and erotic magazines, literary erotica, or other media occasionally referred to as "soft porn."

Hard core pornography has absolutely no redeeming literary or social value. It is clearly injurious to the physical, emotional, and spiritual health of individuals. It is so virulent and harmful that we are compelled to focus our full attention on it, and we call upon Christians to do all they can to eradicate it.

A Resolution

Being deeply concerned about the far reaching effects of pornography on persons and on society, we:

1. Commend the U.S. Department of Justice for its establishment of a Commission on Pornography, and for its stated determination to take effective action against illegal obscenity while protecting the free speech rights of individuals under the First Amendment to the U.S. Constitution.

2. Commend the Surgeon General of the United States for his efforts to make the public health dangers of pornography known to the public.

3. Commend the Governing Board of the National Council of Churches of Christ in the USA for passing a strongly worded policy statement condemning violence and sexual violence in media.

4. Commend the work of the Religious Alliance Against Pornography (RAAP), a broadly based interfaith group composed of Protestants, Jews, Orthodox, Roman Catholic, ecumenical, and evangelical groups who are united in their stand against pornography portraying sexual violence and against child pornography.

5. We call upon American Baptist congregations to take seriously their responsibility for ministering to individuals and families to help them develop an accurate knowledge of sex and healthy attitudes toward it which include an understanding of sex as a gift of God. We also call upon American Baptist congregations to lift up the name and cause of Christ as they take prophetic action in their communities against the presence of pornography.

6. We call upon American Baptist national program boards and the boards of American Baptist regions to help develop resources that will be useful to the churches in carrying out their ministry of holistic sex education among individuals and families, and in the churches' action against pornography in their communities.

7. We call upon law enforcement officials and prosecutors to take strong action in eradicating illegal obscenity.

8. We call upon individual citizens to become directly involved in the distasteful activity of informing themselves about pornography, understanding its effects, and developing strategies for taking direct legal action against it by becoming plaintiffs in anti-pornography legal proceedings.

9. We commit ourselves as individuals to understand the scourge of pornography, to seek the courage to take specific action against pornography, and to be teachers and motivaters of persons who are in a position to be effective opponents of it in our society.

Adopted by the General Board of the American Baptist Churches - December 1988.

166 For, 1 Against, 1 Abstention

(General Board Reference # - 8162:12/87)

Policy Base:

American Baptist Policy Statement on Family Life - June 1984:

"A vision of marriage as monogamous, life-long, one flesh union is affirmed by Jesus . . .

A vision of the parent-child relationship as one of tender care, mutual responsibility, and mutual benefit . . .

We affirm children are a gift from God, entrusted to parents for love, care and nurture . . .

We affirm Christian families as agents through which God's Good News is proclaimed, received, and lived out so that persons might fulfill God's redemptive purpose in history . . .

We affirm . . . family groups experiencing conflict within marriages or between generations are . . . helped to find resources for healing . . .

We are committed to providing programs of education . . . to empower parents striving to raise children according to Christian principles . . . and to sustain parents when young children struggle with sexual orientation . . .

We are committed to advocating the rights of all families, and especially those with dependent children and aging members, to the necessities of life: shelter, safety, medical care, and education."

American Baptist Policy Statement on Human Rights - December 1976

"The right to the basic necessities of food, shelter, clothing, and health care . . . the right to develop family structures, to build mutually satisfying human relationships and to nurture, train and educate children . . .

The right to grow in mind and self-fulfillment . . .

The right to follow the dictates of conscience . . .

The right to privacy in one's home . . .

The right to human dignity . . . "

American Baptist Policy Statement on Women and Men as Partners in Church and Society - December 1985:

" . . . the father and the mother should model mutual love and respect for the gifts and qualities that each brings to their marriage and the home they have established. . . . It also means that parents should teach their sons and daughters to love and respect all persons, seeking to free them from stifling male and female stereotypes and encouraging them to develop skills and talents according to their individual gifts. . . ."

"We affirm that both men and women in church and society should share concern for strong family units and consistent child care. . . ."

Footnotes:

[1] For example, Miller v. California (1973) and other decisions described in the report of the Attorney General's Commission against Pornography. Paris Theater v. Slaton (1973) states: "The Sum of experience . . . affords an ample basis for legislatures to conclude that a sensitive, key relationship of human existence, central to family life, community welfare, and the development of the human personality, can be debased and distorted by crass commercial exploitation of sex."

[2] As cited in the report of the Attorney General's Commission on Pornography.

Notes: *This 1988 resolution from the American Baptists clearly differentiates between "erotic magazines, literary erotica, or other media occasionally referred to as 'soft porn,'" and hard core pornography, and only advocates the elimination of the latter. Hard core pornography is defined as that which portrays violent and coercive sex or children engaged in sexual acts and has no redeeming social value.*

AMERICAN FAMILY ASSOCIATION

TESTIMONIALS (UNDATED)

Christian Leaders Commend American Family Association

The American Family Association was founded in 1977. It is a member of the Evangelical Council for Financial Accountability. It's monthly magazine has a circulation of approximately 380,000, including approximately 170,000 pastors and churches. AFA has over 500 local chapters in communities across America. Below are comments from 39 Christian leaders with very diverse theological perspectives who are personally acquainted with the AFA ministry.

The American Family Association has kept before all of us the tragedy of television, movies, and printed materials which attack the very plan and design of God for each human being and God's wonderful creation of family life. May these efforts continue forward so that God's power working within all of us can help change the tone, themes, and contents of modern television programming to reflect more clearly God's life in and among us.

Most Rev. Roger Mahony, Catholic Archbishop of Los Angeles

On behalf of the Assemblies of God, I wish to express appreciation to the Reverend Donald E. Wildmon, executive director of AFA, for his efforts to promote a constructive change in network television programming. The 2.5 million Assemblies of God adherents in the U.S.A. are very desirous that the networks would reverse the unwholesome trend in programming which, we feel, is adversely affecting the morality of our nation.

Dr. G. Raymond Carlson, Gen. Supt., Assemblies of God

When many in today's society are apathetic about the increasing amount of sex and violence on television and pornography on the newsstands, Donald Wildmon has spearheaded a moral witness against this evil. It is good to work with him in the CLeaR-TV effort. I hope you will join in this witness.

Bishop Louis W. Schowengerdt, The United Methodist Church

Donald E. Wildmon, executive director of American Family Association, has provided unique, unselfish and understanding leadership on behalf of CLeaR-TV's efforts to reduce sex, violence and profanity in TV programs. His perception, professionalism and persistence are to be commended. I appreciate his efforts and salute him for the outstanding leadership he provides AFA and CLeaR-TV.

Dr. Melvin Worthington, Executive Secretary
National Association of Free Will Baptists

I have known Donald Wildmon for many years. He is a man of highest integrity and always lives by the highest ethical standards. He is leading a needed crusade for decency and integrity in our American life. I encourage you to listen to what he says.

Dr. James T. Draper, Past Pres., Southern Baptist Convention

I heartily support the American Family Association's effort to bring needed changes to television programming. The time for bringing family values back to television has never been more appropriate—and indeed urgent. Donald Wildmon is on the front lines, fighting the good fight.

Charles "Chuck" Colson, Chrm., Prison Fellowship Ministries

Donald E. Wildmon and the American Family Association are to be commended for their steadfast commitment to the promotion of decency and morality in the media industry.

John Cardinal O'Connor, Catholic Archbishop of New York

Donald Wildmon is one of the most courageous, faithful examples of what I believe our Lord had in mind when He commanded us to be salt and light in our society. He has done more to awaken the Christian world to the incredible onslaught of all that is evil and anti-Christian through the media of anyone of our time. I believe he is to be applauded and encouraged in every possible way. I count it a privilege to stand with him and encourage you to do the same.

Bill Bright, Pres., Campus Crusade for Christ International

Don Wildmon has been at the forefront of the moral and social issues, especially television, long before many other Christian leaders and people awakened to the crucial problems we face related to the violence, sex, etc. on television. I applaud him.

Dr. Thomas A. McDill, Pres.' Evangelical Free Church in America

For five years I have known Don Wildmon as a courageous and fearless crusader for a decent and moral America. He has one purpose, to awaken the conscience of our people to join the battle against forces, especially in the media, which would undermine our Judeo-Christian values.

Bishop Clyde E. Van Valin, The Free Methodist Church

Rev. Donald E. Wildmon is a man of integrity and dedication. I strongly support his ministry. Our denomination is highly indebted to him for his efforts to clean up television programming.

Dr. Robert Kline, Gen. Supt., Churches of Christ in Christian Union

The effort of Don Wildmon and the American Family Association in promoting constructive change in network television programming could prove to be one of the most effective means we have of bringing back a direct influence of positive morality on American society.

Dr. John Moran, President, The Missionary Church

I commend to you the ministry of the American Family Association and Donald Wildmon, executive director. In a generation of deteriorating morals we desperately need to be salt and light. The American Family Association is a vehicle assisting us in making a difference.

Dr. Robert S. Ricker, Gen. Sec., Baptist General Conference

I consider Donald E. Wildmon a good Christian man deeply committed to a very troublesome moral issue that threatens the existence of the Christian family and brings untold hurt to our Lord's churches. We are all indebted to him for his tireless efforts to clean up TV programming.

Ray O. Brooks, Past President, American Baptist Association

Rev. Donald E. Wildmon is a sincere servant of the Lord, dedicated to making America better through promoting family values that are in keeping with the Judeo-Christian tradition.

Rev. Clifford R. Christensen, Conference Minister
Conservative Congregational Christian Conference

Donald E. Wildmon, executive director of the American Family Association, is a modern-day John the Baptist speaking out fearlessly against the moral corruption in our decadent society. He is appreciated and commended.

Thomas D. Thurman, Director, Christian Restoration Association

Be assured that Donald E. Wildmon is in touch with the issues that really count. He is unrelentingly involved, and doggedly determined to do something about it. Wisdom would mandate hearing him out.

Rev. Tom Grinder, General Overseer
International Pentecostal Church of Christ

The American Family Association, under the leadership of Donald E. Wildmon, was among the first to focus the Christian community's attention upon the evils of pornography and to discern the consistent anti-Christian bias in much of today's motion pictures and television.

Dr. Robert D. Rasmussen, Executive Minister
American Baptist Churches of the West, A.B.C.E., in the U.S.A.

I have known of the work of the Rev. Donald Wildmon for several years, and have heartily endorsed it and have been very happy to assist him from time to time. His work is basic to preserving a Christian, moral America.

Most Rev. James Parker Dees, Presiding Bishop
The Anglican Orthodox Church

I have been associated with Mr. Donald Wildmon for approximately five years. He is a proven leader deeply committed to strong Judeo-Christian values. Through the American Family Association, a strong and clear call is going forth to call this nation back to morality and decency. We believe there is a need to return to the principles that have made this nation great.

Dr. Don Sauls, Gen. Supt., Pentecostal Free Will Baptist Church

Don Wildmon has focused his attention on an important ministry and has devoted his considerable talent and ability to it quite effectively. He is truly blessed, because many have reviled him, persecuted him and said all manner of evil against him falsely (Matthew 5:11). But he is truly appreciated by many Christians who applaud his straightforward, fact-backed, well-executed attacks on obscenity, profanity and anti-Christian depictions in the media and arts.

Ben Johnston, Moderator, Associate Reformed Presbyterian Church

I have been personally acquainted with the work of the American Family Association for years, and am personally acquainted with The Rev. Donald Wildmon, with whom I have worked for the past several years. I commend this effort and Don's good offices to your support.

Rt. Rev. William C. Wantland, Episcopal Bishop of Eau Claire

Don Wildmon represents us all. He is our John the Baptist in the field, whether that field be pornography or decency in radio, television, the Hollywood movie industry or motel movies. I would hate to think where we would be without him.

Dr. Ray E. Smith, Gen. Supt., Open Bible Standard Churches

I appreciate the stand that Rev. Wildmon takes on moral issues. Television programs have become offensive, vulgar and immoral. We need to support him as he is attempting to clean up the airways.

Rev. Gary Thornton, Executive Director
Association of Independent Methodists

In my opinion, AFA is impacting change for the better toward wholesome family values in current media. I commend AFA to you for prayerful and financial support.

Dr. O. Dale Emery, General Superintendent, The Wesleyan Church

I write to share with you my respect for the person and the work of Donald E. Wildmon. His efforts in leading others in a combined attempt to improve the quality of TV programming in the U.S.A. have the hearty endorsement of myself and of my church.

Dr. Robert Hess, General Superintendent
Evangelical Friends Church, Eastern Region

I regularly thank the Lord for Donald Wildmon, and the work that's done through the American Family Association. The Lord has placed a humble servant in this difficult post and he accomplishes his work with remarkable grace.

Dr. David Mains, President, Chapel of the Air

I should like to encourage Donald E. Wildmon in his tremendous efforts to seek the highest possible ethical standards in the television programs that are coming into our homes. I think everyone will agree there has been an erosion of good taste and basic morality in the television programs that are coming into the homes of our nation. Someone must take a leadership role in this challenge. I am pleased to see Rev. Donald E. Wildmon take on this challenge. May his work be successful.

Most Reverend Daniel E. Sheehan, Catholic Archbishop of Omaha

Don Wildmon and the AFA are providing an essential service to the evangelical Christian community by keeping us informed about current events that are in direct opposition to our moral and spiritual values. He gives us constructive actions to take and makes us feel that our response makes a difference. I applaud his sincerity and commitment so we can be the "salt" Jesus called us to be to the world.

Dr. Tim Blanchard, General Director
Conservative Baptist Association of America

I thank God for Donald Wildmon, his dedication to family values, and his determination to make a difference in our society. His concern is sincere, and I believe this latest strategy is sound.

Mark Taylor, Editor, The Lookout, Standard Publishing Company

Rev. Donald Wildmon and the AFA have for several years taken a strong stand on the subjects of pornography and its distribution, both in the printed word and through television. Their efforts have succeeded time and again in removing pornographic maga- zines from stores and in alerting Americans to the insidious creeping of pornography into our lives. Rev. Wildmon is to be commended for his high standards and willingness to step up to the formidable challenge of cleaning up network programming.

Rev. L. Edward Davis, Stated Clerk, Evangelical Presbyterian Church

Never before in history has Satan fought so hard for the very souls of this generation. Never before have we needed ministries like American Family Association. Don, keep fighting, the TBN family is with you.

Paul F. Crouch, President, Trinity Broadcasting Network

Pornography is a major moral problem in the U.S.A. at this time. I believe that the American Family Association is a powerful opponent of pornography and is therefore worthy of support.

Most Reverend John F. Whealon, Catholic Archbishop of Hartford

Don Wildmon is committed to Jesus Christ in his specialized ministry. His ministry is most effective in meeting a real need in our society. Don Wildmon is a Christian example to all of us in the spiritual warfare.

Bishop Leon Stewart, General Superintendent
International Pentecostal Holiness Church

Don Wildmon and the American Family Association are an essential voice in promoting a constructive change in network television programming and upholding traditional family values. They are helping awaken Christians to the need to be involved in addressing vital issues in our society. I strongly recommend your participation with millions of other Americans who care about the future of our society.

Rev. David Krogh, Pres., Church of God (General Conference)

We support Don Wildmon and the ministry of the American Family Association. We join them in striving to uphold high ideals and Biblical moral values before our nation.

Dr. J. Eugene Kurtz, General Supervisor
International Church of The Foursquare Gospel

It is a great joy to endorse Donald Wildmon and the American Family Association for the outstanding work that they are doing in attempting to solve one of the greatest problems of our day: the elimination of the filth, profanity, pornography and blasphemy from our media. Not only every Christian, but every decent minded American should be delighted to support them.

Dr. D. James Kennedy, Senior Minister
Coral Ridge Presbyterian Church

Donald Wildmon is a sincere, devout Christian. His ministry is marked by intensity and integrity of Spirit.

Andrew Miller, National Commander, The Salvation Army

As General Secretary of the Assemblies of The Lord Jesus Christ, we heartily commend Don Wildmon for the work he and American Family Association are doing in regards to cleaning up the television programs which so greatly affect the households of our nation. Keep up the good work!

Rev. M.L. Walls, Gen. Sec., Assemblies of The Lord Jesus Christ

Notes: *The American Family Association is an ecumenical, evangelical Christian group which works against pornography, particularly what it believes to be the portrayal of objectionable values on television. Its more liberal counterpart is the Religious Alliance Against Pornography.*

BAPTIST GENERAL CONFERENCE

RESOLUTION ON OBSCENITY (1973)

In the light of the recent United States Supreme Court decision on obscenity whereby states and local communities have been given greater authority to set their own standards on obscenity and mindful of the serious nature of this problem in the United States today, BE IT RESOLVED:

A. That we commend the United States Supreme Court for its decision reversing a trend of recent decisions on obscenity.

B. That we urge our Conference churches, pastors and members to contact local authorities, making known our serious concern on this problem and requesting prompt action to control or eliminate this evil practice in our nation.

Notes: *This 1973 resolution from the Baptist General Conference (approximately 137,000 members) was issued in response to a Supreme Court ruling in which the court replaced the "utterly without redeeming value" test with a standard requiring only that the work lack "serious" literary, artistic, political, or scientific value. This resolution called for the elimination of obscenity in general.*

BAPTIST GENERAL CONFERENCE

RESOLUTION ON PORNOGRAPHY (1986)

Whereas the problem of pornography has continued to be a crisis in this nation as identified by the United States Attorney General's Commission.

And whereas many children and families have suffered from the consequences of pornography.

And whereas the preponderance of media reviews of the Attorney General's Commission on Pornography have been critical, resulting in a curtailment of full implementation of the recommendations of the committee.

Therefore, be it resolved that the delegates of the 108th annual meeting of the Baptist General Conference direct the general secretary to send telegrams, on behalf of the Baptist General Conference, to the Attorney General of the United States and to the President of the United States urging them to quickly implement the recommendations of the Attorney General's Commission on Pornography and that the responsibility for implementation be kept at the Attorney General level to ensure their accomplishments.

Further be it resolved that the delegates of the annual meeting of the Baptist General Conference write, and encourage others to write, to the Attorney General of the United States and the President of the United States, urging them to quickly implement these recommendations and their implementation be retained with the Attorney General.

Notes: *This 1986 Baptist General Conference resolution supports U.S. Attorney General Ed Meese's report on pornography, including the report's harsh estimate of the dangers and harms of pornography. The conference recommends the implementation of the report's proposed measures to restrict pornography.*

BAPTIST GENERAL CONFERENCE

RESOLUTION ON PORNOGRAPHY (1987)

Whereas the problem of pornography has continued to be a crisis in this nation as identified by the United States Attorney General's Commission on Pornography, and whereas many men, women and children have been victimized by pornography, therefore be it resolved that the delegates to the 1987 annual meeting of the Baptist General Conference hereby urge other members of the Baptist General Conference to inform themselves about the evils of pornography and to work toward instituting state and local laws which are enforceable and constitutional to remove hard core pornography from our land.

Notes: *In 1987, the Baptist General Conference again responded to U.S. Attorney General Ed Meese's report on pornography. Unlike its 1986 resolution, the 1987 resolution speaks of "hard core pornography" rather than general obscenity.*

CHRISTIAN CHURCH (DISCIPLES OF CHRIST)

CONCERNING PORNOGRAPHY (1976)

APPROVED by the General Assembly

WHEREAS, pornography in various forms has increased dramatically in recent years, and

WHEREAS, this exploitation constitutes an intrusion into the lives of citizens of the community, and

WHEREAS, the influence of pornography results in a confusion of values, causing many persons to substitute eroticism for sexuality, lust for love, and self-gratification for the dignity of others, and

WHEREAS, these perversions of human values deny the New Testament understanding of personal worth, and inhibit the development of adequate, loving male/female relationships.

THEREFORE BE IT RESOLVED, that the General Assembly of the Christian Church (Disciples of Christ) meeting in San Antonio, August 15-20, 1975, request the church to refine and intensify its program of sex education and wholesome family life, and

BE IT FURTHER RESOLVED, that individual congregations of the church be urged to assert their strong moral opposition to pornography wherever they perceive it to appear in their local community.

Notes: *This 1976 resolution from the Christian Church (Disciples of Christ) disapproves of pornography in its "various forms" and urges members to show their opposition to it. The church has approximately 1,120,000 members.*

CHRISTIAN CHURCH (DISCIPLES OF CHRIST)

RESOLUTION CONCERNING PORNOGRAPHY (1985)

WHEREAS, pornographic materials are degrading to women, men, and children, and exploit all involved in their production and consumption; and

WHEREAS, pornography is often linked to the incidence of rape, incest, and the sexual abuse of children; and

WHEREAS, materials judged to be obscene are not protected under the First Amendment to the Constitution, and their transport, distribution, and sale are prohibited by Federal Law;

THEREFORE BE IT RESOLVED, by the General Assembly of the Christian Church (Disciples of Christ) meeting in Des Moines, Iowa, August 2-7, 1985, that

1. the Division of Homeland Ministries be requested to make available information on the effects of pornography on society in general and specifically the effect of the pornographic exploitation of children; and

2. members of the Christian Church (Disciples of Christ) be encouraged to express their

concern over pornography and to take appropriate action in their communities to curtail the distribution of such materials; and

3. the General Minister and President be asked to write a letter to the President of the United States encouraging him to enforce existing laws concerning the transport, distribution, and sale of obscene materials.

Notes: *This 1985 resolution of the Christian Church (Disciples of Christ) condemned pornography because of its degradation of individuals and its connection to sexual abuse and violence directed at women and children. It encouraged greater enforcement of existing laws regarding obscene materials.*

CHRISTIAN REFORMED CHURCH IN NORTH AMERICA

STATEMENT AND RESOLUTION ON PORNOGRAPHY (1988)

II. Overtures

A. *Pornography*

1. Material: Overture 15, p. 368

2. Background:

   Classis Grandville overtures synod to adopt a Statement on Pornography. The matter came to synod last year and now appears in revised version.

3. Recommendation:

   That synod adopt Overture 15.

A Statement on Pornography

The *American Heritage Dictionary* defines pornography as "the presentation of sexually explicit behavior as in a photograph, intended to arouse sexual excitement." Literally, "pornography" is the combination of two Greek words *porné*, "prostitute," and *graphé*, "to write" or "to picture."[1] The verbal root of *porno* means "to sell," "to harlot for hire."

The word *pornography* is not mentioned in the Scriptures, but the Greek word *porneia* is repeatedly used in the New Testament to embrace this form of sexual behavior as a sin of the flesh (Gal. 5:19).

This implies, of course, that there is a healthy view of sexuality. The Bible teaches us that sex is neither an accident of nature nor an invention of the devil. And though there is a distinction in gender between animals as well, our human sexuality is in no way equivalent to that of the animals. Our sexuality is distinctively human. It was designed by the Creator. It is God's gift to a unique creature whom the Bible describes as created in God's image and after his likeness. (Cf. CRC Publications, *Sex, Marriage, and the Family.*) As such, sex is not evil. It is a gift from God to be exercised within the marriage bond. It is our heart that makes sex the jungle that it has become. "For out of the heart," says Jesus, "come evil thoughts, murder, adultery, sexual immorality, theft, false testimony, slander" (Matt. 15:19).

In view of the fact that the CRC has as its basis of authority for faith and practice the Holy Scriptures, we believe that what the church says about sexual behavior should honor both God and our neighbor. Therefore, Christians do well to recognize the church's important role in providing instruction on questions of human sexuality.

We also believe that the Bible clearly condemns sexual perversions[2] which pornography glorifies and promotes as normal and healthy.[3]

Pornography contributes to the break-up of marriages and families, the molestation of children, rape, and other forms of criminal sexual conduct.[4] It victimizes women, children, and men.

The pornography industry is primarily controlled by and contributes millions of dollars in profit to organized crime.[5]

We as Christians are called upon by God to defend the weak and defenseless (James 1:27), and stand against unrighteousness (Heb. 1:9).

Jesus declared that if we have done it for the least of these we have done it for him (Matt. 25:40-45).

It is our obligation as Christians to stand against evil, promote human dignity, protect our children from sexual exploitation, and provide healthy roles for human sexual expression.[6]

The use of any form of pornographic material to arouse sexual desire is a sin.[7]

"You have loved righteousness and hated wickedness, therefore God, your God, has set you above your companions by anointing you with the oil of joy" (Heb. 1:9).

A Resolution Concerning Pornography

WHEREAS, the appended statement is a true representation of the position of the Christian Reformed Church in North America on the matter of pornography:

THEREFORE BE IT RESOLVED:

- That synod urge the members of the church, through its teaching and preaching ministry, to closely examine their life-styles and attitudes on human sexuality from a biblical perspective as well as in light of the negative messages that come from modern media and pornography.

- That synod urge each congregation to choose at least one of their members to become actively involved with a local or national decency organization and keep the congregation informed on specific issues and steps to be taken to promote decency.

- That synod urge all of our members who use or view any form of pornographic material to arouse sexual desire to recognize that such is a sin, to repent of that sin, and to seek forgiveness and healing from Jesus Christ, our Lord.

- That synod urge all church members to become actively involved in stemming the tide of pornography by:

  a. praying for the individuals directly involved in the battle against pornography in all its varied forms; for the many innocent victims; for those who sell, produce, and distribute pornographic material;

  b. educating themselves to become more aware of the impact that pornography is having on society;

  c. withholding patronage from establishments that deal in or support pornography;

  d. actively involving themselves in the public debate over pornography by contacting public officials, writing letters to the editors of magazines and newspapers, and speaking openly with friends, neighbors, and family members, and in so doing, holding forth the biblical standards for sexuality, and

BE IT FURTHER RESOLVED, that synod instruct the stated clerk to publish and distribute to each congregation a copy of the Statement on Pornography and a copy of this resolution, and

BE IT RESOLVED, that synod prepare and distribute a list of available resource materials to further equip both clergy and laity to become better informed and more effectively involved.

—Adopted

Endnotes

[1] *Theological Dictionary of the New Testament,* edited by Gerhard Kittel.

[2] Eph. 5:3, 5; Col. 3:5; Lev. 18:6, 23; 19:29; 20:10-16; Rom. 1:24; 1 Cor. 5:9-13; Ex. 22:19

[3] *Final Report of the Attorney General's Commission on Pornography* (AG), Rutledge Hill Press Edition, 1986, p. 489; *A Strategy for Decency* (SFD), by Brad Curl, 1986, pp. 72-82.

[4] While behavioral science cannot offer proof of harm in the form of empirical evidence showing a direct causal relationship to pornographic materials, the preponderance of research verifies that sexually explicit and graphically violent material significantly changes the attitude of the viewer toward healthy human sexuality.These attitudinal changes are often made manifest in deviant sexual behavior. Refer to Chapter 18 of *AG* and pages 63-71 of *SFD* for a summary of that research.

[5] *The Seduction of Society,* 1984, by William A. Stanmeyer, pp. 29-32; AG, pp. 40, 199-210.

[6] Ezek. 33:8; Matt. 18:5-9.

[7] Matt. 5:28; Ex. 20:14; Phil. 4:8; Prov. 6:23-25.

Notes: *This 1988 statement by the Christian Reformed Church in North America (approximately 220,000 members) condemns as a sin the use of any pornography to arouse sexual desire. While the church feels that sex in itself is not evil, it believes that pornography glorifies perversions and supports organized crime. Members are urged to join decency organizations and actively work against the pornography industry.*

CHURCH OF GOD IN CHRIST, MENNONITE

THE CHURCH AND THE WORLD (UNDATED)

The Church and the world are distinctly separate institutions with aims, tastes, and attachments essentially different; for members of the Church to be conformed to the world by way of dress, socials, picnics, shows, fairs, and such worldly amusements is sinful. "Ye cannot serve God and mammon." Matt. 6:24; John 18:36; Rom. 12:1,2; II Cor. 6:14-18; I John 2:15,16; Titus 2:11,14; Eph. 5:11.

The Church is an organization called out from the world. Jesus said to His disciples, "If ye were of the world, the world would love his own: but because ye are not of the world, but I have chosen you out of the world, therefore the world hateth you" (John 15:19). It is well to think of the Church as the mystical Body of Christ and every member an integral part of it.

The aim of the Church is to glorify its Redeemer " . . . seek those things which are above, where Christ sitteth on the right hand of God" (Col. 3:1). "Knowing this, that our old man is crucified with him . . . " (Rom. 6:6). "I am crucified with Christ: nevertheless I live; yet not I, but Christ liveth in me: and the life which I now live in the flesh I live by the faith of the Son of God, who loved me, and gave himself for me" (Gal. 2:20). A true Christian does not follow the carnal desires of the flesh.

A spiritual house—"Ye also, as lively stone, are built up a spiritual house, an holy priesthood, to offer up spiritual sacrifices, acceptable to God by Jesus Christ" (I Pet. 2:5). " . . . be ye transformed by the renewing of your mind, that ye may prove what is that good, and acceptable, and perfect, will of God" (Rom. 12:2).

It is not the worldly ambitious who " . . . may sit, the one on thy right hand, and the other on the left, in thy kingdom. . . . Ye know that the princes of the Gentiles exercise dominion over them, and they that are great exercise authority upon them. But it shall not be so among you . . . '' (Matt. 20:21, 25, 26).

The unregenerated seek and love to promote the things of this world. ''They are of the world: therefore speak they of the world, and the world heareth them'' (I John 4:5).

''Love not the world, neither the things that are in the world. If any man love the world, the love of the Father is not in him. For all that is in the world, the lust of the flesh, and the lust of the eves, and the pride of life, is not of the Father, but is of the world. And the world passeth away, and the lust thereof . . . '' (I John 2:15-17). ''And the devil, taking him up into an high mountain, shewed unto him all the kingdoms of the world in a moment of time. And the devil said unto him, all this power will I give thee, and the glory of them: for that is delivered unto me; and to whomsoever I will I give it. . . . And Jesus answered and said unto him, Get thee behind me, Satan: for it is written, Thou shalt worship the Lord thy God, and him only shalt thou serve'' (Luke 4:5,6,8). '' . . . that which is highly esteemed among men is abomination in the sight of God'' (Luke 16:15). Moses valued true riches in Christ above the glories in Egypt (Heb. 11:26). The Apostle Paul thought of his inheritance in Christ as an excellency not comparable to any earthly glamour or esteem (Phil. 3:8). He admonished the brethren to '' . . . condescend to men of low estate . . . '' (Rom. 12:16).

'' . . . lovers of pleasures more than lovers of God'' (II Tim. 3:4), could include voluptuous and sensual living, which are classed under unlawful pleasures for Christians. Living in pleasure or going to places where sensual pleasure is promoted is not conducive to spiritual life. ''For the flesh lusteth against the Spirit, and the Spirit against the flesh . . . '' (Gal. 5:17). ''For they that are after the flesh do mind the things of the flesh; but they that are after the Spirit the things of the Spirit. For to be carnally minded is death; but to be spiritually minded is life and peace'' (Rom. 8:5,6).

There are the worldly places of amusement such as ballrooms, theaters, movies, gambling dens, circuses, bowling alleys, skating rinks, and Sabbath desecration in the form of joy rides, motor boating, racing, popular games, dissipation in parks and swimming pools, and such. We also think of the hundreds of thousands of girls disappearing from year-to-year as victims of seductive pleasures and vice in this carnal, pleasure-loving age. Let us turn once more to the Word of God: '' . . . but know thou, that for all these things God will bring thee into judgment'' (Eccl. 11:9).

Notes: *This statement by the Church of God in Christ, Mennonite (approximately 10,000 members), while not specifically mentioning pornography, emphasizes that spiritual life is not compatible with worldly amusements. Those places or things which promote sensual pleasure are "unlawful" for Christians.*

CHURCH OF THE BRETHREN

UNFINISHED BUSINESS (1966)

A. The Theological Basis of Personal Ethics

Request for a Study, 1963

Annual Conference, in light of an appeal from the Western Pennsylvania board of administration and elders and moderators' council, and upon recommendation of Standing Committee, appoints a committee to make a thorough theological study of the concerns related to the Church of the Brethren's historic position with regard to personal ethics and conduct, which have been noticeably altered by the impact of rapid social and technological change, which thus cause the erosion of ethical standards and practices of the personal and corporate life of the church.

Committee: Clemens Rosenberger (chairman), Mrs. W. Newton Long, Sr., Donald E. Miller, Paul S. Hoover, Robert McFadden.

1966 Report of the Committee

The Church of the Brethren historically has seriously attempted to guide its conduct in personal ethics by a careful and considered study of the New Testament. Brethren have always believed that the faith of the New Testament should be expressed in the many and varied situations of life. Your committee has therefore approached the query by looking first of all to the Biblical witness regarding personal conduct, and then to a historical and theological consideration of the Brethren understanding of the style of the Christian life.

Believing that the query is calling for more than general suggestions, we have consulted Brethren across the Brotherhood to discover those problems of personal conduct that are most pressing in contemporary life. The major portion of our report is given over to those problems. In keeping with the instruction of Annual Conference we have incorporated an answer to the query on gambling and games of chance within the larger report.

I. The Biblical Witness

Christian ethics begins with the freedom, holiness, and steadfast love (*chesed*) of God, who has revealed himself most clearly in the historical life of Jesus Christ. He is the beginning and the end, the creator, sustainer, and ruler of all. Conduct is right as it comes under the claim of God in His holiness and righteousness. The relationship of men to one another is defined by God's self-disclosure to men. Because God is love we ought to love one another, and because He is holy we are called to be a holy people.

However, in their freedom men sin against God by ignoring and revolting against his claim, through living by their own self-centered standards of righteousness and freedom rather than doing what is pleasing in his sight. The consequence of sin for mankind is a life of anxiety, rebellion, meaninglessness, social injustice, and death (John 1:10-13; Romans 1:24-27). Men prefer sloth and alienation to the freedom that comes from a covenantal relationship to God.

In the face of human despair God comes as One who in suffering love redeems and reconciles men, restoring them to right relationship with Him. The character of God's freedom and self-giving love is seen most clearly in Jesus of Nazareth, in whom the whole fullness of deity was pleased to dwell. He who has seen the Christ has seen the Father. His life and teaching, His cross, His resurrection, and His Spirit are the basis for all Christian ethics.

The Christian seeks to respond to God's claim, to live in harmony with him, to glorify Him, to do what is pleasing in His sight, to love Him, and to be faithful to Him. Jesus' summary of personal ethics is that "you shall love the Lord your God with all your heart, and with all your soul, and with all your mind," and "you shall love your neighbour as yourself" (Matthew 22:37-39). The twofold commandment makes brilliantly clear that love of God always entails love of neighbor; personal ethics always involve social ethics.

The Gospels expose any attempt to separate an act from its motive. God looks not simply upon the external act, but upon its wholeness, including its motive.

Some of Jesus's severest condemnation came upon those who pretended to be faithful, while their intentions were corrupt. Bitter anger is subject to the penalty of murder, and lust to the penalty of adultery (Matthew 5:21-30). So also worthy intentions are not sufficient but must be accompanied by "good fruit." Motives, means, and consequences must be viewed in their interrelatedness in assessing whether they are pleasing to God. The act is always to be considered in its fullness.

The gospel is not a new code of conduct. Legalism looks to a law or principle to find the specific requirements of God in a particular situation, but love supersedes the most exacting legal description of an act. Love will not steal or kill or commit adultery. It is patient and kind, not arrogant or rude; it rejoices in the right. Love does not ignore injustice, but always seeks justice for the neighbor.

The New Testament points to the Spirit of Christ renewing community, prompting men to do what is pleasing in His sight. We have died to the ways of sin and now are raised in His Spirit, so that we are to walk in newness of life. One who lives under the Spirit fulfills what the law requires without slavish and deadening adherence to the law. Galatians 5:22-25 may be taken as a remarkably precise statement of the new Spirit that Jesus Christ has released into the world. "The harvest of the Spirit is love, joy, peace, patience, kindness, goodness, fidelity, gentleness, and self-control. There is no law dealing with such things as these. And those who belong to Jesus Christ have crucified the lower nature with its passions and desires. If the Spirit is the source of our life, let the Spirit also direct our course" (N.E.B.).

The New Testament recognizes that prayerful thought and wisdom are required in making right ethical decisions. Paul continually urges his fellow Christians to learn what is pleasing to God and to be filled with a knowledge of His will. Our decision can be responsive to God only when we constantly consider the Scriptures and when we constantly confer with those of like faith, whose judgment can often correct our own (Matthew 18). At the same time we need to be thoroughly familiar with the facts of a situation, including whatever scientific understanding or professional services may be available. Responsible choices must be well informed.

Honest Christians may well differ about the claim of God in a particular situation. In such cases we need to exercise charity and patience, remembering that we are not our brother's final judge. Such forbearance need not lead us to abandon the attempt to find group consensus and thus to leave morality to individual decision alone. Although many variations are to be found in the New Testament, it is full of accounts of those who sought a consensus in the Lord's will for them. Those who live in His Spirit will seek consensus without forcing their views upon one another.

II. The Christian Life in the Contemporary World

History has brought changes into modern life that have critical bearing upon personal ethics and conduct. These changes include the terror of possible nuclear destruction, the increasing secularization of religious values, impersonalization of human relationships, the industrialization and automation of work, the gulf between the affluent and the poor, the conformism of mass culture, and the widespread loss of identity and meaning. New situations call for new ways of expressing traditional Brethren concerns for brotherhood, mission, and service.

Brethren at times have responded more clearly to God's call for holy separation from the world than to His example of active reconciling love in the world. Personal ethics and conduct have often been guided by ideals of abstinence, cleanliness, and purity that are unaffected by the standards of the world. At other times, and especially in recent years, Brethren have come to acknowledge that God's claim for separation also passes through self-giving engagement within the world. This new attitude among Brethren is surely a recognition that God separates a holy people to himself in order that He might send them forth as agents and witnesses of His redeeming love among men. The same obedient devotion that prompts Christians to be separate from the world also calls the church into reconciling engagement within the world.

Consideration of the New Testament faith and of the conditions of the contemporary world suggests a style of life that might be characterized along the following lines:

1. *Self-giving engagement with the world.* An attitude of servanthood can be joined with a forthright and active mission in the world. Christians may be actively, even aggressively, engaged in a work of reconciliation in all realms of life.

2. *Reconciling love joined with a sense of justice.* Love that is genuine goes not overpower the other person, nor does it gloss over genuine interpersonal difficulties. Though we allow for differences, still we are called to act unashamedly in the face of injustice.

3. *An obedient devotion that transcends legalism and remains open to new situations.* Devotion that is patient, humble, and sincere may be a part of careful attention to one's daily work. At the same time the Christian has a confidence that allows him to be open to the variety of new situations in the modern world.

III. Special Areas of Concern

Areas of personal life that have been especially challenged by the rapid changes in contemporary life may be grouped under the following headings: personal integrity, family relationships, concern for the neighbor, life, and property. Each of these topics is treated directly in the Sermon on the Mount and the Ten Commandments, as well as throughout the Bible.

Personal Integrity

God's call brings man into responsible selfhood. The Bible describes personal maturity as a relationship of complete and wholehearted devotion to God (Exodus 20:3; Matthew 22:37) that is always coupled with a loving concern for one's fellowman (Matthew 22:39). True selfhood comes in being centered in Christ, willingly accepting the way of the cross, having the same mind as Christ, and growing in every way into the fullness of his stature. In the power of God's presence we are delivered from the massive powers of depersonalization in our time (Romans 8:2).

The primary vocation of every person is to accept God's claim upon his life. Brethren have long recognized the integrity, humility, and servanthood that are entailed in God's call. What is so very much needed today is the realization that God's claim is upon every person in his secular occupation in the world. Be it in home or office, field or factory, every Christian is being claimed and judged by God within the special activities of that occupation.

The Bible repeatedly calls for integrity of speech (Exodus 20:7; Matthew 5:33-37). Continued use of profane language will certainly impair one's relationship to God. And yet it must be remembered that no speech is really truthful unless it springs from an open love of God and neighbor. Truth is not to be narrowly defined in terms of adherence to a fixed pattern in a day when the network of obligations is increasingly complex. Those who are faithful to God's truth become more responsive to their obligations in both word and deed. Duplicity in filling out income tax forms or cheating in the classroom can hardly be a truthful use of language.

Oaths indicate weakness in the integrity of speech rather than strength. Slander and other malicious speech do not proceed from the Spirit of Truth. Both the hiding and the expression of deep feelings become a misuse of speech outside responsibility to one's fellowman (Ephesians 4:25-29).

Family Relationships

The love of a man and a woman is one of God's most sacred gifts to mankind. Such love can be fulfilled only in marriage, which is a reflection of the relationship between Christ and His church. The fidelity of man and wife is a cornerstone of personal ethics for the Christian. To divorce sexuality from personal commitment and to use it as a passing pleasure or as a means of making material products more marketable is a violation of God's gift to man. While the Bible does not advocate the repression of sexual impulse, it does make clear that sexual intimacy belongs to a lifetime covenant between a man and a woman (Matthew 19:3-9). In a culture that is saturated with sexual stimulation, youth are asked to consider whether the intimacy they express in courting reflects the degree of commitment that they have made. The closest intimacies must be reserved for a lifetime public promise to care for and love one another.

A concern for the proper expression of the relationship between man and woman has often led Brethren to raise questions about dancing. Social dancing, square dancing, or folk dancing carried out in well-supervised and well-planned settings can afford a healthy environment for normal heterosexual development among young people. On the other hand, many types of modern dance are overly provocative and indiscreet and still others reflect the meaninglessness and nihilism of much contemporary life. The decision between proper and improper dancing must be made by the individual in the light of Christian ideals after careful consideration of the issues involved and in conversations between parents and youth, Christians and their fellow Christians. Some will choose not to dance at all. An important consideration is that the physical not be elevated above the social and the esthetic. Married persons will need to consider how their marriage and home life will be affected by dancing with the spouse of another. In the matter of dancing or in any form of recreation the Christian will want to do what is wholesome and healthful.

The sale of pornography is a serious social problem in our day. The Christian is called away from that literature and those entertainments of which the primary purpose and effect are sexual stimulation with no real concern for the persons involved. On the other hand Christians should not quickly label "filth" or "pornography" works of literature of which the primary aim is social reform but which use the realistic language of the times.

Like the love of man and wife, so also is love between parents and children a sacred gift from God. When the relationship between parents and children is lost, then the continuity between generations is impaired (Exodus 20:12). Parents who love their children will instruct them in the way of the Christian life, and children who love their parents will honor and respect them, even when they disagree (Ephesians 6:1-4; Colossians 3:20,21). The instruction of no church or school can replace that of the parents.

The delinquency of youth seems most often to be a flight from the uncaring authority or neglect of an adult generation. Delinquency becomes the symptom of the failure of love between husband and wife, parents and their children. Parents of youth should care for them by setting limitations without being repressive, and by encouraging them toward independence without abandoning them. Youth are to respect the authority of their parents, while striving for true personhood through independence of judgment.

Concern for the Neighbor

The Bible makes it abundantly clear that personal ethics must never be divorced from concern for the neighbor. Personal ethics must include the individual's responsibility toward the larger social issues of our day. The individual believer is bound together with others in such a way that the concern of one is the concern of all (I Corinthians 12). The gospel proclaims the presence of the Kingdom of God the new society among men. The whole of mankind shall finally be bound together in Jesus Christ. In Him the Old Testament distinction between the neighbor and the stranger is overcome (Luke 10:29-37). All men have become neighbors. The Christian is to associate freely with those of every race and class. The Christian today should use every opportunity to alter those social customs, practices, and attitudes by which whole groups of people are discriminated against.

Education to the very limit of a person's capacity and opportunity is desirable for service to one's fellowmen. However, education in our day is often only a vehicle for wealth, prestige, and power. Without loving concern for the neighbor, educational procedures become a sham and the educational degree a means to social domination. The Christian is called to realize that responsible love for one's neighbor is at the heart of all genuine education. The Christian will not pursue a course of education primarily for power and prestige, nor will he use devious means for the attainment of an educational degree.

The profit motive in business does not change the fact that the primary duty of man is service and loving concern for his neighbor. The Christian businessman is called to conduct his business primarily for the service of his neighbor, and to consider his employees and competitors as those for whom he has responsibility. He will not engage in a business that does not truly serve the consumer, nor will he conduct his business in a way that ignores his neighbor's welfare. So, also, the Christian laborer will care for his employer as well as for fellow laborers. He will not engage in labor that clearly and directly disregards the neighbor, nor will be misrepresent his labor to his employer.

The art of secular government should be of major concern to every Christian especially in a democratic society in which all men have the right of free speech and where the will of the majority rules. Though insistent upon separation of church and state, Christians will regard local, national, and world government agencies as subject to God's reign. Political involvement for the purpose of achieving reconciliation and peace in our time is one of the marks of the true work of the church in the world. Christians are called to speak out on public issues and to vote for candidates, laws, and platforms after careful consideration of the issues. Politically minded Christians are called to run for office but must avoid committing the sins of slander and misrepresentation. Once in office the Christian politician must not manipulate the state to further any of the church's peculiar ends. Through an active participation in politics at many different levels, from individual voter to top officeholder, challenges prevail in countless areas where Christians can act: righting social wrongs; revealing greed and exploitation for what they are; raising money to help heal the numerous ills of our society; and allowing the church the freedom to carry out her mission. However, the Christian, whether voter or officeholder, must not use the much abused "Render to Caesar" (Mark 12:17) and "Let every person be subject to the governing authorities" (Romans 13:1) to justify clearly un-Christian acts that are contrary to the total message of the New Testament. Responsible statesmanship in the interests of peace and order is a lonely task, but one that must be taken up at the risk of misunderstanding, persecution, or the loss of public support.

The question of war and peace has become an issue of survival in this generation. The official position of the Church of the Brethren continues to be that in the light of the spirit and the teachings of the New Testament, war is sin. Christians are called to work for those conditions and climates within which international problems can be resolved without resort to violent force. Recognizing the difficulties of the ethical dilemmas that often arise between love and justice, the church allows for difference of conscience regarding military service. Nevertheless, Brethren are called to witness to their faith that the Servanthood of Christ, the way of reconciling love, is of ultimate power and relevance in today's world. We need a sense of urgency in working for alternatives to military destruction. Youth are encouraged to elect alternative service. To find the means for peace is the call of God for our epoch of history.

Life and Property

Life and property are gifts to man from God. As a living soul and by God's grace, man is enabled to have dominion over the earth and to care for his fellowman. Separation from God brings thorns and thistles, anxiety, sickness, isolation, and death to man (Genesis 3). In Jesus Christ man gains abundance of life, the hope of resurrection, and the promise of a new heaven and a new earth. Life and property assume their rightful significance when man recognizes that he is to be a good steward of God's gifts, using them in nourishment of and care for his fellowman.

One of the threats to life in our day is the widespread use of stimulants and narcotics. Such drugs often represent a way of escaping from the one's own selfhood. Christians should be aware of those drugs that have power to draw men into slavery and ought to use them only with medical advice. Although a Christian's faith cannot be judged simply upon an issue such a smoking, Brethren are encouraged to consider matters of health and the avoidance of what is offensive to others in their decision about smoking. Christians are to have freedom not only from legalistic codes, but also from enslavement to deleterious habits.

In our time the use of beverage alcohol and the consequences of its use have become one of the greatest of social problems. Because it impairs mental and physical acuity, drinking is the cause of a large share of the injuries and fatalities that occur on the highways. Because it is a depressant drug, alcohol dulls sensibilities, releases inhibitions and causes man to be unable to respond to the love of God or neighbor. Because it is a habit-forming drug to many people, alcohol has resulted in the disease of alcoholism, the incidence of which is exceeded only by heart disease and cancer in the United States. It is urgent that Christians use every opportunity to point up the need for greater attention to and care for those who are subject to alcoholism. In his care for the neighbor the Christian is called to witness in his personal life against the evils of beverage alcohol and to oppose the massive social and economic pressures that promote its use.

In an affluent society in which many persons are seeking security through possessions, it must be affirmed again and again that life does not consist of the abundance of things and that the Good Life is not found in material possessions. Christians must see affluence as either a potential blessing in the establishment of the Good Life among all men and nations, or a possible peril greater than poverty. Luxurious living must not be allowed to crowd out involvement in social issues such as civil rights, poverty, or urban decay, nor must materialism divorce us from the great issues of our day. In his search for security the Christian is called to resist the many pressures of our materialistic living and to practice the "simple life" as God's faithful stewards of our time: to purchase within his reasonable financial means; to beware of excessive deficit spending and long-term, high-interest installment buying; to renounce luxuries which are inconsistent with the life of service and suffering; to set aside first his responsible giving to the church and its world ministries.

One of the most critical social problems of today is the widespread popularity of small lotteries and policy games, from which organized crime receives its major source of income. The hope to gain something for nothing is a flight from reality, so much so that for many persons gambling is habitual and uncontrollable. Life before God is not an unrealistic hope for a lucky break, but is a way of facing the future in the confidence that Jesus Christ discloses God's steadfast love and care for man. The risks it runs are those of faith undertaken in loving concern for one's fellowman and the surprises it expects are not those of chance but the free operation of God's grace. The Spirit of Christ is that of charity, sacrifice, and self-giving rather than of gaming in order to gain the property of the neighbor, no matter how worthy the use to which the gain is put. Christians are called to act and speak openly against the sources of organized crime and to work for the release of those who are so economically oppressed that they are inclined to gamble. It must be recognized that some prizes appeal primarily to recognition or enjoyment rather than to chance gain. The Christian is to distinguish between gambling and innocent games in conversation with his fellow Christians.

Conclusion

The above discussion of special concerns may be helpful only so long as Brethren "hunger and thirst after righteousness" under God's loving claim, as a servant people in the midst of the world, with the assurance that the Spirit of Christ is alive and active in every realm of contemporary life reconciling men to one another and to God.

W. Clemens Rosenberger, Chairman
Mrs. W. Newton Long, Sr.
Donald E. Miller
Robert McFadden
Burton Metzler
Kurtis F. Naylor

Action of the 1966 Annual Conference: Report adopted.

Notes: *This 1966 statement by the Church of the Brethren (approximately 160,000 members) mentions pornography as part of a general study of personal ethics. The statement indicates that material which is primarily intended to sexually arouse is* *improper, but that which employs sexuality in an artistic manner in an attempt to bring about social reform should not be judged as harshly.*

CHURCH OF THE BRETHREN

GUIDANCE TOWARD A RESPONSE TO VIOLENCE AND PORNOGRAPHY IN THE MEDIA (1985)

WHEREAS: God intends our interpersonal relationships to be just, non-violent, wholesome, and mutually affirming;

WHEREAS: Pornography, violence, use of profanity, sexual suggestiveness, and anti-Christian attitudes, all of which promote disregard for persons and promote acts of injustice among them, are reaching epidemic proportions in the mass media as well as in local communities;

WHEREAS: Many in the local church do not know how to deal with these problems locally and/or nationally, and are therefore unable to fulfill the redemptive role in society to which they believe God has called them;

THEREFORE: We, the Morgantown Church of the Brethren, in Council on July 8, 1984, request Annual Conference to undertake a study in order to:

1. discover the scope of these problems which make it difficult for Christian values to be taught;

2. provide guidance to the local churches as to how best to deal at the local level with violence and pornography in the media;

and we pass this query to the 1984 West Marva district conference for consideration.

Anna Lee Reed, Board Chair
Dennis Overman, Clerk

Action of the West Marva District Conference meeting at the Elkins, West Virginia, Church of the Brethren, September 21-22, 1984: Moved and passed to send this query to the 1985 Annual Conference in Phoenix, Arizona.

William Bane, Moderator
Linda Davis, District Clerk

Action of the 1985 Annual Conference: Ramona Pence, a Standing Committee delegate from the Shenandoah District, presented the recommendation from Standing Committee. *The 1985 Annual Conference delegates adopted the recommendation that the concern of the query be approved and implemented in the following ways:*

1. The General Board, through the General Services Commission, within the next six months, appoint a volunteer and provide the funds for the volunteer to fulfill the assignment of

—coordinating the existing Television Awareness Training (TAT) Leaders.

—disseminating information to TAT Leaders.

—making congregations aware of the availability of TAT Leaders and information which helps congregations deal with issues of violence and pornography in the media.

—keeping informed of current development through workshops, publications, etc.

2. Staff persons whose portfolios deal with related areas of concern, e.g., women's issues, youth, young adults, and the study committee for Conditions of Childhood in the United

States, give attention to the growing concern about violence and pornography in the media.

3. The Goals and Budget Committee, in reviewing the Goals for the 80s, consider including the issue of violence and pornography in the media.

4. District boards continue raising the concern of violence and pornography in the media with local congregations and continue promoting the use of resource persons and materials, especially where there is no TAT Leader in the district.

Notes: *This 1985 statement from the Church of the Brethren explains the church's desire to monitor and challenge the content of some television programming through a "Television Awareness Training" program. Pornography is grouped with other items the church finds undesirable, including violence, use of profanity, sexual suggestiveness, and anti-Christian attitudes.*

CHURCH OF THE NAZARENE

STATEMENT ON PORNOGRAPHY (1985)

33. We hold specifically that the following practices should be avoided:

33.1. Entertainments which are subversive of the Christian ethic. Our people should govern themselves by three principles. One is the Christian stewardship of leisure time. A second principle is the recognition of the Christian obligation to apply the highest moral standards to the Christian family. Because we are living in a day of great moral confusion in which we face the potential encroachment of the evils of the day into the sacred precincts of our homes through various avenues such as current literature, radio, and television, it is essential that the most rigid safeguards be observed. The third principle is the obligation to witness against social evils by appropriate forms of influence, and by the refusal to patronize and thereby lend influence to the industries which are known to be the purveyors of this kind of entertainment. This would include the avoidance of the motion picture theater (cinema). We should also avoid such other commercial ventures including television programs which feature the violent, the sensual, and the pornographic and thus undermine God's standard of holiness of heart and life [Romans 14:7-13;1 Corinthians 10:31-33; Ephesians 5:1-18; Philippians 4:8-9; 1 Peter 1:13-17]. (904.7, 904.9)

Notes: *The Church of the Nazarene is one of the largest holiness groups, and, as such, it is very concerned with inward and outward purity. This 1985 statement urges that all motion pictures be avoided because the industry is known to provide unwholesome entertainment. The statement further indicates that all types of sensual or pornographic films or literature are to be avoided.*

EPISCOPAL CHURCH

RESOLUTION ON SEXUALITY AND PORNOGRAPHY (1982)

Human Sexuality

Whereas, the Church believes and affirms the teaching of Holy Scripture that "the body is the temple of the Holy Spirit", and affirms that human sexuality is a gift of God that blesses and enriches the whole of life and that sexual union is a Holy Bond of commitment and fidelity between man and wife through the blessing of the Holy Estate of Matrimony; and

Whereas, pornography lacks respect for the body, debasing and soiling this good gift of God by advertising deviate forms of vice, which tend to increase the amount of addition to such vice; and

Whereas, pornography undermines the Holy Estate of Matrimony and the divinely ordered family life, equating human sexuality with temporary pleasure, disregarding the responsibility and abiding affection that distinguishes sexuality from promiscuity, prostitution, and degeneracy; and

Whereas, pornography has created an insatiable lust which now extends to the use of children, exploiting and debasing them and advocating incest and sexual relations between children and adults; therefore be it

Resolved, The House of Bishops concurring, That the 67th General Convention reaffirms the Church's biblical conviction that human sexuality is a gift of God intended to bless and enrich the whole of life, and urges all priests, educators and parents to provide an ethos in which children may mature in a healthy and responsible understanding of their sexuality counteracting the dehumanizing influence of exploitive pornography.

Notes: *This 1982 resolution from the Episcopal Church (approximately 2,750,000 members) condemns pornography because it undermines family life by equating sexuality with temporary pleasure that does not include responsibility and affection. It also states that pornography creates "an insatiable lust which now extends to the use of children."*

EPISCOPAL CHURCH

RESOLUTION ON PORNOGRAPHY (1985)

Resolved, the House of Bishops concurring, That the 68th General Convention commend the report of the Standing Commission on Human Affairs and Health on "consumerism and sexual behavior" and urge the Commission to develop actions in the next triennium to combat pornography and other forms of sexual exploitation that treat persons as commodities to be used and discarded; and be it further

Resolved, That the Standing Commission on Human Affairs and Health be asked to communicate to dioceses and congregations their findings with positive plans that would enable effective responses to those exploitive forces that corrupt us, our children, and our culture.

Notes: *This 1985 resolution from the Episcopal Church expands upon the church's earlier anti-pornography stand by establishing a commission to study and recommend actions against pornography and "other forms of sexual exploitation."*

EVANGELICAL CONGREGATIONAL CHURCH

STATEMENT ON PORNOGRAPHY (1983)

144.6 Pornography

Although it may be difficult to define precisely what is pornographic or obscene, it is clear that books, magazines, movies and language, which distort and degrade human sexuality, impose a harmful influence upon individuals, especially the young, upon the family, and upon society as a whole.

The production and use of obscene materials violate the Biblical injunction against carnal lust (Galatians 5:16), falsify the place of sexuality in human relations, and transform persons made in God's image into impersonal things to be used in gratifying sinful human passions and weaknesses.

The legalization of pornographic materials or of prostitution in unacceptable to the Christian since these activities necessarily involve the exploitation of persons—willingly or unwillingly—for degrading and dehumanizing purposes which border upon blasphemy against God himself through the degradation of persons made in His image (James 3:9). Out of love for God and neighbor, then, the Christian has the right and obligation to oppose pornography in all its forms through available legal means.

It must be remembered, however, that obscenity goes beyond the area of the sexual. It includes violence and all acts and attitudes, including prejudice, which demean the worth of a fellow human. We must also guard against the less obvious but more pervasive and potentially more subversive influence of books, motion pictures and TV programs which glorify, or portray as normal, situations, attitudes and living arrangements which flout the Biblical teaching regarding the sanctity of marriage and the family.

Notes: *This statement of the Evangelical Congregational Church (approximately 36,000 members) recognizes the difficulty involved in defining pornography and obscenity in detail, but generally describes them as distorting sexuality by emphasizing carnal lust. Obscene and pornographic materials are dehumanizing and must be opposed. The statement further notes that prejudice and violence, too, are obscene.*

EVANGELICAL FREE CHURCH OF AMERICA

RESOLUTION ON PORNOGRAPHY (1985)

INASMUCH as the Evangelical Free Church bases its standard of morality upon the authority of the Word of God; and

WHEREAS the Bible condemns fornication (Eph. 5:3, Col. 3:5), adultery (Lev. 20:13, Rom. 1:24), incest (Lev. 18:6, I Cor. 5:1), homosexuality (Lev. 20:13, Rom. 1:24), bestiality (Lev. 18:23), and prostitution (Lev. 19:29, Eph. 5:5) as immoral; and since pornography is known to condone and promote all these forms of immorality; and

WHEREAS through God created both men and women in His own image, pornography is essentially a degradation of both sexes (especially women and children), since most pornography involves the use of women and children in subordinate, degrading poses for sexual exploitation, and even the sadistic and violent pleasures of men and women and fosters the mentality which considers the human being, not as a person, but as an object which exists to gratify the selfish interest of others and reflects hostility toward women and children; and

WHEREAS pornography is known to be both seductive and addictive, desensitizing its victims, leading them to greater consumption of pornographic material; and

WHEREAS research shows that pornography incites violence, contributes to many violent crimes such as rape and child abuse, and encourages illicit and abusive sexual activity; and

WHEREAS this seriously undermines family structure as well as church and community values; and

WHEREAS the Supreme Court has established that obscene material is *not* protected by the First Amendment (Roth vs. United States, 1957); and that material can be judged as a whole to determine whether it lacks serious literacy, artistic, political or scientific values (Miller vs. California 1973); and that juries can judge obscenity by local community standards rather than by a National Standard (Hamling vs. United States 1974); that indecent language in broadcasting can be prohibited (FCC vs. Pacifica 1978); and affirms the protection of children against sexual exploitation and abuse, (New York vs. Ferber, 1982); and

WHEREAS pornography has increased in the past several years to where it is now a multi-billion dollar business often linked to organized crime; and

WHEREAS modern technology is rapidly expanding access to pornography in our homes through cable T.V., video cassette recorders, the telephone and even personal computers; and

WHEREAS this expanded access means increased consumption of pornography not only by adults but by unsupervised children in our homes; and

WHEREAS the use of children in pornographic materials is growing at an alarming rate;

BE IT AFFIRMED that we as members of the Evangelical Free Church do hereby condemn pornography as evil, exploitive, offensive and totally unacceptable in any form.

THAT we insist that the President of the United States, the Postal Services, and the Department of Justice and all proper authorities enforce all obscenity, pornography, and indecency laws; and

THAT we encourage continuing legislative efforts to eliminate the destructive influence of pornography, obscenity and indecency; and

FINALLY, we urge our congregations to patronize and publicly support those businesses which refuse to benefit financially or in any other way from the sale, production, or distribution of pornography, and conversely—in accord with our first amendment rights to freedom of speech—we urge our congregations to enter the public debate in opposition to the growing evil of pornography, to oppose its growing intrusive presence in our public life, to insist on the enforcement of the laws which regulate it, and to protest against those who profit by it.

Notes: *This resolution of the Evangelical Free Church of America (approximately 110,000 members) condemns all forms of pornography as degrading, exploitive, inciteful of violence, and destructive of the family structure.*

EVANGELICAL LUTHERAN CHURCH IN AMERICA

SEX, MARRIAGE, AND FAMILY (1970)

Adopted by the Fifth Biennial Convention
Minneapolis, Minnesota
June 25-July 2, 1970

Sex, marriage, and family are gifts of God in which to rejoice. Their essential goodness cannot be obscured by any crisis of our time.

As traditional moral codes are being challenged, there is a profound struggle to formulate bases of ethical judgment which have meaning for contemporary man. Powerful forces of social change, joined with discoveries in the medical and life sciences, influence all aspects of human existence. The church is concerned not only with specific issues and controversies, but with the basic Christian understanding of man's sexuality.

Human Sexuality

Who is man? Man is a responsible person made in the image of God. God created male and female, making sexual interdependence serve the divine intention for life-in-community. Scripture portrays man as a relational being whose true humanity is realized in faith and love with God and neighbor.

True humanity is violated by sin, which is man's broken relationship with God and fellowman. This alienation expresses itself in all facets of life, including sex, marriage, and family. At the same time God works in these broken relationships, healing and freeing the forgiven to devote their efforts to the well-being of others.

Human sexuality is a gift of God for the expression of love and the generation of life. As with every good gift, it is subject to abuses which cause suffering and debasement. In the expression of man's sexuality, it is the integrity of his relationships which determines the meaning of his actions. Man does not merely have sexual relations; he demonstrates his true humanity in personal relationships, the most intimate of which are sexual.

Marriage

Christian faith affirms marriage as a covenant of fidelity—a dynamic, lifelong commitment of one man and one woman in a personal and sexual union. While hereafter in this report the phrase "covenant of fidelity" is employed, and we recognize it as expressing a key insight about Christian marriage, in biblical language, it may also be helpful at times to express the same emphasis in other terminology through such a phrase as "mutual commitment to lifelong faithfulness" as a substitute for a "covenant of fidelity." Marriage is not simply a legal transaction which can be broken when the conditions under which it was entered no longer exist. It is an unconditional relationship, a total commitment based on faithful trust. This union embodies God's loving purpose to create and enrich life. As the needs of the partners change, the covenant of fidelity must be renewed by God's grace and continually reaffirmed by husband and wife.

This view transcends the civil understanding of marriage as a legal contract. A marital union can be legally valid yet not be a covenant of fidelity, just as it can be a covenant of fidelity and not a legal contract. Such a covenant is also to be distinguished from an identification with the marriage pattern of any particular culture, from the idea that an established structure is normative for all times, and from the legalistic notion that because two people have had sexual intercourse they are bound together forever. The existence of a true covenant of fidelity outside marriage as a legal contract is extremely hard to identify.

Marriage is ordained by God as a structure of the created order. Thus the sanction of civil law and public recognition are important and beneficial in marriage, as checks against social injustice and personal sin. The marriage covenant, therefore, should be certified by a legal contract, and Christian participants should seek the blessings of the church.

The relationship between husband and wife is likened in Ephesians 5:21-23 to the relationship between Christ and the church. This depicts a communion of total persons, each of them living for the other. As with the covenant between Christ and the church, the promise of fidelity is fundamental. Therefore, Christians regard marriage as a primary setting in which to live out their calling from the Lord.

However, many persons are single for varied reasons. There should be no exaltation of either the single or the married state, one over the other. It is a matter for gratitude when the conditions of life make possible free and open choices.

Family

The family has the function of nurturing human being in relationships which are rich with creative possibilities. It provides the surrounding in which persons enhance rather than exploit one another, in which mistakes may be made and forgiveness realized.

The family appears in many forms in different times and places. It develops in response to the need of men, women, and children, whether married or unmarried, for a primary relationship in which they may have a sense of intimacy and belonging. There is no greater challenge today than in the family, for it is intended by God to be that basis community in which personhood is fostered. The family should not become centered on itself, but should be seen as a base from which its members move out to participate in society.

Ethical Decision

The Christian's ethical decisions are made in the context of his relationships with God and other persons. The Christian acts knowing that he daily becomes alienated from God and daily needs God's forgiveness. Under God's grace, however, he is freed to choose how best to serve his fellowmen in Christian love.

The Christian needs more than love to guide him. In making decisions he should recognize that he and the other persons with whom he acts are unique men, women, and children with particular gifts and responsibilities, living in particular places and relationships. Furthermore, he draws his guidance and strength from the Christian revelation, bringing to each situation the benefits of the accumulated wisdom and supporting fellowship of the church.

Human life must be regulated by just laws because man is finite and sinful. Such laws, enacted by reason and enforced by power, can never be the direct expression of Christian love. Nevertheless, Christians as citizens and the church as institution should join with others in advocating and supporting just laws. In this process, however, it is not proper for any church to impose its sectarian views on the general community.

Some Current Issues

The following statements are not to be thought of as categorical laws or "Christian" solutions to the problems involved. Nor are they intended to furnish easy answers to hard questions. They are offered as guidance to pastors and laymen in their ethical decision-making.

1. *Some Issues Related to Sexual Expression*

    Within the realm of human sexuality, intercourse is a joyful means of giving oneself in the mutual expression of love. It is within the permanent covenant of marital fidelity that the full potential of coitus to foster genuine intimacy, personal growth, and the responsible conception of children is realized.

    Because the Lutheran Church in America holds that sexual intercourse outside the context of the marriage union is morally wrong, nothing in this statement on "Sex, Marriage, and Family" is to be interpreted as meaning that this church either condones or approves premarital or extra-marital sexual intercourse.

    Scientific research has not been able to provide conclusive evidence regarding the causes of homosexuality. Nevertheless, homosexuality is viewed biblically as a departure from the heterosexual structure of God's creation. Persons who engage in homosexual behavior are sinners only as are all other persons—alienated from God and neighbor. However, they are often the special and undeserving victims of prejudice and discrimination in law, law enforcement, cultural mores, and congregational life. In relation to this area of concern, the sexual behavior of freely consenting adults in private is not an appropriate subject for legislation or police action. It is essential to see such persons as entitled to understanding and justice in church and community.

    Sexual exploitation in any situation, either personally or commercially, inside or outside legally contracted marriage, is sinful because it is destructive of God's good gift and man's integrity.

    The church recognizes the effects of social environment and cultural traditions on human behavior. It seeks, therefore, to respond understandingly to persons who enter into relationships which do not demonstrate a covenant of fidelity.

2. *Some Issues Related to Marriage*

    It is the quality of interpersonal relationships within marriage that is the concern of the church. A covenant of fidelity can be broken in reality whether the union terminates formally through legal action or displays external solidarity. In ministering to persons affected by a broken covenant the church is called to assist them to perceive their problems more clearly and, hopefully, to experience forgiveness and reconciliation.

If the outcome is formal dissolution of the marriage, the church should continue to minister to all persons involved. To identify the legal action of divorce as sinful by itself obscures the fact that the marital relationship has already been mutually undermined by thoughts, words, and actions. Although divorce often brings anguish to those concerned, there may be situations in which securing a divorce is more responsible than staying together.

When the question of the remarriage of a divorced man or woman arises, the church and the individuals themselves will do well to concentrate upon the potential of the new rather then the collapse of the former marriage. A clear understanding of the dynamics which led to the breakdown of the first union helps a person prepare more adequately for the second. A divorced man and woman, of course, should fulfill all legitimate obligations to the members of the broken family.

A shared Christian faith contributes to the strength of a marriage. Even more, marriage and family provide a primary setting for Christian nurture and maturity. Before a man and woman enter into an interfaith marriage, each should strive to understand and respect his own faith and the faith of his partner. They should become intelligently informed about factors which can cause special difficulty.

Theologically, marriage between persons without reference to racial and ethnic differences and background is a witness to the oneness of man under the one God, and as such should be fully accepted in both church and society.

3. *Some Issues Related to Conception Control*

The ethical significance of the use of any medically approved contraceptive method within a covenant of marital fidelity depends upon the motivation of the users. A responsible decision for or against having a child will include evaluation of such factors as the health of the potential mother, a reliable prognosis concerning the health of a possible child, the number and spacing of other children, the family's economic circumstances, and the rapid growth of population. People have a right not to have children without being accused of selfishness or a betrayal of the divine plan: and every child has a right to be a wanted child.

All persons are entitled to receive from governmental and voluntary agencies information about conception control.

4. *Some Issues Related to Abortion*

In the consideration of induced abortion the key issue is the status of the unborn fetus. Since the fetus is the organic beginning of human life, the termination of its development is always a serious matter. Nevertheless, a qualitative distinction must be made between its claims and the rights of a responsible person made in God's image who is in living relationships with God and other human beings. This understanding of responsible personhood is congruent with the historical Lutheran teaching and practice whereby only living persons are baptized.

On the basis of the evangelical ethic, a woman or couple may decide responsibly to seek an abortion. Earnest consideration should be given to the life and total health of the mother, her responsibilities to others in her family, the state of development of the fetus, the economic and psychological stability of the home, the laws of the land, and the consequences for society as a whole.

Persons considering abortion are encouraged to consult with their physicians and spiritual counselors. This church upholds its pastors and other responsible counselors, and persons who conscientiously make decisions about abortion.

5. *Some Issues Related to Family Life Education*

There is need for competent education to understand sexuality and to prepare for courtship, marriage, and family.

This kind of education properly begins in the home, where parents teach their children not only by words but by their actions and expression of feeling. But children and young people also learn from other sources, such as the peer group, books, movies and television, which often convey incomplete or distorted information. Parents have the right to expect help from the church in their roles as educators in sex, marriage, and family, particularly in relating their Christian convictions to this task.

The church supports responsible family life education in the public school, so long as religious and moral commitments are respected. Helping young people grow into mature men and women is so important that every possible resource must be involved, including competent, voluntary agencies. But it is the public school that can furnish an education reaching most children and young people. Family life education in the school should include parents in its planning and execution. It should also offer courses for them, coordinated with those their children are taking.

The task of education in sex, marriage, and family requires that the home, the church, and the school prepare themselves for effective fulfillment of their appropriate roles.

A Call

The Lutheran Church in America calls upon its pastors to reinforce the covenant of fidelity in their liturgical leadership, preaching, teaching, and counseling. It calls upon its members to study this statement and the booklet *Sex, Marriage, and Family: a Contemporary Christian Perspective;* and to give support to one another amid the painful ambiguities of making ethical decisions relating to sex, marriage, and family. It calls upon its agencies of education and social service to develop specific plans for helping synods and congregations incorporate the major emphases of this statement into their lives. It calls upon the church, both as a corporate body and as individual members, to witness to the civic community in behalf of just laws and policies affecting sex, marriage, and family, and in behalf of legislation that will improve the economic and social conditions which influence the lifestyles of people.

Notes: The Evangelical Lutheran Church in America was created by a merger on January 1, 1988, of the American Lutheran Church, the Lutheran Church in America, and the Association of Evangelical Lutheran Churches. The new church, with about 5,300,000 members, has yet to make any new statements on the many social issues before it. In the interim, it has circulated the statements of the previously existing bodies for their continuing wisdom and support.

This 1970 statement from the Lutheran Church in America refers obliquely to pornography with the comment that "sexual exploitation in any situation, either personally or commercially, inside or outside legally contracted marriage, is sinful because it is destructive of God's good gift and man's integrity."

EVANGELICAL LUTHERAN CHURCH IN AMERICA

STATEMENT ON PORNOGRAPHY (1974)

A statement of the Seventh General Convention of The American Lutheran Church adopted October 12, 1974, by action GC74.12.48, as a statement of comment and counsel addressed to the members of the congregations of The American Lutheran Church to aid them in their decisions and actions.

1. Pornography often is equated with obscenity. Pornography indeed may be obscene, but so are other matters not related to sex. Violence, war, double talk intended to deceive, exploiting or treating any other human being as a thing, engaging in manipulative selling, placing material interests ahead of human values—these too are obscene. Christians make a mistake when they leave the impression that it is only sex-oriented obscenities, not the whole range of offenses done to other human beings, which arouse their opposition.

2. Appeals to clamp down on pornography cause problems for Christians. They understand pornography to be material that depicts or describes erotic behavior in ways deliberately intended to stimulate sexual excitement. They regard human sexuality too highly to see it trifled with as a thing for the market place. Thus Christians easily respond to calls for sexual purity and morality in print, on the screen, and on the stage. However, deeper questions are involved in the usual efforts to curb pornography, such as:

   a. is it either right, necessary, or salutary to use civil laws to set standards for thoughts, tastes, and attitudes toward sexual practices?

   b. how can persons and communities be protected against sex-saturated materials and outlets which offend the sensitive or exploit the gullible?

   c. what room is there, with both freedom and responsibility, to explore issues and problems in human sexuality even though they run counter to current taboos and standards?

   d. why is so much of the sexual relegated to the realm of the forbidden and why is it made so difficult for people to appreciate their sexual selves and their sexual feelings?

   e. how does the Gospel liberate the believer from crippling enslavement both to prevailing sexual stereotypes and to self-centered pursuit of erotic pleasures?

3. Christians as citizens need to give thoughtful consideration to the issues involved in pornography. Two recent major events served to focus public attention on these issues. The first was the 1970 *Report of the Commission on Obscenity and Pornography,* including the vigorous dissents registered by minority members. In summary, the Commission advocated "the right of adults who wish to do so to read, obtain, or view explicit sexual materials." It recommended legislation both to regulate "the sale of sexual materials to young persons who do not have the consent of their parents" and "to protect persons from having sexual materials thrust upon them without their consent through the mails or through open public display." Beyond these exceptions, the Commission recommended the repeal of all legislation prohibiting "the consensual sale, exhibition, or the distribution of sexual materials to adults."

4. The second major event was the June 21, 1973, series of decisions by the Supreme Court of the United States reaffirming previous decisions that "obscene material is unprotected by the First Amendment." Acknowledging "the inherent dangers of undertaking to regulate any form of expression" the majority of the Court agreed to "confine the permissible scope of such regulations to works which depict or describe sexual conduct." The Court set three guidelines; "(a) whether the average person, applying contemporary community standards, would find that the work, taken as a whole, appeals to the prurient interest. . . . (b) whether the work depicts or describes, in a patently offensive way, sexual conduct specifically defined by the applicable state law, and (c) whether the work, taken as a whole, lacks serious literary, artistic, political, or scientific value." Far from settling the situation, the Court decisions raised further critical issues yet to be resolved.

5. Persons seriously interested in attacking the evils associated with pornography wisely would consider such points as the following:

a. Pornography is a big business, supplying a product for which there is evident demand. Refusal to buy the product, and withholding patronage from those who offer the offending goods or services, strike at the profit core.

b. By most standards pornography is a low-grade, low quality, overpriced product that prostitutes the sexual side of human life. Good judgment and good taste argue against spending good money for inferior, shabby, degrading products.

c. Pornography preys on sexual ignorance, fears, and frustrations. Positive acceptance of oneself as a sexual being, and healthy attitudes and orientation to human sexuality, reduce the lures of pornography.

d. The influence and example of parents and other trusted adults in their reading, viewing, leisure-time, and entertainment habits communicate powerfully to children and youth. Parental guidance, to be effective, needs reliable information concerning issues, materials, and curiosities currently in tension.

e. The law, the police, and the courts are the legal resources available for combating pornography. Cooperation between citizens and personnel in law enforcement systems is essential if a specific alleged violation is to be given its due judicial decision.

6. The church has the opportunity through the Spirit of God for creating new human beings who are free and responsible to live and act because of the power of the Gospel. The church teaches, on the basis of the whole of God's counsel, the importance of controls arising from within because of a person's relationship with the Living Lord. It stresses a person's right to make free choices, under God, accountable to God, considerate of the neighbor. Such choices take civil law into account, but take even more seriously God's Law and the Gospel revealed in his Son. Human freedom of course carries the risk that some persons will misuse their freedom. Human freedom also insures opportunity for many persons to grow in wisdom, knowledge, and favor with God and neighbor. Such freedom, applied to pornography, carries risks of misuse and exploitation. Such freedom, applied to pornography, also insures opportunity for many persons to grow in understanding and appreciation for God's gift of human sexuality.

7. For civil legislators the difficult task is (a) to balance freedom and responsibility, (b) to protect the sensitive and the gullible, (c) to assure a climate for open and honest discussion of issues related to human sexuality, (d) to define clearly that which is a scandal and an offense to standards of morality and integrity, and (e) to provide channels for adjudicating between competing sets of standards and values. How to achieve these goals is a perplexing exercise in political realities. Christian citizens will offer their counsel, their prayers, their support for what is good and wholesome, and their energies to correct what is evil and destructive in public policies dealing with pornography.

Notes: *This statement was issued by the American Lutheran Church, which in 1988 merged with the Lutheran Church in America and the Association of Evangelical Lutheran Churches to form the Evangelical Lutheran Church in America (approximately 5,300,000 members). This statement recognizes the difficulty caused by the desire to regulate pornography while at the same time leaving room for the responsible exploration of human sexuality. While the statement offers no answers, it does raise several important questions.*

EVANGELICAL LUTHERAN CHURCH IN AMERICA

HUMAN SEXUALITY AND SEXUAL BEHAVIOR (1980)

E. Defiling God's Gift

1. Human beings are capable not only of good but also of evil uses of their sexuality. People are ready to exploit this fact to their own power or profit. Major industries are

built up around satisfying "the lust of the flesh and the lust of the eyes and the pride of life"(1 John 2:16).

2. Among forms of exploitive sexual behavior against which Christians should be ready to work are those which:

a. exploit children and youth, men and women, as in pornography and prostitution;

b. take advantage of persons who are ill, helpless, dependent, handicapped or of little power;

c. endanger, cause physical or emotional injury, or do long-term harm;

d. use threat, force, or prestige to persuade an otherwise unwilling person to engage in sexual behavior;

e. engage promiscuously in a public quest for new sexual partners;

f. break promises and violate commitments which people have made in the responsible exercise of their free will;

g. build trade and commerce based on satisfying prurient interest;

h. violate standards of public decency;

i. invade the privacy and self-respect of others;

j. magnify sexuality and sexual behavior in print, on screen, and on the state in ways irrelevant to the product or incidental to the dominant theme.

3. Particularly despicable is behavior which uses the threat or the reality of physical and mental harm. Persons thought to be homosexual are harassed, beaten, even killed. Pimps force the prostitutes beholden to them to remain loyal or to suffer the consequences, including physical harm and abuse, even death. Preschool and young school-age children are lured into serving ruthless adults who profit from the sexual cravings of the child pornography market. ALC members must act against these evils in their communities.

F. Expressing Concerns Through Law

1. Laws express society's recognition that sexual behavior affects not only the participants but also the health, strength, and survival of the society itself. Christians must beware, however, of equating sin with crime. Nor dare they accept the proposition that because behavior is not against the law it therefore must be acceptable. Their concern must be for laws that foster justice, mercy, equality of opportunity, and the protection of basic human rights. Particularly difficult, in this light, is the task of attempting to draft laws which bear upon moral convictions not shared by all persons in the community. Reasonable persons can and must decide together what laws most likely will assure justice and mercy, opportunity and rights, for all.

2. In most American communities today the consensus of reasonable persons overwhelmingly would support laws that in the quest for justice and mercy, opportunity and rights:

a. prohibit use of force or other forms of coercion in inducing persons to participate in sexual behavior against their will;

b. protect children, youth, the retarded, the handicapped, and others unable to give informed consent against seduction, exploitation, or abuse;

c. forbid entrapment and other illegal activities used to obtain evidence;

d. require correcting or ending conditions that have been judged through due processes to be a public nuisance;

e. safeguard public decency against actions or conduct patently offensive or likely to be offensive to the moral sense of the community;

   f. insure the civil and legal rights of every person so long as their exercise of these rights does not infringe on the privacy and the civil and legal rights of other persons.

3. On the other hand, there is much difference of opinion among reasonable persons as to the wisdom, fairness, or indeed the enforceability of laws that purpose to:

   a. label as criminal the private behavior of mutually consenting adults;

   b. eliminate or control trade in pornography that appears in print, on stage, or on the screen;

   c. outlaw adultery, incest, prostitution, sodomy, bestiality, and "offenses against nature";

   d. remove from the realm of criminal justice those forms of sexual behavior regarded as non-violent, non-coercive, non-exploitive, or "victimless";

   e. add "affectional preference" to the basic list of "sex, creed, race, color, or national origin" on the basis of which a person's civil liberties are protected;

   f. put the community on record as to the standards it upholds but expecting that the laws will not be enforced.

4. The foregoing outlines goals. Much discussion will be needed to apply these goals to specific situations. Christians ought to participate gladly in the consensus-seeking processes by which good laws are drafted.

Notes: *This statement was issued by the American Lutheran Church, which in 1988 merged with the Lutheran Church in America and the Association of Evangelical Lutheran Churches to form the Evangelical Lutheran Church in America. It is an excerpt from* Human Sexuality and Sexual Behavior *which includes pornography on a list of exploitive sexual activities and supports laws against coercive sexual behavior, child pornography, and behavior which is a nuisance to the community. It notes that significant differences of opinion exist regarding laws that would regulate consensual, nonviolent adult behavior and other activities. It recognizes the difficulty inherent in "attempting to draft laws which bear upon moral convictions not shared by all persons in the community."*

EVANGELICAL LUTHERAN CHURCH IN AMERICA

THE VICTIMS OF PORNOGRAPHY (1985)

An analysis commended by the Standing Committee, Office of Church in Society. The American Lutheran Church, as a supplement (1985) to "Pornography," a statement of comment and counsel addressed to members of ALC congregations for study and action as they deem appropriate (1974).

1. Introduction

1.1 In 1974 the Seventh General Convention of The American Lutheran Church adopted a statement of comment and counsel entitled "Pornography." In this statement, pornography is equated with obscenity and defined as depicting erotic behavior in ways deliberately intended to stimulate sexual excitement. ALC members are urged to "give thoughtful consideration to issues involved in pornography" and to "offer their counsel, their prayers, their support for what is good and wholesome, and their energies to correct what is evil and destructive in public policies dealing with pornography."

1.2 Since the 1974 statement was adopted, both the nature of pornography and the social climate in the United States have changed. On one hand, commercial sex-oriented materials and services have increased in volume, in variety of media used, and in brutality. The content of sex-oriented materials has become more varied. They now include graphic, explicit portrayals of genitals, sex acts among all combinations of participants (e.g. male/female, adult/child, group sex, child/child, with animals), masturbation with foreign objects such as guns, sadomasochism, torture, rape, murder, dismemberment, sexual domination/submission/humiliation, sexual parodies and caricatures of generally respected entities (e.g. government, law, church, scripture, sacraments), and graphic portrayals of illegal acts (e.g. a patient being sexually abused by both doctor and nurse during an office visit, a child being molested, a parishioner being sexually abused by a clergyperson).

1.3 On the other hand, the social climate in the United States of America has become both more tolerant of sexual expression and less tolerant of it. What was once called "pornography" is now common fare in movies and television. However, several groups in our society—in the face of increased documentation of rape, incest, murder, bondage, torture, family violence, and discrimination against women—have become unwilling to accept explicit sexual material as harmless or victimless. Certain kinds of sexual material have been shown by scientific studies and crime analysis to have contributed to the commission of crimes against women and children, perpetrated mostly by men who purchase and consume such material.[1] Interestingly, some studies have shown that mildly erotic sexual materials appear to have the effect of lessening aggression by men against women.[2]

1.4 The present document seeks to call attention to these and other considerations for the purpose of aiding ALC members in their discussions, decisions, and actions regarding sexually oriented material.

2. Definitions of Pornography

2.1 The word "pornography" is compiled from two Greek words, "pornay" and "graphay." "Pornay" is a form of "peraymi" which means "to sell," usually in reference to a slave or harlot for hire. "Graphay" refers to that which is written, inscribed, or pictured. "Pornography," then, literally means picturing or describing prostitutes, with the connotation of an unequal slave/master relationship. Such portrayals have occurred throughout human history.

2.2 A 1973 United States Supreme Court decision offered these guidelines to define sexual obscenity: a) the work, taken as a whole, appeals to prurient interests; b) the work depicts or describes, in a patently offensive way, sexual conduct defined by applicable state law; and c) the work, taken as a whole, lacks serious literary, artistic or scientific value.[3] These guidelines have proven to be difficult to apply to particular cases or items.[4]

2.3 The 1974 ALC statement defines pornography as "material that depicts or describes erotic behavior in ways deliberately intended to stimulate sexual excitement." Some therapists now argue that stimulating sexual excitement can be therapeutic and materials that assist that purpose need not always be classified as "pornographic."

2.4 City governments in Indianapolis and Minneapolis have recently tried to differentiate pornographic material from erotic material, even though the two may sometimes coincide. Their tentative definitions also try to differentiate pornography from obscenity, even though they, too, may coincide. Rather, these efforts would define pornography in terms of a violation of civil rights, that is, as sexually explicit descriptions or portrayals of women or children in dehumanized, mutilated, animalistic, submissive, distorted, sadistic and/or masochistic positions through which women or children are placed and kept in a subordinate role and status (paraphrased). Pornography is thus defined as demeaning and destructive in its portrayal of women and children. Its major focus is physical and psychological violence against others.

2.5 Erotic material, in differentiation from pornography, may depict arousing, sexually explicit relationships between consenting people of equal status and respect for each other.[5] Erotic portrayals need not to be demeaning and can be edifying and therapeutic. They can also contribute to dramatic presentations and be aesthetically pleasing. Yet, some erotic portrayals are demeaning of all participants, by virtue of their casual, disdainful or trivial attitude toward human nature and human sexuality.

2.6 Obscenity refers to any excess, not necessarily sexual, that is an offense against decency. It can also refer to sexual portrayals which, on the whole, appeal to prurient interests. Obscenity is based on a value judgment which is difficult to prove in court.[6]

2.7 Definitions vary in focus and legal force. The more vague and inclusive the definition, the less useful it is as a tool in controlling offensive materials and services. Yet, a narrow definition, such as focusing on violence against women and children as portrayed in sexual settings, does not address other important questions which explicit sexual materials may raise for Christians, such as sexually explicit parodies and misrepresentations of Christian sacraments, scriptures and people. Perhaps several narrow definitions are needed at this time, in view of the complexity of both content and media used by purveyors of sexual goods and services.

3. Arguments for Allowing or Prohibiting Explicit Sexual Materials

3.1 There are several types of arguments which have been used by various people in favor of or against sexual materials considered pornographic by certain segments of the population. These arguments are based on different criteria, assume different definitions, and serve different purposes. Some of these arguments can be summarized as follows:[7]

3.2 Scientific studies form the basis for one type of argument, including that of the President's Commission on Obscenity and Pornography (1970). The Commission concluded that scientific studies showed little evidence that the use of pornography (as they define it) is harmful to the user or to society, and therefore few restraints should be placed on its dissemination. Countering this argument are more recent scientific studies of Victor B. Cline (University of Utah), Edward Donnerstein (University of Wisconsin), and many others,[8] which indicate that consumption of certain types of violent sexual portrayals does have a negative effect on both the individual user and society. Therefore, they contend certain verifiably harmful types of materials which combine violence and sex should be controlled.

3.3 A second type of argument bases its case on the First Amendment of the United States Constitution, which insures freedom of speech. It is maintained by some civil liberties advocates that any abridgement of freedom to communicate—for example, controlling freedom to communicate any and all forms of sexual expressions—would jeopardize the freedom of all other fields of communication. For that reason, even the worst "pornography" must be tolerated, so that censorship does not become a precedent. Those who argue against this stance point out that customary interpretations of the First Amendment have excluded certain forms of expression, such as prohibitions against libel, slander, sedition, perjury, advocating illegal acts, false advertising, copyright violations, etc.[9] The First Amendment does not guarantee absolute freedom to express everything in all cases. Arguments have also been made that the rights of some adults to choose an option should be balanced by the rights of other adults and children not to have that opinion thrust upon them unwillingly, or to have any resulting harm inflicted upon them. One person's freedom must be balanced by another person's freedom and by responsibility.

3.4 A third type of argument bases its support for allowing distribution of sexually explicit materials upon therapeutic considerations. Some counselors and social scientists have argued that, while many people find what they call pornography distasteful, it should be available because it serves as a sexual substitute or outlet for lonely, maladjusted, and confined persons, and may serve as a safety valve for society.[10] It may also serve as a stimulus for rejuvenating jaded relationships, and help solve a variety of sexual problems. Arguing against these claims are those who agree that the carefully structured use of erotica in therapeutic settings can be an aid to overcoming sexual dysfunctions, but that the distortions, violence, and callousness towards human dignity present in much of today's commercial sexual merchandise does more harm than good, *especially* to sexually maladjusted and immature people who purchase such goods and services instead of seeking professional help.

3.5 A fourth of arguments in favor of allowing the publication of sex-oriented materials is based on the desire to promote the publication of its author's or publisher's underlying philosophy.[11] Some people believe that the ideology of sex merchants will help to liberate society from certain "repressive" influences, such as religion, the nuclear family, sexual taboos, age discrimination (i.e. children should be allowed to choose having sex with adults), romanticized love, and a search for beauty and dignity. These are seen as having caused undue restraint and distress, and thus must be changed to a more liberal configuration which freely allows sexual contact between people of all ages, family relationships, sexual orientation, etc. Those arguing against such positions do not see the sex merchant's emphasis on secularism, non-committed relationships, ugliness, violence, hatred, and routine sex techniques as an improvement over previous options. They see such an approach as an insult to God, to human dignity, and to decency.

3.6 A fifth argument in favor of allowing the dissemination of all sexually explicit goods and services is profitability. In 1981, for example, the sex-oriented industry grossed almost as much money as the legitimate record and movie industries combined.[12] The argument is that society must want this product if it pays such a high price for it. Those who argue against violent sexual portrayals point out that saleability alone should not determine the availability of a product of service, especially if monetary profit for some is gained through physical, spiritual, and social harm to others, both individually and collectively.

3.7 One challenge that stands before Christians who would deal responsibly with sexual materials and services is that of becoming informed as to what the various people are selling: A positive attitude toward sexuality? A world-view in conflict with Christianity? A (possibly) protected expression of views? A (harmless) entertainment option? A danger to society and its citizens? Part of the challenge is to evaluate the Christian options, to see whether we are doing our best, or whether more needs to be done in teaching healthy sexuality, nurturing spirituality, forming human dignity and mutual respect.

4. Biblical/Theological Considerations

4.1 Biblical theology on the whole understands sexuality positively as a gift from God (Gen. 1:26-31). Some biblical passages (e.g., Song of Solomon) can be considered erotic in a positive sense, in that they celebrate the beauty of the human body and the creativity of human love and sexuality. Biblical theology affirms marriage as the appropriate arena for such sexual expression, but also affirms the option of remaining single (1 Cor. 7:36-40). The basis of biblical covenant theology is the building up of human dignity and respect for all people (Ex. 6:2-9, "I have heard the groanings of the people . . . I will bring you out from under the burdens"; 1 Peter 2:9-10, "Once you were no people, but now you are God's people.") It is a theology of grace in which God redeems and accepts the unrighteous, i.e., all people (1 Cor. 6:9-11, "The unrighteous will not inherit the kingdom of God . . . and such were some of you. But you were washed, you were sanctified . . . "; Mt. 21:28-32, " . . . the tax collectors and harlots go into the kingdom of God . . . "). It views all people as blessed (Gen. 1:27, "God created male and female, and blessed them"), all believers as members of the body of Christ (1 Cor 6:13-20) and temples of the Holy Spirit (1 Cor. 3:16-17). Biblical theology recognizes that demeaning behavior is inappropriate for the people of God to perpetrate upon others or to accept for themselves (1 Cor. 6:10-20, 8-9-13; 10:23-24; 12:4-26; 13:1-13; Lk. 9:46-48; 10:38-42).

4.2 Biblical theology speaks out against such practices as incest and the public or inappropriate display or viewing of nakedness in a way that would demean someone (Gen. 3:7-11; 9:20-23; Ex. 20:26; 28:42; Lev. 18:6-30). Similarly, biblical theology warns against lust (Mt. 5:27-30), against sexual relations with animals (Lev. 18:23) or prostitutes (1 Cor. 6:15-16), against various bizarre relationships (Rom. l:18-32) and against murder (Ex. 20:13; Mt. 5:21, Jas. 2:8-13), practices which are vividly portrayed and implicitly promoted by some commercial sexually explicit material.

4.3 Biblical theology has been ambivalent toward the treatment and status of women. On one hand, women in the Bible are affirmed as leaders and supporters of the religious community (e.g. Deborah, a prophetess and military leader, Judges 4-5; Phoebe, Paul's assistant and deaconness at Cenchreae, Rom. 16:1-2, the Samaritan woman who witnessed to Jesus' identity and thereby converted a whole town, Jn. 4:4-42, women as first witness to the resurrection, Mt. 28:1-10; all women, who are viewed as equal partners in Christ, Gal. 3:28; etc.).

4.4 On the other hand, there are elements in biblical writings which have been used to justify subordination, disrespect, humiliation, rape, and brutal violence against women (e.g. ''Wives, be subject to your husbands, as to the Lord,'' Eph. 5:22; ''Let a woman learn in silence with all submissiveness,'' 1 Tim. 2:11-12; ''Women should keep silent in the churches,'' 1 Cor. 14:34; ''But he would not listen to her, and being stronger than she, he forced her, and lay with her. Then Ammon hated her with a very great hatred . . . ,'' 2 Sam. l3:1-22; ''Here are my virgin daughter and his concubine; ravish them and do what seems good to you, but against this man do not do such a vile thing. . . [after his concubine was found dead] he took a knife, and laying hold of his concubine he divided her, limb by limb, into 12 pieces and sent her throughout the territory of Israel,'' Judges 19:11-21:25[13]).

4.5 These sections are part of the biblical canon and some are read to the present day in our churches. For some hearers they perpetuate the perception that women can legitimately be treated as subordinates, victims, and sex objects—the property of men. Therefore, Christians cannot entirely exempt themselves from the guilt of promoting violence against women. We cannot place all blame on purveyors of pornography. Even such a biblical passage as the injunction to keep silent is potentially damaging to women, since ''silenced'' women may be reluctant to speak out against sexual abuse and humiliation.

5. Conclusions

5.1 In light of the preceding considerations, several conclusions can be drawn regarding the responses and actions Christians might consider:

5.2 Human sexuality itself is a gift from God; portrayals of respectful, even erotically explicit, sexual encounters may be edifying. The development of a healthy sexuality within the church is one way to counteract the more damaging portrayals in the commercial sex-oriented material.

5.3 Portrayals of sexual encounters which demean and humiliate women or children or men, which undermine human dignity, or which promote hatred or violence, should be seriously challenged by direct action and by indirect education, since such portrayals are damaging to all parties—to the models who pose for such material, to the reader or viewer or hearer, and to the members of the general public who become victims when consumers of explicit materials seek to act out scenarios they have seen, read, or heard.

5.4   Focusing on the positive and affirming aspects of biblical theology will help Christians gain self-esteem and self-confidence, so they will be able to resist appeals to pose for, purchase, or act out materials that are sexually demeaning.

5.5   Focusing on the goodness of God's gift of sexuality in positive sex education can help Christians accept their sexuality as healthy and wholesome, leaving no need to turn for stimulation to sex-oriented materials which demean others and promote violence.

5.6   The rapid increase in volume, viciousness, and variety of violent sexual material calls for a response from Christians for the sake of human dignity and respect for all persons. Appropriate available means to address this problem should be considered, including *boycotts* (don't patronize stores which handle offensive, sexually violent materials); *legal action* (where applicable, sue producers and vendors for damages done to person, neighborhood, social climate, reputation); *ordinances* (pass legislation restricting "adult" stores); *protest* (demonstrate nonviolently at government zoning and licensing hearings); *education* (stress the destructive character of portraying sex-connected violence); *coalitions* with other groups (one need not agree on all issues to join together on one issue); *counseling* (both victim and perpetrator need grace and understanding to break the cycle of violence); *promotion of viable alternatives* (be more aggressive about the promotion of the love and acceptance available within Christianity). As a last resort, consider such direct actions as picketing "adult" stores or standing in their doorways with a camera.

5.7   Renewed enthusiasm for communicating the gospel of grace can hold out a beacon of hope for victims of sexual assault and violence who are left with feelings of guilt, fear, shame, and uncleanness. Victims, as well as perpetrators, should be welcomed, forgiven, and affirmed in a new life-style when seeking help from the church.

5.8   Elements in our own religious tradition which are demeaning to people should be recognized and addressed. To the extent that the church has set the climate for, and actively perpetuated, the subordination of women and children, the burden of guilt must be shared with the perpetrators of commercial, violent, sexual products.

5.9   To the extent that we, as Christians, have declined to keep informed about the growing threat of demeaning and violent sexual material and about the growing numbers of women and children who are directly or indirectly hurt by this industry, we should confess our indifference, naivete, and complicity in its burgeoning presence.

5.10   As Christians, we should be extremely concerned about the explicit anti-Christian element in such of the commercial sex products, insofar as the industry itself identifies symbols, persons, quotations, and rites as Christian and the object of ridicule.

5.11   The First Amendment to the U.S. Constitution, which guarantees the freedom of churches to speak their message of love and peace, also protects the rights of others to communicate potentially violent and slanderous material. Care must be taken to guard the rights of freedom of expression, while at the same time protecting citizens from violation of their rights to respect, integrity, and safety. There needs to be a balance between freedom of expression on one hand, and freedom from oppression on the other hand. To the extent that pornography portrays and incites insults and violence against women, it encroaches upon a women's right to a safe and peaceable life. To the extent that pornography perceives, shapes and exploits men as primarily interested in voyeurism, violence, and viciousness, men are also its victims. To the extent that pornography portrays children as objects of sexual activity, rather than as powerless dependents needing care and protection, children are its most pathetic victims. And, to the extent that pornography attacks the fabric of our society, our faith, and our respect for one another, we are all its victims.

Notes

[1] See, for example, Victor B. Cline, "Aggression Against Women: The Facilitating Effects of Media Violence and Erotica," an unpublished paper available from Dr. Cline at the University of Utah, Edward Donnerstein and Daniel Linz, "Sexual Violence in the Media: A Warning," *Psychology Today*, January 1984.

[2] Diana E.H. Russell, "Pornography and Violence: What Does the New Research Say?" *Take Back the Night, Women on Pornography*, ed. Laura Lederer, New York: William Morrow and Company, Inc., 1980, p.219.

[3] Paul J. McGeady, "Obscenity Law and the Supreme Court," *Where Do You Draw the Line?*, ed. Victor B. Cline, Provo, Utah: Brigham Young University Press, 1974, p. 97.

[4] Wendy Kaminer, "Pornography and the First Amendment: Prior Restraints and Private Actions," *Take Back the Night*, pp. 241-247.

[5] Diana Russell, "Pornography and Violence," *Take Back the Night*, pp. 218-219.

[6] Wendy Kaminer, "Pornography and the First Amendment," *Take Back the Night*, pp. 243-244.

[7] For a fuller treatment of typical arguments for and against pornography, see John H. Court, *Pornography: A Christian Critique*, Downers Grove, IL; InterVarsity Press, 1980.

[8] See, for example, Diana Russell, "Pornography and Violence," *Take Back the Night*, pp. 236-237, for others working in this area.

[9] Victor B. Cline, "Where Do You Draw the Line? An Introduction," *Where Do You Draw the Line?*, pp. 7-8.

[10] John Court, *Pornography*, pp. 16-17ff.

[11] See, for example, John Court, *Pornography*, pp. 18, 20, 23, 25, etc.; Laura Lederer, "Playboy Isn't Playing," An Interview with Judith Bat-Ada," *Take Back the Night*, pp. 121-133.

[12] Paul C. McCommon, III, CDL Legal counsel, "Pornography, 1983: Its Pervasive Presence in American Society," quoting Linda Tschirhart Sanford and Mary Ellen Donovan, "You Can Stop Pornography," *Reader's Digest*, June, 1982.

[13] For a discussion of this and other anti-feminine texts, see Phyllis Trible, *Texts of Terror: Literary-Feminist Readings of Biblical Narratives*, Philadelphia: Fortress Press, 1984.

[14] See also Andrea Dworkin, "For Men, Freedom of Speech; for Women, Silence, Please," *Take Back the Night*, pp. 256-258.

A Selected Annotated Bibliography

Cline, Victor B., ed. *Where Do You Draw the Line? An Exploration into Media Violence, Pornography, and Censorship*, Brigham Young University Press, Provo, Utah 1974. An anthology of articles related to the legal and psychological issues surrounding pornography, including a summary of the Report of the National Commission on Obscenity and Pornography (1970).

Court, John H. *Pornography: A Christian Critique*, InterVarsity Press, Downers Grove, Illinois, 1980. An Australian author treats the various arguments made against pornography, and the counter-arguments defending the rights or benefits of explicit sexual materials. A conservative Christian conclusion is drawn after surveying the arguments.

Fortune, Marie. *Sexual Violence: The Unmentionable Sin*, Pilgrim Press, New York, 1983. About all aspects of sexual violence against women and children, with a section suggesting appropriate pastoral response to those involved. Brief section on definitions and effects of pornography.

Gallagher, Neil. *The Porno Plague*, Bethany House Publishers, Minneapolis, 1981. A Christian perspective on pornography, including strategies for combating the presence of explicit materials, sample letters, etc.

Griffin, Susan. *Pornography and Silence*, Harper and Row Publishers, New York, 1981. A challenging book on the philosophy which the author believes is underlying much of pornography, and other areas of life.

Lederer, Laura, ed. *Take Back the Night: Women on Pornography*, William Morrow and Company, New York, 1980. An anthology by women on various aspects of pornography, such as definitions, victims, research, legal issues, strategies, beneficiaries, and effects, from a feminist perspective.

Trible, Phyllis. *Texts of Terror*, Fortress Press, Philadelphia, 1984. A study of selected texts from the Old Testament which portray women in a negative light. A responsible book that wants to take seriously the need for churches to hold up positive role models for its members.

Notes: *This 1985 statement was issued by the American Lutheran Church, which in 1988 merged with the Lutheran Church in America and the Association of Evangelical Lutheran Churches to form the Evangelical Lutheran Church in America. The statement attempts to differentiate between harmful pornography and material which can be used in a positive way to stimulate sexual excitement. It also suggests that churches have played a role in maintaining attitudes which demean women and thus cannot entirely separate themselves from the pornography which they condemn. The church urges its members to work against violent, demeaning, or child pornography.*

FREE METHODIST CHURCH

STATEMENT ON PORNOGRAPHY (1985)

13. Pornography

336.3 Pornography appeals to the lustful desires of the lower nature. It depicts and encourages indecent and deviant sexual conduct such as adultery, bestiality, incest, rape, sodomy, and child molestation. Its effects are a progressive decay of moral values, beginning with addiction, followed by a desensitizing of conscience, and tending toward the wanton acting out of illegitimate or perverted sexual conduct, often victimizing the innocent and unsuspecting.

For society, pornography is a virulently degenerative force. It damages and destroys. For Christians, pornography is an abomination which must be opposed by any legitimate means.

Notes: *This statement of the Free Methodist Church rejected pornography for its promotion of deviant sexual conduct, which leads to a decay of moral values. The Church urged its members to combat pornography "by any legitimate means."*

GREEK ORTHODOX ARCHDIOCESE OF NORTH AND SOUTH AMERICA

ORTHODOXY VS. PORNOGRAPHY: HOW CAN I HELP? (UNDATED)

As waves of pornography engulf our society and intrude upon our homes, good people ask, "What can be done?"

The answer:

- Avoid personal and family exposure to pornography.
- Know its effects and dangers.
- Take effective personal and community action.
- Support enforcement of constitutional antipornography laws.

How to Avoid Personal and Family Exposure to Pornography

- Set personal and family standards based on the teaching of the Fathers of the Church that focus on human dignity and wholesome living.
- Have open family discussions with children of suitable age about pornography and its dangers.
- Emphasize the sacred nature of the human body and the joy of proper sexual relationships.
- Avoid places where pornography is believed to exist.
- Control and monitor television viewing.
- Select movies and other entertainment based on reliable reviews.
- Read good books, . . . and read them to your children.
- Be aware of unsuitable music and lyrics. Discuss their impact on young people and others.

Know the Effects and Dangers of Pornography

Those who treat pornography victims report that many who are exposed to pornography progress through four stages:

1. Addiction. This addiction of the mind can be as powerful as any drug, alcohol, or cigarette addiction of the body.
2. Escalation. Progressively coarser material may be sought to satisfy the addiction.
3. Desensitization. With continued exposure, what at first offends becomes acceptable and then craved.
4. Acting Out. The thought is father to the deed. There is a great tendency to translate thoughts into action.

Many reliable studies and wide experience in law enforcement and personal counseling show that pornography is a significant contributing factor—often the triggering cause—of child abuse, violent crimes against women, teenage pregnancy and suicide, drug abuse, broken marriages, and broken lives.

How to Take Effective Personal and Community Action

Your most effective personal tools are your voice, your pen, your patronage, and your participation.

Pornography is a $10 billion per year industry in the United States. It will fail when it is unprofitable.

- If a local store sells or rents offensive materials, tell the manager (kindly but firmly) that you want to patronize that business but cannot it if undermines your family's values. A personal visit is most effective. Individualized letters also help.

  Merchants interpret each customer's expression as representing 100 other who feel the same way but who remain silent.

- Join with others in urging merchants to discontinue marketing offensive materials and in encouraging enforcement of constitutional laws relating to pornography.

  Parish Philoptochos, G.O.Y.A.L., Bible and Study groups, etc. are often more successful than larger organizations.

- Write or visit radio and television station managers, newspaper editors, and others to express concerns or commendations.

- Write to companies sponsoring advertisements in offensive publications or shown with offensive television programs.

Remember, obscene materials are illegal. They are not constitutionally protected. Indecent materials may be regulated by law. And you are free to let your patronage reflect your values as to what you personally find offensive.

How To Support Enforcement of Antipornography Laws

- Understand that obscenity is illegal. Material is "obscene," as defined by law, if—
  1. The average person, applying *local community standards*, would find that the material appeals to the prurient (lustful) interest.

     AND
  2. It depicts or describes, in a patently offensive way, sexual conduct specifically defined by state law.

     AND
  3. Taken as a whole, it lacks serious literacy, artistic, political, or scientific value.

All states have laws making obscenity illegal.

Material that is not "obscene" but is "indecent" can be legally limited as to time, place, and manner of presentation.

- Let law enforcement personnel know that you and your neighbors want antipornography laws enforced. Enforcement requires proof that the materials offend local community standards. Speak out so those standards will be known.

- Alert officials to the sources of obscene materials coming to your attention. If unsolicited materials are mailed to you, forward them to your postmaster with your complaint.

- Encourage legislators to enact additional laws where needed in such areas as telephone and computer pornography, cable television, and so forth.

From our neighbor is life and from our neighbor
is death.
If we win our neighbor we win God, but if we
cause our neighbor to stumble we sin against
Christ.

St. Anthony of Egypt

Notes: *This undated pamphlet of the Greek Orthodox Archdiocese of North and South America (approximately 2,000,000 members) stated that pornography contributes to "child abuse, violent crimes against women, drug abuse, teenage pregnancy and suicide, broken marriages and broken lives." The Archdiocese urged its members to speak out for stricter enforcement of obscenity laws.*

GREEK ORTHODOX ARCHDIOCESE OF NORTH AND SOUTH AMERICA

STATEMENT ON PORNOGRAPHY (UNDATED)

The unprecedented flow of pornography in our country confronts us both as Greek Orthodox church persons and as concerned citizens.

Religion and morality are indispensable supports of our form of government. Pornography constitutes a vicious assault on those supports. It dehumanizes the human person, reduces him to an animalistic level, and is therefore contrary to the will of God. It is destructive of the institution of marriage, and so of the family. It is destructive of love, preaching a doctrine of ugly lovelessness to our children.

Religion and morality are the resources on which our government must draw. When we look at the freedom with which pornography flows today, when we look at our spiritual and moral capability, then we see a depletion of that capability.

We are equally concerned about the crime of pornography as citizens. We see how it adds to the soaring crime rate. There are so many areas is our cities where people no longer have the use of their streets because of this fear to walk them.

Contrary to the view expressed by some, pornography debases society and its growing influence threatens our view of life and all that true religion teaches about human relationships. As pornography has grown in popularity its content has worsened considerably. Much of it now portrays violence, degradation and humiliation in addition to explicit sexual content. Common pornographic themes now include sadism, incest, child molestation, rape and even murder.

So called adult bookshops in the United States now total more than 15,000 . . . three times the number of the nation's largest restaurant chain. In 1983 the industry was estimated to have taken in $6 billion, almost as much money as conventional movie and record industries combined.

What Can be Done?

We must stop looking through our fingers as if to say this cannot happen with our people. It already has. Let us become aware of it. Pray that we may be all of one mind and accord before God. We must stop the degeneration of the term sex and return it to its proper light as taught by the Holy Orthodox Church.

1. This can be accomplished by realizing these facts and urging our spiritual leaders speak out on the subject.

2. We can draw attention to the smut rackets in our communities by the spreading of valuable information about them which are accessible from such publications as *The Readers Digest*.

3. Greek Orthodox can write letters to the leading publishers and producers of films to restrain the production of such materials.

4. The local chapters of our organizations can form committees who will investigate their local distributors of books and movies and should such pornographic material be available, try to discourage such businessmen from distributing it.

5. In many communities there are already groups which have been organized to challenge the spreading of this trash. Our local churches should do everything possible to aid these groups.

Let us practice our Faith, not with words alone, but with positive action by not becoming contributors to the spreading of this evil. Let us challenge such conditions and say we are positively opposed to it!! Our brother is our concern; Lead him not into temptation but deliver him from evil.

Notes: *This undated statement by the Greek Orthodox Archdiocese of North and South America (approximately 2,000,000 members) depicts pornography as destructive of morality by dehumanizing people and as contributing to the high rate of crime. The archdiocese encouraged its members to take positive action to challenge the spread of pornographic literature.*

INDEPENDENT FUNDAMENTAL CHURCHES OF AMERICA

RESOLUTION ON WORLDLINESS (1979)

WHEREAS, the Word of God instructs believers that we be not conformed to this world, but that we be transformed by the renewing of our minds (Romans 12:2); and

WHEREAS, we recognize that the lives of Christians are adversely affected through the influence of the press, radio, and television programming;

WHEREAS, our Christian homes, marriages, testimony, influence, godly living and spiritual effectiveness are being undermined through our acquiescence to the world-system;

BE IT RESOLVED, that the delegates to the 50th Annual Convention of the Independent Fundamental Churches of America, meeting at Schroon Lake, New York, June 23-29, 1979, reaffirm our historic committment to separated Christian living.

BE IT FINALLY RESOLVED, that we urge our constituency to shun the love of the world (I John 2:15-17), seek a Biblical philosophy by the renewing of our minds (Romans 12:2), and perfect holiness in the fear of God (II Corinthians 7:1).

Notes: *This 1979 resolution by the Independent Fundamental Churches of America (approximately 120,000 members) does not specifically mention pornography, but it clearly would be part of the adverse effects of the worldwide media. The press, radio, and television are generally considered part of the "world-system" from which Christians should maintain a distance.*

LUTHERAN CHURCH-MISSOURI SYNOD

HUMAN SEXUALITY: A THEOLOGICAL PERSPECTIVE (1981)

The union of husband and wife extends to the most intimate sharing in the act of sexual intercourse. The complete physical sharing of husband and wide is characterized by relaxation, enjoyment, and freedom from guilt. Decisions relative to this physical sharing should be made by husband and wife after prayerful discussion, as they keep in mind always that mutual enjoyment of God's beautiful gift is the goal they both seek (1 Thess. 4:4-5; 1 Cor. 7:5). Couples need to remember that their physical commitments are *personal* commitments. The act of intercourse is described in the Bible as an act of knowing: "Adam knew Eve his wife" (Gen. 4:1). This is no mere euphemism; or, if it is, it has an uncanny aptness. In the intimate sharing of the sexual act, a union in which the self is naked before the other, a unique knowing takes place. This is not knowledge *about* sex. It is knowledge of the self and the other as sexual beings united with one another in this most intimate union of giving and receiving.[19] The man and the woman, two different beings, while retaining (even accenting) their differences, nevertheless become one. The knowledge of that fellowship—like the knowledge of that fellowship in which God "knows" those who are His—can never be fully communicated apart from the experience of the union itself. It can only be said that in this union the partners come to know themselves even as they know the other. They know themselves only "in relation" to each other.

It is, of course, possible to forget that we are here talking of mutual *love* and to imagine that nothing more than a satisfaction of sexual appetite is involved. Clearly, however, though we might settle for no more than that, to do so would be to fall short of the personal relationship for which God has created us. The satisfaction of appetite alone, apart from any commitment of love, has not yet risen from the animal to the human, personal sphere.[20].

*To view our sexuality in the context of a personal relationship of mutual love and commitment in marriage helps us to evaluate the practice of masturbation. Quite clearly, chronic masturbation falls short of the Creator's intention for our use of the gift of sexuality, namely, that our sexual drives should be oriented toward communion with another person in the mutual love and commitment of marriage. By its very nature masturbation separates sexual satisfaction from the giving and receiving of sexual intercourse in the marital union and is symptomatic of the tendency of human beings to turn in upon **themselves** for the satisfaction of **their** desires.*

In childhood, masturbation may often be a form of temporary experimentation. However, children of God are warned against the voluntary indulgence of sexual fantasies as endangering faith and spiritual life. Such inordinate desires are clearly called sin by our Lord (Matt. 5:28). As the child grows and matures, youthful lusts and fantasies (2 Tim. 2:22) are left behind.

For those who are troubled by guilt and who seek God's help in overcoming problems in this area, pastors and Christian counselors need to stand ready to offer Christ's forgiveness, remind them of the power of the Holy Spirit to help them lead "a chaste and decent life in word and deed," and hold before them the joys of remaining faithful to what God's Word teaches about His intention for the good gift of sexuality.

The satisfaction of sexual appetite does not necessarily involve a personal relationship at all. At that level the man, for example, need not be concerned with woman as woman, as a personal being who calls him to fellowship, but simply with her physiological functions and capacities. And at that level it is quite understandable that people should regard their partners as essentially interchangeable. C.S. Lewis has described the situation quite well:

We use a most unfortunate idiom when we say, of a lustful man prowling the streets, that he "wants a woman." Strictly speaking, a woman is just what he does not want. He wants a pleasure for which a woman happens to be the necessary piece of apparatus.[21]

When the church condemns such as casual approach to sexual encounters as contrary to the will of God, it does more than take recourse in some special "religious" insight. It calls people back to a realization of the human, personal significance of the sexual act. A society in which casual sexual encounters and divorce prevail is on its way to viewing sexual partners as interchangeable. Its tendency is to dehumanize people and treat them solely in terms of their sexual functions, abstracting such functions from any content of personal significance.

The relationship of mutual love, one of the purposes for the fulfillment of which the Creator ordains marriage, is something very different. "Eros makes a man really want, not a woman, but one particular woman. In some mysterious but quite indisputable fashion the lover desires the Beloved herself, not the pleasure she can give."[22] And, indeed, lovers— however fickle they may prove to be at some future moment—are genuinely captivated by one another. They will quite naturally swear fidelity to each other. They rightly recognize the immense human and personal significance of the encounter with the beloved. It is this mutual love, implanted by the Creator in His creatures, with its original tendency toward permanent commitment, which marriage institutionalizes and seeks to make permanent.[23] Thus does the Creator continue today to deal with the predicament of "aloneness" within the human creation. He continues to give men and women to each other in the one-flesh union of marriage.

Endnotes

[19] Cf. Helmut Thielicke's fine discussion (*The Ethics of Sex*, trans. John W. Doberstein, [New York: Harper and Row, 1964], pp.66 ff.) of the distinction between sexual knowledge and knowledge about sex.

[20] Thielicke, pp. 20-26.

[21] C.S. Lewis, *The Four Loves* (New York: Harcourt Brace and Company, 1960), pp. 134 f.

[22] Ibid., p. 135.

[23] We have, of course, described marriage as we in our culture ordinarily experience it. It is equally possible that it might not be preceded by mutual love (e.g., marriages might be arranged by parents), but the institution of marriage would still be ordered toward such a relationship of mutual love, and we would expect it to give rise to this love.

Notes: *This excerpt from a longer statement on human sexuality by the Lutheran Church-Missouri Synod (about 2,660,000 members), while not speaking directly to pornography, does condemn a "casual approach" to sex which treats the partner as a physical apparatus outside of a loving relationship.*

NATIONAL ASSOCIATION OF EVANGELICALS

RESOLUTION ON PORNOGRAPHY AND OBSCENITY (1985)

In recent years there has been a growing portrayal of sexual immorality and deviation in the cinema, television, radio and the print media. The lifestyle modeled for our children on mass media outlets portraying these excesses is dehumanizing and morally destructive. Such ideas and ideals promoted by mass media are in direct contradiction to the biblical lifestyle.

Furthermore, the eight billion dollar pornography industry has grown to epidemic proportions and is invading all the segments of our society. Pastors, counselors, social agencies and law officers are seeing families broken and lives adversely affected as well as persons of both sexes victimized by this plague of pornography and obscenity. This industry, controlled largely by organized crime, is responsible for corrupting the lives of children as well as adults, and most alarming of all is the proliferation of child pornography.

Aware of this insidious evil in our society and seeking to be obedient to our prophetic task as God's people, the National Association of Evangelicals therefore declares itself as follows:

1. We are committed to Jesus Christ who calls us as the "salt of the earth" and "the light of the world" to be involved in the solution of the problem of pornography.

2. We are committed to speak out against pornography and obscenity at every opportunity.

3. We encourage our congregations and denominations to observe a Pornography Awareness Sunday or Week.

4. We urge our congregations to become involved in appropriate plans of action in their communities.

5. We commit ourselves to participate as an Association in the National Coalition Against Pornography.

6. We call upon the President of the United States to declare publicly his support for the enforcement of obscenity laws and to order the Justice Department to enforce the existing obscenity laws.

7. We urge Christians everywhere to seek ways to minister more effectively to both the victims and perpetrators of obscenity and pornography.

Notes: *This statement by the National Association of Evangelicals, an ecumenical body which is the more conservative counterpart to the National Council of Churches, condemns pornography as an "insidious evil" and especially corruptive of young people. It supports greater enforcement of existing obscenity laws.*

NATIONAL ASSOCIATION OF FREE WILL BAPTISTS

RESOLUTIONS ON PORNOGRAPHY (UNDATED)

III. WHEREAS, the greatest needs of our nation are spiritual revival and return to God and Biblical values, and

WHEREAS, the current movements for rights of homosexuals, disregard for the sacredness of human life as created by God, such as abortion on demand and euthanasia, the equal rights amendment, pornography, secular humanism, and other such evils are in direct conflict with a return to God and spiritual renewal,

BE IT RESOLVED, that this body go on record as opposing the said evils, and

BE IT FURTHER RESOLVED, that our people be encouraged to work for the election of public officials, regardless of political party, who are supportive of Biblical values. (*Adopted as amended*)

IV. WHEREAS, the American home is experiencing a deterioration in foundation, and

WHEREAS, this moral decay is greatly effecting our Free Will Baptist homes, therefore,

BE IT RESOLVED, that this body encourage and admonish our pastors to assist our people in establishing and conducting Christian homes. (*Adopted as amended*)

V. WHEREAS, offensive television programs continue

BE IT RESOLVED, that we reaffirm our position as stated in Resolution #1 in 1975:

1. That the National Association of Free Will Baptists hereby express its firm conviction that television programs which degrade sex, glorify violence, and deny moral decency have no place on the airways.

2. That we strongly oppose programming which undermines the moral values and ideals of our great nation.

3. That we urge all Free Will Baptists to enthusiastically express appreciation to producers, networks, and sponsors for morally wholesome television programs.

4. That we call on Free Will Baptists to vigorously oppose the showing of offensive movies on television through:

   a. Letter writing (to the Federal Communications Commission, legislators, local station managers, and sponsors),

   b. Selective buying practices,

   c. Selective viewing, and

   d. Supporting worthy organizations that are opposing such programs.

5. That we regard this issue with such intense concern that we commit ourselves to work to secure its implementation. (*Adopted*)

Notes: *In these three resolutions by the National Association of Free Will Baptists, which* *has approximately 201,000 members, pornography is associated with such things as euthanasia and the Equal Rights Amendment as part of the current "disregard for the sacredness of human life." The moral decay affecting Christian homes is acknowledged, and the television sex and violence which also contributes to this decay is condemned.*

NATIONAL COUNCIL OF CHURCHES OF CHRIST IN THE U.S.A.

VIOLENCE AND SEXUAL VIOLENCE IN FILM, TELEVISION AND HOME VIDEO (1986)

A Policy Statement of the National Council
of the Churches of Christ in the U.S.A.
Adopted by the Governing Board
November 6th 1986

About NCC Policy Statements

A policy statement of the National Council of the Churches of Christ in the U.S.A. expresses the Council's basic position with respect to Christian principles and their general application to today's society and world. The 260-member Governing Board, made up of delegations representing the NCC's 32 member communions, is the only body that can approve such statements. Developed through an extended study process that generally culminates with readings at two successive Governing Board meetings, a policy statement:

● guides the work of the Council,

● is commended to member church for their consideration, and

● helps influence public opinion.

Policy statements have a wide scope and form the basis for resolutions addressing current and more specific situations facing church and society.

Forward

The National Council of the Churches of Christ in the U.S.A. recognizes the powerful influence of television, film, cable TV and videocassettes on the opinions, tastes and values of Americans. The Council first addressed the functions and responsibilities of the electronic media through a Policy Statement, "The Church, Television and Radio Broadcasting", June 8, 1963 (updated to include cable-TV, June 10, 1972). These media have now become the dominant forms of visual communication, and the Council reiterates its conviction that, as instruments of God's creation, they must be held in trust by those who use them. Their stewardship is of inescapable concern to all Christians, especially in those situations where their capacity to enhance the common goal is diminished by the use of gratuitous violence and sexual violence for commercial gain.

Therefore, in 1983, The NCCC's Communication Commission established a Study Commission to examine more specifically the problems of violence and sexual violence in the media. The Commission's report, entitled "Violence and Sexual Violence in Film, Television, Cable and Home Video," was received by the Governing Board of the Council in November, 1985. The Governing Board now addresses itself to the substance of this report, including conclusions about research, guiding principles for consideration by member communions and recommendations for action.

If it is to respond constructively to the use of violence and sexual violence in the media, the church must first understand the reasons why this material attracts and holds audience interest. Research indicates that all of us, and children in particular, have been conditioned by the visual media to demand action, movement and rapid resolution to conflict. But the problem goes deeper than media as a method of transmitting images. Throughout history, humankind has manifested an attraction to violence. Societies are organized around the maintenance of security. Militarism and consumerism both reflect the need for security and needs to be powerful, to be in control and to be accepted.

The Christian understanding of sin recognizes that we are created whole but become alienated from God, from one another and from ourselves. We would like to be rescued from this condition but instead we act in ways that increase our alienation from others and from ourselves. Part of this alienation comes from a self perception that we are not valued, or are over valued in comparison with others. We are insecure, proud, unable to trust or to accept gifts of God's grace. When we perceive ourselves and others as of little value, or of too much value, we are led to rest our power by measuring it against others. We use our freedom to assert our will against others and against God's will for our lives.

If as a Christian community we are to address the damage from this misuse of freedom, then we must approach the issue of violence and sexual violence in the media not from a prior commitment to censorship, but with an understanding of underlying causes. And we are committed to a process of education and sensitization of the public to help individuals recognize their own complicity in the media's messages of violence.

I. Violence and the Media

America is a violence prone society. Between 1963 and 1973, while the war in Vietnam was taking 46,212 American lives, firearms in America killed 84,644 civilians. If the United States had the same gun homicide rate as Japan, our 1966 gun death toll would have been 32 instead of 6,855; if our suicide rate by gun were the same, only 196 persons would have killed themselves with a gun instead of 10,407. Since 1933 the per capita rate of rape in the United States has increased more than 700%. There were eight handgun murders in England in 1980 and 10,012 in the United States.

Much violent behavior is learned. The mass media are powerful teachers and conditioners of individual attitudes and behavior. But Christian doctrine emphasizes the importance of seeking non-violent ways to reduce conflict between individuals, groups and nations. The use of violence turns individuals into things, objects of force or coercion, allowing one individual or group to dominate another. Such domination is counter to Christianity's teaching of human equality and the power of love and its commitment to justice and equity to resolve differences between individuals and groups.

Therefore, we deplore the increasing depiction of violence and sexual violence in the visual media. Violent behavior by media models gives negative guidance when such behavior fails to show consequences, and encourages violence as a superior choice in human relations. Such portrayals demean human interchange and harm our social environment by objectifying persons and undermining harmonious community life. Media leaders must recognize that their violent portrayals damage the common good and threaten media freedom. We support this freedom not only because it is guaranteed by the First Amendment, but also because if our society allows itself to become fettered by censorship, it may no longer be receptive to the new promptings which come from God.

The National Commission on the Causes and Prevention of violence wrote in 1969, "Violence on television encourages violent forms of behavior, and fosters moral and social values about violence in daily life which are unacceptable in a civilized society." In 1972, Dr. Jesse Steinfeld, Surgeon General, told a Senate hearing that three years of research by his office had provided him with sufficient data to establish a causal relationship between television violence and aggressive behavior. He concluded: "the broadcasters should be put on notice. The overwhelming consensus and the unanimous Scientific Advisory Committee's report indicate that television violence, indeed, does have an adverse effect on certain members of our society."

Industry leaders have resisted this charge that violence and sexual violence in broadcasting and films contribute to violence in the society. Broadcasting representatives hold that the evidence is not conclusive, that there is disagreement among researchers, and that there are many factors other than media involved in the social equation of violent anti-social behavior. Film industry leaders point out that no one is obligated to see films which are violent and that films are voluntarily rated by the motion picture industry in order to provide guidance for parents.

We believe that the weight of research over the past thirty years supports the following conclusions about the relationships between televised violence and aggression:

1. Laboratory studies show conclusively that there is a causal relationship between viewing violence on television and subsequent aggressive behavior.

2. The vast majority of field studies demonstrate a positive association between exposure to media violence and aggressiveness.

3. The positive association between viewing TV violence and aggressiveness is small but consistent. Looked at across the entire population and over an extended period of time, such a modest statistical relationship implies a substantial negative social effect.

4. The conclusion that media violence encourages antisocial and aggressive behavior is consistent with accepted theories about the nature of social learning.

5. Laboratory studies show that violent sexual material stimulates aggression toward women; also, violent material stimulates sexual violence.

6. Media *can and often do* create insecurity, vulnerability and dependency, and thereby the overall conditions in which violence is facilitated in society. Most children and adults who are heavy viewers of television express a greater sense of insecurity and apprehension about their world than do light viewers: the "mean world" syndrome.

7. Because music video often combines teen idols with erotic material and violence in a repetitive context, this new format requires careful research and monitoring. (We believe existing research on media violence in general implies a detrimental effect of violent and sexually violent music video on children and youth.

II. Freedom, Censorship and Corporate Responsibility

Both the Christian faith and the democratic philosophy of government emphasize the freedom of the individual person from compulsory conformity of belief, thought and life-style. On the other hand, both Christian and democratic traditions recognize that individual freedom is limited by, and in fact is only fulfilled through, the requirements of a just and orderly community. A society that values freedom promotes not only the independence of individuals, but also the mutual responsibility of every individual for each other and for the welfare of the community as a whole.

The Governing Board does not favor censorship, by which we mean governmental prior restraint of speech. Those who favor censorship argue that society needs conformity to some standard of decency and morality, and that the Constitution does not guarantee individuals or groups the freedom to undermine the society by advocating or attractively describing ideas or practices, which, would result in harmful changes in the society. Those who are against censorship argue that while freedom of expression may be abused by some, the dangers of limiting it are even greater. We oppose government intervention to determine the content of programming, since it opens the door to compromise of political and religious issues. On the other hand, we believe that holding broadcasters to a higher level of responsibility to the viewing public by providing specific categories of program service does not contravene the First Amendment.

We oppose compromise with the guarantees of the First Amendment. At the same time we deplore the activities of those in the media industries who hide behind these protections to make money at the expense of the public welfare. The public, acting through its governmental institutions, must provide protection for freedom of expression; however, that freedom is not a license to exploit and demean the common good.

We recognize that many professionals within the communication industry *are* concerned about the amount of exploitative sex and gratuitous violence in the media in which they work, and are doing what they can to serve positively the needs and interests of the viewers. These people deserve and require our support, our encouragement and our commendation. But these individuals are themselves only a small part of a vast and complex system which parcels out responsibility, a little bit to everyone, so that in the end, *no one* is ultimately responsible.

The fact of corporate irresponsibility must be addressed. The "business war" which constantly is being waged among broadcasters and cable operators often leads them to place the public interest second to corporate profit. Law and governmental regulation must redress the balance by insisting that *all* stations, networks and cable systems must put public interest before private profits. Communication corporations must expand their sense of responsibility beyond that of their stockholders to include the interests of the larger national community.

The electromagnetic spectrum is a limited resource. Only impartial regulation of its use can guarantee the First Amendment objective of an open marketplace of ideas. As the Supreme Court said in the landmark Red Lion case: "It is the right of the viewers and listeners, not the right of the broadcasters, which is paramount. It is the right of the public to receive suitable access to social, political, esthetic, moral and other ideas and experiences which is crucial here."

III. Guiding Principles

Christians have no simple and easy answers to these complex issues. We cannot formulate a solution which can be claimed to be *the* Christian solution. However, we can articulate some principles which may serve to guide the churches as they seek solutions to the problem.

A. The Christian Calling and the Media

Christians are called to preserve, perpetuate and share the moral values which have come from their families of faith. We are also called to bring prophetic judgment to bear on threats to the public welfare which come through the moral pollution of our media environment. In addition, we are called to be informed, to encourage research so that society will have accurate information as the basis for action, and to participate in constructive responses to the problems posed by the new media environment.

B. Freedom and Responsibility

We affirm our adherence to the principles of an open marketplace of ideas and the guarantees of the First Amendment to freedom of speech, of the press and of religion. These freedoms are the right of citizens, both individually and corporately. It is the nature of these freedoms that they be exercised within a framework of social responsibility and of concern for the public welfare.

We support industry self-regulation as a means of solving many of the problems related to violence in the media. But we believe that self-regulation can be only a partial solution because without some governmental oversight the industry's self-interests will take precedence over the public interest. Laws and regulation, within the constraints of the First Amendment, are essential because they can place all competitors on an equal basis.

C. Special Responsibility of Television and Cable

Television and cable may deliver unexpected images into homes. Because of this fact and because the broadcast spectrum and wiring systems are limited, the television and cable industries have a special responsibility for the public interest.

The airwaves are held in trust for the public by radio and television broadcasters, with licenses regulated by government. The broadcaster is therefore responsible for the content of programming. However, this right does not abridge the public's "right to know" and to be fairly represented.

Some argue that cable TV is legally similar to a newspaper and has the same First Amendment protection; however, we hold that since cable depends upon the use of city streets, it has a special public service obligation. Others argue that television should no longer be regulated because there is no scarcity of frequencies. We believe that scarcity argument has not been proved; that broadcast stations need to be licensed; and that they have an obligation to serve the public interest. If either cable or television were allowed to have monopoly control in our communities, the public's concern about violence in these media would be ignored in the interest of making greater profits.

D. The Needs of Children

Children are especially threatened by the pervasiveness of violence and sexual violence in media. Both ethically and constitutionally it is the responsibility of the entire society to protect the interest of children and to provide for their education and welfare. The need to protect children extends into the home, including protection from both the unexpected images of television and the paid cable services and those of rented video cassettes and films.

We believe children should legally be barred from theatre showings of films deemed unsuitable for them. Parents should be helped to avoid the showing of that same material in their homes via television, cable and videocassette. At the same time, broadcasters should be required to make available regularly scheduled programming to enlighten and entertain children.

IV. A Call to Action

The nation's communication system is our lifeline for the preservation of our freedom and our system of democratic government. Communication, by whatever means, must be free, open, constructive and creative, and must be easily accessible to members of the public. Media leaders, the government and the public are all responsible for keeping it so.

When one or another errs or falls short of fulfilling its responsibility to guard the common goal, the others are required to call it to accountability.

There is compelling reason for the public at this time to demand a reformation of the conduct of the producers and disseminators of film, television and home video. Gratuitous violence, and especially exploitative sexual violence, must not be allowed in homes without clear and advance information to viewers as to the nature of the material. Also, viewer control over what is seen by children should be guaranteed. But since this control will never be absolute, it is imperative that our member communions assess the level of violence and sexual violence in such programming and help parents, educators and others to counter their negative effects. Churches should develop educational activities to help both adults and children analyze and deal with the content of video programming and formulate their own standards of program excellence.

The National Council of the Churches of Christ calls on the Federal Communications Commission (FCC) to fulfill its statutory and moral obligation to protect the public interest with respect to the industries it regulates. Its failure to adhere to its own rules and thus its failure fully to regulate its licensees is adverse to the public welfare. Responsible regulation is essential to reduce violence in television and cable. The FCC should fulfill its legally-required oversight of its licensees and enforce its time-honored standards of broadcast practices.

The Council further calls upon Congress and the Federal Communication Commission

1. to study the incidence of violence in programs and its effects on both adults and children, and to regularly publish the findings of such studies;

2. to require broadcasting, cable-TV and other electronic distribution systems to warn audiences about the character and intensity of violence in their entertainment programs;

3. to reinstate the historic process of broadcaster ascertainment of community needs and interests to give the communities process by which they can register their concerns about community needs including the problems of violence and sexual violence in programming; and

4. to require cable-TV companies to provide means by which parents may exercise their right to prevent their children from viewing programs deemed unsuitable.

Churches should participate in communication affairs more actively than they do now. They should take cognizance of the influence the media exert on problems whose resolutions may determine the future of humanity. They should put the public interest above considerations of institutional advantage and should ally themselves with those elements in the media that discern our mutual responsibility to serve the public good and are willing to labor for maximum diversity of programming and services that are of social significance and artistic merit.

As an alternative to the plethora of violent material directed toward children, television stations and cable services should provide a substantial amount of programming which serves the educational and information needs of children, is directed to specific are groups, and is reasonably scheduled through the week. Citizens should concern themselves with the content of entertainment programs and should participate locally in analyzing and evaluating programs and their effects. Only by careful, long-term attention to the content and perceived objectives of programs can individuals and communities make mature and discriminating judgments about them. Public groups should encourage those sponsors, producers and program outlets that strive for artistic excellence and the uplifting of ethical values in their programs, and should challenge, through the Federal Communications Commission and the courts, those federally licensed outlets, that fail to serve the public interest.

The movie industry, which is not regulated by Congress, should voluntarily expand and clarify the present rating system.

The National Council of the Churches of Christ further urges holders of stock in companies which advertise on television or Cable-TV to call the attention of the officers and directors of those companies to the importance of adopting voluntary guidelines which would avoid sponsorship of programs with excessive violence and gratuitous sexual violence. Such corporate stockholder action is equitable and could become increasingly effective if a large number of sponsoring corporations were to adopt such voluntary guidelines.

The Governing Board urges the member communions of the Council, acting in concert through the Council's Communication Commission, to produce and distribute programs of high artistic merit which illuminate the human condition without resorting to gratuitous violence and exploitative sex.

The Governing Board recommends that the leaders of the member communions launch a continuing program of information and education to make their membership aware of the seriousness of the problems society faces from the depiction of violence and sexual violence in the visual media.

Finally, the Governing Board believes that the state has a compelling interest in the impact on society of excessive violence and sexual violence in film, television and home video. Considering the public concern over this matter, we expect the media industry to take voluntary action, so as to avoid any involuntary restraint that might have an adverse effect on First Amendment rights.

Notes: *This pamphlet of the National Council of the Churches of Christ in the U.S.A. (an ecumenical body which is the more liberal counterpart to the National Association of Evangelicals) focuses, not on general pornography, but specifically on violence and sexual violence. While not favoring government control of media content, the council does favor holding broadcasters to a higher standard of responsibility, since studies have shown a link between viewing violence and subsequent aggressive behavior. The council especially advocates protecting children in the home from unexpected media presentations of (sexual) violence. Citizens are urged to let their concerns be heard.*

PRESBYTERIAN CHURCH (U.S.A.)

RESOLUTION ON MEDIA PORNOGRAPHY (1984)

Overture 157-84, On Making Known the Church's Strong Disapproval of Mass Media's Portrayal of Sexuality, Sexual Exploitation, Violence, Drug and Alcohol Abuse and on Establishing a Council to Formulate New Voluntary Standards—from the Presbytery of Elizabeth; and *Overture 161-84*, On Taking Action Against Obscenity and Pornography—from the Presbytery of Cincinnati.

The committee recommends that the 196th General Assembly (1984) take no action and that the following resolution be adopted:

"Whereas, in the last few years there has been an explosive escalation of the portrayal of sexual immorality and deviation, profanity, alcoholism and other drug abuse, and demonic violence on television and radio; and

"Whereas, the lifestyle that is modeled for our children on the mass media outlets, which portray these excesses without regard for time of day or age of audience, is potentially dehumanizing and morally destructive; and

"Whereas, many of the ideals lifted up on mass media programming are in direct contradiction to those lifestyle ideals that are proclaimed and modeled in the gospel of Jesus Christ; and

"Whereas, we are called as members of the church of Jesus Christ to name the principalities and powers that are seeking to claim our allegiance; and

"Whereas, the General Assemblies of both the former UPCUSA and the PCUS have acted in response to violence, sexual exploitation for commercial purposes, and lax morality in the public media; and

"Whereas, the former PCUS at its 121st General Assembly (1981) recorded its opposition to themes of violence and immorality in the public media and further called for appropriate federal agencies to employ their influence to eliminate extreme portrayals of these themes in the public media; and

"Whereas, the former PCUS at its 189th General Assembly (1977) adopted a resolution, 'to take a public stand against the use of pornography and violence in the media and to reinforce the dignity of human beings, and thereby strengthen the Christian faith;' (*Minutes*, 1977, Part I, p.118); and

"Whereas, among the comments that have been made by past General Assemblies, the 185th General Assembly (1973) noted a concern for the following problem areas as they are portrayed in the mass media:

"a. glorification of violence and its numbing effect on ethical standards;

"b. commercialization and exploitation of sex;

"c. overt appeals to materialism as the ideal style of life;

"d. emphasis on advertising instant relief of problems through medication; and

"Whereas, pastors, counselors, social agencies, and law officials are seeing families broken and lives adversely affected, as well as persons of both sexes and of all ages victimized by pornography and obscenity; and

"Whereas, pornography, 'kiddie porn' and materials depicting excessive violence and murder combined with sexual content are part of a growing $6 billion industry (more than the movie and record industries combined) controlled largely by organized crime (ranked as their third largest money-maker); and

"Whereas, the Supreme Court of the United States in 1973 established basic guidelines for determining ''what is obscene''; and

"Whereas, the Supreme Court of the United States has traditionally held that obscenity is not protected by the First Amendment and that obscenity is not protected expression; and

"Whereas, there are existing federal and state laws to stem the rampant flow of obscene materials and to control their availability; therefore, be it

"*Resolved*, That the 196th General Assembly (1984) of the Presbyterian Church (U.S.A.):

"1. Direct the Stated Clerk to notify the President of the United States that it is the desire of the General Assembly of the Presbyterian Church (U.S.A.) to have the laws related to obscenity enforced by the U.S. Attorney General and the U.S. attorneys, the U.S. Postal Service, the Commerce Department, and the Customs Department, and that the Presbyterian Church (U.S.A.) is supportive of current efforts to include obscenity under the R.I.C.O. Statutes. (R.I.C.O. Statutes: Racketeering Influenced and Corrupt Organizations statutes currently cover obscenity. Legislation to this effect was introduced into the House and Senate on 11-14-83.)

"2. Mandate the Council on Women and the Church and the General Assembly Mission Board (Office of Women) to persevere in their work in the areas of pornography and obscenity and the education of the church and society to combat the abusive treatment of women.

"3. Establish official, visible relationship with other denominations and their leaders who are taking action against obscenity and pornography;

"4. Encourage every Presbyterian to:

   "a. develop awareness of the depth of the problem and its implications for the church and the world;

   "b. take an active supportive role in one of the organizations working to establish the enforcement of current laws;

   "c. refrain from supporting economically all motion pictures offensive to that individual's personal and moral convictions, and refrain from supporting economically companies that sponsor TV or radio programs or advertise in media in ways offensive to that individual's personal moral convictions;

   "d. file objections with the management or refuse to patronize those businesses that they personally feel contribute to the moral decay of our homes and families;

   "e. write personally to those against whom the above action has been taken, informing them of the action and the reason for it.

"5. Call on our churches to minister both to those who have become victimizers and to those who are or who have been victimized by violence, pornography, and sexual abuse, affirming the love of God and the new life in Jesus Christ that is for all persons.

"6. Instruct the Stated Clerk to send a copy of this action to the appropriate executives of denominations in the United States with whom we are in correspondence, informing them of our concern and commitment and encouraging their consideration of this matter."

Notes: *The Presbyterian Church (U.S.A.) was formed through the 1983 merger of the United Presbyterian Church in the U.S.A. (UPCUSA) and the Presbyterian Church in the United States (PCUS). In this statement, the Presbyterian Church (U.S.A.), which has about 3,000,000 members, repudiates the pornography, violence, and other immorality portrayed in the media, and encourages political response and personal education to combat the problem. The statement notes previous comments on this issue by the UPCUSA in 1973 and 1977, and by the PCUS in 1981.*

PRESBYTERIAN CHURCH (U.S.A.)

RESOLUTION ON PORNOGRAPHY (1986)

Commissioners' Resolution 3-86. On Reaffirming the Actions of the 196th and 197th General Assembly (1984 and 1985) Regarding Pornography.

[The General Assembly adopted *Commissioners' Resolution* 3-86.]

Whereas, the United States Attorney General's Commission on Pornography has documented that sexually explicit and violent materials are addictive and demoralizing to individuals, victimize children, women and men, and contribute to the destruction of family life . . . in essence, pornography is not a victimless crime;

Whereas, the content of pornography is antithetical to the Judeo-Christian calling and values;

Whereas, the 196th and 197th General Assemblies (1984,1985) declared their awareness and growing concern for the devastating affects of pornography on the social, moral and spiritual conditions of our Nation by adopting strong overtures with definitive recommendations;

Whereas, the 197th General Assembly (1985) mandated that a $45,000, three-year study be undertaken by the Council on Women and the Church (COWAC) to develop resources to inform and equip congregations in the battle against pornography,but the General Assembly Finance Committee has not funded this work by COWAC;

Whereas, the proposed Mission Design specifies ''pornography'' as an area of concern of the Social Justice and Peacemaking Ministry Unit (second draft, p. 16:91); therefore, be it

Resolved, That the 198th General Assembly (1986) of the Presbyterian Church (U.S.A.) reaffirm the actions of the 196th and 197th General Assemblies (1984 and 1985) related to pornography; and

Mandate the appropriate agency (Advisory Council on Church and Society or Social Justice and Peacemaking Ministry Unit) to advocate the public policy position of the General Assembly in the area of pornography and assist the Church in its social witness (this includes the immediate funding of work to implement the actions of the two previous General Assemblies).

Sharlyn W. Stare—Presbytery of Cincinnati
William R. Stepp—Presbytery of Tropical Florida

Notes: *The Presbyterian Church (U.S.A.) was formed through the 1983 merger of the United Presbyterian Church in the U.S.A. (UPCUSA) and the Presbyterian Church in the United States (PCUS). This resolution reaffirms that ''the content of pornography is antithetical to the Judeo-Christian calling and values,'' and acts to ensure funding for the major three-year study called for in 1985.*

PRESBYTERIAN CHURCH (U.S.A.)

PORNOGRAPHY: FAR FROM THE SONG OF SONGS (1988)

A. 42.254-.684 Report of the Council on Women and the Church and the Committee on Women's Concerns, "Pornography: Far from the Song of Songs."

That the report be adopted as amended, so that it shall then read as follows:

1. paragraphs 42.254-.629

    a. 42.266—insert the following paragraph above the dotted paragraph which begins with "the inherent goodness":

       "that God calls human beings to positive expressions of mutual affirmation and commitment, especially as typified in the calling to faithful, respectful marital and family relationships."

    b. 42.271—change "The traditional patriarchal"in the ninth line to *"Historically, the predominant* interpretation of the story". . .

    c. 42.292—insert the following in the second line after "relating to women": *"and other issues addressed later in this report"*

    d. 42.294—strike "that is produced for monetary profit and" and add the following at the end of the sentence: "or mistreatment of any person, male or female, *and is usually produced for monetary profit."*

    e. 42.319—in the 5th dotted paragraph change "about" to *"including"* so that it reads: "male and female persons, *including* exploitation of" . . .

       42.319—in the last dotted paragraph insert the following after "children": "materials that depict children (*previously defined as pornography)*". . .

    f. 42.374—change title to read, "Harm to Children *and Youth"*

    g. 42.375—add *"and youth"* to "children" at several points:

       line 2—"harm it has on children *and youth. Young people* in". . .

       line 6—"by adults to coerce children *and youth* into". . .

       line 8—"children *and youth* include". . .

    h. 42.453—add the following sentence at the end: *"(Note: the use of the words, 'Sex Education,' in step one of the following figure does not refer to competent sex education that is factually accurate and sensitive to personal responsibility.)"*

    i. 42.595—substitute the following sentence for the first sentence of the section: *"Some men constantly test sexual prowess in an attempt to boost a poor self-image."*

    j. 42.596—strike in the first line at the top of the right column the phrase "particularly by men who rely on" and insert the following to read:

       "can be used in compulsive ways, *creating and facilitating* masturbatory fantasies". . .

    k. 42.605—strike the second sentence and insert the following: *"Pornography is an extreme variation on common attitudes and beliefs. It reflects and reinforces certain injurious stereotypes:"*

    l. 42.612—in line 7 insert the following after "caring, warmth": "caring, warmth, *commitment*, and genuine mutual pleasure". . .

    m. 42.614—insert the following before "standard" in line 3:

       "vulnerable to this *false* standard of masculinity."

n. 42.617—in line 3 strike the phrase which begins the second sentence of the section, "Homosexual images are not inherently pornographic and". . . The second sentence now begins: "*H*omophobia should not motivate". . .

o. 42.624—change beginning of sentence which starts in the seventh line from the end of section to read, "*Children, youth, and adults* need opportunities". . .

p. 42.626—change phrase in line 7, "on adults and children" to read, "of pornography on *children, youth and adults.*"

q. 42.627—change last sentence to read: "Efforts to address the dehumanizing power of pornographic images should be matched with *continuing* efforts to promote full human dignity through *masculine and feminine religious images.*"

2. paragraphs 42.630—646

a. 42.632—insert the following phrase after "Receive the report": "Receive the report, *with deep appreciation for the work of the Task Force*, and recommend it". . .

b. 42.633—change "2." to "*4.*"

—substitute the following recommendation:

"*Reaffirm that the 200th General Assembly (1988) of the Presbyterian Church (U.S.A.) opposes pornography as stated by previous General Assemblies (1984, 1985, 1986, and 1987) and as defined in this report (paragraph 42.294).*"

c. 42.634—change "3." to "*5.*"

—strike "such as the National Coalition Against Censorship" and insert the following, to read, "protecting First Amendment rights *as outlined in this report.*"

d. 42.635—change "4." to "*6.*"

e. 42.636—change "5." to "*7.*"

—strike "such as the Religious Alliance Against Pornography, to" so that the sentence shall then read, "interfaith efforts *which* study and address the issue". . .

f. 42.637—change "6." to "*8.*"

g. 42.638—change "7." to "*9.*"

h. 42.639—change "8." to "*10.*"

—insert the following in the first line after "General Assembly": "the General Assembly, *since sexism is perceived as a fundamental cause of pornography,* address the systemic roots". . .

i. 42.640—change "9." to "*3.*"

—change final line to read, "*203rd* General Assembly (*1991*)."

—add after this a new sentence: "*Recommendations adopted by the 200th General Assembly (1988) for action by the Presbyterian Church (U.S.A.) and its members are to be regarded as interim policy until recommendations are prepared for the 203rd General Assembly (1991) in response to study of this report.*"

j. 42.641—change "10." to "*11.*"

k. 42.642—strike the entire section.

l. 42.643—strike the section beginning with "a. develop". . .

—change "b." to "*a.*"

—change "c." to "*b.*"

—change "*d.*" to "*c.*"

—add the following word in the second line of new section c: "on counseling children, *youth*, and adults". . .

    m. 42.646—change "15." to "2."

So that the amended paragraphs 42.630-.646 of the Joint Report of the Council on Women and the Church and the Committee on Women's Concerns, "Pornography: Far from the Song of Songs, " shall then read as follows: [See 42.630-.646 for text as amended.]

3. paragraphs 42.647-.684

    a. 42.648—insert the following paragraph at the beginning of the section: "*Section XIV includes a number of items found to be valuable in the study of the Task Force. It includes materials and conclusions that are not necessarily in agreement with positions taken by the General Assembly of the Presbyterian Church (U.S.A.) and are not to be taken as the policy of the Presbyterian Church (U.S.A.) or of any other church.*

I. Introduction

42.255

General Assembly Actions

42.256

Responding to overtures from the Presbyteries of Elizabeth and Cincinnati, the 196th General Assembly (1984) adopted a resolution on pornography that mandated the Council on Women and the Church (COWAC) and the General Assembly Mission Board (Office of Women) to "persevere in their work in the areas of pornography and obscenity and the education of the church and society to combat the abusive treatment of women."

42.257

Taking action to provide the budget necessary for this study in both 1985 and 1986, the 198th General Assembly (1986) directed the Council on Women and the Church and the Committee on Women's Concerns to complete the work approved in 1984. In addition, the 1985 action directed the two women's advocacy groups as follows:

. . . to present the results of their research and proposals to develop educational materials and plans to distribute them to sessions and congregations;

. . . to develop material for education purposes concerning obscenity, pornography, sexual harassment, and other forms of sexual exploitation of persons, appropriate for study within sessions and congregations;

. . . to make the church aware of educational resources already in existence that cover the topics of obscenity, pornography, sexual harassment, and other forms of sexual exploitation. (The entire texts of the 1984, 1985, and 1986 General Assembly actions are in the Background Material of this report.)

42.258

These actions were consistent with the work done by the women's advocacy groups since their establishment in 1972 in the PCUS and in 1973 in the UPCUSA. Previous General Assemblies had assigned studies on rape and battering, reported in 1978, on sexual harassment (1982), and sexual exploitation of women (1986).

42.259

The 198th General Assembly (1986) assigned "the appropriate agency (Advisory Council on Church and Society, [or] the Social Justice and Peacemaking Ministry Unit) to advocate the public policy position of the General Assembly in the area of pornography, and assist the church in its social witness.''

42.260

Process of the Study

42.261

In July 1986, following action by the General Assembly Council to provide funding for the pornography study, COWC and COWAC initiated the formation of a task force, with Sylvia Thorson-Smith, of Grinnell, IA, a former member of COWAC, serving as coordinator. In consultation with COWAC and COWC, the following persons were invited to serve on the task force:

The Rev. Anne Callision, R.N., Santo Domingo, Dominican Republic; Ms. Doris Carson, Kingsport, TN; Ms. Patsy H. Correll, Spartanburg, SC; Ms. Carol E. Davies, Independence, MO; the Rev. Barbara Horner-Ibler, Mt. Vernon, NY; Ms. Diana Lim, Cupertino, CA; the Rev. Dr. Allen Maruyama, Denver, CO; Ms. Faye McDonald Smith, Atlanta, GA; Ms. Elizabeth McWhorter, Atlanta, GA; Dr. Cheri Register, Minneapolis, MN; and the Rev Dr. James Spalding, Iowa City, IA; Dr. Elizabeth H. Verdesi and Ms. Judith Mead-Atwell, New York staff for COWAC, and the Rev. Carole Goodspeed, Atlanta staff for COWC, have also worked with the task force.

42.262

The Task Force on Pornography held four meetings: December 2-4, 1986, in New York, NY; March 18-20, 1987, in Minneapolis, MN; June 29-July 6, 1987, at Ghost Ranch in Abiquiu, NM, and September 20-22, 1987, in Atlanta, GA. In addition to these sessions, members and staff attended numerous events and spoke to many people with expertise or interest in the issue of pornography. These meetings included presentations by persons with diverse viewpoints. Bibliographies were prepared, books and articles were read, and members shared with each other written reviews of what they had read. (A more detailed report of the process may be found in the Background Materials.)

42.263

Task force members who attended the 199th General Assembly (1987) conducted Hearings, in order to head opinions directly from Presbyterians on the issue of pornography. During its meeting at Ghost Ranch, the task force held an informal session to discuss the issue with those attending other seminars there. It met with Mr. Keith Wulff of the Communications United of the Support Agency concerning the preparation of a survey on pornography to be distributed to the members of the Presbyterian Panel in September 1987.

42.264

Progress reports of the work of the task force were presented to COWC and COWAC at their joint meetings in March and July 1987. The report was adopted by both groups in November 1987, and approved for recommendation to the 200th General Assembly in 1988. The Advisory Council on Church and Society reviewed the report at its December 1987 meeting and took action to support it.

42.265

Affirmations that Guided the Study

42.266

The work of the Task Force on Pornography was rooted in the following affirmations:

We affirm:

● that God is the source of human dignity.

● the equal dignity of women and men as being created equally in the image of God.

- the created goodness of the human body, both male and female.

- that God calls human beings to positive expressions of mutual affirmation and commitment, especially as typified in the calling to faithful, respectful marital and family relationships.

- the inherent goodness of naked flesh in all of its infinite forms, colors and conditions.

- that human beings were created with the possibility for ultimate acts of celebration and joy in sexuality.

- that the historic pattern of dominance and subjugation in human relationships is a distortion of God's intended creation.

- that images and portrayals of sexual behavior are not in themselves evil or offensive.

- that God's gift of sexual pleasure is fulfilled in acts of human love and mutual respect.

- that God demands sexual responsibility, balancing love for the self and love for the other.

- that God calls us to promote the dignity of all persons and to confront the circumstances in society that negate the integrity of human life.

- the Christian calling to love across all the boundaries of human limitation, modeling our relationships after God's covenant with us and the example of Jesus Christ.

- that Christians are called to study the complex relationship between pornography and contemporary society.

- that Christians are called to understand the issue of pornography today within the context of its history and the history of religious attitudes.

- that Christians face the challenge of living in a pluralistic society that warrants our commitment to the protection of diversity and freedom.

- that Christians are called to model the covenantal, compassionate community.

- our belief as Christians that the love of Jesus Christ is the Good News, empowerment in a world filled with conflict, alienation, and fear.

II. Theological Statement

42.267

Preface

42.268

As a result of its research and study, the Task Force on Pornography is convinced that pornography is a powerful symptom of injustice and alienation in human society. Through words and images, pornography debases God's intended gifts of love and dignity in human sexuality. Although humankind was created male and female, equally and fully in the image of God, the history of humanity reveals a fundamental pattern of dominance and subjugation. While this historic pattern of systematic oppression has been exposed more fully in our time than ever before, we live in an age also marked by the shattering of many norms of behavior and the subsequent loss of moral restraints. In such a time pornography has proliferated. The task force believes that the church is called to give serious attention to this issue, to reject all forms of dominance and subjugation, and to witness to loving respect and equality in human relationships. Reflected in the title of this report is the conviction that pornography represents human discord, far from the mutual sexual delight depicted biblically in the Song of Songs.

42.269

Pornography is a striking sign of human brokenness and alienation from God and from one another. This particular form of brokenness and alienation discloses a distortion of male and female relationships rooted in a pattern of dominance and subjugation. The central issue of pornography is not so much the disturbance of traditional norms of sexual morality as it is the gross distortion of power revealed in its graphic sexual images.

42.270

From the perspective of biblical understanding and the Reformed tradition, pornography represents a vivid expression of human alienation: from the creator God who makes covenants and from one another as covenant partners of God.

42.271

The creation story presents male and female as created in the image of God (Gen. 1:27). The image of God is not complete without both male and female. Man and woman, as made in the image of God, are to reflect in their relation to each other the relation of God to human creatures. If male and female related to one another in this way, sexual relationships between women and men, as well as all other relationships, would reflect the wholeness of God's creation. Historically, the predominant interpretation of the story of the creation had indicated that God created the human race with the image of God somehow less complete in the female. Such as interpretation guarantees that the inferiority of the female will always be seen as inferior to the male, and it fosters the exploitation of women, one form of which is pornography.

42.272

In Genesis 3, the story of the Fall portrays the breaking of the relationship of wholeness expressed in creation. Here is a parable of the false and egocentric attempt of human beings to "play God" that results not only in breaking the covenant relationship with God but also in distorting the human sexual relationship. The man and the woman felt threatened by each other and sought to hide their nakedness as they sought also to hide from God. Theology which interprets this story as a paradigm of man's vulnerability to the temptress woman legitimizes the domination, control and exploitation of all women. Pornography reinforces the same images of power.

42.273

The sexual relationship of male and female is central in the story of Creation and the Fall; it can also be viewed as a way of expressing the covenant relationship of God with people. God is said "to know" the covenant people. The Hebrew verb "to know" is a term that, as the Genesis account shows, refers to the sexual encounter between a man and a woman (in Genesis the relation of Adam and Eve). "To know" connotes mutuality and intimacy. Closely tied to the eros quality of love in human relations, it is also connected with agape love as concern and care for the other.

42.274

God's covenant concern for Israel is characterized by the term "compassion", expressed in Hebrew by the word that means "womb." In sexual terms compassion is not a superficial feeling but one felt deeply within the body, an eros love. The highly sensual love poetry of the Song of Songs in the Hebrew Bible, where man and woman take pleasure in and celebrate one another's bodies, has been seen through the centuries as symbolic of the relationship of God and the people of Israel, of Christ and the church.

42.275

The God of the covenant has compassion and saves the people. So too, God forges a covenant relation with loving kindness (hesed), an agape love. In covenant relationship, God's love (hesed) is given, returned, and shared with those in the covenant community, thus becoming the model of the compassion expressed among those in the community for each other, and for others. The people of the covenant are to show compassion for one another in ways that express both dimensions of love.

42.276

The old covenant and the new expect human beings to live in such a way that they express toward each other the compassion that God has extended to them. The term for this life is shalom, which means health, wholeness, unity, peace. In living as covenant people in shalom, there can be no separation of body and spirit. And there can be no easy separation of eros and agape or connecting sexuality only to eros, surrounding it with taboos, or expressing it through patriarchal oppression or pornographic exploitation.

42.277

How does God deal with the disruption of creation and the breaking of the covenant? The Law (Torah) was given as a remedy for the human hardness of heart. But we humans, in our alienation, in both biblical times and today, turn the law into a legalistic system, and often use it to exploit, oppress, and degrade other human beings.

42.278

Jesus came seeking to restore shalom, the wholeness of human relationships in creation and in covenant. The acceptance of the annointing by the woman in Bethany (Mark 14:3-9), the lifting up of the woman taken in adultery (John 8:3-11), the healing of the woman who touched his garment (Mark 5:25-34), and the affirmation of children (Mark 9:35-37, 42; 10:13-16) all indicate Jesus' compassion ("womb love") for victims of a patriarchal, alienated society. Jesus dealt both firmly and lovingly with those who were the exploiters and oppressors of his day, the tax collectors and the religious authorities. In, the death and resurrection of Jesus Christ the compassion of God reaches out to all to the oppressor and the oppressed the exploiter and the victim.

42.279

God establishes the church as the community of covenant and compassion, the community in which all divisions are overcome and all conflicts are healed. In the covenantal Christian community, members share the "womb love" of God with both the oppressor and the oppressed in order to heal the wounds of society. The alienation that is expressed in pornography, sexual exploitation and violence is to be overcome in the community marked by wholeness, compassion, eros and agape.

42.280

The *shalom* of the covenant community, seeking to fulfill its created nature in the relationship of woman and man, is also a sign for the larger community, a witness to God's intention for the whole created order. The achievement of such wholeness, free from pornography and sexual exploitation, is also the task of the Christian community and its members as they fulfill their calling day by day and as they seek to change the systems that debase and distort the life of persons and communities.

III. Why Study Pornography Now?

42.281

Pornography is not a new phenomenon in human history, nor is it a new issue for the church. During the 1970s both the PCUS and the UPCUSA conducted studies on issues related to human sexuality, including pornography. In 1973, the PCUS General Assembly adopted a paper, "Pornography, Obscenity, and Censorship," and recommended it for study and action. In 1974, the Advisory Council on Church and Society (ACCS) of the UPCUSA prepared a document, "Dignity and Exploitation: Christian Reflections on Images of Sex in the 1970s" which was commended for churchwide study by the General Assembly. In addition, the 1977 UPCUSA General Assembly adopted a resolution opposing the use of pornography and violence in the media; it also urged that "Christians should make a response to such activity that will reflect their faith more than their fears.'' (The entire text of the 1977 General Assembly action is found in the Background Materials.)

42.282

Previous Studies

42.283

The 1973 PCUS paper begins:

> We worship a God who creates and loves, judges and saves human beings. Therefore we stand for the dignity and welfare of human life, and work not only for the physical and spiritual health of individuals but also social circumstances which promote it. This concern for the integrity of human life and for social conditions which support it leads us to be concerned about pornographic or obscene literature and movies.[1]

42.284

The 1974 UPCUSA paper affirms three principles of the Christian tradition to be used as guidelines in studying pornography and obscenity:

1. the idea of the image of God as the source of our human dignity and of our protest against all forms of exploitation of our sexual nature;

2. Christian neighbor love, which is distinguished from but may include *eros*, the love we more commonly associate with sexual relationships; and

3. the covenant in which God gives a promise and a hope to us, and by which we are drawn into loving relationship with both God and other people.[2]

42.285

Both study documents examined the problems of defining pornography and obscenity, and they explored the legal "tightrope" between those issues and censorship. They recognized the difficult balance between individual freedom and community responsibility, and they presented guidelines for Christian decision making on these issues. (Guidelines from both the 1973 and the 1974 studies are included in the Background Materials of this report.)

42.286

In light of these studies in the 1970s, why did the Presbyterian Church (U.S.A.) direct COWAC and COWC to do additional study one decade later? Several reasons stand out.

42.287

Increased Proliferation of Pornography. In the last decade, both the amount and variety of pornographic materials have burgeoned. These materials have been marked by increasingly violent themes. It is also clear that it becomes more and more difficult to escape exposure to them.

42.288

Intensity of the Debate Over Pornography. Pornography is an issue that polarizes individuals of diverse political and religious beliefs. Disagreement over definitions, effects, and regulation divides some groups and makes unlikely allies of others. A report on pornography by a commission established by the U.S. Attorney General (sometimes referred to as "the Meese Report") and increased anti-pornography activity by law enforcement officials have both sparked vigorous reaction on all sides.

42.289

Rising Voices of Fear. The issue of pornography has become a focal point for the escalation of fear among many people—fear of violence and abuse, fear of women and children victimized and endangered, fear of vanishing values and uncontrollable change, fear of loss of spiritual authority, and fears of a culture exposed for its greed and exploitation.

42.290

Increased Denominational and Interfaith Response. Many religious bodies, including the Lutheran Council in the USA and the United Church of Canada, have developed study materials on the issue of pornography. Others have adopted statements and held educational events. In 1985 the National Council of the Churches of Christ adopted a study paper entitled, ''Violence and Sexual Violence in Film, Television, Cable and Home Video.'' In 1986 the Religious Alliance Pornography was formed to proclaim that ''hardcore and child pornography, which are not protected by the Constitution, are evils which must be eliminated.'' (The Background Materials contain the foundational statement of the Religious Alliance Against Pornography, as well as a more detailed summary of interfaith activity.)

42.291

Thus, given the seriousness of the issue, the General Assembly has called for new resources on pornography. The task force believes that, in its call for resources, the church is looking also for new words of hope, faith and action based on a deeper understanding of the nature of pornography.

42.292

Aware of the interconnectedness of pornography with other issues relating to women and other issues addressed later in this report, and recognizing that no study of pornography will ever be complete, the Council on Women and the Church and the Committee on Women's Concerns has found this study to be both challenging and satisfying. Challenging, because of its complexity, and satisfying because it deals with the central core of our being, our sexuality as persons. The Task Force on Pornography offers this report to the 200th General Assembly of the Presbyterian Church (U.S.A.) (1988) for its consideration and approval.

IV. What is Pornography? A Discussion of Definition

42.293

Discussion of pornography begins with the question, ''What is it?'' There is much debate over its definition but scant consensus on a precise set of words that adequately describe what it means.

42.294

As a result of its study, the task force recommends the following definition of pornography:

Pornography includes any sexually explicit material (books, magazines, movies, videos, TV shows, telephone services, live sex acts) for the purpose of sexual arousal by eroticizing violence, power, humiliation, abuse, dominance, degradation, or mistreatment of any person, male or female, and is usually produced for monetary profit. Any sexually explicit material that depicts children is pornography.

A Look at Origins

42.295

While excavating near Naples in 1748, searching for the remains of three cities buried by volcanic ash from Mount Vesuvius in 79 A.D., workers found artifacts that identified one of the sites as Pompeii. Among the artifacts were frescoes and statues of an explicitly sexual nature. These paintings and statues were found not only in brothels and nuptial chambers but also on street corners and in the entry ways and living areas of private homes. Public buildings exhibited drawings of landscapes and still lifes mixed together with sexually explicit drawings and statues. The total effect confused historians of the eighteenth and nineteenth centuries who were not accustomed to seeing representations of sexual acts in places to which every one had access, i.e., homes, public buildings, and the marketplace.

42.296

Social commentators and historians debated the original purpose of these works, as well as their effect upon those exposed to them. A problem developed regarding what to do with the controversial artifacts, since the excavation site had become a popular tourist attraction. To prevent women and children from seeing the frescoes and statues, the works were locked inside a secret museum within the National Museum of Naples.

42.297

Once they acquired a residence and because they were authentic and rare, it was necessary to classify them. A name for this particular type of art was required. While writing about the representations in 1850, a German art historian, C.O. Muller, called the producers of the works "pornographers," from the Greek words meaning whore and painting, or portrayal. The term caught on and, in 1864, the newly published edition of *Webster's Dictionary* defined pornography as "licentious painting employed to decorate the walls of rooms sacred to bacchanalian orgies, examples of which exist in Pompeii."[1]

42.298

Current Efforts to Define Pornography

42.299

The 1987 *Random House Dictionary of the English Language* defines pornography as "obscene writings, drawings, photographs, or the like, especially those having little or no artistic merit."[2] It also refers to the Greek derivation of the word, from *porno* meaning harlot and *graphos* meaning graph (writing or picture). In its linguistic root, pornography is linked to women, to the graphic portrayal of sexuality, and to economics (porno is a form of *peraymi*, meaning "to sell").[3] Pornography, quite literally, means picturing or describing prostitutes.

42.300

United States Supreme Court Justice Potter Stewart uttered a memorable remark in 1964 when he said, "I cannot define pornography, but I know it when I see it."[4] Identifying pornography is an intensely individual experience, dependent on subjective interpretation of images and on individual values. Dr. Ann Welbourne-Moglia, former executive director of the Sex Information and Education Council of the United States (SIECUS), stated in her testimony before the U.S. Attorney General's Commission on Pornography in 1985:

> Just as each individual's sexual health is an integration of factors unique to him/her, so too is the meaning of pornography a very personal one, depending on the background and life experience of the individual rendering the judgement. Because pornography is based on a subjective, emotional, and physical response, one person's pornography could also be another person's art form. Thus, we have a problem in defining pornography in a way which is acceptable to all.[5]

42.301

Focusing on the economic exploitation involved in the production of pornography, Welbourne-Moglia defines pornography as "commercially available writings, pictures, films, etc., intended to arouse sexual feelings and fantasies for the purpose of monetary profit."[6] She acknowledges different kinds of sexually explicit material (pornography and erotica) but makes clear the inescapable exposure to widespread commercial sexual materials.

42.302

Several terms are used to label sexually explicit material. Sometimes the intent is to separate material that is acceptable, or less offensive, from that which is unacceptable, or very offensive. A discussion of terms such as pornography, erotica, hard-core, soft-core, and obscenity is presented here in order to demonstrate opinion on the differences between sexually explicit materials.

42.303

Pornography and Erotica

42.304

Distinction is often made between the terms erotica and pornography. In 1974, the American Lutheran Church (ALC) defined pornography as "material that depicts or describes erotic behavior in ways deliberately intended to stimulate sexual excitement." In 1985, the ALC updated its statement in an effort to differentiate between pornographic material that focuses on "physical and psychological violence against others" and erotic portrayals that "need not be demeaning,"and may be "edifying," "therapeutic," and "aesthetically pleasing." The 1985 statement indicates that "some therapists now argue that stimulating sexual excitement can be therapeutic, and materials that assist that purpose need not always be classified as 'pornographic'."[7]

42.305

The United Church of Canada, in formulating its 1984 definition, also sought to distinguish "pornographic materials from other sexually explicit materials":

> Pornography is material that represents or describes degrading, abusive and/or violent behavior for sexual gratification so as to endorse and/or recommend the behavior as depicted.[8]

42.306

The National Organization for Women (NOW) in 1984 adopted a resolution stating that "pornography, as distinct from erotica, is a systemic practice of exploitation and subordination based on sex which harms women and children."[9]

42.307

For many feminists, it is not the graphic image of sexuality that is objectionable so much as the content of the imagery, i.e., the systemic oppression of women that it represents. Such feminist interpretation identifies pornography as depictions of sexual violence, dominance, and conquest. This view maintains that pornography uses images of sex to reinforce power, inequality, and humiliation. On the other hand, erotic portrayals are acceptable if they depict mutually pleasurable sexual interaction between persons of equal power. Such images may visualize egalitarian sexual relationships that communicate feelings of love and caring.[10]

42.308

In its 1986 report, the Attorney General's Commission did not distinguish between pornography and erotica in its working definition of pornography as "predominantly sexually explicit and intended primarily for the purpose of sexual arousal."[11]

42.309

Although the commission "struggled mightily to agree on definitions of such basic terms as pornography and erotica, it never did so."[12]

42.310

The commission recognized that the term "pornography" is "undoubtably pejorative" and that to call something pornography these days is to condemn it. Conversely, commission members stated that to use the term "erotica" is to describe sexually explicit materials of which the user of the term approves. For some, the word erotica describes any sexually explicit material that contains neither violence nor subordination of women. For others, the term refers to almost all sexually explicit material and, for still others, only material containing generally accepted artistic value qualifies as erotica.[13]

Hard-Core and Soft-Core

42.311

Effort is sometimes made to distinguish between hard-core and soft-core pornography. The term ''soft-core pornography'' is sometimes used to identify sexually explicit material that displays nudity or suggests sexual activity. The term ''hard-core pornography'' may be found in reference to material that depicts or describes explicit sexual activity such as intercourse, masturbation, oral sex, or lewd exhibition of the genitals.[14]

42.312

The Attorney General's Commission states that ''if we were forced to define the term, 'hard-core pornography', we would probably note that it refers to the extreme form of what we defined as pornography and, thus, would describe material that is sexually explicit to the extreme, intended virtually exclusively to arouse, and devoid of any other apparent content or purpose.'' However, the commission acknowledged that ''this definition may not be satisfactory'' since application of this term to a range of material is ''far broader than we would like.'' Commission members concluded that ''careful analysis will be served if we use this term far less than more.''[15]

42.313

Pornography and Obscenity

42.314

The terms ''pornography'' and ''obscenity'' are often used together and the difference between them is not always clear. Unlike the word ''pornography,'' the word ''obscenity,'' need not necessarily suggest anything about sex at all.[16] Therefore, anything from some aspects of war to the number of people filled by drunk drivers to certain sexually explicit material may be described as ''obscene,'' or deserving of moral condemnation.

42.315

The Supreme Court has given the term ''obscenity'' legal definition for purposes of identification and regulation of objectionable materials. Intense debate exists over the adequacy of this definition, its effectiveness as applied to particular materials, and its usefulness in regulating materials regarded as pornographic. A discussion of the legal definition of obscenity and its historical development as a standard to regulate pornography is presented in the section of this report entitled ''A History of Pornography Regulation in the United States.''

42.316

The Task Force's Struggle

42.317

Throughout its work the task force struggled to find words to describe what constitutes the essence of pornography. Efforts to define pornography proved frustrating since definition would describe an aspect of nature that most people cannot articulate—sexuality, its freedoms and its limits.

42.318

As the task force discussed the diverse definitions of pornography, it was faced with countless questions, each one prompting others and compounding the dilemma:

- If pornography is defined by some as 'sexually explicit material intended primarily for the purpose of sexual arousal'' and if labeling something ''pornography'' is to cast a tone of condemnation over it, as the Attorney General's Commission suggested, what would such interpretation reveal about our sexual values?

- What is the purpose of sexuality and sexual behavior?

- Why are negative meanings attached to materials that have no other purpose than sexual arousal?
- As Christians, what is our understanding of sexuality and its purpose?
- Considering other words associated with pornography such as "lewd," "lascivious," "filthy," "prurient," "wanton," "lustful," and "impure," how can Christians interpret these words and apply them to images?
- Is all sexually explicit material lewd and filthy?
- What is the difference between healthy sexual desire and prurient lust?
- How are our perceptions regarding images influenced by our values regarding sexual behavior?
- What makes the picture different from the act? Or is it?
- Since values regarding pornography can be found in conflict across time, culture, religion, race, class, and sexual preference, whose definitions prevail in discussions of pornography?
- If pornography is not only about heterosexual relationships, but also about homosexual relationships, how does homophobia influence one's entire understanding of pornography?
- Is it possible to apply distinctions between erotica and pornography to homosexual images as well as heterosexual images?

42.319

As the task force considered these and other questions, it felt keenly the tension between the need to define pornography and the risks in defining it. Nevertheless, the task force produced a definition that indicates our understanding of the issue:

- This definition is consistent with the theological position stated earlier, one that values human dignity and human sexuality.
- It recognizes that to label anything "pornography" is to cast a tone of condemnation over it.
- It rejects judgments that condemn all sexually explicit materials.
- It seeks to narrow the focus on those materials that deserve to be labeled "pornography."
- It affirms that pornography is essentially about power and the dehumanization of both male and female persons, including exploitation of human sexuality for economic profit.
- It affirms that sexually explicit materials that depict children (previously defined as pornography) constitute a separate category outside the debate over material that depict adults.

42.320

The task force's definition may elicit significant disagreement when applied to particular materials and images since defining and identifying pornography involves intensely individual, personal judgment. There needs to be latitude in applying words such as "degrading," "dehumanizing," and "humiliating" to specific materials.

42.321

This definition is presented apart from the discussion of the effects of pornography or efforts to regulate it. These are separate issues that are addressed in subsequent sections of the report.

How to Recognize Pornography

42.322

The task force offers the following guidelines for applying this definition to particular material. This means that material will be characterized as pornography if it

- includes graphic displays of sexual behavior (graphic, meaning vivid, exaggerated, or excessively descriptive) that eroticize (make sexually arousing) self-pleasure through the exploitation of power over another person.

- involves words that are written or spoken, whether in still or moving pictures, actual sexual activity or performance.

- involves the sexual subordination or mistreatment of women or men.

- includes material intended to be sexually arousing by depicting any of the following:

  —women or men as sexual objects, things, or commodities to be used for personal gratification;

  —women or men in ways that suggest they enjoy pain or humiliation;

  —women or men in ways that suggest they experience pleasure in being raped;

  —women or men as tied up, cut up, mutilated, tortured, bruised, or physically hurt;

  —women or men in ways that communicate force, threat, or intimidation;

  —women or men in ways that suggest erotic appeal in victimization and sexual submission;

  —women or men penetrated by sexual paraphenalia or using penetrating objects or animals;

  —women or men reduced to body parts through exaggerated exhibition of breasts and genitals;

  —women or men in ways that suggest pleasure in dehumanizing acts involving urination, excretion, or any foul treatment. (The Minneapolis Civil Rights Ordinance, found in the background of this report, was the source for these guidelines.)

42.323

The term "child pornography" is limited to material that visually depicts sexual conduct by real children. Any sexually explicit material depicting children is pornography in its most serious and intolerable form. There are no distinctions between pornography and erotica in material that depicts children.

V. Current Statistics on the Pornography Industry

42.324

Pornography is an $8-billion-a-year industry.[1,2] Other sources indicate a $9 billion annual estimate.[3]

42.325

About Motion Pictures

42.326

It costs $30-150,000 to produce a film ($75,000 average).[4]

Performers earn $250-$500 per day, famous stars up to $2500.[5]

In 1984 there were 400 film titles, in 1985 there were 1700.[6]

There are twenty-five national adult film production companies; 80 percent of the filming occurs in and around Los Angeles, CA.[7]

There are ten to fifteen national distributors of pornographic films.[8]

There are approximately 600 adult theaters in the United States.[9]

Motion pictures account for over $500 million in annual receipts.[10]

42.327

About Videotape Cassettes

42.328

A 90-minute video takes three days to produce; average cost: $12,000.[11]

It was estimated in 1986 that over 2,000 new videos would be produced that year.[12]

The profits range from a minimum of $200,000 to millions for each video.[13]

Of the 14,000 video stores nationwide, 75 percent sell pornographic cassettes, which account for 50-60 percent of all prerecorded cassette sales.[14]

Other sources indicate 30,000 video-rental stores in the U.S.[15]

In 1984 over fifty-four million pornographic videos were rented. In 1985 over seventy-five million adult videos were rented (20 percent of market).[16]

More than 2.5 million people view pornographic movies each week.[17]

42.329

About Magazines

42.330

There are between 50-60,000 adult magazine titles, hundreds of new titles each month.[18]

One pornographic magazine costs twenty-five cents to fifty cents to produce and retails between $3.00 and $12.00.[19]

The 13 most popular magazines sell 12 million copies per month: *Playboy, Penthouse, Hustler, Playgirl, Gallery, Club, Forum, Oui, High Society, Cheri, Genesis, Chic, Club International.*[20]

Playboy and Penthouse have a combined readership of twenty-four million.[21,22]

Two hundred million issues of the over 800 different soft-core and hard-core pornographic magazines were sold in 1984 in the U.S., principally at news-stands, grossing over $750 million for the industry.[23]

There are an estimated 400 "skin" magazines on the market. Two of the leading ones had a monthly readership of as high as 7.6 million.[24]

42.331

About Cable and Satellite Television

42.332

Cable is in forty million homes (available to 70 percent of all households).[25]

In 1983 an estimated two million American households subscribed to cable television services featuring pornography.[26]

Playboy Cable Channel is the largest pornographic service, in 700,000 homes.[27]

Satellite networks distribute pornography to 50,000 subscribers.[28]

42.333

About Dial-A-Porn

42.334

In 1983, the New York Telephone Company received 500,000 calls a day as a carrier of a Dial-A-Porn Message, earning the company $25,000 a day and the supplier of the message $10,000 a day.[29]

The New York Telephone Company facilitated 96 million calls in 1985, generating $56 million in income for the utility.[30]

Problems in Using Statistics on Pornography

42.335

Statistics offered on pornography often use raw, unevaluated data as a basis for authoritative presentation. Without thorough analysis it is difficult to interpret clearly the implications of the data. For instance, books, articles, newsletters, and reports begin with statistical evidence on the proliferation of pornography; the statistic that pornography is an eight to nine billion dollar industry often stands alone. In both instances, there is no indication of how the term "pornography" is being used or what kind of materials are included in such a statistic. These statistics may include any material that might be considered by some to be pornographic, even though there is great diversity in the material. By grouping all commercial sexually explicit material together, the diversity is never considered, much less analyzed.

42.336

Another problem is that there is significant discrepancy in the statistics themselves. One source lists 14,000 video stores nationwide, another lists 30,000. One source lists 400 adult theaters, another lists 600. As part of a list of pornography statistics, one source notes only that cable television is available in forty million homes, but does not reveal the critical additional statistic (found in a different source) that two million homes subscribe to cable pornography services. At first glance, the reader may think that forty million homes subscribe to cable pornography since the statistic stands independently in a list of data. Nor is there any indication of the kind of pornography shown in the two million homes that subscribe.

42.337

Some statistics are not dated, and some sources quote outdated statistics as current data. This is particularly true of statistics related to child pornography. Increased attention to child pornography led to significant legal changes in 1982, and yet statistics from the 1970s are still presented as if they are the present reality. Often the reader can determine this only by reading the footnotes and fine print with great care.

42.338

Statistics are also frequently used to imply causal relationship between pornography and other social problems by placing statistics on rape, incest and battering next to those on the proliferation of pornography. While the discussion of pornography must include consideration of the question of harm and the effects of pornography on human attitudes and behavior, oversimplification may result if statistics are presented in too limited a context.

42.339

Anti-pornography efforts have produced "a crackdown on adult bookstores, x-rated movie theaters, massage parlors"[31] and other pornographic outlets and materials in several areas. Statistics may be used to support claims that a "clean-up" of pornography bears a direct relationship to lowered crime rates. For example, one source maintains that a "crackdown" in Cincinnati "resulted in a 42 percent decrease in assaults, prostitution, and drug trafficking, and an 83 percent drop in rapes, robberies and aggravated assaults."[32] These statistics do not indicate the year the crimes occurred, when the crackdown began, or what is being compared.

42.340

According to statistics of the Federal Bureau of Investigation, the number of rapes, for example, in Cincinnati increased by 19 percent from 1983 to 1984 (up from 308 to 367), decreased by 1.9 percent from 1984 to 1985 (down from 367 to 360) and decreased by 19 percent from 1985 to 1986 (down from 360 to 291). Between 1983 and 1986, FBI statistics indicate that robberies decreased by 13 percent and aggravated assaults increased by 11 percent.[33] Although prosecution efforts have been directed against pornography in Cincinnati since the late 1960s, organized community activity began in 1983.[34]

42.341

The *Uniform Crime Reports* of the FBI reveal that statistics on rape, assault, and other offenses go up and down in any given year in most areas where efforts have been made to curb the availability of pornography. The relationship between pornography and criminal activity is a complex one and many factors, other than pornography, are involved in understanding crime rates. How, then, does one take seriously the influence of pornography while not oversimplifying the consequences of its presence or absence?

42.342

Statistics reveal the magnitude of the issue and challenge the reader to ask questions and seek further analysis. Questions for consideration include: What definition of pornography is used to determine the reporting of statistical data? What particular material is included in a statistical report? Do the statistics cited here include materials that fit the criteria of the definition developed by the Task Force on Pornography? Do they include materials that would not fit the definition in this report? Is it possible to make such a distinction? What can be concluded from statistics about the relationship between pornography and human behavior? What do statistics contribute toward an understanding of our society in the 1980s? What is a faithful Christian response to such an understanding?

VI. What Are the Effects of Pornography? A Discussion of Harm

42.343

Central to the study of pornography is the issue of harm. Pornography includes a variety of sexually explicit material that finds an open market in contemporary culture. What are the influences of this material? How can its influence be measured and understood? Is the degree of harm related to the content of the imagery?

42.344

These and many other questions provoke considerable debate over both the individual and societal harms that can be attributed to pornography. One attempt to resolve the debate is found in the report of the Attorney General's Commission on Pornography. Its findings serve as an introduction to the discussion.

Findings of the Attorney General's Commission on Pornography

42.345

The commission prefaced its findings on "the question of harm" with the acknowledgement that "the world is complex, and most consequences are 'caused' by numerous factors."[1] Therefore, in analyzing the influence of pornography, members concluded "that some forms of sexually explicit material bear a causal relationship to both sexual violence and sex discrimination, but we are hardly so naive as to suppose that were these forms of pornography to disappear the problem of sex discrimination and sexual violence would come to an end."[2]

42.346

Having defined pornography for the purpose of their report as material that is "predominantly sexually explicit and intended primarily for the purpose of sexual arousal," the commission was faced with making some distinctions in assessing the harm of sexually explicit materials. Commission members presented their findings on the issue of harm by dividing the materials into four categories:

42.347

Sexually Violent Material

42.348

This category features "actual or unmistakably simulated or unmistakably threatened violence presented in sexually explicit fashion with a predominant focus on the sexually explicit violence."[3] Citing "virtually unanimous" clinical and experimental research, the commission concluded that exposure to sexually violent materials increases the likelihood of aggression and that a causal relationship can be shown between such material and aggressive behavior towards women. Therefore, this kind of material is harmful to society.

42.349

Nonviolent Materials Depicting Degradation, Domination, Subordination, or Humiliation

42.350

This category "depicts people, usually women, as existing solely for the sexual satisfaction of others, usually men, or that depicts people, usually women, in decidedly subordinate roles in their sexual relations with others, or that depicts people engaged in sexual practices that would to most people be considered humiliating.[4] The commission acknowledged that there is less evidence linking this material causally with sexual aggression, but concluded that "substantial exposure . . . bears some causal relationship to the level of sexual violence, sexual coercion, or unwanted sexual aggression in the population so exposed.[5] Furthermore, it stated that substantial exposure to material in this category is related to "the various non-violent forms of discrimination against or subordination of women in our society."[6] As such, this category is subtle and dangerous, because it constitutes some of "what is currently standard fare in heterosexual pornography, and is a significant theme in a broader range of materials not commonly taken to be sexually explicit enough to be pornographic."[7]

42.351

Nonviolent and Nondegrading Materials

42.352

This category, consisting of materials "in which the participants appear to be fully willing participants occupying substantially equal roles in a setting devoid of actual or apparent violence or pain,"[8] gave the commissioners the most difficulty. A significant increase in sexually explicit material involves videos available for home use, reported by many couples to be a mutually pleasurable source of sexual stimulation. Acknowledging a fair conclusion from social science research, commission members stated that "there is no persuasive evidence to date supporting the connection between nonviolent and non-degrading materials and acts of sexual violence, and that there is some, but very limited evidence, indicating that the connection does not exist."[9] Commissioners disagreed about the general harm to society in the public display of acts traditionally regarded as private, as well as the harm to the "moral environment of society" resulting from the public display of sexual activity regarded by many as immoral. Some members believed that some of the material in this category is educational or artistic and could be seen as beneficial, especially when used for therapeutic purposes.

42.353

Nudity

42.354

While some of the commissioners found the use of nudity in art or for educational purposes to be harmful, they expressed concern about the impact that "portrayals of nudity in an undeniably sexual context" have on "children, on attitudes toward women, on the relationship between the sexes, and on attitudes toward sex in general."[10] They differed on the extent of these harms.

Evidence for Assessing Harm

42.355

Social Science Research

42.356

The value of social science research in determining causal relationship is often debated. One commission member, Dr. Judith Becker, herself a Columbia University psychologist, said, "I don't think there is in the social science data any conclusive causal relationship between this type of material and the commission of sexual crimes. The data show that in certain experiments attitudes change, and I think one makes a quantum leap from attitudinal changes to committing serious crimes."[11] Becker and Ellen Levine, another commission member, also contended that "studies have relied almost exclusively on male college student volunteers, which means that the 'generalizability' of this data is extremely limited."[12]

42.357

Debate continues to be spirited over the conclusions drawn from research on pornography and human behavior. While such experiments reflect limited investigation at this point, they represent valuable attempts at understanding sexually explicit materials as one of many factors influencing human attitudes and actions. Significant work in this area has been contributed by Edward Donnerstein, Victor Cline, Dorf Zillmann, Jennings Bryant, and others. Brief summaries of some of their findings may be found in the Background Material of this report.

42.358

Testimony of Women and Men

42.359

Some of the strongest indictments against pornography are found in the testimony of those who have felt its influence. Women have told intimate stories of their victimization at hearings in Minneapolis and Indianapolis, before the Attorney General's Commission, and elsewhere. Their testimony bears witness to the feelings of some women that pornography has played an important role in their being coerced into sexual activities. Dr. Pauline Bart, professor of sociology, has cited the following statements of women describing what they were asked to do:

> Miss C: "He'd go to porno movies, then he'd come home and say, 'I saw this in a movie. Let's try it.' I felt really exploited."

> Miss F: "He'd read something in a pornographic book, and then he wanted to live it out. It was too violent for me to do something like that. It was basically getting dressed up and spanking. Him spanking me. I refused to do it."

> Miss P: "My boy friend and I saw a movie in which there was masochism. After that he wanted to gag me and tie me up. . . . He literally tried to force me, after gagging me first. . . . I started crying and struggling, got loose, and . . . ran out of the house."[13]

42.360

Witnesses before the commission made allegations about rape, forced sexual performance, battering, torture, imprisonment, murder, disease, self-abuse, and prostitution related to pornography. The commission report contains excerpts of testimony to psychological harm (i.e., suicidal thoughts, fears, shame, guilt, amnesia, nightmares) and societal harm (i.e., sexual harassment, financial loss, racism, family problems) attributed to pornography.[14]

42.361

Critics of victim testimony observe that these are often "truly pathetic glimpses of lives lost—drug abuse, bad marriages, child molestation, beatings, forced sex, and incest."[15] For these individuals, pornography may be simplistically identified as a cause, rather than an accessory, of their pain.

42.362

Victim testimony stands as a collection of intimate stories told with profound conviction. For centuries, women's testimony about rape, battering, incest, and harassment has been silenced and repudiated. Women's stories (and in lesser numbers, those by men) reveal, in stark description, individual perceptions about the harmful power of pornography in their lives. As a record of personal witness, they stand as evidence that must be heard.

General Discussion of the Question of Harm

42.363

In addition to experimental research by social scientists and the personal testimony of individuals, further insight is provided by those who have studied this issue. Discussion of these views is divided into three areas: harm to women and men, harm to persons in the pornography industry, and harm to children.

42.364

Harm to Women and Men

42.365

Much debate centers on the role that pornography plays in influencing the attitudes and behavior of people. Some analysts draw direct connections between pornography and the lives of real people. Catherine MacKinnon, speaking for some feminists, writes:

> Everything you see in pornography is being done to a real woman right now. Look at the data on rape, child sexual abuse, sexual harassment, forced prostitution, and battery. . . . Now go look at the pornography again. If you don't see rape, battery, sexual harassment, child sexual abuse, and forced prostitution there, it is because you have accepted these treatments as the nature of women, as the nature of sex, as our sexual fulfillment, as what sexual equality really looks like.[16]

42.366

John Stoltenberg confronts the power of pornography to damage the sexual identity of men and, consequently, their relationships with women:

> Pornography institutionalizes the sexuality that embodies and enacts male suprema-cy. Pornography says . . . men are masters, women are slaves; men are superior, women are subordinate; men are real, women are objects; men are sex machines, women are sluts. . . . When equality is an idea whose time has come, we will perhaps know sex with justice, we will perhaps know passion with compassion, we will perhaps know affection and ardor with honor.[17]

42.367

While acknowledging that offensive, sexist images are presented in pornography, other writers, such as Dierdre English, regard such images as fantasy, not behavior. She contends that fantasy is multidimensional and symbolic, and that through fantasy, people imagine acts that they would not perform because they are socially banned sexual expressions. In this way, society allows a refuge from repression and a means for venting aggression in a non-harmful way.[18] Supporters of English's view believe that pornography is not directly correlated to acts of sexual coercion, and conversely, many acts of coercion occur apart from pornography.

42.368

Dr. Godon C. Nagayama Hall, a Presbyterian elder in Seattle and a clinical psychologist with the Sex Offender Program at Western Washington State Hospital, wrote an article for the newsletter of the Presbyterian Health, Education and Welfare Association entitled, "Pornography: A Cause of Sexually Aggressive Behavior or an Effect of a Sexist Society?" Citing the work of psychologist Martha Burt, he reports that "sexist attitudes, in assumedly normal persons, [are] associated with an acceptance of sexual aggression against women. . . . Thus, persons with sexist attitudes may be more accepting of sexual aggression than are persons with more egalitarian attitudes concerning gender roles."[19]

42.369

Nagayama Hall's most compelling analysis involves the role of the Christian church in the relationships between pornography, sexist attitudes, and sexually aggressive behavior. Maintaining that the church has long propagated sexist attitudes, he contends that some fundamentalist Christians appear to "emphasize the possibly equivocal relationship between pornography and sexual aggression, while ignoring the evidence of a relationship between sexism and the acceptance of sexually aggressive behavior." He concludes:

> Many sexual offenders are not the immoral beasts depicted by the media, but often have been very active church participants and have been exposed to church doctrine. While sexual offenders have ostensibly violated church doctrine in their sexual aggression, in another sense such aggressiveness against women may be supported by church doctrine. . . . The exploitation of women that occurs both in pornography and sexual aggression may only be the effects of the more general problem of the unequal status of women in our society, and it is to this broader issue that the Christian church should address itself.[20]

42.370

Harm to Persons in the Pornography Industry

42.371

In discussing harm to women and men, attention also needs to be directed toward the effect of pornography on those in the pornography industry. The Attorney General's Commission describes its impact on the lives of women who participate in its production:

> It may very well be that degradation led a woman to being willing to pose for a picture of a certain variety, or to engage in what appears to be a non-degrading sexual act. It may be that coercion caused the picture to exist. And it may very well be that the existing disparity in the economic status of men and women is such that any sexually explicit depiction of a woman is at least suspect on account of the possibility that economic disparity is what caused the woman to pose for the picture that most people in this society would find embarrassing.[21]

42.372

The commission report provides lengthy discussion on the quality of the lives of people in the industry. Victims are most often girls in their late teens from broken homes, who have experienced sexual abuse, frequently incest. Unable to find work, they may respond to "modeling" ads and discover that the job involves posing nude or acting in a sexually explicit film. They may or may not be coerced into performing, and if they continue this work, it is often with no guarantees, no benefits, long hours, the risk of disease, and the escape to drugs.

42.373

Reports of the victimization of women (and men with similar histories) are often countered with the contention that these people are free adult persons who are satisfied with their choice. To the argument that these are merely "women with the freedom to bargain . . . simply exchanging the use of their bodies for money," an article in the *Harvard Women's Law Journal* counters that "this attitude is refuted by those involved in the industry who are often victimized and exploited by photographers, producers of films and the men they have relationships with."[22]

42.374

Harm to Children and Youth

42.375

One of the overriding concerns related to the effects of pornography is the harm it has on children and youth. Young people in this culture are exposed to sexually explicit material of all kinds before they are emotionally able to understand and evaluate it. Other concerns focus on the use of pornography by adults to coerce children and youth into acts of sexual abuse. Three examples of its harmful influence on children and youth include rock videos, Dial-a-Porn, and "slasher" movies.

1. *Rock Videos*. A study of "Violence and Sexual Violence in Film, Television, Cable and Home Video," conducted by The National Council of Churches of Christ, reported testimony that heavy viewing of music videos may significantly increase violence in our society because it closely links erotic relationships with violence performed not by villains, but by teenage idols. These programs, which combine the attraction of music, dancing, and exotic and creative backgrounds, become a powerful "selling" of violence.[23]

2. *Dial-a-Porn*. Since deregulation of the telephone company in 1982, Dial-a-Porn services have become increasingly available. Sexually explicit material of all kinds is offered, either in conversation with a paid performer (credit card billing) or prerecorded messages, usually one minute in length (charged on the phone bill). Children, some very young, reportedly find Dial-a-Porn phone numbers in such places as school bathrooms. Many people are concerned that distorted sexual messages in these calls produce a harmful effect on children. Blocking devices, costing about $100, are available to prevent such calls.

3. *"Slasher" Movies*. Horror films, often popular with teenagers, combine images of sexuality and violence that present powerful messages to young people. Some people argue that such films are escapist; others contend that themes linking sexual pleasure and violence, particularly towards women, create and reinforce harmful attitudes that affect behavior.

42.376

Dr. Ann Welbourne-Moglia, referred to earlier, contends that most exposure to pornography is by choice and that both teenagers and adults use pornography to obtain sexual information. Unfortunately, most of these materials depict sexuality primarily in physical-genital terms, and their understanding is greatly distorted. Young people learn from many sources in society that women are sexual objects, and that men are physically driven, violent, uncaring creatures. She concludes that

> we have no choice as to whether children and youth will be exposed to erotic or pornographic material. It is virtually impossible to shield them from sexual stimuli today. What we need to do is give children, young people, adults, and parents the information and skills they need and are asking for, so that their sexuality will be healthy.[24]

VII. A History of Pornography Regulation in the United States

42.377

Early Regulation of Pornography and Obscenity

42.378

The development of laws to regulate obscenity began in England.[1] Although there were no established standards for identifying obscene materials or acts, a current dictionary definition indicates moral assumptions that have influenced the identification of obscene materials and acts:

> Offensive to modesty or decency; indecent; lewd, as obscene pictures. Causing, or intended to cause, sexual excitement or lust. Abominable; disgusting; repulsive; and obscene exhibition of public discourtesy.[2]

42.379

The first report obscenity decision in England involved Sir Charles Sedley in 1663, who was convicted of obscene exposure for disrobing in front of a crowd and urinating on them. In 1727, nakedness was found to be a breach of the peace, and in 1770 a man was jailed for publishing an obscene poem entitled, "Essay on Women."

42.380

Prior to the American Revolution, only one state had an obscenity law. Since the First Amendment to the Constitution guarantees that "Congress shall make no law . . . abridging the freedom of speech, or of the press,"[3] any regulation of pornography and obscenity challenges the constitutionally allowable limits of these freedoms. Obscenity laws have repeatedly tested the meaning of constitutional rights.

42.381

In 1711, censorship laws in Massachussetts were extended to include the "wicked, profane, impure, filthy and obscene."[4] The earliest reported American case to confront obscenity was in 1815, when it was declared an offense to exhibit for profit a picture of a nude couple. Beginning in 1821, states began to pass obscenity statutes and this trend accelerated after 1868, when New York adopted an obscenity law.

42.382

While nineteenth century Victorian drawing rooms espoused a vast array of rules and regulations designed to keep everyone and everything in their proper places, a small select group of upperclassmen pursued their investigation into the profane and pornographic.[5] In secret these men collected erotic and esoteric memorabilia, built libraries and debated the nature of pornography. Some believed that all representations are potentially harmful because they distract from the real world. Others thought that representations are a self-contained experience and do not influence real life.

42.383

As long as this debate remained within the select privileged group, concern about pornography's ill effects on society did not arise. Generally the powerful of that era believed that poor people, all women, and children could not understand the world of grand passion. To expose them to it would be harmful and would engulf their lives, creating chaos. Therefore they had to be shielded from such literature.

42.384

In the late 1800s, pornography regulation was largely due to the efforts of one individual, Anthony Comstock. In 1873, he organized the New York Society for the Suppression of Vice and started a movement that succeeded in enacting laws that, with some modification, remain in effect today. Also in 1873, President Grant signed "An Act for the Suppression of Trade in, and Circulation of, Obscene Literature and Articles of Immoral Use," better

113

known as the "Comstock Law." This law targeted materials sent through the mail from information on contraception and abortion to lewd books and advice on sexuality.

42.385

In his role as a special agent for the Department of the Post Office, Comstock took a direct hand in the arrest and conviction of many people, including Margaret Sanger, who came to his attention because of her birth control pamphlets and other materials. Sanger fled the country after being indicted for nine charges of obscenity, but she returned to assist her estranged husband, who was arrested when he distributed a pamphlet to a man working for Comstock. Shortly after she returned, Comstock died, and the movement appeared to collapse without his zeal. Public opinion shifted away from censorship and charges against Sanger were dropped.

42.386

Comstock's death in 1915 reduced the vigorous suppression of materials, but prosecutions continued on a sporadic basis. In 1879, U.S. law enacted a British legal principle, that "a publication could be banned solely because of the sexual content of isolated passages." This principle held until the 1930s when a federal court ruled against suppression of a book that would become a modern classic, *Ulysses*. This ruling maintained that "obscenity must derive from a reading of the work as a whole," and the law must look at the work's effect "on a person with average sexual instincts, not a young or especially susceptible reader."[6]

42.387

Other books and magazines, such as *Lady Chatterly's Lover*, *An American Tragedy*, and *Esquire*, were prosecuted as obscenity. Courts labored to separate materials of literary and scientific merit from those written merely to excite lust. Panels of experts gathered to judge the value of questionable literary pieces.

42.388

At the same time, courts declared that juries must set the standards and contradictory decisions were found from one jurisdiction to another. Cases were referred to the Supreme Court in the search for standardized interpretation of the law regarding obscenity.

42.389

Current Obscenity Law

42.390

In 1957, the Supreme Court was confronted with the tension over constitutionally allowable limits on First Amendment guarantees. In deciding the case of *Roth v. United States*, the Court issued a landmark pronouncement delineating obscenity regulation.

42.391

Roth—a distributor of unauthorized and slightly altered books, including *Ulysses* and *Works in Progress* by James Joyce and Balzac's *Contes Drolatiques*—appeared before the Supreme Court to appeal his conviction for mailing obscene circulars and books. The Court upheld Roth's conviction, ruling that it was illegal to mail "obscene, lewd, lascivious, or filthy" materials or "other publications of an indecent character."[7] In another 1957 case, *Albert v. California*, the Supreme Court upheld a law banning the publication, advertising, sale, or distribution of "any obscene or indecent" material.[8]

42.392

Establishing new judicial precedent in the Roth opinion, the Supreme Court ruled that obscene materials are those that are "utterly without redeeming social importance," which meant that some material was outside protection of the First Amendment.[9] Material was held to be legally obscene if "to the average person, applying contemporary community standards, the dominant theme of the material taken as a whole appeals to prurient interest."[10] Prurient interest was defined as a "shameful or morbid interest in nudity, sex or excretion which goes substantially beyond customary limits of candor in description or representation."[11]

42.393

This decision did not serve to end the debate. The phrase, "utterly without redeeming social importance," opened the door to repeated challenges. In the decade following the Roth decision, books that had previously been declared obscene were reexamined for traces of socially redeeming qualities.

42.394

Writers not only wrote pornography; they wrote *about* pornography—analyzing it, defining it, condemning it:

- It is fantasy writing, wish-fulfillment writing, differing from other forms of fantasy writing, such as romantic fiction by being explicitly sexual. . . . Pornography is transcribed masturbation fantasy.[12]

- Pornography is the representation of directly or indirectly erotic acts with an intrusive vividness which offends decency without aesthetic justification.[13]

- Pornography, then, is a certain kind of obscenity—it is sexual obscenity in which the debasement of the human element is heavily accentuated, is depicted in great psychological detail, and is carried vary far toward its upmost logical conclusion.[14]

42.395

In their 1959 book, *Pornography and the Law: The Psychology of Erotic Realism and Pornography*, Eberhard and Phyllis Kronhausen added a new phrase to the discussion of pornography:

> In pornography [hard-core obscenity], the main purpose is to stimulate erotic response in the reader. And that is all.[15]

42.396

In the opinion of some, hard-core pornography fits the criterion of the Roth decision by being "utterly without redeeming social importance." Furthermore, it was regarded as infantile. The warnings to protect children from Satan, issued earlier by Anthony Comstock, shifted to warnings about the individual who read pornography and was characterized as mentally defective and probably a lower-class male. This kind of individual was assumed to be immature, to have no taste for art or literature and to live in a fantasy world that would be twisted to suit reality. Opinion was expressed that these individuals had to be restrained and their access to pornographic representations controlled.[16]

42.397

Following the Roth decision, books that had previously been banned or available only "underground" began to surface. *Fanny Hill* by John Cleveland, *Tropic of Cancer* and *Tropic of Capricorn* by Henry Miller, *Lady Chatterly's Lover* by D.H. Lawrence, and *The Story of O* by Pauline Reage all found their way onto community bookshelves and public libraries. Community standards appeared to be changing as pornography, and obscenity boundaries, were repeatedly tested.

42.398

Throughout the 1960s the Supreme Court heard repeated challenges to obscenity law. In 1973 two cases that added to the Court's interpretation have since undergirded obscenity law opinion. The ruling in *Paris Adult Theatre I v. Slaton* established that speech which is obscene may be regulated if these is merely a "rational basis" for the regulation, and not according to the more stringent legal standards of "clear and present danger,"or for "compelling interest," which apply to speech protected by the First Amendment.[17]

42.399

The ruling in *Miller v. California* set the standards for a test of whether material is legally obscene. In order to be judged obscene, and regulated as such, material must fit all three of three following criteria:

1. The average person, applying contemporary community standards, would find that the work, taken as a whole, appeals to the prurient interest [in sex]; and

2. The work depicts or describes, in a patently offensive way, sexual conduct specifically defined by the applicable state [or federal] law; and

3. The work, taken as a whole, lacks serious literary, artistic, political, or scientific value.[18]

42.400

The Supreme Court also gave examples of the types of sexual conduct that could be defined and regulated as obscenity under part two of the standard:

a. Patently offensive representations or depictions of ultimate sexual acts, normal or perverted, actual or simulated.

b. Patently offensive representations or descriptions of masturbation, excretory functions, and lewd exhibition of the genitals.[19]

42.401

Subsequent to these opinions, the Supreme Court has required that this legal definition of obscenity be used only under "close judicial scrutiny" in order "to insure that non-obscene material is not erroneously determined to be obscene."[20] A leading case involved the Supreme Court's overturning a Georgia conviction against the film *Carnal Knowledge*. In its ruling, the Court made clear that the First Amendment prohibits any community from finding against a movie such as this, regardless of its standards.[21]

42.402

Because of this concern, subsequent cases have been limited to those involving "hard-core" material, that which is "devoid of anything except the most explicit and offensive representations of sex."[22]

42.403

In 1982, the Supreme Court ruled in *New York v. Ferber* that the standard of obscenity bears no relevance to child pornography. Since child pornography involves the sexual abuse of real children, the Court upheld a New York statute "prohibiting the distribution of material which depicts children engaged in sexual conduct without requiring that the material be legally 'obscene.'"[23]

42.404

In so ruling, the Court made a significant exception to the obscenity formula by placing children in a protected category.

42.405

Several laws related to obscenity and pornography have been passed by Congress. Federal statutes make it a criminal act to mail obscene material, to import or transport obscene material in interstate or foreign commerce, to broadcast obscene language, or to transport obscene material for the purpose of sale or distribution.[24]

42.406

The U.S. Customs Service, the U.S. Postal Service, the Federal Communications Commission, and the Federal Bureau of Investigation are responsible for enforcement of these obscenity statutes. In 1984, Congress added "dealing in obscenity" to the federal Racketeer-Influenced Corruption Organizations law (R.I.C.O.), which covers racketeering activities involved in murder, extortion, gambling, narcotics, bribery, robbery, and kidnapping.[25]

42.407

As of October 1987, two obscenity cases have been filed by the Justice Department under this provision.[26]

42.408

While there is broad consensus on the regulation of child pornography by government and law enforcement agencies, opinion is divided over the identification and regulation of material depicting adults by use of the obscenity standard. Furthermore, new court opinion continues to be written, as additional cases testing existing obscenity standards are presented. Two challenges were made in 1987.

42.409

The Constitution of the State of Oregon sets forth in plain language that no law shall be passed restraining the free expression of opinion, or restricting the right to speak, write or print freely on any subject whatever; but every person shall be responsible for the abuse of this right.[27]

42.410

Following seizure of the inventory of an adult bookstore and a subsequent jury trial in which the owner was found guilty of disseminating obscene material, the Oregon Supreme Court rejected the precedent established in *Miller v. California*, and overturned the conviction. In its January 1987 opinion, the Oregon Court disagreed with previous United States Supreme Court rulings and declared that "although the Miller test may pass federal constitutional muster . . . , the test constitutes censorship forbidden by the Oregon Constitution."[28] The Oregon Court further argued that "obscene speech, writing or equivalent forms of communication are 'speech' nonetheless . . . it may not be punished in the interest of a uniform vision on how human sexuality should be regarded or portrayed."[29] In its ruling, the Oregon Court challenged United States Supreme Court opinion, which the Oregon Court argued violates both the Oregon Constitution and the First Amendment to the Constitution of the United States.

42.411

In a case decided May 4, 1987, the Supreme Court altered its three-tier test for judging obscenity. While presumably continuing to allow community standards to determine whether a work appeals to the prurient and is patently offensive, it shifted the third criterion by ruling that the proper inquiry in determining obscenity is not whether an "ordinary member of any given community" would find serious literary, artistic, political, or scientific value in the work, but whether a "reasonable person" would find serious value.[30] Opinion on this ruling suggests that the standard for determining a work's value has been shifted from one based on a community's values to one based on the values of an individual not necessarily in the community.[31] This adjusted definition, according to columnist James J. Kilpatrick, succeeds in "obscuring the already obscure."[32]

Alternative to Obscenity Law: The Civil Rights Ordinance

42.412

In 1983, the city of Minneapolis held hearings on a new zoning regulation to curb the sale of pornography in certain neighborhoods. Attorney Catherine A. MacKinnon and author Andrea Dworkin, feminists who were teaching a course on pornography at the University of Minnesota Law School, were asked by neighborhood groups to testify. Neither MacKinnon nor Dworkin believed that zoning regulations or existing obscenity laws would address their major concern: the harm of pornography to women.[33] In their opinion, zoning regulations seemed to legitimize pornography as long as it was kept out of specified areas.

42.413

As a result of their testimony, the City Council of Minneapolis hired Dworkin and MacKinnon to draft an ordinance to amend the Minneapolis Civil Rights Ordinances to include pornography as sex discrimination. Under this new law, trafficking in pornography, coercion into pornographic performances, forcing pornography on a person, and assault or physical attack due to pornography would be defined as violations. Rather than as a criminal law, which depends on police action and state prosecution, the ordinance was drafted as a civil law in which an aggrieved person may enforce its provisions by means of a civil action or suit. After hearing testimony, primarily by women who believe themselves to be harmed and victimized by pornography, the City Council adopted the ordinance, which defined pornography as "the sexually explicit subordination of women, graphically depicted, whether in pictures or in words." The ordinance is prefaced with the following findings on pornography:

> The council finds that pornography is central in creating and maintaining the civil inequality of the sexes. Pornography is a systematic practice of exploitation and subordination based on sex which differentially harms women. The bigotry and contempt it promotes, with the acts of aggression it fosters, harm women's opportunities for equality of rights in employment, education, property rights, public accommodations and public services; create public harassment and private denigration; promote injury and degradation, such as rape, battery and prostitution, and inhibit just enforcement of laws against these acts; contribute significantly to restricting women from full exercise of citizenship and participation in public life, including in neighborhoods; damage relations between the sexes; and undermine women's equal exercise of rights to speech and action guaranteed to all citizens under the constitutions and laws of the United States and the state of Minnesota.[34]

42.414

Immediately following approval of the ordinance by the City Council, the mayor vetoed it, holding that it conflicted with First Amendment rights and would be overturned by the courts. A second, slightly amended ordinance was adopted by the Council, and was also vetoed by the mayor.

42.415

In 1984 and 1985, the City of Indianapolis struggled with a different version of the ordinance. Indianapolis legislators narrowed the definition to concentrate on violent, "hard-core" pornography, excluding action against "soft-core" pornography. This ordinance was passed by the city, signed by the mayor, and immediately became the target of a suit filed by a coalition of booksellers, distributors, and publishers.[35] Both a federal district court and the U.S. Court of Appeals then upheld the suits ruling against the ordinance. The Supreme Court declined to review the case.

42.416

In its opinion, the Court of Appeals held that the ordinance's definition of pornography was its essential flaw:

> The ordinance discriminates on the ground of the content of the speech. Speech treating women in the approved way—in sexual encounters "premised on equality"—is lawful no matter how sexually explicit. Speech treating women in the disapproved way—as submissive in matters sexual or as enjoying humiliation—is unlawful no matter how significant the literary, artistic, or political qualities of the work taken as a whole. The state may not ordain preferred viewpoints in this way. The constitution forbids the state to declare one perspective right and silence opponents.[36]

118

42.417

The Court of Appeals sympathized with the contention that "pornography is not an idea; pornography is the injury."[37] The fact that "depictions of subordination tend to perpetuate subordination . . . simply demonstrates the power of pornography as speech."[38] However, the court contended that "the image of pain is not necessarily pain," and "depictions may affect slavery, war, or sexual roles, but a book about slavery is not itself slavery, or a book about death by poison a murder."[39] Even though the ordinance, as civil law, did not include prior restraint (a hallmark of censorship), the court ruled that "a law awarding damages for assaults caused by speech also has the power to muzzle the press."[40]

Pending Legislation: The Pornography Victims Protection Act

42.418

Currently pending in the Congress is legislation entitled "The Pornography Victims Protection Act" (H.R.1213, which is included in the Background Papers of this report). The purpose of this proposed legislation is to provide legal means for prosecuting those who engage in specific harmful behaviors related to the production of pornography. The legislation would make it "a criminal offense for any person to coerce, intimidate, or fraudulently induce any person, adult or minor, to engage in any sexually explicit conduct for the purpose of producing any visual depiction of such conduct."[41] Sponsor of the House bill, Representative Bill Green, has maintained that this legislation "will effectively combat such sexual exploitation, particularly of women and children in the United States, while giving victims the opportunity to recover significant compensation for their injuries."[42]

VIII. Government Studies of Pornography

The 1970 Report of the Presidential Commission on Pornography and Obscenity

42.419

An eighteen-member commission, appointed in 1968 by President Lyndon B. Johnson to study the issue of pornography and obscenity, submitted its report to the Nixon administration in 1970. The highly controversial report, which followed two years of study funded by a two million dollar budget, was fully endorsed by twelve of the seventeen voting members. Two members accepted the content of the report but disagreed with the legislative recommendations. Three members rejected the majority decision and filed sharply-worded minority dissents.

42.420

The majority report concluded that there is no causal relationship between sexually oriented material and criminal or antisocial behavior. It called for a repeal of laws forbidding the sale of erotic material to adults, which were found to be a source of entertainment and information for substantial numbers of adults. The report was rejected by the Nixon administration, and the United States Senate rejected the commission's finding that government interference in the sale of pornography to adults was unjustified.[1]

42.421

The 1971 yearbook of *Collier's Encyclopedia* presented comparative data that are helpful in seeing the differences between majority and minority views of commission members:

Legislation

The Majority Report

. . . The commission recommends that federal, state, and local legislation should not seek to interfere with the right of adults who wish to do so to read, obtain, or view explicit sexual materials. On the other hand, we recommend legislative regulations upon the sale of sexual materials to young persons who do not have the consent of their parents, and we also recommend legislation to protect persons from having sexual materials thrust upon them without their consent through the mails or through open public display.

Minority Objections

The commission's majority report is a Magna Carta for the pornographer. . . . The commission leadership and majority recommend that more existing legal barriers between society and pornography be pulled down. In so doing, the commission goes far beyond its mandate and assumes the role of counsel for the filth merchant—a role not assigned by the Congress of the United States. (Hill, Link Keating)

Sex Education

The Majority Report

The commission believes that accurate, appropriate sex information provided openly and directly through legitimate channels and from reliable sources in healthy contexts can compete successfully with potentially distorted, warped, inaccurate and unreliable information from clandestine, illegitimate sources. . . . The commission recommends that a massive sex education effort be launched.

Minority Objections

Sex education, recommended so strongly by the majority, is the panacea for those who advocate license in media. The report . . . notes that three schools have used "hard-core pornography" in training potential instructors. . . . Will these instructors not bring the hard-core pornography into the grammar schools? (Hill, Link, Keating)

Public Opinion

Majority Report

There is no consensus among Americans regarding what they consider to be the effects of viewing or reading explicit sexual materials.

Minority Report

Credit the American public with enough sense to know that one who wallows in filth is going to get dirty. This is intuitive knowledge. Those who will spend millions of dollars to tell us otherwise must be malicious or misguided, or both. (Keating)

Antisocial effects of pornography

Majority Report

Extensive empirical investigation . . . provides no evidence that exposure to or use of explicit sexual materials plays a significant role in the causation of social or individual harms such as crime, delinquency, sexual or non-sexual deviancy or severe emotional disturbances.

Minority Report

. . . Data from a number of studies which show statistical linkages between high exposure to pornography and promiscuity, deviancy, affiliation with high criminality groups, etc., have gone unreported. This suggests a major bias in the reporting of results. . . . (Hill, Link, Keating)

Morality

Majority Report

The commission is of the view that it is exceedingly unwise for government to attempt to legislate individual moral values and standards independent of behavior, especially by restrictions upon consensual communication. . . . Governmental regulation of moral choice can deprive the individual of the responsibility for personal decision which is essential to the formation of genuine moral standards.

Minority Report

Not only does every individual reflect a certain moral character, but so does every group of individuals . . . the essence of which is determined by a general consensus of individual standards. . . . It is this level, this distillation, this average, this essence, which the state has an interest in protecting. . . . The obvious morals protected are chastity, modesty, temperance, and self-sacrificing love. The obvious evils being inhibited are lust, excess, adultery, incest, homosexuality, bestiality, masturbation, and fornication. (Hill, Link, Keating)

The 1986 Report of the Attorney General's Commission on Pornography

42.422

In May of 1985, Attorney General Edwin Meese III announced the appointment of an all-member commission, with a $500,000 budget, whose stated objective was to determine the nature, extent, and impact on society of pornography in the United States, and to make specific recommendations to the Attorney General concerning more effective ways in which the spread of pornography could be contained, consistent with constitutional guarantees.[2]

42.423

In his press statement announcing creation of the commission, Attorney General Meese declared that reexamination of the issue of pornography is long overdue. Its impact upon society was last assessed fully fifteen years ago. Since then, the content of pornography has radically changed, with more and more emphasis upon extreme violence. Moreover, no longer must one go out of the way to find pornographic materials. With the advent of cable TV and video recorders, pornography now is available at home to anyone—regardless of age—at the mere touch of a button.[3]

42.424

For one year the commission gathered information, including testimony presented at public hearings in Washington, D.C., Chicago, Los Angeles, Miami, and New York City. In July of 1986 the commission released its report, published in one volume by Rutledge Hill Press for public distribution. This edition, entitled *Final Report of the Attorney General's Commission on Pornography*, begins with an introductory discussion of the issue of pornography and its definition. Although commission members acknowledged the futility of their attempt to define pornography, and minimized use of the word throughout their report, they also indicated that their reference to material as "pornographic" meant "only that the material is predominantly sexually explicit and intended primarily for the purpose of sexual arousal."[4]

42.425

The report continues with a history of pornography and a discussion of the constraints of the First Amendment, including an analysis of obscenity laws as established by the Supreme Court. While concluding that there are First Amendment concerns created by obscenity regulation, the Commission supported efforts to regulate sexually explicit material according to established obscenity law standards.[5] (Thorough discussion of obscenity law regulation may be found in the section of this report entitled "A History of Pornography Regulation in the United States.")

42.426

The commission's report represents the most recent governmental effort to document evidence of the proliferation of pornography in the 1980s. Introductory comments to the chapter on "The Market and the Industry" state that "More than in 1957, . . . more than in 1970, . . . more than just a year ago in 1985, we live in a society unquestionably pervaded by sexual explicitness."[6]

42.427

Because of this proliferation, the commission precedes its discussion of the pornography industry with a survey of other forms of sexually explicit material that ''are usefully contrasted with the more unquestionably pornographic.''[7]

42.428

The Market for Sexual Explicitness:

42.429

The Motion Picture Industry. Sexuality, in varying degrees of explicitness or offensiveness, is part of many mainstream motion pictures. The rating system has no legal force, but it is designed to provide information on the content of films. ''R'' rated films are restricted to viewing by persons over the age of seventeen, unless accompanied by a parent or guardian. Such films may be devoted to themes of sex or violence, including scenes of nudity, but they do not contain explicit sexual activity. If a film is sexually explicit or has extreme amounts of violence, it is rated ''X,'' and no one under the age of seventeen may be admitted.

42.430

The rating system is virtually ineffective in categorizing pornographic films. Only rarely are such films even submitted for rating. Many of these are self-labeled ''XXX'' for promotional purposes. Furthermore, many of the films that receive an ''X'' rating are intended for adult viewing but are not commonly considered to be pornographic.

42.431

Sexually Explicit Magazines. Most magazines with sexual content are directed to the attention of men, although some variations have recently been aimed at a female audience. Some combine sexual content with a substantial amount of nonsexual material. Some limit sexual content to photographs of female nudity, while others show significant amounts of simulated or actual sexual activity. Commission members believed that virtually all of the magazines they categorized as ''sexually explicit'' contain at least some material considered to be ''degrading,'' and some magazines contain large amounts of degrading, as well as sexually violent, material.

42.432

Television. The advent of cable and satellite television added a new availability for sexually explicit materials. Under current law, cable and satellite television are not subject to the same range of Federal Communications Commission content regulation and are, therefore, more free to offer sexually explicit material than is broadcast television. This may include films, talk shows offering sexual advice, and music videos with stronger sexual and violent themes. What is available varies according to area and channel.

42.433

The commission classifies videotape cassettes as a form of television, since that is the means by which they are viewed. Video cassettes may encompass anything from standard motion picture fare to material that might be shown in an ''adults only'' theater. The commission acknowledged that material found in video stores tended in the past to be ''more on the conventional end'' and reflected desires of patrons to be offered a full range of video material. More recently, however, ''less conventional material has become available in some full range of video outlets.''[8]

42.434

The Pornography Industry

42.435

The commission contends that in the past ten to twenty years, there has been ''a dramatic increase in the size of the industry producing sexually explicit materials that would generally be conceded to be pornographic.''[9]

42.436

While the industry is not as clandestine as it was in earlier years, the production of pornographic materials is still a substantially underground business. Although the commission indicates that 80 percent of the production of pornographic motion pictures and videos is done in and around Los Angeles, members maintain that "there is virtually no overlap between this industry and the traditional motion picture industry."[10]

42.437

The production of standard pornographic magazines and books also operates according to a partially clandestine process.

42.438

The method of distributing films is rapidly changing as "adults only" theaters decrease in popularity and video tape cassettes become an increasingly popular medium. Videotapes that could be considered pornographic are often available at regular video stores, as well as at "adults only" pornographic outlets, or sex shops. Entry to "adults only" establishments is usually limited to those over eighteen years of age. "Peep shows" are often available and provide booths that allow some degree of privacy for patrons to masturbate or engage in sexual activity with others while viewing films or live sex acts (male-female, two men, two women, more than two people). Anonymous sex acts are also possible through holes in the walls of the booths.

42.439

Books and magazines are available at these outlets, although many magazines are sold through the mail. Magazines that in the recent past sold for $10 to $20 each are discounted, a reflection that videotapes are becoming the preferred medium. Sexual paraphernalia and newspapers are also for sale.

42.440

Dr. Park Elliot Diet, associate professor of law, behavioral medicine, and psychiatry at the University of Virginia and a member of the Attorney General's Commission, summarized in his personal statement the extremes that pornography may depict:

> A person who learned about human sexuality in the "adults only" pornography outlets of America would be a person who had never conceived of a man and a woman marrying or even falling in love before having intercourse, who had never conceived of two people making love in privacy without guilt or fear of discovery, who had never conceived of tender foreplay, who had never conceived of vaginal intercourse with ejaculation during intromission, and who had never conceived of procreation as a purpose of sexual union. Instead, such a person would be one who had learned that sex at home meant sex with one's children, stepchildren, parents, stepparents, siblings, cousins, nephews, nieces, aunts, uncles, and pets, and with neighbors, milkmen, plumbers, salesmen, burglars, and peepers, who had learned that people take off their clothes and have sex within the first five minutes of meeting one another, who had learned to misjudge the percentage of women who prepare for sex by shaving their pubic hair, having their breasts, buttocks, or legs tatooed, having their nipples or labia pierced, or donning leather, latex, rubber, or child-like costumes, who had learned to misjudge the proportion of men who prepare for sex by having their genitals or nipples pierced, wearing women's clothing, or growing breasts, who had learned that about one out of every five sexual encounters involves spanking, whipping, fighting, wrestling, tying, chaining, gagging, or torture, who learned that more than one in ten sexual acts involves a party of more than two, who learned that the purpose of ejaculation is that of soiling the mouths, faces, breasts,

abdomens, backs, and food at which it is always aimed, who had learned that body cavities were designed for the insertion of foreign objects, who had learned that the anus was a genital to be licked and penetrated, who had learned that urine and excrement are erotic materials, who had learned that the instruments of sex are chemicals, handcuffs, gags, hoods, restraints, harnesses, police badges, knives, guns, whips, paddles, toilets, diapers, enema bags, inflatable rubber women, and disembodied vaginas, breasts, and penises, and who had learned that except with the children, where secrecy was required, photographers and cameras were supposed to be present to capture the action so that it could be spread abroad.[11]

42.441

The Role of Organized Crime

42.442

After spending "a considerable amount" of time "attempting to determine whether there is a connection between the pornography industry and what is commonly taken to be 'organized crime,'" the commission concluded that "such a connection does exist."[12]

42.443

Although there was disagreement about the involvement of organized crime, much of it involved varying assessments of what constitutes organized crime. Some people believe that "organized crime" means organizations directly related to the elaborately structured system knows as La Cosa Nostra. For others, it is any well organized enterprise that engages in criminal activity.

42.444

The commission felt there was "strong evidence that significant portions of the pornographic magazine industry, the peep show industry, and the pornographic film industry are either directly operated or closely controlled by La Cosa Nostra members or very close associates."[13] While its lack of resources made it impossible to investigate these matters directly, the commission felt sufficiently persuaded by the work of federal and state authorities.

42.445

Child Pornography

42.446

The Attorney General's Commission subtitles its discussion of child pornography "That Special Horror." It establishes at the outset that "the distinguishing characteristic of child pornography, as generally understood, is that actual children are photographed while engaged in some form of sexual activity." To understand child pornography is to understand its "special harm [which is] largely independent of the kinds of concerns often expressed with respect to sexually explicit materials involving only adults."[14]

42.447

During the 1970s, increasing amounts of sexually explicit material involving children began to appear in adult bookstores and other channels of distribution. Testimony before Congress in 1977 revealed that "child pornography and child prostitution have become highly organized, multimillion dollar industries that operate on a nationwide scale."[15] At that time, over 200 different magazines were produced each month. Thousands of children were being sexually exploited, and witnesses before Congress told of pornographers who kidnapped children and parents who sold them.

42.448

The commission acknowledged that drawings of children engaged in sexual intercourse with adults and written descriptions of children engaged in sexual activity can be dated from ancient civilization. Even though these portrayals and accounts may offend modern sensibilities, they are not "child pornography" in the current legal and clinical sense. In 1982 the Supreme Court, in its *New York v. Ferber* decision, wrote that child pornography is "limited to works that visually depict sexual conduct by children below a specified age."[16] The commission makes clear that the court's language defines "child pornography" as appropriate only if it describes material depicting real children.

42.449

Because real children are involved in the actual production, the Supreme Court ruled that child pornography is a special category of material that may be regulated apart from obscenity standards used to regulate adult material. In 1977, Congress passed "The Protection of Children from Sexual Exploitation Act," which was a beginning effort to prohibit the production of sexually explicit material involving children. Enforcement of this act was of limited practical value, and Congress later passed the Child Protection Act of 1984. The commission declared that "virtually every state . . . now prohibits by its criminal law the production, promotion, sale, exhibition, or distribution of photographs of children engaged in any sexual activity."[17]

42.450

Title 18 of the United States Code prohibits the use of any minor in sexually explicit conduct for the production of any visual materials, as well as the transportation, distribution, or reception of any visual depiction of a minor engaged in sexually explicit conduct. A "minor" is defined as any person under the age of eighteen and "sexually explicit conduct" as sexual intercourse, oral or anal sex, bestiality, masturbation, sadistic or masochistic abuse, or lascivious exhibition of the genitals or pubic areas.[18]

42.451

In the late 1970s, increased public attention and concern had a significant impact upon law enforcement initiatives against child pornography. Those efforts accelerated after the Supreme Court ruling in 1982, and the commission reports that these law enforcement efforts curtailed "substantially the domestic commercial production of child pornography."[19] However, the domestic industry still continues as does a significant foreign industry. This material is not available openly, but it may be obtained "under the counter."

42.452

Child pornography is produced not only through commercial channels. The commission contends that the greatest amount is produced noncommercially in a kind of "cottage industry." Many children suffer from sexual abuse, and when photographs are taken, child pornography is the photographic record of that abuse. Child pornography often involves photographs taken by child abusers who either share them or distribute them informally to other child abusers. It is very difficult to determine the size of this trade because this network is so clandestine.

42.453

The commission report uses a diagram to show a cyclical pattern by which children become engaged.[20]

(Note: the use of the words, "Sex Education," in step one of the following figure does not refer to competent sex education that is factually accurate and sensitive to personal responsibility.)

Cycle

One of the most common questions asked from a public that knows very little about child pornography is: "How does child pornography begin?" This diagram explains one of the most common ways a child is introduced to pornographic activity:

1. Pornography is shown to the child for "sex education."

2. Attempt to convince child explicit sex is acceptable, even desirable.

6. Photographs or movies are taken of the sexual activity.

Cycle of Pornography

3. Child porn used to convince child that other children are sexually active—it's ok.

5. Some of these sessions progress to sexual activity.

4. Child pornography desensitizes—lowers child's inhibitions.

Source: S. O'Brien, *Child Pornography*, 89. (1983).

42.454

The report declares that, while "the legislative assault on child pornography drastically curtailed its public presence" and the "sexual exploitation of children has retreated to the shadows, . . . no evidence before the commission suggests that children are any less at risk than before. The characteristics of both perpetrators and victims, combined with the extremely limited state of professional understanding, make it unlikely that child pornography is a passing phenomenon."[21]

42.455

Findings and Recommendations

42.456

1. The commission rejected the First Amendment interpretation that holds that all sexually explicit materials involving consenting adults, no matter how offensive, should be protected from regulation according to principles of freedom of speech and the press. It upheld interpretation of the Supreme Court in defining obscenity and permitting its regulation.[22]

42.457

2. The commission advanced ninety-two recommendations for stricter enforcement of existing obscenity law, including those for the justice system and law enforcement agencies, for the regulation of child pornography, for victims of pornography, for civil rights legislation, and for regulation of "adults only" pornographic outlets.

42.458

The commission addressed the relationship between pornography and behavior in a section entitled "A Question of Harm." Findings by the commission on this aspect on the pornography issue are presented in the section of this report entitled, "What Are the Effects of Pornography? A Discussion of Harm."

IX. What Should Be Done About Pornography? Four Divergent Views

42.459

The debate over the definition of pornography and its effects culminates in debate over what should be done about it. Efforts to regulate it confront the delicate balance between individual freedom and public welfare, between personal decision making and community responsibility. Regulation also challenges the rule of law and calls for interpretation of the most basic legal principles. Both the 1973 PCUS statement on "Pornography, Obscenity, and Censorship," and the 1974 UPCUSA statement on pornography address the challenge that this balance between individual and society presents for Christians:

> Both the Christian faith and the democratic philosophy of government emphasize the freedom of the individual person from compulsory conformity of belief, thought, and lifestyle. On the other hand, both the Christian and democratic traditions recognize that individual freedom is limited by, and in fact only fulfilled in, the requirements of a just and orderly community. A free society is not only a society which promotes the independence of individuals, but a society in which individuals live in mutual responsibility for each other and for the welfare of the community as a whole. (1973 PCUS statement).

> Most ethical discussion affirms the balance between rights and responsibilities, between concern for the individual and concern for the community. The reason is simple; we believe two complementary realities: Jesus said, " . . . without your Father's leave, not one [sparrow] can fall to the ground. As for you, even the hairs of your head have all been counted." Along with God's care for the unique individual, we also affirm our inescapable corporateness. "Now you are in Christ's body, and each of you a limb or organ of it."

> As Christians therefore, we are required to deal intelligently and faithfully with the two sometimes conflicting civil interests of individual freedom and public welfare. We cannot, on the one hand, simply declare that our freedom as Christians makes legislative issues [that bear on the exploitation of sex] of no interest or consequence for us: nor can we, on the other hand, impose our views on others without regard to the integrity of their interests, even when they may be in conflict with our own. (1974 UPCUSA study).

42.460

The same tensions between individual freedom and community regulation confront Christians in the 1980s. A review of the history of pornography and obscenity in American society reveals the continuing debate over approaches to regulating pornographic material.

42.461

The agendas for addressing the issue of pornography reflect widely divergent value systems and goals. They constitute radically different views of sexuality, freedom, legality, morality, history, and the status of women and men. Because the issue is set into such divergent frameworks, conflict exists in analysis of both the problem of pornography and the solution to it. Furthermore, there is fundamental disagreement even among those who appear to be on the same side of the issue.

42.462

For Christians studying the issue of pornography, all approaches need to be examined through theological values about sexuality, morality, individual freedom, legal restraint, and male-female relationships. Presbyterian Christians also look at these various analyses through their particular Reformed theology and history. Religious values are clearly articulated in some of these perspectives, but they are not mentioned in the essential framework of others. However, all of them reflect theological values, and each of them challenges Presbyterians to examine their faith in relationship to the issue of pornography.

42.463

In an effort to give shape and understanding to this complex issue, Dr. Elizabeth Fox-Genovese of Emory University has categorized four different "camps" into which views of pornography and its regulation can be placed.[1] Two can be labeled "opponents" of pornography; two can be labeled "tolerators." Two advocate or support governmental regulation through the legal system; two reject any governmental regulation.

42.464

Advocate Regulation: A Morality View

42.465

Fox-Genovese distinguishes the first "camp" as primarily "conservatives of various persuasions who view pornography as certain testimony to the degradation of our moral life. . . . For the conservatives, moral decency is at stake, and behind moral decency, the institutions, notably family and church, that have sustained it in the past. With varying degrees of enthusiasm, they are willing to risk the perils of censorship, which some view less as perils than as the reimposition of minimal social and political order."[2]

42.466

The Rev. Dr. Jerry R. Kirk, pastor of the College Hill Presbyterian Church in Cincinnati, OH, and the organizing president of the National Coalition Against Pornography (N-CAP), entitles his book on pornography *The Mind Polluters*. In the first chapter he describes his realization that "the moral behavior of the nation has shifted" and that the problem that confronted him as a pastor was having "no answer for the avalanche of immorality that was crushing my people."[3] In his view, "the new American lifestyle" has turned us "away from the sanctity of the home, the security of marriage, from modesty and chastity." Kirk says, "When did those words become trite, humorous, old-fashioned? What happened to the innocence of youth, to blushing young brides, to heroes who were admired for faithfulness and self-control?"[4]

42.467

William A. Stanmeyer, in his book, *The Seduction of Society*, describes his view of America's changing society:

> In retrospect, it is clear that our national morals have changed considerably since World War II. Prior to 1940-1945, the country as a whole adhered to the Judeo-Christian ethic of self-control. Generally speaking, our sexual relations were monogamous, our music wholesome, our films unobjectionable, our adolescent entertainments innocuous.
>
> There was no open display of sexual materials. The calendar "pin-up" pictures of athletic girls on gas station walls were tame enough, and surely not obscene by any reasonable standard.
>
> Whatever went on in private, public sexual morality (save perhaps among some

indiscreet members of the movie industry) was uniformly straight-laced and even virtuous. Even in the mid-60s, people wondered out loud whether Nelson Rockefeller, an otherwise-qualified candidate for President, would lose too many votes because of his divorce.

Departures from basic morality caused scandal, not invitations onto the talk show circuit.

The moral tone of society was fairly high. During World War II people's energies focused on economic struggles and the national battle against the Axis powers. Immediately after the war, our national energies focused on economic expansion, building families in the suburbs, and acquiring that second car. There was a discipline in building one's assets even as, during the Depression years, there was a discipline in fighting to preserve one's assets. Whatever else they do, depression and war and subsequent economic growth bring austerity and demand stamina, not dissipation and hedonism.

Looking back, it seems that for about fifteen to twenty years, from the end of the war till around 1960-65, society remained on a moral plateau. We built a marvelous highway network. Much of the middle class fled the cities for the sprouting suburbs. Population expanded. Incomes went up. Despite the perceived Soviet threat, people came to take domestic tranquillity and material advancement for granted. Moral problems did not especially preoccupy us. If they existed in any serious way, they lay below the surface of our national public life.[5]

42.468

According to Kirk, Stanmeyer, and those who share their views, something happened in the 1960s and 1970s to shift American society radically from an essentially moral culture to an immoral one. "The social consensus on moral values was shattered" and "public decency began to collapse."[6]

42.469

Promiscuity, drugs, and divorce are seen as evidence of a society that has lost its moral authority. Consensus among those who hold this view targets pornography as responsible for society's moral collapse. The "source of immorality" that is "shattering people's marriages and slaughtering our young people" is pornography.[7]

42.470

Stanmeyer cites numerous examples of what pornography is: exploitation films involving graphic sexual acts, magazine photos dehumanizing women, live sexual performances, adult bookstores with peep shows and sexual paraphernalia, films that mix sex and violence, films and photos of explicit sex by children, and magazines depicting rape, which serve as technique manuals.[8]

42.471

Examples of pornography by proponents of this view include the whole range of sexually explicit material: child pornography, men's magazines, cable television movies, videotapes, Dial-a-Porn phone messages, films, and everything in adult book stores.

42.472

While there is some recognition of the debate over definition and the distinction between hard-core and soft-core pornography, all sexually explicit material is believed to contribute to the immorality of society and is only less dangerous by degree. Kirk quotes the conclusions of researchers Park Elliott Diet and Barbara Evans that "sadism and masochism, in the broadest sense, play a part in all pornography."[9]

42.473

Child pornography and pornography's influence on children constitute a primary focus of this approach. Quoting Matthew 18:5-6, Kirk holds pornography's producers, actors, models, purchasers, advertisers, tolerators, and defenders responsible for the "millstone" fastened around the necks of our children.[10]

42.474

The *Playboy* philosophy, advertising, rock lyrics and videos are linked to child molestation, incest, teen-age pregnancy, drugs, illicit sex, and suicide. Child pornography is a special concern, but all pornography is the target. According to Bruce Taylor of Citizens for Decency Through Law, "You'll never get rid of child pornography until you get rid of the general pornography industry. It's the same people producing it. If the federal government is serious about wiping out kiddie porn, it ought to put the producers and distributors in jail."[11]

42.475

Proponents of this approach believe not only that pornography has a connection to the evils of society but that it is the primary identifiable source. Statistics on the proliferation of pornography are accompanied by statistics on the sexual abuse of children, rape, abduction of children, runaway children, sexually transmitted diseases, and homosexuality.[12]

42.476

James Dobson, president of Focus on the Family and a member of the Attorney General's Commission, identifies pornography as the target in "combatting the darkness," since "what is at stake here is the future of the family itself."[13]

42.477

Broken families, violence, and abused children are seen as consequences of pornography's wickedness.

42.478

This view takes a protective approach to pornography's consequences for women. It acknowledges the "devastation" and "exploitation" of women that result from both the production of pornography and the impact of its images on all women.[14]

42.479

Pornography is labeled a "male obsession" that women find "offensive." Feminists such as Andrea Dworkin and Susan Brownmiller are cited in establishing the relationship between pornography and violence toward women. Pornography is held responsible for the "desensitization of men" and the distorted images men have of women.

42.480

However, this is essentially a "morality view" and not a feminist one. While appearing to support the feminist argument, closer examination reveals a departure from feminist analysis. Kirk, is contrasting "the pit and the pedestal," attacks the pit of violence and abuse that pornography creates for women, while implying that the pedestal is the ideal place for women. Feminists reject the pedestal (supra-human elevation) as well as the pit.

42.481

In spite of expressed protective concern for women who are victimized by pornography, women are ultimately viewed as the seducers, the source of male victimization. Kirk appears to be addressing a male audience when he refers to the Book of Proverbs, warning of the danger of "constant exposure to pornographic material" and the lure of the Playboy bunny and her associates:

> Do not desire her beauty in your heart,
>   and do not let her capture you with her eyelashes;
> for a harlot may be hired for a loaf of bread,
>   but an adulteress stalks a man's very life.

. . .

for many a victim she laid low; yea all her slain
  are a mighty host.
Her house is the way to Sheol,
  going down to the chambers of death. (Prov. 6:25-26;
  7:26-27)[15]

42.482

Stanmeyer further distances this approach from feminism. While feminists are affirmed for recognizing the antifemale essence of pornography, they are charged with overlooking "the fact that it also degrades children of both sexes and degrades young men as well (homosexual pornography)."[16] Feminists are suspected of tolerating pornography that does not involve women and are accused of not discerning the "common thread" of "predatory hedonism," or the exploitive pleasure without moral and cultural restraint that "connects all forms of pornography." Because "sexual liberation" appears to him to be part of the feminist program, he contends that "a by-product of feminism is the notion that women should have the same opportunity as men to be sexually promiscuous." Feminist views are rejected because they "have not embraced a traditional view of public morality and public decency."[17]

42.483

Because this "camp" recognizes pornography's evil influence on society, an extensive agenda is advocated for regulating and eliminating it. It sees a legal difference between hard-core and soft-core pornography and accepts the established definition of the Supreme Court on obscenity. Pornography is seen as unprotected, obscene speech since it is "nothing more than a means whereby one is titillated or sexually stimulated."[18] The essence of regulation is the strict legal enforcement of current obscenity law.

42.484

Kirk, however, recognizes the difficulty of regulation by means of existing laws and proposes an ultimate solution:

> While the current law clearly does permit effective action to be taken, *Miller v. California* contains phraseology that often has been exploited to wriggle free from the law. This is why our job would be greatly facilitated if legislation were enacted forbidding the distribution through interstate commerce, whether by printed material or filmed material, by air waves or by wireless communication, of any visual portrayal of ultimate sexual acts for purposes of commercial entertainment.[19]

42.485

Kirk's National Coalition Against Pornography (N-CAP) states the following as its focus:

> As a coalition, we are in unanimous agreement that hard-core and child pornography, which are not protected by the Constitution, must be eliminated. . . . N-CAP encourages and supports the enactment and the full, fair enforcement of constitutional laws prohibiting obscenity and child pornography, and effectively regulating indecency and sexually explicit material that is harmful to minors.[20]

42.486

N-CAP prepares materials and sponsors events that present information and rationale for governmental enforcement of obscenity laws, as well as extensive suggestions for individual and community involvement against pornography. In 1987, a two-year "community-by-community crusade across America" was launched to Stand Together Opposing Pornography (STOP).[21]

42.487

Supporters are being trained and encouraged to build a team of community leaders to assess the problem in their communities, work with law enforcement officials and the media, and raise funds.[22] Suggestions from the Attorney General's Commission regarding citizen and community action are recommended, such as education about pornography, economic boycotts and picketing, advocacy for antidisplay and zoning laws, conducting a Court Watch to monitor obscenity cases, patronage of antipornography businesses, parental monitoring of rock music, and working to limit availability of pornography in taxpayer-funded institutions, particularly schools.[23]

42.488

With regard to schools, these suggestions allow that "content-based restrictions . . . need not be limited to the legally obscene."

42.489

This approach is represented by a wide diversity of individuals and groups. The Religious Alliance Against Pornography (RAAP), an organization of Protestant, Catholic, and Jewish leaders of both conservative and liberal views, have united around a narrow focus: "That hard-core and child pornography, which are not protected by the Constitution, are evils which must be eliminated."[24] (The foundational document and list of organizing leaders of RAAP is in the Background Materials of this report.)

42.490

Supporters of this view are found in largest numbers among a variety of both theologically and politically conservative organizations. In a brochure accompanying materials describing *A Winnable War*, the 1987 film on pornography produced by James Dobson and Jerry Kirk, identification is made of organizations that are "dedicated to the preservation of traditional family values": American Life Lobby, Christian Action Council, National Right to Life Committee, Christian Legal Society, Concerned Women for America, the Eagle Forum, Family Research Council, Morality in Media, National Association of Evangelicals, National Coalition Against Pornography, National Federation for Decency, the National Pro-Family Coalition, and Focus on the Family.[25]

42.491

Proponents reject charges that "those who oppose the spread of obscene material in our society are . . . grim, scissor-happy reactionaries who bludgeon their opponents with the Bible." In an editorial criticizing the media's depiction of this approach, Steve Hallman writes, "We are liberals and conservatives, women and men, Christian, Jew, and nonbeliever who, with a genuine concern for the Constitution and the danger of excessive zeal, have yet become very alarmed over the proliferation of pornography. . . ."[26]

42.492

In their view, the most traditional values of society are being assaulted by a "flood of pornography" and the battle against it is nothing less than a "war against impurity."[27]

42.493

Advocate Regulation: A Feminist View

42.494

The second "camp" that Fox-Genovese identifies consists of "militant feminists who view pornography as one of the principal weapons in the systematic oppression, objectification, and degradation of women. . . . For the militant feminists, pornography should be understood exclusively as a powerful support of men's brutalization and oppression of women, which they frequently equate with male sexuality in particular and mandatory heterosexuality in general."[28]

42.495

The issue of pornography is a divisive one for feminists. Sexism is a reality that feminists understand and articulate with some degree of consensus. However, on this particular issue, feminists divide sharply on both analysis of the problem and its solution.

42.496

For feminists in this "camp," pornography cannot be understood as simply pictures, images, and words. Pornography is completely interwoven with behavior. It is the image, but the image is also the act. One feminist slogan sometimes seen on buttons is "Pornography is the theory, rape is the practice."

42.497

Andrea Dworkin, one of the foremost articulators of this approach, entitles one of her books *Pornography: Men Possessing Women*. In her first chapter, she introduces the feminist analysis of sexism, which is fundamentally rooted in the power that men have over women. Male power is embodied in seven tenets of male supremacy ideology:

1. Men have power of self which women lack.

2. Men have power of physical strength.

3. Men have the power to terrorize, from rape to war.

4. Men have the power to name and define experience.

5. Men have the power of owning.

6. Men have the power of money.

7. Men have the power of sex.[29]

42.498

Dworkin contends that "male sexual power is the substance of culture" and that a man's sexual power over women "illuminates his very nature."[30] All of these tenets of male-supremacy ideology are the essence of pornography. Pornography is the representation of male power in both the image and in the actual lives of real women. For Dworkin and others, image and behavior are one. In her testimony before the Attorney General's Commission, Dworkin said,

> I am a citizen of the United States, and in this country . . . every year millions of pictures are being made of women with our legs spread. We are called beaver, we are called pussy, our genitals are tied up, they are pasted, makeup is put on them to make them pop out of a page at the male viewer. Millions and millions of pictures are made of us in postures of submission and sexual access so that our vaginas are exposed for penetration, our anuses are exposed for penetration, our throats are used as if they are genitals for penetration. In this country where I live as a citizen real rapes are on film and are being sold in the marketplace. And the major motif of pornography as a form of entertainment is that women are raped and violated and humiliated until we discover that we like it, and at that point we ask for more. . . . When your rape is entertainment, your worthlessness is absolute. You have reached the nadir of social worthlessness. The civil impact of pornography on women is staggering. It keeps us socially compliant, it keeps us afraid in neighborhoods; and it creates a vast hopelessness for women, a vast despair. One lives inside a nightmare of sexual abuse that is both actual and potential, and you have the great joy of knowing that your nightmare is someone else's freedom and someone else's fun.[31]

42.499

Catherine MacKinnon, feminist legal scholar, writes extensively in explaining this view. She describes the impact that pornography has, not only on the women who produce it, but on all women:

> What pornography does goes beyond its content: It eroticizes hierarchy, it sexualizes inequality. It makes dominance and submission sex. Inequality is its central

dynamic; the illusion of freedom coming together with the reality of force is central to its working. Perhaps because this is a bourgeois culture, the victim must look free, appear to be freely acting. Choice is how she got there. . . .

From this perspective, pornography is neither harmless fantasy nor a corrupt and confused misrepresentation of an otherwise natural and healthy sexual situation. It institutionalizes the sexuality of male supremacy, fusing the eroticization of dominance and submission with the social construction of male and female. To the extent that gender is sexual, pornography is part of constituting the meaning of that sexuality. Men treat women as who they see women as being. Pornography constructs who that is. Men's power over women means that the way men see women defines who women can be. Pornography is that way. Pornography is not imagery in some relation to a reality elsewhere constructed. It is not a distortion, reflection, projection, expression, fantasy, representation, or symbol either. It is a sexual reality.[32]

42.500

Because feminists who support this view see pornography as inseparable from behavior, they regard regulation as the only means of ending the systematic oppression of men over women. Pornography and women's powerless status, in their view, are mutually reinforcing of each other. Regulation is the only means to break the cycle.

42.501

Yet, Dworkin and MacKinnon speak perhaps for most feminists in rejecting obscenity law as a method for regulating pornography. The problem with pornography is not sexual pleasure but misused power. Obscenity legislation regulates material that has no other purpose except sexual arousal, usually of men. Dworkin explains in unmistakable language feminist criticism of obscenity law:

To be obscene, the representations must arouse prurient interest. Prurient means itching or itch; it is related to the Sanskrit for "he burns." It means sexual arousal . . . empirically, prurient means causes erection. . . .

What is at stake in obscenity law is always erection: under what conditions, in what circumstances, how, by whom, by what materials men want it produced in themselves. Men have made this public policy. Why they want to regulate their own erections through law is a question of endless interest and importance to feminists. Nevertheless, that they do persist in this regulation is simple fact. . . .

Pornography, unlike obscenity, is a discrete, identifiable system of sexual exploitation that hurts women as a class by creating inequality and abuse. This is a new legal idea, but it is the recognition and naming of an old and cruel injury to a dispossessed and coerced underclass. It is the sound of women's words breaking the longest silence.[33]

42.502

Women have organized to fight pornography through groups such as Women Against Pornography (WAP), Women Against Violence in Pornography and Media (WAV/PM), Feminists Against Pornography (FAP), and Women Against Violence Against Women (WAVAW). They conduct tours of establishments that market pornography in order to educate and sensitize people to the issue. They organize protests, boycotts, and marches, sometimes under the banner "Take Back the Night."

42.503

The National Organization for Women (NOW) has endorsed the civil rights ordinance approach to regulating pornography and has affirmed its support for the Pornography Victims Protection Act currently pending in Congress. In a statement following release of the Attorney General's Commission report, NOW expressed support for the commission's findings that pornography harms women and children. However, NOW rejected the commission's emphasis on obscenity law enforcement and repudiated the "undertone" in some commissioners' statements that suggested that pornography is any "sexually explicit material that does not reflect 'traditional family values.'"[34]

42.504

Proponents of this approach believe that support for civil remedies and other protests tactics are all within constitutional guarantees. A statement by Women Against Pornography maintains that:

> Women can protest pornography without violating the First Amendment as long as they do not invoke or advocate the exercise of government authority. Only the government, by definition, can violate a First Amendment right. The First Amendment does not apply to interactions between two private parties; for example, feminists promoting a boycott of a pornographic movie. We are working hard, in the exercise of our own First Amendment rights, to develop strategies for effective private action against the pornography industry. We are working to make people aware of the implications of the violent misogynist pornography that has become an accepted part of our culture. Our movement against pornography is an anti-defamation movement against the perpetuation of negative and destructive images of women in the media.[35]

42.505

These feminists not only believe that they can oppose pornography within the limits of the First Amendment but also challenge the patriarchal foundation in which the First Amendment is rooted. MacKinnon maintains that the Constitution and the Bill of Rights were conceived by white men who had power and wrote the First Amendment to make sure that Congress would not take away the freedoms they wanted to protect. Those who did not have those freedoms (women and racial ethnic persons) didn't get them. MacKinnon asks the questions: If the First Amendment is a guarantee of free speech, whose speech is protected? Who has the power of speech and of the press? Whose voices are silenced by that unlimited power and "freedom"?[36]

42.506

Feminists who support the regulation of pornography recognize the difficulties that are involved. An article in the Harvard Women's Law Journal prefaces a discussion of regulation with three reminders: feminists cannot rely on patriarchal society to enforce laws on behalf of women; the suppression of pornography cannot cure all sexism even if it stops one means of perpetuating it; any regulation of speech presents a potential for unacceptable censorship of ideas.[37] Methods other than obscenity law are proposed by some feminists for regulating pornography: wider enforcement of laws against rape, statutory rape, slavery, and prostitution; criminal statutes under a feminist definition of pornography rather than the current obscenity standard; public civil nuisance statutes; zoning laws; tort suits and libel suits; taxation; and corrective funds to aid victims of pornography.[38]

42.507

This approach is centered in a concern for the harm pornography does to women. It does not ignore the harm done to children and men; it includes them as potential victims in proposed civil rights ordinances. However, pornography is at its core a graphic representation of male power over women, which many feminists regard as not imagery but the real-life brutalization that women experience in our society. Poet Adrienne Rich has written:

> but when did we ever choose
> to see our bodies strung
> in bondage and crucifixion across the exhausted air
> when did we choose
> to be lynched on the queasy electric signs

of midtown when did we choose
to become the masturbator's fix
emblem of rape in Riverside Park
the campground at Bandol the beach at Sydney?

. . .

I can never romanticize language again
    never deny its power for disguise for mystification
but the same could be said for music
    or any form created
    painted ceilings beaten gold worm-worm Pietas
reorganizing victimization frescoes translating
violence into patterns so powerful and pure
we continually fail to ask if they are true for us.[39]

42.508

Oppose Regulation: Libertarian and Feminist Views

42.509

Elizabeth Fox-Genovese described the third and fourth ''camps'' which advocate tolerance for pornography because of strong opposition to its regulation. The third ''camp'' consists of radical individualists or libertarians, from the far left to the far right of the political spectrum, who celebrate the lifting of sexual repression and the rights of individuals of any age to participate in the sexual expression of their choice.[40] Fox-Genovese's fourth ''camp'' consists of ''uneasy liberals who fear the consequences of censorship in any sphere and perhaps also fear being dismissed as sexual prudes. . . . The liberals resemble the libertarians in their mistrust of censorship, but they remain queasy about whether it would be possible to place some limits on the spread an escalating violence of pornography.[41]

42.510

The lines of the libertarian and liberal camps are not as easily distinguished as those of the morality and feminist camps. For both libertarian and liberals, whom Fox-Genovese terms ''tolerators,'' pornography is not the primary issue in this debate. What is at stake is freedom—of individual sexual expression, of speech, and from censorship.

42.511

In describing her own conflict with the issue, Fox-Genovese writes:

> To avoid confusion, let me begin with the end. I abhor pornography. It represents an obscene degradation of women, increasingly of children, and of our conception of ourselves as a society. In principle, I would ban it without a second thought, and with precious few worries about the expressions of healthy sexuality that might be banned along with it. But we live in a society that is based on individualist principles that do not easily permit action in the name of the collectivity. . . . Abuses of individual right have riddled our history, but, however heinous those abuses, individual right has survived as the cornerstone of our most positive visions of justice and order.[42]

42.512

The opponents of regulation articulate their views through the leadership of a variety of individuals and groups. The first can be classified as liberal and libertarian legal opinion, most visibly represented by the American Civil Liberties Union (ACLU) and the National Coalition Against Censorship (NCAC). The second is comprised of alternative feminist opinion, which radically divides itself from feminist views that advocate regulation of pornography. Both of these approaches share a belief that consensus is impossible to find and that any problems related to pornography should not be used as license to curtail individual freedom.

42.513

A Civil Liberties View

42.514

The American Civil Liberties Union (ACLU) maintains that "all forms of expression, no matter how objectionable or offensive they may be to some or even to most of us, are protected by the First Amendment's guarantees of freedom of speech and press."[53] Its supporters hold the view that pornography, because it is material, composed of words and images, is speech and, as such, is guaranteed protection to the full extent of the First Amendment freedom. This opinion rejects any attempt to regulate pornography through legislation or any form of government action, whether through use of the Court's definition of obscenity or through civil rights ordinance. It would oppose all forms of pressure or harassment on producers or distributors of pornography, out of the fear that such measures function to muzzle and silence freedom of speech and press.

42.515

The civil liberties view would support the legal opinion that ruled Indianapolis's attempt at a civil rights ordinance unconstitutional. Pornography, in this opinion, may influence behavior, but it is not itself behavior. It is imagery, and regardless of how vile the images or the idea expressed, a free society that guarantees individual freedom of expression faces unacceptable risk in curtailing any form of speech. "The 'civil rights' approach to pornography may seem novel, but it amounts, as every other antipornography measure does, to giving the state the power to control speech—a power which will not be limited to the kinds of racist, anti-Semitic or sexist speech we may abhor."[44] (See further discussion of the civil rights ordinance ruling elsewhere in this report.)

42.516

In material prepared by the ACLU, pornography is argued to be entitled to constitutional protection because it is most often sex-related publications that are the target of obscenity law.[45]

42.517

In the past, materials related to birth control, abortion, women's bodies, reproduction, and homosexuality have all been labeled obscene and their removal from many communities has been sought. Even though the courts have held that not all forms of expression are protected by the First Amendment, the ACLU works "as much as possible to limit the scope of obscenity laws, to mitigate penalties, and to assure that they are implemented only with full attention to due process of law."[46]

42.518

The issue of harm to women and children is given consideration. They question the causal links between exposure to pornography and subsequent criminal behavior, but they reject any censorship of books, magazines and films because of the effect they might have on some people. They maintain that violent images are found in the Bible, Shakespeare, and countless other sources, and "if we hold images or words responsible for the stimulus they might provide to some disturbed people, there is no reason to stop with pornography."[47]

42.519

Regarding child pornography, this approach contends that "sexual exploitation of children is a crime" and "it is criminal acts which should be vigorously prosecuted, not the books or films which depict the criminal event."[48]

42.520

Any effort to restrict accessibility of material to minors is seen as an invariable restriction on adult access as well. It is believed that such monitoring should be a matter for parental, not governmental, regulation.

42.521

The ACLU is a member organization of the National Coalition Against Censorship (NCAC), an alliance of groups concerned about the threat to First Amendment freedoms. Highly critical of the Attorney General's Commission report and its findings, Leanne Katz, NCAC director, challenged the commission's process and what it failed to consider:

> Restrictions on sexually related expression invariably affect literature and the arts, communication and entertainment, education and intellectual inquiry. . . . So it is a real scandal that the commission has made no attempt on its own to invite testimony from, for example—not a fiction writer, a journalist, or a reporter—nor so far as I am aware, a single artistic group, or any writers' organization in this entire country. In fact, the American Society of Journalists and Authors issued a statement charging that the preoccupation with attacking pornography distracts us from efforts to deal with the real causes of serious problems; and the Society urges sexuality education rather than sexual repression.[49]

42.522

Suggestions in a newsletter to members of NCAC on ways to "combat censorship" include a reminder that "stopping sexually explicit expression in this day of the Xerox machine and VCR"are no more effective "than Prohibition was in stopping bootlegging and bathtub gin."[50] Members are encouraged to enlist individuals and groups in the "fight against censorship"; to write letters to magazines and newspapers; to keep alert for local, state and national efforts to regulate; and to oppose harassment of community merchants who are pressured to remove offending materials. The same newsletter lists the following groups as participating organizations of the National Coalition Against Censorship:[51]

Participating Organizations (Partial listing)

Actors' Equity
American Association of School Administrators
American Association of University Professors
American Civil Liberties Union
American Ethical Union
American Federation of Teachers
American Jewish Committee
American Library Association
Modern Language Association
National Council of the Churches of Christ
National Council of Jewish Women
National Education Association
People for the American Way
Union of American Hebrew Congregations
Unitarian Universalist Association
United Church of Christ
United Methodist Communicators, United Methodist Church

42.523

A Feminist View

42.524

Sharp disagreement divides the feminist community on this issue. Taking a position in direct opposition to anti-pornography feminists are other feminists who evaluate pornography differently and reject its regulation. Such persons share a deep concern for sexual violence. Feminists have spent decades raising society's consciousness about rape, battering, sexual harassment and all forms of behavioral violence toward women. However, as Dierdre English writes: "Opposing violence against women is obvious. Opposing pornography is not as easy—because pornography is fantasy, not action, and because no one seems to be able to define pornography satisfactorily."[52]

42.525

Gloria Steinem writes for many feminists in trying to make distinctions between pornography and erotica. "Erotica," she says, "is rooted in eros or passionate love, and thus is the idea of positive choice, free will, the yearning for a particular person. . . . Pornography begins with a root meaning 'prostitute' or 'female captives,' thus letting us know that the subject is not mutual love, or love at all, but domination and violence against women."[53]

42.526

The problem, as English continues, is that "the line between pornography and erotica is hopelessly blurred. Such intangibles as intention, experience and context are everything in this. . . . Women Against Pornography define pornography as that which is violent and degrading to women, (but) . . . degradation, after all, is highly subjective. Without a reasonable effort to separate negative from positive sexual images, the movement will inevitably begin to see everything that is sexually suggestive as something that is tending toward rape."[54]

42.527

Other feminists, such as Ellen Willis, reject the stereotypes inherent in distinctions between erotica and pornography: "The view of sex that most often emerges from talk about 'erotica' is as sentimental and euphemistic as the word itself: Lovemaking should be beautiful, romantic, soft, nice, and devoid of messiness. . . . This goody-goody concept of eroticism is not feminist but feminine. It is precisely sex as an aggressive, unladylike activity, and a specific genital experience that has been taboo for women."[55] The ideas of Willis and others challenge centuries of patriarchy in which female sexuality has been narrowly defined and restricted and represent the affirmation of the newly discovered freedom of women to experience fully their own sexuality.

42.528

Because of this commitment to sexual liberation for women, groups such as the Feminist Anti-Censorship Task Force (FACT) "view the free speech accorded to pornographers as a necessary bedfellow to free speech for feminists and to the creation of [their] own erotica."[56] As with other liberals and libertarians, these feminists fear that anti-pornography efforts will ultimately be directed at their efforts to find new sexual expression. Barbara Kerr, FACT member and filmmaker, contends that "feminists trying to create an erotica concurrently with the anti-porn movement have been very beleaguered,"[57] and worries that their attempts at creativity will be increasingly silenced.

42.529

While some feminists accept studies suggesting that exposure to depictions of sexual violence does promote aggression, they do not support efforts to regulate pornography as a solution to such violence. English calls for an understanding of the complex motivations of male violence towards women and repudiates the "hope that by changing pornography [women] can reform the sexual nature of men."[58] She continues with a scenario:

> A man and a woman look at a sexually explicit picture. The woman is horrified. The man is delighted because the woman is horrified. The woman is horrified because the man is delighted. But the issue is not the picture they view. This issue is them.[59]

Not only is the feminist community divided over analysis of pornography and its effects but also over specific attempts to regulate it via the feminist-inspired civil rights ordinance. The

Venn diagram below has been used as a means of challenging the assumptions behind such laws:

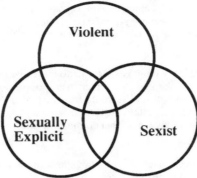

The Venn diagram above illustrates the three areas targeted by the [Minneapolis] law, and represents a scheme that classifies words or images that have any of these characteristics: violence, sexual explicitness, or sexism. Clearly, a text or an image might have only one characteristic. . . . Areas can also intersect, reflecting a range of combinations of the three characteristics.[60]

42.530

These feminists believe the diagram reveals the flaws in regulating only material that is sexually explicit and violent or sexually explicit and sexist while ignoring material that is violent and sexist, only violent, or only sexist.

42.531

Betty Friedan, founder of the National Organization for Women (NOW), addresses another concern when she writes, ''Get off the pornography kick and face the real obscenity of poverty.'' She also fears that banning books and movies for sexually explicit content will be far more damaging than beneficial to women. Furthermore, Friedan contends:

The pornography issue is dividing the women's movement and giving the impression on college campuses that to be a feminist is to be against sex. . . . I think the secret this obsession with pornography may mask for women alone, for aging women and for women still more economically dependent on men than they would like to be, is fear of poverty, which is the ultimate obscenity for Americans. . . . I sat at a dinner table recently with several women, . . . and could not believe their venom against the young rock star Madonna. I suggested that teenagers identified with her gutsiness, strength and independence as well as her not-at-all-passive sexuality, which to me was not a retreat from women's liberation, but a celebration of it. Whoever said that feminism shouldn't be sexy.[61]

42.532

Many feminists, like Betty Friedan, fear any alliance on the issue of pornography with conservatives and the Religious Right, those who have a long history of opposition to other significant women's issues, such as battered wives' legislation and shelters, pay equity, child care, abortion rights, textbook images of women, and the Equal Rights Amendment. Fear exists that radically different goals—for feminists an end to sexism and sexual violence, for conservatives a return to traditional moral and family values—cannot be compromised or pursued apart from otherwise competing agendas for social change. For many with such fears, tolerance of pornography is preferable to being co-opted by a movement that is fundamentally antifeminist.

42.533

Comparative Analysis of These Views

42.534

The Task Force on Pornography believes that pornography can be understood in all of its complexity by examining the divergent approaches that individuals and groups advocate for addressing it. Each approach is shaped by its emphasis on certain values and principles. We have seen the strengths of each reflected in the concerns of its supporters and the sense of caring that motivates their involvement in this issue. While we believe that classification of opinion into four "camps" is useful to understanding the debate over pornography, we also believe that these divisions should not be seen as rigid groupings into which individuals can easily be placed. The opinion of any person can move in and out of these four "camps," and all four inform the issue of pornography. Furthermore, the task force believes that all of these approaches are, to some degree, single-minded and incomplete. Analysis reveals fundamental differences in values, goals, and methods. As Presbyterians who are seeking to understand the whole of this issue and to develop an ethical approach that reflects the values of our faith, we have examined each of these approaches and present what we believe are their strengths and weaknesses.

42.535

Regulate Pornography: A Morality View

Strengths

- Serious attention to moral climate of nation and personal moral responsibility of individuals.

- Sincere religious motivation by many holding this view.

- Willingness to risk labeling—anti-sex, prudish—to confront issue of pornography.

- Early recognition of the exploitation and dehumanization of pornography; leadership in promoting study and education about the issue, including in the PC(USA).

- Intensive focus on children, both child pornography and pornography's effects on all children.

- Demonstrated ability to organize concerned individuals and groups for government and interfaith efforts to address pornography issue.

- Concern for effect of pornography on women, men, and family values; commitment to preserving the "goodness" of traditional society.

Weaknesses

- Attention to moral values fails to take seriously the lack of moral consensus in contemporary society.

- Religious motivation can be insensitive to moral pluralism of society.

- Uncritical acceptance of traditional sexual mores.

- Appears to have an uncritical acceptance of causal effects of pornography on behavior; simplistic belief in elimination of pornography as solution to immorality.

- Emotional appeal on issue of child pornography can be distorted and used to simplify what are complex issues involving adult pornography.

- Dangers of "crusade" on this issue; unintentionally contributes to climate of repression; excessive reliance on legal means without attention to potential legal abuse; insufficiently critical of obscenity law as a means of regulating pornography today; leadership overwhelmingly reflects a white male cultural and theological view.

- Limited understanding of role of traditional family and oppression of women; blindness to traditional society's history of sexism, racism, economic evils; focus on current moral issues of pornography ignores its systemic history and meaning.

Regulate Pornography: A Feminist View

Strengths

- Serious attention to the centrality of women to pornography issue; fundamental analysis of sexism in sexual history of men and women; focus on pornography as exploitation and abuse of both some women and all women.

- Supporters include men who oppose sexism and who address the ways in which men exploit women through pornography, and are themselves exploited.

- Willingness to risk pejorative labeling—militant, prudish, anti-sex—to confront issue of pornography.

- Creativity in developing civil rights ordinance; serious recognition of the failure of legal tradition to guarantee justice for women.

- Consciousness-raising efforts to sensitize people to the issue of pornography; powerful impact of tours to sex shops.

- Women organizing for women's issue and highly motivated to end victimization of women; empowerment for powerless women; attention to class, race and homosexual issues.

- Willingness to confront attitudes on both the "left" and "right" that exploit women in traditional roles, as passive wives, mothers, and sex objects.

Weaknesses

- Lines are not easily drawn between sexual imagery that is exploitative and that which is consensual; imbalance in view that women are essential victims of male sexual power; lack of attention to women's increasing understanding of their own sexuality and their own power in making sexual decisions.

- Loss of credibility; alienates more moderate views, including other feminists.

- Fundamental conflict of ordinance with historical precedent in interpreting First Amendment rights; inherent conflict in interpreting speech as behavior.

- Perception, if not the reality, of separatism intent on goals; sees women only as victims of abusive male sexuality; refusal to include men in some organizations and activities.

- Divisiveness of challenging political and feminist credentials; singleminded zeal lacking serious recognition of alternative concerns.

Oppose Regulation: A Civil Liberties View

Strengths

- Fundamental attention to protection of every individual's First Amendment rights, regardless of the offensiveness of the idea or image; guardians of a pluralistic society that tolerates all speech.

- View is defined with clarity; all speech is protected.

- Represents history of legal efforts to protect the voices of political dissidents and those likely to be silenced by regulation efforts.

- Broad ecumenical support for these principles among denominations in closest communion with Presbyterians.[6]

- View stimulates understanding the complex web of influences and patterns in society; seeks deep-rooted solutions rather than the simple prohibition of materials; promotes sexuality education as a solution to disempowering pornography's influence.

Weaknesses

- Unwillingness to compromise protection of ideas for protection of persons alleging harm from the ideas; uncritical tolerance for the marketing of all ideas regardless of their consequences or effects; exaggerated emphasis on freedom of individuals; inattention to issues of community and social welfare.

- Clarity can be insensitive to other concerns; too easily dismisses historical precedent for constitutionally restricting speech.

- Legal history one of failure to give inclusiveness to women's equality and justice; women's speech is often the voice of the powerless with inadequate legal protection.

- Inadequate attention to pornography as a powerful influence, even if it is not the only influence or even the most important influence on society's ills; refusal to address pornography as a contributing influence.

Oppose Regulation: A Feminist View

Strengths

- Understands the dangers and risks of censorship, particularly for potentially dissident views; recognizes the threat to publications and films of feminists, racial ethnic persons, and homosexuals.

- Suspicious of sex-role stereotyping in regard to sexuality; affirms possibility of new behaviors by men and women; refuses to see women only as victims of male sexual power and men only as oppressive in their treatment of women; affirms egalitarian sexual relationships between women and men as desirable and possible.

- Early attention to uneasy alliance with antifeminists on this issue; concern for co-optation of feminists by those who oppose their other goals and values; concern that pornography is a diversionary strategy against feminist goals of economics and reproductive rights.

- Emphasizes raising status of women as a solution to power of pornography; focus on comprehensive strategy rather than simplistic one; analysis of complex web of issues.

- Exposes the double standard of targeting sexually explicit material while tolerating material that is exclusively sexist or violent.

Weaknesses

- Attention to protection of materials more than to actual harm to persons.

- Lack of focus on actual women who are victimized by pornography industry and women who continue to exist in unequal power relationships with men.

- Fears of alliance with antifeminists prevents attention to pornography issue that it deserves by feminists; implication that it is better to ignore the issue than find common ground with political opponents; perception that women cannot maintain their values and denial of pornography as a legitimate women's issue and not a diversionary one.

- Attention to complex web of issues obscures the importance of this particular issue; raising the status of women dependent on many strategies, including serious attention to the issue of pornography.

X. Pornography and Culture

42.536

In a paper entitled "Pornography and Individual Rights: the Issues," Elizabeth Fox-

Genovese writes, "Pornography is . . . obscene, not so much because it exposes naked flesh, but because it exposes our society naked."[1] Indeed, pornography is not an aberration; it is the expression of mainstream cultural attitudes and realities in an exaggerated, distorted, and extremely vivid form. Looking at the pictures in a pornographic magazine is somewhat like seeing American culture in a carnival funhouse mirror. The image reflected is a vision of dominance and subjugation. It is consonant with a highly individualistic culture in which people compete with each other for power, prestige and possessions.

42.537

Whatever else it may tell us, pornography offers irrefutable evidence that this culture is patriarchal. Not only the materials themselves, but the industry that supplies them and the market that consumes them, are built on an inequality of power between men and women. It is primarily men who produce and consume images that, at best, depersonalize and objectify women and, at worst, encourage violence and brutality against them. The task force believes that pornography both reflects and magnifies a range of cultural phenomena, including the following:

—a mystification of sex based on ignorance of human sexuality;

—the association of sex with sin and evil;

—the use of sex as an instrument of power;

—economic discrimination against women;

—the acceptance of violence as natural and inevitable;

—desensitization to images of horror;

—the commercialization of human needs;

—widespread addiction to obsessive compulsive behavior;

—unequal responsibility for human relationships.

42.538

Mystification of Sex

42.539

Published erotic or pornographic materials are the most accessible, and for many, the only, source of information about sex. Most of us respond with familiarity to stories of young boys hovering over an issue of a "girlie" magazine, or of girls reading aloud to each other the juicier passages of a romance novel. The silence that our cultural institutions—church, school, and family—have long practiced about sexual matters has bred an intense curiosity about sex and unleashed an explosion of sexual information and misinformation in the commercial media. Misleading ideas are not confined just to pornography; they easily become governing assumptions in many people's private sexual relationships. The belief that women are naturally passive and are sexually stimulated by domination gives men the privilege of initiating and controlling sexual activity. As women begin to break their silence about sexuality, many of them realize that their sexual expression has been inhibited by this myth. Theologian Mary Pellauer writes, "In our society, let alone in our theologies and churches, we have barely begun to explore women's sexuality from the inside out. Ignorance about the simplest facts of female biology is rampant, and our culture spreads strange ideas about women's sexuality in many more ways than in pornography."[2] Candid discussions of female sexuality, of what women truly enjoy in sexual relationships, can do much to challenge the myths about women that pornography perpetuates.[3] Equally open and honest testimony about male sexuality can debunk the myth that men must be aggressive to be sexual and can free young men from the pressure to tally up sexual conquests. Responsible education about sexuality, drawing on the way people experience it in loving and committed relationships, might well diminish pornography's appeal. For example, Ann Welbourne-Moglia, in her testimony, cites studies that show that "young

144

people who obtain sexual health information and education from their parents are less likely to use pornography.''[4]

42.540

Ironically, some of the voices raised in alarm over pornography also oppose sex education. Many fear that removing sexuality from the realm of the secret and private will bring on a flood of pornographic images and will lead to rampant practice of sexual behaviors labeled "deviant." On the contrary, recognizing sex as a basic human longing and discussing it publicly would allow us as a society to attain a more compassionate understanding of human sexuality and the kinds of sexual behavior that contribute to people's health and well-being. A society that does not claim that right forfeits sexuality to those who profit from its distortion.

42.541

Association of Sex with Sin and Evil

42.542

Christians partake in a long heritage of sexual shame, dating at least as far back as the Patristic Period, when the Fall from Paradise was interpreted as a sexual sin, a notion preserved in the phrase "carnal knowledge." This notion is derived from a dualistic world view that associates the spirit, reason, cultural restraint, and maleness with good, while the body, emotion, unbridled nature, and femaleness are associated with evil. To attain the good, human beings must overcome the longings of the flesh. The secular counterpart of this religious belief is known to us as "Victorian morality," a double standard of behavior that confines sex to marriage while tolerating prostitution as a necessary outlet for men's baser instincts.

42.543

There were no such tacitly approved outlets for women, because healthy women were not supposed to feel sexual desire. Women were divided, on the basis of their sexual behavior, into two categories, often denoted "Madonnas" and "whores." "Fallen women" were subject to social control through laws prohibiting prostitution that were almost never enforced against their male customers. Even after the "sexual revolution" of the 1960s, this Madonna-whore dichotomy remains. Many women have internalized it, so that they feel shame when they behave as sexual beings. This dichotomy is certainly prevalent in pornography. A common scenario shows a prim and prudish woman or a childlike, innocent one, being exposed as savage and lustful by the sexual skills of a man who can then claim victory over her.

42.544

This view of sexuality as the sin lurking in otherwise respectable people is implicit even in some of the anti-pornography literature that the task force read in both Christian and feminist sources. Proceeding from the belief that sexuality is a gift of creation to be affirmed, the task force is uncomfortable with antipornography appeals that warn against the spectre of temptation, often in female guise, or that arouse fear of sex as a male instinct for oppression.

42.545

Cloaking sex in secrecy and shame would probably be counterproductive as a tactic to eliminate pornography. This legacy of shame, perpetuated by both church and society, is what gives pornography its power. Calling this legacy "the ancient but still popular heresy that human sexuality is dirty," the authors of the 1973 report to the General Assembly of the PCUS maintained that greater emphasis on "the beauty and goodness of the human body and its functions" could be pornography's undoing. "Pornography or obscenity then loses its power and fascination as it is exposed for what it really is: not some tremendous and delicious evil which is secretly relished even as it is righteously opposed but a stupid, trivial and boring parody of the real joy, excitement, pleasure, and wonder of authentic human life as God has willed and created it."[5]

42.546

Use of Sex as an Instrument of Power

42.547

Organizing Against Pornography, a grassroots network in Minneapolis, makes the claim that "pornography eroticizes inequality."[6]

42.548

Subduing women with physical strength or the force of social privilege is shown to be sexually exciting in itself. Sex is commonly depicted as an adversarial relationship. Even where the people involved seem to be enjoying the act mutually, this is often prefaced by a scene in which the man subdues the woman. Mary Pellauer writes, "The basic plot of many kinds of porn is the overcoming of a woman's resistance so thoroughly that she is gratefully orgasmic."[7]

42.549

Some pornography depicts acts that are clearly hostile and have little to do with mutual pleasure, such as a man ejaculating in a woman's face.

42.550

Sexism is not the only injustice that pornography "eroticizes." A special genre of openly racist magazines and films simulates Nazi concentration camp scenes or shows white slavemasters laying claim to black or Oriental slaves. Child pornography depends for its very existence on adults' ability to manipulate children.

42.551

As shocking as it may be to look at images of sexual subjugation for the first time—the experience of some of the task force members—there is still something frighteningly familiar about them. Pornography that celebrates men's sexual dominance over women offers a graphic reminder of women's condition in the world at large. It tells us just why women are afraid to go out alone at night or why women feel strangely vulnerable when they are the only woman in a roomful of men. One woman on the Task Force, for example, told of stopping at a doughnut shop on her way to work one morning and then driving away out of a self-protective instinct when she saw that there were only men inside.

42.552

This is a culture where harassment by sexual innuendo and intrusive touching is common-place and rape is epidemic, where the four-letter word describing sexual intercourse is often used to offend or degrade another person. It is sobering for women to think that "ordinary" men enjoy images of dominance and concur in this view of women and sexual relationships.

42.553

Marie Fortune, a United Church of Christ minister who has studied sexual violence, contents that "male dominance has become eroticized as has its corollary, female submission. . . . The belief is that together dominance and submission and power and powerlessness create the formula which sparks erotic desire in both men and women." Fortune looks forward to an eroticization of equality, in which "both women and men will find erotic pleasure in approaching each other as equals, sharing both proactive and receptive sexual activity."[8]

42.554

The patriarchal attitudes and habits that pornography illustrates so graphically are, like sexual shame, of ancient origin. There has been no time in recorded history when men and women were free to define and live out sexual relationships based on social equality without interference from the culture around them. Attempts to eliminate pornography by returning to previous codes of moral "decency" fail to challenge the deeply embedded assumption that men have a right to wield power over women.

42.555

Some Christians suggest that a restoration of the nuclear family, with the father as head of household and the mother in the role of housewife, would counter the impact of pornography on sexual attitudes and behavior. This would replace a risk-filled liberation with fatherly protection. Lisa Duggan and Ann Snitow offer a succinct argument against that view: "Protection and respect are not substitutes for the power to protect ourselves, to control our lives. If men are allowed to 'protect' us, then we are also at their mercy."[9]

42.556

The task force did not find the patriarchal family to be a safe refuge for women; it is a place where sexual power can be exercised in private. As more women have begun talking about the sexual abuse they experienced in childhood and adolescence, or as battered wives, it has become evident that incest and marital rape are not rarities, nor are they confined to obviously decadent families. Recent studies show that at least 25 percent of adult women in the United States, and 10 percent of adult men, were sexually molested as children, mostly by relatives or other trusted adults.[10]

42.557

In some studies, nearly 40 percent of women reported child sexual abuse.[11]

42.558

As far as women's safety is concerned, there is no "golden age" to return to.

42.559

There is sound reason to speculate that many of the women who work in the pornography industry have previously been subject to sexual abuse. This is certainly true of women leaving the practice of prostitution and of female criminals.[12]

42.560

No thorough census can be taken of a subculture as evanescent as that which produces pornographic materials. Nevertheless, testimony from former models and actresses, and other anecdotal evidence suggest that many of the women who perform in scenes of sexual dominance and hostility come to the job believing that sex has to do with power and that they themselves are powerless.[13]

42.561

Economic Discrimination Against Women

42.562

Another way in which women today experience powerlessness is economically. Previous reports to the General Assembly have described the structure of economic inequality and the practice of sex discrimination.[14]

42.563

The pornography industry also profits from this inequality. The daily wage for an actress in an adult movie may sound good, but the films are shot fairly quickly, and the wage represents a minute percentage of the film's earnings. Performers in live peep shows may earn wages somewhat higher than those earned in other unskilled and disproportionately female jobs, but they do not get rich. They move rather, from poverty to subsistence, or from subsistence to a modicum of comfort.

42.564

When the task force visited a Times Square sex shop, its members were struck with how ordinary and unexotic the women seemed. The same women might well be seen behind the counters in the fast food restaurants, and that sort of low-wage work may be their other best option.

42.565

Masturbating behind a screen in a sex shop is surely safer than street prostitution, which poses constant dangers to health and safety. The Dial-a-Porn telephone outlets offer an even safer work environment for women. One task force member interviewed a former clerical worker for the Presbyterian Church who worked as a telephone "fantasy girl" so that she could provide a home for herself and her young daughter. (The interview is in the Background Materials of this report.) In sum, the pornography industry draws from a populous labor market of unskilled and economically needy women whose other options are not especially promising.

42.566

Rumors of big money may, nevertheless, be an enticement for women to take part in the production of sexually-explicit films and videos. The million dollars that *Playboy* allegedly paid Jessica Hahn for baring her breasts and telling about her sexual encounter with television evangelist Jimmy Bakker is more money than she could hope to make in a lifetime as a church secretary. Such expectations, however, usually prove to be illusory. According to a recently broadcast television documentary, the will to do pornographic modeling or acting is often sustained by drug use, since the work itself is arduous, risk-filled, and perceived as demeaning. Even the relatively highly paid stars may find themselves destitute because of chemical dependency.[15]

42.567

The distribution of pornographic materials has a race and class dimension that affects women differentially. It is quite easy for middle-class suburban families to insulate themselves from pornographic imagery. Adult bookstores and movie theaters tend to be located in low-rent neighborhoods populated by racial ethnic persons and by single parent families, most of which are headed by women.[16]

42.568

The women who live in these neighborhoods report that they are frequently harassed on the street or solicited for sex by men patronizing the bookstores and theaters. Some of the grassroots efforts to change zoning laws and relocate pornography outlets in nonresidential areas have been initiated by women who cannot afford to move out of the neighborhoods themselves.

42.569

The Acceptance of Violence as Natural and Inevitable

42.570

One of the most controversial aspects of the report of the Attorney General's Commission on Pornography was its emphasis on sexual violence, which, its critics argue, leaves the impression that all or most sexually explicit material also has violent content. The bulk of the material that the task force viewed consisted of redundant "plumbing shots"—close-ups of genital organs. Dehumanization—the reduction of sex to a mechanical bodily function with no emotional dimension—seemed more prevalent than violence, and its impact was more boring and disheartening than frightening. The task force found cause for alarm in some of the violent images that appeared in films we viewed, especially those that linked sex and violence in such a way as to make them seem synonymous. A particularly horrifying image, from which some members looked away, was a film of a woman being forced to suck the end of a pistol as though she was performing fellatio on it. It is not easy to dismiss such blatantly violent pornography as simple fantasy when real women are being raped and murdered in equally bizarre ways. The news accounts in August 1987 of an apartment in Philadelphia strewn with female corpses and pornographic magazines should certainly give pause to all.

42.571

Much of the debate about pornography has focused on the question of harm. Attempts have been made to prove and disprove the contention that specific images of sexual violence result in specific acts of sexual violence. It is a difficult proposition to test since it often relies on the testimony of people convicted of sexual crimes, who are not generally credible witnesses. For obvious ethical reasons, the test cannot be replicated in a laboratory by showing subjects violent images and then sending them off to act them out if they choose. Pursuing the question of harm seems fruitless as long as it focuses on specific cause-and-effect relationships and postulates that pornography is the immediate cause. There are many other contributing factors.

42.572

American society tolerates violence as inevitable, and it condones sexual violence as intrinsic to male nature. Rape is not the exclusive province of hardened criminals; it is practiced by gangs of teenagers testing their sexual prowess, by soldiers in wartime, by fervent suitors frustrated by their dates' resistance. "Boys will be boys" is the proverbial justification for such behavior.

42.573

Images of rape are not, however, the exclusive province of pornography. In an episode of the television drama *Hunter*, police sergeant Dee Dee McCall was raped. When the producers decided to have her raped again, the actress who portrays her, Stefanie Kramer, threatened to leave the show. The first rape was dramatically justified, but the second was, in her words, "pure exploitation."[17]

42.574

Vicarious violence is, indeed, a high grossing form of entertainment, as the box-office success of movies such as *Rambo* and the *Dirty Harry* series illustrate. The horror movie genre popular with teen-age audiences has been transformed in just a decade or two from suggestive tales of the supernatural to realistic simulations of gross and bizarre violence, much of it with sexual connotations. Dr. Edward Donnerstein, whose psychological research demonstrates that depictions of violence, not of sex, make men aggressive toward women, offers this example of how the "slice and dice" movies work:

> This type of film usually has a sexual scene preceding a very graphically violent scene. For example, one film, *Toolbox Murders*, has a very beautiful bathtub scene. A woman in a bathtub is masturbating; a beautiful song is playing in the background. It goes on for about three minutes when a killer comes in and chases her around with a nail gun.

> Then this song comes back on, and he puts the gun to her head and blows her brains out. But it's interesting that when a clip of the movie is shown on television, the women's breasts will be covered up because you can't show anything sexual. Yet they will show the entire scene to the point of the nail being driven through her head. . . . The problem with this is that kids watching this movie are being told you can't see a woman's breasts on television, but it's fine to see her blown apart, mutilated, or raped.[18]

42.575

Stanley Kubrick's movie about the Vietnam War, *Full Metal Jacket*, gives female viewers a rare, instructive, and frightening look into how men entering the United States military forces are trained to think of violence as sexually exciting. The soldier's ditty, "This is my weapon, this is my gun; one is for business, the other for fun," is only one of many examples of a military folklore that links sex and violence. Even at the highest levels of military strategizing, more subtle but equally phallic imagery is used to describe the "thrust" of a missile or its "penetration" capability.[19]

42.576

Violent imagery is so deeply embedded in popular culture that rooting it out of the public consciousness would take far more than restricting publication and distribution of violent pornography alone. Yet, whether or not pornography causes violent sexual behavior, it does help purvey an ideology of violence that encourages toleration of an extraordinarily high incidence of violent crime. But television and Hollywood movies, because of their wider distribution and the stamp of legitimacy they carry, do even more to support the belief that violence is natural and inevitable. Regardless of what conclusions psychologists draw about actual one-to-one harm, women seem to know instinctively, by the fears aroused, that depicting acts of violence for their entertainment value, in whatever medium, keeps women at risk of rape and murder.

42.577

Desensitization to Images of Horror

42.578

In November 1963, millions of Americans, without expectation, became witnesses to an actual murder. Those who saw it will never forget seeing Lee Harvey Oswald walking quietly but reluctantly alongside the guard escorting him, then suddenly doubling over, his face contorting into a grimace. His shock and pain were so vivid that the television audience could almost feel them. But then the scene was played again—and again and again, until we could anticipate every little change in his facial expression. The more it was shown, the less real it seemed. Some people grew accustomed to watching it without feeling horror.

42.579

Over the next several years, television viewers watched the Vietnam War up close, in their living rooms—even in their kitchens and dining rooms while they ate their meals. After the news was over, they could watch Westerns or crime dramas in which people were routinely shot and killed. This daily blending of reality and fantasy could have had a desensitizing effect on some adults and caused confusion in children, who could not distinguish the actual violence from the feigned.

42.580

Every age has had its version of pornography, but recent technological advances have led to greater arousal of physical responses without emotional inhibitions. Film and television have so inundated us with realistic images of horror that we have been conditioned to respond with indifference, perhaps in self-protection. Those who seek to shock or arouse, as some of the producers of pornography do, must invent fresh and exciting images. In the case of violent pornography, this means moving far beyond the knife-at-the-throat rape to slicing off nipples or shoving scorpions into vaginas. Frequent, routine exposure even to these images soon dulls their impact.

42.581

When the space shuttle challenger exploded on the television screen, ending the lives of the seven human beings aboard, the television commentator maintained his professional objectivity and reported flatly: "A major malfunction has occurred." This makes a glaring contrast to the tearful cry of the radio reporter at the crash of the dirigible Hindenburg in 1937: "Horrible! Horrible! Oh, the humanity! Oh, the humanity!" One response to violent pornography that might motivate public activism would be to look at the human beings pictures and cry "Oh, the humanity!"[20] on their behalf.

42.582

Commercialization of Human Needs

It is by now commonplace to think of advertising as the manipulater, for profit, of human desires. In recent years, as the United States has changed from an industrial to a service economy, the creation of new "needs" has been considered crucial to economic stability. These needs have become seemingly more psychological than utilitarian and as new needs are created, new products are offered to fill them. For example, teenagers buy expensive designer jeans not for their sturdiness or comfort but for the image they convey. A significant element of this desired image is sex appeal. Thus, advertising offers the subtle promise of sexual fulfillment.

42.584

What advertising only hints at, pornography makes vivid. For $10, a customer can nourish fantasies of sexual fulfillment by looking at a magazine full of color photographs of people he does not know, personally engaged in any conceivable sexual activity. For $2 a minute, the patron of a live sex shop can stand in a private booth and "command" an anonymous women behind a plastic screen to take off her clothes and act out his fantasies.

42.585

The danger here is not the sex itself but the risk that a manufactured need for instant, no-strings-attached sexual gratification will reduce the complex gift of human sexuality to a purely physical response. Pornography is, as one movie title puts it, "not a love story." The PCUS statement of 1973 describes it as "the intrusion of a stranger who neither knows nor cares about the people involved in intimate physical processes and thus reduces what is happening to bare physical functions without meaning or personal involvement."

42.586

In offering photographs or films of real women and men as anonymous sex objects, pornography reduces these human beings to commodities. The compassion that pictures of sexual abuse would ordinarily arouse is undermined, because there is nothing to be known about the reality behind the visual image.

42.587

In contrast, Mary Pellauer writes, "I will never be able to see another item of pornography without being flooded by questions about the women pictures: Was this one an incest victim? Was that one coerced into this by violence or poverty? What was it like for her to be filmed chained, smiling, with a knife at her genitals? What was her pay? What percentage of the profit was that? Does she have colitis as a result of the nervous stress? When I go into a porn shop to investigate, the questions multiply: Who are the men in this shop? Why do they look so furtive? Why do they scamper away from me and my companions?"[21]

42.588

Having the answers to these questions would make the image ineffective, because caring would negate the promise of disengaged, noncommittal gratification.

42.589

Widespread Addiction to Obsessive-Compulsive Behaviors

42.590

The objectification or abuse of women is not the only troubling aspect of pornography. What it suggests about the state of males and their sexuality is quite alarming. A forty-eight billion dollar industry has to draw from the pockets of a very large number of income-earning men. It cannot rely solely on a sleazy underworld. The clientele the task force members saw on the trip to Times Square included men who would fit easily into our home neighborhoods. Why do men choose to spend their money this way? What do they get out of

151

anonymous, vicarious sex that they do not get from a committed relationship? What psychological needs does pornography serve, and how else might those needs be met?

42.591

The authors of the best-selling study of contemporary American culture, *Habits of the Heart*, claim that, "American cultural traditions define personality, achievement, and the purpose of human life in ways that leave the individual suspended in glorious, but terrifying, isolation."[22]

42.592

Astonishing numbers of people soothe that terrifying isolation through obsessive-compulsive behavior with alcohol, drugs, food, and abuse of their spouses and children.

42.593

Many new "Twelve Step" treatment programs have sprung up on the model of Alcoholics Anonymous, which establishes a community of recovering peers in which individuals can safely admit their powerlessness over the addiction, surrender control of their lives to God or a "higher power," and make "a searching and fearless moral inventory" of themselves.[23]

42.594

One of these, Sex Addicts Anonymous, posits that people who are obsessed with sex have unmet, essential human needs that have nothing to do with sex per se. Women with feelings of inferiority may rely on sexual attractiveness as a measure of their worth and seek out constant validation from different sexual partners. Some women pose nude or perform in sexually explicit films as a quicker route to male approval.[24]

42.595

Some men constantly test sexual prowess in an attempt to boost a poor self-image. Physical intimacy with a prostitute may allay fears of emotional intimacy with wives or mothers or daughters. Frequent orgasm may produce a euphoria that eases the stresses of life.

42.596

It is often said that pornography itself is addictive, but this confuses cause and effect. Certainly, pornography can be used in compulsive ways, creating and facilitating masturbatory fantasies as an outlet for emotional frustration or a cure for loneliness. The impulse to masturbate is natural and can be used positively in maintaining a healthy sexual life. But when it or any other human activity—even work or church attendance—becomes obsessive, filling a void left by lack of self-esteem, the failure of relationships, or a sense of meaninglessness, there is cause for concern. Such concern should be expressed compassionately, with attention to the person's human condition. Finding fault with the images themselves misses the point and leaves suffering people unhealed.

42.597

Unequal Responsibility for Human Relationships

42.598

Over the last thirty years, with improvements in contraception and increased affluence, American women have begun to exercise greater sexual and economic independence. While this has brought about significant changes in their expectations of men and male-female relationships, most women still measure the value of life in relational terms. Many men, on the other hand, seem to be backing away from intimacy with and commitment to women.[25]

42.599

In *The Hearts of Men*, Barbara Ehrenreich claims that American men have been rebelling since the 1950s against the obligations of marriage and family. She traces this tendency in popular culture, particularly through the rapid growth of Hugh Hefner's *Playboy* enterprises. Many men, of course, insist that they read *Playboy* for its high-quality writing and that the nude photographs are only incidental.

42.600

Whether or not they are deliberately fleeing from responsibility for human relationships, there is measurable evidence that millions of men are, at least, avoiding the consequences of their sexual behavior. Late Census Bureau data indicates that currently, 8.8 million American mothers of minor children are raising children in the absence of their fathers. Only 2.1 million of these women, less than a quarter, receive child-support payments in the amount ordered by the court. Another 1.1 million are receiving part of the support due, leaving 5.6 million who are getting no financial support at all from the fathers.[26]

42.601

Some public concern is aroused by the extremely high incidence of teen-age pregnancy, but the focus is still on the girls' sexual behavior, rather than the responsibility of the boys, who abandon their pregnant partners about ninety percent of the time.[27]

42.602

The quest for "free" sex is, of course, not new. Pornography has not brought it about, but it does give it vivid ideological expression. Despite the availability of contraception, which is still neither entirely effective nor entirely safe, there is no such thing as free and unencumbered sex for women. It has costs: possible pregnancy, loss of esteem, the risk of abuse and violence. The AIDS epidemic has brought new risks to both sexes.

42.603

Yet the greatest human cost of a commercialized, dehumanized, and abusive sexual ideology may be the loss of complex and challenging human relationships. Some opponents of pornography appear to offer solutions to the crisis in male-female relationships by restoring women to their traditional roles, at the cost of gains made in freedom and equality since the 1950s. The task force, however, agrees with Elizabeth Fox-Genovese that "the chasm between men and women results from the breakdown of an old society, not from the birth of a new one."[28]

42.604

Summary

42.605

The consensus of the task force is that pornography is primarily a symptom of problems that are very deeply embedded in our culture. Pornography is an extreme variation on common attitudes and beliefs. It reflects and reinforces certain injurious stereotypes:

- that women exist to serve men's needs;

- that sex is an adversarial relationship in which one person exercises power over another;

- that violence is natural, acceptable, and sexually stimulating;

- that commitment to human relationships threatens individual freedom;

- that self-gratification is the highest good.

42.606

The proliferation of pornographic materials and the raging debate about their propriety and impact provide an opportunity to address these underlying issues from the perspective of the Christian faith. Perhaps the problems of today's culture can best be summarized as the denial of the compassionate community in which Christians profess to believe. A right relationship with God depends on a right relationship with each other. In this culture, such community is fractured by exaggerated individualism, undergirded by sexism, and fostered by competitiveness that may lead to exploitation.

42.607

Fox-Genovese concludes her paper on pornography by indicting the "failure of individualism," while recognizing that in American culture, community values based on equality and mutuality between women and men to not in fact exist. To reverse destructive individualism and the further polarization between women and men, she claims that " . . . we need collective principles and yes, a collective vision, on the basis of which we can demand respect for women on a new basis and as the necessary foundation for our society's respect for itself."[29]

42.608

Christians themselves are a diverse community and the church must examine its own history to understand its role in shaping cultural values. Is it naive to think that Christians can create a compassionate community—a healthy, whole community that models in its own life the values by which it hopes to transform society?

42.609

Karl Barth wrote that what seems to be unnatural from the perspective of the world becomes natural for the follower of Christ.[30] Believers are the body of Christ—a body rent even unto death by compassion. Faithfulness to Christ's doctrine of love and equal regard for women and men as being created in God's image are necessary and effective antidotes to the degradation and abuse that pornography represents.

XI. Findings

42.610

The Task Force on Pornography has examined this issue from as many perspectives as it could identify. Not only has it probed psychological, sociological, legal, historical, and feminist opinion on pornography but, throughout the process, it has also sought to look at this complex issue within a biblical and theological framework. Its worship and study have led it to a deeper understanding of the integral relationship between our faith and issues of pornography, sexuality, and human history. It presents the following findings with the hope that others in the Presbyterian Church (U.S.A.) will share what it believes about the significance of this difficult issue for the church in our time.

42.611

1. *Pornography is both a symptom and a cause of human alienation, reflecting the failure of human sexual relationships to fulfill God's intended creation.* Pornography in our culture reflects nothing new in human history, but it exposes in graphic sexual images the systemic distortion of power in human relationships. It not only reflects a historic pattern of dominance and submission in sexual relationships, but it also serves as a reinforcing agent to perpetuate that pattern in human behavior. Pornography's images of sexuality violate God's images of human dignity and sexual pleasure based on mutual love and respect.

42.612

2. *Pornography is not simply the display of human flesh or sexual behavior.* There is nothing inherently sinful or dirty in our physical bodies or sexuality. Neither is there anything inherently evil or offensive in images of our bodies or of sexual behavior. Human beings are created with the possibility for joy and celebration in sexuality; images that convey love, caring, warmth, commitment and genuine mutual pleasure between equals should be seen positively. Such images may be therapeutic and may stimulate healthy, constructive, egalitarian sexual relationships.

42.613

3. *Understanding the historic oppression of women is central to understanding the issue of pornography.* Pornography will continue its appeal as long as sexual arousal is stimulated by images of power over another person, usually male over female. Energy needs to be directed, not only toward confronting pornographic materials that eroticize the subordination of women but also toward raising the status of women in every way possible. This includes education offering alternative images of mutual respect, dignity, and justice in all human relationships, as well as support for economic, legal, and educational programs to empower women.

42.614

4. *Pornography victimizes men as well as women.* By perpetuating the erotic images of power, violence, and abuse, men remain vulnerable to this false standard of masculinity. Pornography represents male sexuality as selfishly brutal, contributing to attitudes that deprive men of full human dignity and prevent them from experiencing the ultimate pleasure found in relationships of loving mutuality. Educational efforts, while exposing the historical pattern of male dominance and female subjugation, should avoid polarization between women and men and seek to restore wholeness in all persons and relationships.

42.615

5. *Pornography must be understood as an issue of people and not only materials.* Pornography is inseparable from the women and men who play a role in producing it, many of whom also become its victims. Increased attention also should be paid to the testimony of those who have been historically silent on this and other issues of sexuality—women, people of color, homosexuals, people with disabilities, and the economically disadvantaged who often live in areas most influenced by pornography. The gospel of grace, forgiveness, and acceptance should be communicated in welcoming anyone who seeks help from church.

42.616

6. *Other broad issues of sexual morality—such as sexual activity between persons not married to each other, homosexuality, and specific sexual practices—need to be addressed in their own right and in terms other than pornography.* A task force established by the 199th General Assembly (1987) is at work examining the wider issues of human sexuality including its moral dimensions.

42.617

7. *Pornography eroticizes power through both heterosexual and homosexual images and affects the lives of women and men of both sexual orientations.* Homophobia should not motivate our concerns and actions regarding pornography.

42.618

8. *Because sexual themes elicit responses that are very personal and intensely subjective, disagreement is to be expected when applying any definition of pornography to specific materials.* Discussion of the pornography issue provides Christians with the opportunity to explore their attitudes toward positive and negative sexual images. Diversity of opinion should be encouraged within a climate of trust and openness.

42.619

9. *Child pornography is the photographic record of actual child sexual abuse. Laws to prohibit its production and distribution need to be supported and vigorously enforced.* The term "child pornography" accurately applies only to material that depicts actual children. It should be restricted to this legal interpretation, which has broad consensus. We may have legitimate concerns about the influence of pornography on children, but our language should not refer to the entire spectrum of these influences as "child

pornography." The picture of an actual ten year-old engaged in sexual behavior is called pornography; a ten year-old child calling Dial-a-Porn is not.

42.620

Increased attention must be paid to all forms of sexual violence, including incest, marital rape and abuse that occur in families. Education and support services must be strengthened to empower children, women and men to resist all forms of sexual coercion. Our concern for abused and exploited children in this society must extend to children around the world who continue to be victims in the production of child pornography.

42.621

10. *Efforts to address the issue of pornography should not rely primarily on the use of law and governmental regulation.* Current methods of regulating pornography depend on existing obscenity law, an approach that is subject to conflict over interpretation that often paralyzes action. Reliance on obscenity law, while calling attention to the issue, requires the tedious examination and prosecution of materials, involving lengthy court hearings and questionable use of limited resources.

42.622

Risks of using the law to regulate pornography are serious ones. Christians in the United States live in a democratic society that places high value on the rights and freedoms of individuals. In a culture rich in diversity, such a value inevitably leads to conflict of rights. The First Amendment to the Constitution guarantees not only freedom for Christians to promote the good news of God's love in Jesus Christ, but also guarantees freedom for others to espouse all manner of ideas that Christians find offensive. Christians live in a pluralistic society that is often disturbing in its lack of common values. However, a review of history reveals that attempts by some to control the speech and writing of others can result in a climate of repression and censorship. The most vulnerable targets are often voices of change. Freedom of expression is a precious right which deserves the strongest constitutional protection from governmental regulation.

42.623

11. *The harm caused by pornography is best understood as part of a complex relationship of human dynamics. The fundamental harm of pornography lies in its influence to perpetuate distorted sexual images and behaviors.* Honest debate is appropriate in trying to determine the effect of pornography on human behavior. It is virtually impossible to ascertain a conclusive correlation between the use of specific pornographic materials and any specific behavior, since human beings act in response to complex sociological, psychological, and biological factors. Pornography may be a contributing catalyst in acts of violence, such as rape, battering and incest, but it is overly simplistic to identify it as a singular target. The strongest correlation to violent or abusive behavior is a personal history of having been abused. Patterns of violence are often learned and perpetuated apart from any connection to pornography. The destructive power of pornography is in providing imagery that produces and reinforces models of sexual violence, exploitation and dominance. The use of pornography, by an individual or a society, insures that attitudes toward sexuality will continue to be influenced by images that negate human dignity and mutuality. On many levels, pornography contributes to alienation in human relationships and distorts the sexual integrity of both women and men.

42.624

12. *Widespread sexuality education provides the greatest hope for disempowering pornography.* Sexually explicit materials of all kinds permeate our society and bombard children and young people with negative images of sexuality. Those who attempt to

protect children from materials need to recognize legal conflict over the interference with adult rights. Efforts to control the display of sexually explicit materials and to provide technical methods for limiting home access to television programs and telephone services are entirely appropriate. However, since it is virtually impossible to escape exposure to all kinds of distorted sexual images, massive educational efforts need to be undertaken. Children, youth, and adults need opportunities to discuss sexuality and sexual materials in families, churches, and schools. Positive Christian values affirming the goodness of human sexuality foster personal feelings of self-esteem and acknowledge respect and dignity of all people.

42.625

13. *Pornography is an issue of profound significance that Presbyterians should seek to understand.* The issue of pornography is one that Presbyterians may be inclined to avoid or regard as irrelevant to themselves and society. Those Presbyterians who called for this study were wise to recognize the need for a thorough investigation of the significance of the pornography issue. A proper study of pornography leads to examination of the broad fabric of society and of the values that affect all intimate human relationships. It provides opportunity for Christians to deepen their understanding not only of pornography, but also of their calling to proclaim God's intended wholeness for individuals and for society.

42.626

14. *The report of the Attorney General's Commission on Pornography should be seen as a valuable educational resource on pornography.* Careful reading of the report reveals the struggles of commission members to define pornography, examine First Amendment issues, investigate current data on the industry, and assess the effects of pornography on children, youth, and adults. Valuable insight is provided in the personal testimony of some of those who appeared before the commission and in the different analyses expressed in each commissioner's personal statement. However, the commission's report is best understood when studied in conjunction with the opinion of its critics, who question the commission's findings on the causal relationship between pornography and behavior and its recommendations for increased regulation of pornography under existing obscenity law.

42.627

15. *The study of pornography provides a unique opportunity for the church to examine its own history and use of images, particularly its language.* For centuries, religious tradition authorizes and perpetuated the dominant rule of men and the subordinate weakness of women. For centuries the church has also used images that are exclusively masculine in reference to both humanity and God. Through such images, Christians have internalized powerful verbal and visual messages that women are not fully human and not fully created in the image of God. Efforts to address the dehumanizing power of pornographic images should be matched with continuing efforts to promote full human dignity through male and female religious images.

42.628

16. *Valuable understanding is found in the study of the pornography issue by other religious bodies.* Exploration of this issue by Jews and Christians of many denominations reveals both a unity of concern about the destructive influence of pornography and a diversity of opinion on the role of religious institutions in addressing it. Interfaith study and activity should promote opportunities for the people of God to affirm their common faith in the goodness of God's gift of sexuality and reject attempts to distort it.

42.629

17. *Two previous studies of the issue of pornography serve as valuable continuing resources for study.* The following theological affirmations are reflected in both the

1973 PCUS statement on "Pornography, Obscenity, and Censorship" and the 1974 UPCUSA study on "Dignity and Exploitation" and are affirmed by this study as well:

a. Human physical life is willed and blessed by God and should be accepted and used with thanksgiving, joy, pleasure, and responsibility.

b. There is nothing inherently dirty, obscene, or sinful about any aspect of our physical existence or relationships.

c. Human beings are created for living together with respect for the dignity and value God gives every human life.

d. Male and female are equally created in the image of God and attempts to prove any intrinsic superiority of the male by referring to masculine language about God are "wrongheaded" and "biblically unsound."

e. Even though dominance and subordination were uniformly the cultural pattern in biblical times, as well as our own, Scripture as a whole does not support a mandate for the suppression of anyone.

f. The image of God contains a mandate for human freedom, self-determination, and fulfillment, and we must be alert to all forms of human exploitation.

g. The point of tension between agape and erotic love is not to put the spiritual and the sensual dimensions of our humanity in opposition but to keep us from self-serving rationalizations that make love a bargain rather than a gift.

h. Covenant love should be a basis for our judgments about sexual materials, measuring both materials and approaches toward them by the intentions expressed and the goals served, not by the degree of explicitness of sexual imagery.

42.630

XII. Recommendations

42.631

As a result of its study, the Task Force on Pornography of the Committee on Women's Concerns (COWC) and the Council on Women and the Church (COWAC) recommends that the 200th General Assembly (1988):

42.632

1. Receive the report with deep appreciation for the work of the task force and recommend it for study throughout the church.

42.633

2. Direct the Office of General Assembly to print this report as a study document (including study guide and response form) and send it to every congregation, presbytery, and synod. (Estimated cost to be carried by the Office of General Assembly.)

42.634

3. Direct the Women's Unit to compile responses to this study (as provided for in the study guide and response form) by congregations, presbyteries, and synods and, with the Committee on Social Witness Policy, to submit a report and recommendations for public policy to the 203rd General Assembly (1991). Recommendations adopted by the 200th General Assembly (1988) for action by the Presbyterian Church (U.S.A.) and its members are to be regarded as interim policy until recommendations are prepared for the 203rd General Assembly (1991) in response to study of this report.

42.635

4. Reaffirm that the 200th General Assembly (1988) of the Presbyterian Church (U.S.A.)

opposes pornography as stated by previous General Assemblies (1984, 1985, 1986, and 1987) and as defined in this report (paragraph 42.294).

42.636

5. Affirm that the Presbyterian Church (U.S.A.) stands opposed to both pornography and censorship and encourages Presbyterians to participate in organizations committed to protecting First Amendment rights, as outlined in this report.

42.637

6. Urge Presbyterians to develop personal and group strategies for action, including:

   a. writing letters to the media with views in opposition to pornography;

   b. communicating with television networks and cable services about opposition to programming considered to be pornographic;

   c. communicating with store owners about opposition to the inappropriate display of pornographic materials;

   d. boycotting materials and companies which market or produce pornographic materials.

42.638

7. Encourage Presbyterians to participate in interfaith efforts, which study and address the issue of pornography.

42.639

8. Encourage Presbyterians to offer support and counsel to persons who believe they have been victimized in any way by pornography and to communicate with members of Congress in support of Pornography Victims Protection legislation. (A copy of this bill, H.R. 1213, is found in the Background Materials.)

42.640

9. Encourage Presbyterians to study the issue of child pornography, become aware of state and federal laws prohibiting it, and support legal authorities in the full enforcement of these laws.

42.641

10. Request that the General Assembly, since sexism is perceived as a fundamental cause of pornography, address the systemic roots of pornography through the following actions related to the status of women in society and in the church:

   a. reaffirm the statement of the 196th General Assembly (1984) which advocated "passage of the Equal Rights Amendment" based on the support of the Assemblies of both former denominations in 1970, 1972, 1974, 1975, 1977, 1978, and 1982, and recommend that Presbyterians communicate with the President and U.S. Senators and Representatives regarding the need for the passage and ratification of the Equal Rights Amendment;

   b. reaffirm support for the United Nations Convention for the Elimination of Discrimination Against Women approved by the 199th General Assembly (1987), and direct that the Stated Clerk communicate this action to all U.S. Senators, urging ratification;

   c. reaffirm the policy of previous General Assemblies regarding the use of inclusive language in the entire life of the Church.

42.642   [Deleted by Assembly action.]

159

42.643

11. Direct the Committee on Justice for Women to review and update previous studies adopted by the General Assembly on issues of women and sexual abuse (rape, sexual harassment, sexual exploitation of women) and to recommend ways of increasing the effective usage of the resources related to those studies by the church.

42.644

12. Request the Education and Congregational Nurture Unit to:

    a. complete the work now in process in developing and producing a proposed sexuality education curriculum for junior and senior high school young people;

    b. review the *Bibliography of Religious Publications on Sex Education and Sexuality* included in the Background Materials of this report and prepare a recommended list of resources which are currently available;

    c. gather and (or) develop (1) materials for pastors on counseling children, youth, and adults on sexual abuse and (2) materials for children on how to resist sexual abuse.

42.645

13. Direct the Mission Responsibility Through Investment Committee to investigate the relationship between business and the pornography industry, including ownership of nonpornography firms by people in the pornography industry and corporate profits generated by pornography such as telephone services, and determine if appropriate stockholder action should be recommended to the 201st General Assembly (1989).

42.646

14. Direct the Women's Unit to request funding up to $10,000 for the Ecumenical Decade for Solidarity with Women, a major effort of the World Council of Churches to address the issues of violence against women.

XIII. Endnotes

42.647

I. Introduction

II. Theological Statement

III. Why Study Pornography Now?

    1. "Pornography, Obscenity and Censorship," *Minutes of the General Assembly*, (PCUS), Part I, 1973, p. 104.

    2. Unsworth, Richard P. *Dignity and Exploitation*, 1974, p. 22 (written for the study committee of the Advisory Council on Church and Society).

IV. What is Pornography? A discussion of Definition: How to Recognize Pornography

    1. Kendrick, Walter, *The Secret Museum: Pornography in Modern Culture*, 1987, p. 13.

    2. *The Random House Dictionary of the English Language*, 2nd ed., 1987, p. 1506.

    3. "The Victims of Pornography," statement by the American Lutheran Church Office of Church and Society, 1985, p. 2.

    4. Unsworth, Richard P. , *Dignity and Exploitation*, p. 12.

    5. Welbourne-Moglia, Ann, "Statement to the U.S. Commission on Pornography, Houston, Texas, September 12, 1985," *SIECUS* (Sex Information and Education Council in the U.S.) *Report*, November, 1985, p. 8.

    6. *Ibid.*, p. 8.

7. American Lutheran Church statement, p. 2.
8. *Pornography Kit*, prepared by the Division of Mission in Canada of the United Church of Canada, 1984, p. 1.
9. Resolution from the National Conference of the National Organization for Women (NOW), July 19-21, 1984, reprinted in the *National NOW Times*, August/September 1985.
10. Steinem, Gloria, "Erotica vs. Pornography," *Outrageous Acts and Everyday Rebellions*, 1983, pp. 219-230.
11. *Final Report of the Attorney General's Commission on Pornography*, Rutledge Hill Press edition, 1986, p. 7.
12. *Ibid.*, pp. 542, 7.
13. *Ibid.*, pp. 7-8.
14. Kirk, Jerry R., *The Mind Polluters*, 1985, p. 108.
15. Attorney General's Commission Report, pp. 7-8.
16. *Ibid.*, 8.

V. Current Statistics on the Pornography Industry

1. "Statistical Fact Sheet," produced by the New York office of Women Against Pornography (WAP).
2. "Significant Facts," Resource Booklet from the *Third Annual Consultation of the National Coalition Against Pornography* (NCAP), September 4-6, 1985, p. 19.
3. *Presbytery of Cincinnati Church and Society Newsletter*, single page reprint of the Special Committee on Pornography, Update 1986.
4. *NAPCRO* (National Anti-Pornography Civil Rights Organization) *Reporter*, September 1986 (1, 5).
5. *Ibid.*
6. *Ibid.*
7. *Ibid.*
8. *Ibid.*
9. *Ibid.*
10. *Ibid.*
11. *Ibid.*
12. *Ibid.*
13. *Ibid.*
14. WAP Fact Sheet.
15. *NAPCRO Reporter*.
16. *Ibid.*
17. *The Cincinnati Enquirer*, September 20, 1984, quoted in the NCAP Resource Booklet, p. 19.
18. *NAPCRO Reporter*.
19. NCAP Resource Booklet, p. 19.
20. *NAPCRO Reporter*.
21. NCAP Resource Booklet, p. 20.

22. WAP Fact Sheet.
23. NCAP Resource Booklet, p. 20.
24. Presbytery of Cincinnati Update 1986.
25. *NAPCRO Reporter.*
26. WAP Fact Sheet.
27. *NAPCRO Reporter.*
28. *Ibid.*
29. NCAP Resource Booklet, p. 19.
30. *NAPCRO Reporter.*
31. *G-CAP Strategies* (handout of the Georgia Coalition Against Pornography), August 12, 1987, p. 1.
32. *Ibid.*
33. Federal Bureau of Investigation, *Uniform Crime Reports for the United States,* 1983 (p. 98), 1984 (p. 94), 1985 (p. 95), 1986 (p. 96).
34. Kirk, Jerry R., *The Mind Polluters,* 1985, pp. 190-191.

VI. What Are the Effects of Pornography? A Discussion of Harm

1. *Final Report of the Attorney General's Commission on Pornography,* Rutledge Hill Press edition, 1986, p. 34.
2. *Ibid.,* p. 34.
3. *Ibid.,* p. 39.
4. *Ibid.,* p. 41.
5. *Ibid.,* p. 42.
6. *Ibid.,* p. 42.
7. *Ibid.,* p. 42.
8. *Ibid.,* p. 43.
9. *Ibid.,* p. 43.
10. *Ibid.,* p. 47.
11. *Ibid.,* pp. XIII-XIV.
12. *Ibid.,* p. 543.
13. *Text of the Public Hearings on Ordinances to Add Pornography as Discrimination Against Women,* Minneapolis City Council, December 12-13, 1983, pp. 19-20.
14. Attorney General's Commission Report, pp. 197-223.
15. Nobile, Philip, and Eric Nadler, *United States of America vs. Sex,* 1986, p. 39.
16. MacKinnon, Catherine A., "Pornography: Reality, Not Fantasy," *Village Voice,* March 26, 1985.
17. Stoltenburg, John, "Pornography and Freedom," *Changing Men,* Fall 1985, pp. 6, 47.
18. English, Deirdre, "The Politics of Porn: Can Feminists Walk the Line?"
19. Nagayama Hall, Gordon C., "Pornography: A Cause of Sexually Aggressive Behavior or an Effect of a Sexist Society?," *PHEWA* (Presbyterian Health Education and Welfare Association) *Newsletter,* p. 7.

20. *Ibid.*, p. 7.

21. Attorney General's Commission Report, footnote 47, p. 41.

22. Jacobs, Caryn, "Patterns of Violence: A Feminist Perspective on the Regulation of Pornography," *Harvard Women's Law Journal*, Spring 1984 (7, 1), pp. 5-24.

23. National Council of the Churches of Christ in the U.S.A., *Violence and Sexual Violence in Film, Television, Cable and Home Video,* study report adopted September 19, 1985, p. 9.

24. Welbourne-Moglia, Ann, *SIECUS Report*, p. 9.

VII. A History of Pornography Regulation in the United States

1. Grossman, Tom, "Obscenity and the Law," Resource Booklet from the *Third Annual Consultation of the National Coalition Against Pornography* (NCAP), September 4-6, 1985, p. 78.

2. *The Random House Dictionary of the English Language*, 1st ed., 1966, p. 994.

3. "Constitution of the United States of American," *Collier's Encyclopedia*, 1966 (7), p. 256.

4. Grossman, p. 78.

5. Kendrick, Walter, *The Secret Museum: Pornography in Modern Culture*, 1987.

6. "The War Against Pornography," *Newsweek*, March 18, 1985, p. 65.

7. Stanmeyer, William A., *The Seduction of Society*, 1984, p. 96.

8. *Ibid.*, p. 96.

9. *Final Report of the Attorney General's Commission on Pornography*, Rutledge Hill Press Edition, 1096, p. 16.

10. Stanmeyer, p. 96.

11. *Ibid.*, p. 96.

12. Allen, Walter, "The Writer and the Frontiers of Tolerance," *Chandos*, 1962, p. 144.

13. Elliot, "Against Pornography," *Harpers*, 1965, pp. 50-51.

14. Color, Harry, *Obscenity and Public Morality: Censorship in a Liberal Society*, Chicago: University of Chicago Press, 1969, p. 242.

15. Kronhausen, Eberhard and Phyllis, *Pornography and the Law: The Psychology of Erotic Realism and Pornography*, 1959.

16. Kendrick, p. 208.

17. Attorney General's Commission Report, p. 17.

18. *Ibid.*, pp. 17-18.

19. *Ibid.*, p. 309.

20. *Ibid.*, p. 18.

21. *Ibid.*, p. 18.

22. *Ibid.*, p. 18.

23. Stanmeyer, p. 88.

24. McMaster, Henry Dargan, "Obscenity Prosecution in the Federal Courts," Resource Booklet from the *Third Annual Consultation of the National Coalition Against Pornography* (NCAP), September 4-6, 1985, pp. 99-105.

25. Kirk, Jerry R., *The Mind Polluters*, 1985, p. 42.

26. "5 Indicted . . . , " *Des Moines Register*, October 9, 1987.

27. *State of Oregon v. Earl A. Henry*, January 21, 1987, p. 3.

28. *Ibid.*, p. 20.

29. *Ibid.*, p. 21.

30. *Richard Pope and Charles G. Morrison v. Illinois*, May 4, 1987, p. 1918.

32. Kilpatrick, James J., "Court makes definition of obscenity muddier than ever," *Des Moines Register*, May 1987.

33. Blakely, Mary Kay, "Is One Woman's Sexuality Another Woman's Pornography," *Ms*, April 1985, p. 40.

34. "An Ordinance of the City of Minneapolis," printed as a single page handout by Women Against Pornography.

35. Blakely, Mary Kay, p. 44.

36. American Booksellers Association v. William H. Hudnut, III (Mayor of Indianapolis), No. 84-3147, August 27, 1985, p. 3.

37. *Ibid.*, p. 10.

38. *Ibid.*, pp. 11-12.

39. *Ibid.*, pp. 13-14.

40. *Ibid.*, p. 19.

41. Rush, Florence, Letter to members of the National Organization for Women, October 27, 1986.

42. *Ibid.*

VIII. Government Studies of Pornography

1. *Collier's Year Book Covering the Year 1970*, 1971, pp. 186-187.

2. "Charter of the Attorney General's Commission on Pornography," *Final Report of the Attorney General's Commission on Pornography*, Rutledge Hill Press edition, 1986.

3. U.S. Department of Justice Press Release, May 20, 1985, p. 1.

4. Attorney General's Commission Report, p. 7.

5. *Ibid.*, pp. 19-21.

6. *Ibid.*, p. 24.

7. *Ibid.*, p. 24.

8. *Ibid.*, p. 26.

9. *Ibid.*, p. 26.

10. *Ibid.*, p. 26-27.

11. *Ibid.*, p. 489.

12. *Ibid.*, p. 29.

13. *Ibid.*, p. 30.

14. *Ibid.*, p. 66.

15. *Ibid.*, p. 132.

16. *Ibid.*, p. 130.

17. *Ibid.*, p. 69.

18. McMaster, Henry Dargan, "Obscenity Prosecution in the Federal Courts," Resource Booklet of the Third Annual Consultation of the National Coalition Against Pornography (NCAP), September 4-6, 1985, pp. 106-109.

19. Attorney General's Commission Report, p. 67.

20. *Ibid.*, p. 138.

21. *Ibid.*, p. 134.

22. *Ibid.*, p. 19-21.

IX. What Should Be Done About Pornography? Four Divergent Views

1. Fox-Genovese, Elizabeth, "Pornography and Individual Rights: The Issues," transcript of a lecture at Grinnell College, Grinnell, Iowa, February 18, 1987, p. 4.

2. *Ibid.*, pp. 4-5.

3. Kirk, Jerry R., *The Mind Polluters*, 1985, p. 14.

4. *Ibid.*, p. 15.

5. Stanmeyer, William A., *The Seduction of Society*, pp. 3-4.

6. *Ibid.*, p. 5.

7. Kirk, p. 17.

8. Stanmeyer, pp. 18-25.

9. Kirk, p. 26.

10. *Ibid.*, pp. 80-81.

11. *Ibid.*, p. 70.

12. "Significant Facts," Resource Booklet of the *Third Annual Consultation of the National Coalition Against Pornography* (NCAP), September 4-6, 1985, pp. 19-21.

13. Dobson, James, "Combatting the Darkness," reprint of an article from *Focus on the Family* magazine, August 1986, p. 4.

14. Kirk, pp. 47-63; Stanmeyer, pp. 67-78.

15. Kirk, pp. 23-24.

16. Stanmeyer, p. 77.

17. *Ibid.*, p. 78.

18. Kirk, p. 108.

19. *Ibid.*, p. 113.

20. Focus of the National Coalition Against Pornography, handout dated February 19, 1987.

21. Kirk, Jerry R., brochure entitled *A Winnable War: How to fight pornography in your community*, 1987, p. 11.

22. *Ibid.*, pp. 11-23.

23. *Ibid.*, pp. 30-42.

24. Foundational document of the Religious Alliance Against Pornography, July 25, 1986.

25. Cizik, Richard, brochure entitled *You Can Make A Difference: A Citizen's Guide to Political Action*, pp. 3-5.

26. Hallman, Steve, "Time misses real point of decency movement." *Concerned Citizens for Community Values Newsletter*, October 1986 (4, 5), p. 2.

27. Kirk, *The Mind Polluters*, pp. 204-205.

28. Fox-Genovese, pp. 4-5.

29. Dworkin, Andrea, *Pornography: Men Possessing Women*, 1979, pp. 13-24.

30. *Ibid.*, p. 24.

31. Attorney General's Commission Report, pp. 198-199.

32. MacKinnon, Catherine A., "Pornography, Civil Rights, and Speech," *Harvard Civil Rights-Civil Liberties Law Review*, Winter 1985 (20, 1), p. 18.

33. Dworkin, Andres, "Against the Male Flood: Censorship, Pornography and Equality," *Harvard Women's Law Journal*, 1985 (8), pp. 7-9.

34. News Release, National Organization for Women, July 9, 1986.

35. Kaminer, Wendy, *Women Against Pornography: Where We Stand on the First Amendment and Obscenity*, 1980.

36. MacKinnon, Catherine A., lecture at Grinnell College, Grinnell, Iowa, February 18, 1987.

37. Jacobs, Caryn, "Patterns of Violence: A Feminist Perspective on the Regulation of Pornography," *Harvard Women's Law Journal*, Spring 1984 (7, 1), p. 44.

38. *Ibid.*, pp. 45-46.

39. Rich, Adrienne, "The Images," *A Wild Patience Has Taken Me Thus Far*, 1981, pp. 3-4.

40. Fox-Genovese, p. 4.

41. *Ibid.*, pp. 4-5.

42. *Ibid.*, pp. 1, 23.

43. *Pornography and the First Amendment*, handout of the American Civil Liberties Union.

44. *Ibid.*

45. *Ibid.*

46. *Ibid.*

47. *Ibid.*

48. *Ibid.*

49. Censorship, Sex and the First Amendment," *NCJW* (National Council of Jewish Women) Journal, Winter 1986 (9, 4), p. 12.

50. National Coalition Against Censorship, *Censorship News*, Fall 1985 (22), p. 3.

51. *Ibid.*, p. 4.

52. English, Dierdre, "The Politics of Pornography: Can Feminists Walk the Line?," p. 50.

53. Steinem, Gloria, "Erotica vs. Pornography," *Outrageous Acts and Everyday Rebellions*, 1983, p. 222.

54. English, pp. 50, 52.

55. Willis, Ellen, "Feminism, Moralism, and Pornography," 1979.

56. Van Gelder, Lindsy, "Pornography Goes to Washington," *Ms.,* June 1986, p. 52.

57. Blakely, Mary Kay, "Is One Woman's Sexuality Another Woman's Pornography?," Ms., April 1985, p. 38.

59. *Ibid.*, p. 57.

60. Duggan, Lise, Nan Hunter and Carol S. Vance, "False Promises: New Antipornography Legislation in the United States," *SIECUS Report*, May 1985 (XIII, 5), p. 2

61. Friedan, Betty, *The Second Stage*, 1986 ed., pp. 357-359.

X. Pornography and Culture

1. Fox-Genovese, Elizabeth, "Pornography and Individual Rights," transcript of a lecture at Ginnell College, Grinnell, Iowa, February 18, 1987, p. 29.

2. Pellauer, Mary, "Pornography: An Agenda for the Churches," *The Christian Century*, July 2-August 5, 1987, p. 654.

3. Kitzinger, Sheila, *Woman's Experience of Sex*, 1983.

4. Welbourne-Moglia, Ann, "Statement to the U.S. Commission on Pornography, Houston, Texas, September 12, 1985," *SIECUS Report*, November 1985, p. 9.

5. "Pornography, Obscenity, and Censorship," *Minutes of the General Assembly of the Presbyterian Church in the United States*, 1973, p. 111.

6. "Pornography: A Practice of Inequality," brochure published by Organizing Against Pornography, Minneapolis, Minnesota.

7. Pellauer, p. 653.

8. Fortune, Marie, *Sexual Violence: The Unmentionable Sin—An Ethical and Pastoral Perspective*, 1983, pp. 18-19, 37.

9. Duggan, Lisa and Ann Snitow, "Porn Law is About Images, Not Power," *Newsday*, September 26, 1984, p. 65.

10. Kohn, Alfie, "Shattered Innocence," *Psychology Today*, February 1987, pp. 54-58.

11. Pellauer, Mary, Barbara Chester and Jane Boyajian, eds., *Sexual Assault and Abuse: A Handbook for Clergy and Religious Professionals*, 1987, pp. 13-14.

12. Chesney-Lind, Meda, "Women and Crime: The Female Offender," *Signs: Journal of Women in Culture and Society*, Autumn 1986.

13. Lederer, Laura, ed. *Take Back the Night*, 1980, pp. 57-70.

14. Previous reports include Violence Against the Image of God: *Exploitation of Women* (1986), *Naming the Unnamed: Sexual Harassment in the Church* (1982), and *A Time to Speak: Resources on Rape and Violence Against Women* (1979).

15. "Death of a Porn Queen," video produced by WOCO-TV, Minneapolis, Minnesota.

16. *Text of the Public Hearings on Ordinances to Add Pornography as Discrimination Against Women, Minneapolis City Council*, December 12-13, 1983.

17. "People" column, *Minneapolis Star and Tribune*, August 21, 1987.

18. "*Penthouse* Interview: Dr. Edward Donnerstein," *Penthouse*, September 1985.

19. Cohn, Carol, "Sex and Death in the Rational World of Defense Intellectuals," *Signs: Journal of Women in Culture and Society*, Summer 1987 (XII, 4) pp. 687-718.

20. Meisel, Donald, in a sermon entitled "The Day Christ Died," Westminster Presbyterian Church, Minneapolis, Minnesota, March 23, 1986.

21. Pellauer, *The Christian Century*, p. 655.

22. Bellah, Robert, et al., *Habits of the Heart: Individualism and Commitment in American Life*, 1985, p. 6.

23. "The Twelve Steps and Traditions," brochure distributed by Al-Anon Family Group Headquarters, Inc., revised 1973.

24. "Death of a Porn Queen" video.

25. Gilligan, Carol, *In a Different Voice*, 1982, and Rubin, Lillian, *Intimate Strangers: Men and Women Together*, 1983.

26. Census data, *Minneapolis Star and Tribune*, August 21, 1987.

27. Gordon, Sol, interviewed on "Twin Cities Live," KSTP-TV, St. Paul, Minnesota, August 1987.

28. Fox-Genovese, p. 30.

29. *Ibid.*, p. 30.

30. Barth, Karl, *Church Dogmatics*, IV, p. 191.

XIV. Background Material

Section XIV includes a number of items found to be valuable in the study of the Task Force. It includes materials and conclusions that are not necessarily in agreement with positions taken by the General Assembly of the Presbyterian Church (U.S.A.) and are not to be taken as the policy of the Presbyterian Church (U.S.A.) or of any other church.

42.648

A. Theological Perspectives

42.649

1. Thoughts on Pornography by Aurelia T. Fule

The theme reminded me of an earlier, seemingly unrelated experience. Three children, five, seven and nine years olds, came to stay with friends of ours while we also were guests. Their parents had to be away from home and arranged for the children to stay four days with this family. After last minute instructions by the mother—to be good, to behave themselves, to be quiet—the parents left. The oldest child then turned to the hostess: "What are the No-Nos?" We all laughed, but it was not a joke. When you have no choice about the land, the lay-out is defined by prohibitions. The children's question haunted us, because in a nutshell this is what Christian ethics means to many people. The No-Nos define the lay of the land of religion.

The story is not unrelated after all. The concern before us is one that we adults often approach by seeking the No-Nos. I suggest that we try a different route.

The study clearly notes the difficulty and necessity of distinguishing obscenity from pornography. I share the affirmations that guide the study (see Introduction), and the definition of the Task Force on Pornography as to what constitutes pornography: " . . . sexually explicit . . . for profit . . . for sexual arousal by eroticizing violence, power . . . dominance . . . of a person. . . ." I deeply appreciate the work of the task force and the result of its work.

"The Hebrew idea of personality," in the rightly famous words of the British scholar, Dr. Wheeler Robinson, "is an animated body, and not an incarnated soul." (*The People and the Book*, ed. A.D. Peake, p. 362), or in the words of J. Pedersen, "The body is the soul in its outward form" (Israel, I-II, p. 171). This is strangely true, strangely because Hebrew had no word for "body". The idea, nevertheless, was communicated.

In the New Testament, the writer who thought through this matter was the apostle Paul. J.A.T. Robinson clearly showed that in Paul's writing, body "is the nearest equivalent to our word 'personality'" (*The Body*, A Study Pauline Theology, SCM Press, p. 28). The body is not something external to me that I may use or misuse; it is not something I have, it is what I am. What happens to my body happens to me, to the whole of me.

The creation story in Genesis, Chapter 1, speaks of human beings as "created . . . in the image of God . . .; male and female . . . " (v. 27). Although no body is alluded to and the image is not physical resemblance, concrete human beings are assumed. Chapter 2 is more specific: "The Lord God formed the human (*adam*, masc.) of the dust of the ground (*Adamah*-fem.) (v.-7). When this chapter recounts the creation of the woman from the rib of the human, women are acknowledged as similar and different: "Bone of my bones, and flesh of my flesh." We are the same substance, equal to each other, says Adam: "she shall be called Woman (*ishshah*) because she was taken out of Man (*ish*)" (v.#23). Yet we are different. The blessing on both of them (1:28) is similar to that of the animal creation: "Be fruitful and multiply and fill the earth . . . " (v. #22) but with added responsibilities for the rest of creation.

The text presents these two persons as the forbears not of a particular people but of humanity. What is said about these two is said about all human beings. We are formed by God—male, female, then and now, here and everywhere. We are formed to reflect the image of God so that looking at the other we may glimpse God's image. We are created for God and for each other, to love in community. We are created as sexual beings. To fill the earth is not said about the fall, it is part of the blessing. Male and female are equal in value and dignity, they are equally valued by God. We are created for responsibility and for freedom. We are to make choices and live with (some of) the consequences of our choices.

When I consider my own body, I do not need convincing that I do not have a body; I am a body. Who I am has to do with my body. A body twenty years older or younger, a foot taller or shorter or twenty pounds lighter would be a person very different from who I am. My self-identity is tied to this body. Would you recognize me tomorrow in another body? This body and I are one. Self-expression is limited by the body, but it is possible only with the body. Body is needed for relationship, for enjoyment—of music, food or love, for engendering or carrying new life. Sexuality partakes of all the above blessings that are given to us by being created as "animated bodies."

For the Christian community, body takes on a hallowed meaning. God comes to us in the person of the Messiah who becomes one of us by being carried in his mother's womb, by sharing the experience of birth with all mothers and all infants. He not only takes on "flesh," he takes a body. For centuries we have recited the creed speaking of Jesus Christ "who . . . under Pontius Pilate was crucified, dead and buried." There is here no soul freed from the body, he was crucified. God's gift of redemption was brought through the body of the suffering, dying redeemer.

"The third day he rose again," we continue. What happened? What does it mean? To believe that "bodily" resurrection means reviving or re-animating a dead body and that this is the miraculous intervention of God is to miss the miracle. The point of the body is identity, self-expression, relationship, touch, feel, love. The gospels assert that the same Jesus who journeyed with and taught the disciples, who was put to death, was alive in their midst. The same Jesus could be recognized by the lakeside and at supper in Emmaus.

Christ's resurrection leads to the concluding promise of the gospel so that we say, I believe "in the resurrection of the body and life ever lasting." Each of us carrying the divine image is created for eternity. Identity, self-expression, sharing in community is understood by the early church in terms of the body. And not just as individual bodies, but the community of faith is spoken of as the body of Christ. The self-expression, though not exclusively, we pray, of Christ here and now is in and through that body.

We who were brought to know God in the face of Jesus Christ have learned that God in Christ has assumed our body and the risen Christ's ascension in some way carried the body—the human person—into the Godhead. These are the Yes-Yes notes of being human, and of belonging to the Body of Christ.

These are my thoughts after reading the report of the task force. I first read the report before it was completed and my response came in terms of the body. On re-reading the completed report, I found myself thinking in these terms still.

Why? I ask myself. Is it that being a woman I live with greater awareness of my body than men do? And as a woman, I am more likely to carry the consequences of my choices than men do. Some women stop menstruating because their diet is faulty or insufficient, while there is no corresponding change in men. Women's biological cycle is evident, we cannot but be conscious of our body. We can carry new life; we watch what we do, what we eat to protect that life; we give birth and nurse babies—all natural to our body, to our deepest self, natural even if we do not in fact become mothers. My body is not external to me; what happens to my body, happens to me.

What pornography does to the body of those photographed, filmed, or watched on stage and to those who watch is done to persons. Dominance, submission, violence, degradation that is suffered by the physical body is suffered by persons. In this way, pornography violates the body and thereby violates the person.

Pornography is not wholly divorced from reality. It is a distorted, exaggerated mirror image of activities fantasized by people who cannot love their own body, because they cannot love themselves. What is fantasized is also a distorted and exaggerated image of social relationships in contemporary society: inequality, exploitation, oppression and violence.

What we need to do about pornography are not simply isolated acts or prohibitions. It is not wholesome—or successful—to treat a symptom and leave the illness. The No-Nos do not work on their own. We—in this land—need to attend to the deep roots of social sickness that burst into violence of many forms. We in this church need to highlight the Yes to life and body, community, and love, and live it in and out of home and church, gratefully, before God.

42.650

2. A Theological Perspective on Pornography from Women of Color by Elizabeth B. Haile

As women of color, we are willing to express the following thoughts to serve as a guide to the Presbyterian Church (U.S.A.) in understanding the perspective of racial ethnic women on the subject of pornography. We believe it is important to relate our feeling to both our Christian heritage and our cultural traditions.

A common factor in all of our racial ethnic cultures is the significance of images. The use of imagery has been essential in transferring the story and the values of a people. So it is not surprising that some manifestation of a god and that god's creations would be expressed. Despite the widespread belief that nonwestern people were heathens before being introduced to Christianity, a critical look might produce some surprising results. The traditional religions on non-western people often contained parallelism with Christianity in religious concepts rituals and symbolism. Thus, not only can we intellectually understand the necessity for a creation story but express it through our senses of seeing and feeling.

The sacredness of all human life is an essential understanding in all our racial ethnic communities. Being "created in God's image" establishes a divine spark in each of us but shows only a reflection of the Divine. The relationship between the Creator and created beings undergirds our perception of "being." God is Spirit and is not limited; we are flesh and are limited to being created male and female.

The biblical story informs us that God intentionally created male and female: moreover, God made them to be sexual beings—not asexual. In the creation story about man and woman being created separately (Gen 2:7-23), there is a distinctly graphic reference to their bodies. Genesis 2:25 tells us, "And the man and his wife were both naked, and were not ashamed." Therefore, what God has created is good—that is, our body is not in itself a reason for us to be ashamed or embarrassed. Unfortunately, it is sometimes what we do with our bodies that is cause for regret. We use our bodies in ways that cause alienation in ourselves and in our relationships with others.

Another way to say this is to examine a section from the Confession of 1967. In *A Commentary on the Confession of 1967: An Introduction to the Book of Confessions*, on page 72, Edward A. Dowey, Jr., of Princeton Seminary writes:

> Male and female are a work of the love of the Creator. Sexuality is not a disaster, although it suffers probably more than most other aspects of the lives of humans from the condition of REBELLION, DESPAIR, and ISOLATION. . . . The two-ness of man and woman, the three-and four- and more-ness of the family group, which leads into a wide complex of social relations, has the blessing promised of the Creator. (Refers to Sections 9.12 and 9.47).

God has endowed male and female with capacities to make the world serve their needs and to enjoy its good things. This has been corrupted so that humans exploit each other, personally as well as one group over another. When sexuality is exploited, that is, when one uses his or her body or another's body for selfish use, then that person has misused the intent of her or his sexuality.

Pornography is one manifestation of sexual exploitation. Pornography, as defined by the Rev. Sandra Mangual of Puerto Rico in an essay for this paper, is "the exploitation of human sexuality utilizing images that are distorting the intrinsic value of human beings, reducing them to objects of pleasure. It is in this process of exploitation that women become the instruments of others' maneuvers, experiencing a loss of control over their lives and therefore a lack of freedom. The ultimate consequence of this disempowerment is the absence of resources to affirm their authentic humanity."

Pornography is a justice issue for women and especially for women of color. In our racial ethnic communities, we are informed about human sexuality by the traditions of our cultures. According to traditional values, it is understood that the individual does not have absolute rights if these violate the integrity of the community. The multitude of generations which preceded us have shaped our consciousness of who we are and of our values. The stories of our peoples also inform us as we respond to issues about injustice against the well-being of our communities.

Pornographic images are destructive because, in the best sense of our traditions, the individual is not the most important, instead the good of the community is primary. For example, both biblical and traditional African theology stress the value of belonging to a community of believers. (When we refer to African traditional religion or theology, we mean the indigenous beliefs and practices on the continent before the advent of Christianity and Islam.) Many African theologians agree that in traditional African religion, humanity is concerned as "being in-relation." Writing in "The Origins and Development of African Theology," (G.H. Muzorewa, Orbis Press, p. 17), Mercy Oduyoye says:

> Africans recognize life as life-in-community. We can truly know ourselves if we remain true to our community, past and present. The concept of individual

success or failure is secondary. The ethnic group, the village, the locality, are crucial in one's estimation of oneself. Our nature as being-in-relation is a two-way relation: with God and with our fellow human beings.

Being-in-relation is seen over and against individual gratification. The relationships that lead to *shalom* in its fullest theological sense are based on *agape* or *phileo* connectedness. This can be seen in covenantal relationships as described in Scripture and reinforced through traditional cultural values. The welfare of persons is a concern of the God who acts in history.

Women of color are beginning to reexamine the Bible for passages which contain both racist and sexist exploitation. A prominent example is the treatment of Hagar by Abraham and Sarah. Sarah and Abraham are credited with being the spiritual ancestors of the peoples of the Old and the New Testaments. They were given a direct promise by God but they attempted to expedite it. And as often happens, the powerless woman, Hagar, became a pawn as Abraham and Sarah played the game of fulfilling their desires.

Sarah's treatment of Hagar portrays the victimizing of the Black woman by the slave owner's wife. Hagar, the Egyptian slave, was never to be the equal of the wife, yet was permitted to become the breeder for Sarah and Abraham's first child (Gen. 16:1-16). Nevertheless, the exploited woman of color was ''disposable'' when no longer sexually useful to the master.

God, however, made a promise also to Hagar and her son, Ishmael: Hagar's worth to God was more than how she could be used sexually. God was merciful and supportive of Hagar when she suffered from her captivity and lack of options (Gen. 21:14-21). God heard her prayers and was present in Ishmael's life as well.

Hagar's story illustrates how being reduced from full personhood to a mere sexual object is destructive. However, the power of one sex or one group over another is often justified by distortion of the reference to dominion in Genesis 1:26, 28. For women of color, this is exacerbated by the misunderstanding of the intent of Genesis 2:16. People must be informed again and again that the concept of male dominance-female subjugation is a result of sinful humanity and not God's intention for being-in-relation.

Whenever human dignity is disregarded, it provides an environment for destructive images. Images have a way of redefining reality; injustice can be created through imagery. For example, harlotry in the Bible is frequently associated with non-Hebrew or foreign women. The cultures of those women were denounced as morally inferior. Therefore, women of a non-dominant culture have been victimized by this image.

The story of Ruth shatters some of the unhealthy images. In patriarchal systems, one of the precious few places a woman has authority is in the management of the home. There she is mother, mother-in-law, and grandmother. Our cultures teach us who we are as we go into another's home. Each culture has specific expectations of the bride and mother-in-law relationship. Ruth agreed with Naomi that ''your people shall be my people and your God by God'' (Ruth 1:15-18). This equality of status afforded to each woman a commitment to fairness in their relationship regardless of the dangers and challenges they would confront in the future, traveling alone without male protection. Ruth, as a foreign, single woman, was vulnerable, particularly to unsolicited sexual advances.

Looking at the parallels between these two women and the modern situation, we women of color need to be the Naomis for our own young women, by guiding them into using whatever skills they may have to assure their independence without being sexually exploited. We include in our concern our foreign sisters who are victimized by the tourism industry.

The Bible has harsh language about the ''mighty'' who victimize the widows, the orphans and a variety of ''humble and meek'' who were perceived as powerless in the secular society described in the Old and New Testaments. Still, church systems have

172

produced damaging images of women and have even looked the other way when these images resulted in violent acts against women of color. Thus, it is not enough simply to hear the gospel. The gospel message needs to be understood, and skills are needed to transfer the relevance of the particular people in a particular time and place.

The Rev. Sandra Mangual-Rodriquez, in an essay written for this paper states:

> I reject pornography for being an exploitation of sexuality which mainly legitimates women as objects of pleasure. This action violates women and denigrates their personhood. The gospel, at the core of its message portrays Jesus denying any reduction to the fulfillment of humanity. He says, "I came so that they might have life and might have it abundantly" (John 10:10). Any Christian discourse that denies this dimension of Jesus' praxis falls short of understanding the depth and value of the christological message.
>
> The abundant life to which Jesus is referring is not a life filled with material things nor satiating our erogenous senses. The abundant life which Jesus promises comes through our relationship with Jesus and through our response to his commandment to love one another as he has loved us. In the abundant life, racial stereotypes are not perpetuated in sexual imagery.

The biblical calling to abundant life is a challenge to Christians living in the United States. America allows the rights to create pornography but it does not take responsibility for dealing with the effects of it. The church must affirm its calling because society has not taken responsibility for the social problems it has created. In claiming a division between church and state, corporate America can profit from pornography yet wash its hands of any moral responsibility.

Basic pornographic ideology permeates the rest of society in general. This can be seen in western understanding of utilitarianism, a private property mentality and a social, economic and class structure. It reflects a patriarchal construction in social-class and economic format which delineates the role of women as subservient to men.

Today, pornography has become a lucrative business for individuals and small "corporations" that try to maintain or increase their existing capital. At the same time pornography becomes an open door for individuals (men and women) who are trying to meet their financial and existential needs in an unjust society characterized by a profound gap between the rich and the poor, a society that stresses individualism and the need for self-realization.

Our opposition to the profiteers of pornography is not to be equated with censorship. We affirm the separation of church and state which our Constitution maintains. Moreover, we do not unconditionally condemn sensual arousal, since sensuality in itself is a part of human sexuality. This applies to what is written in very erotic terms. For example, The Song of Songs, which is replete with sensuous imagery, is poetry that does not promote sexual behavior but acknowledges the strong feelings of love, binding the lovers in-relation.

We do, however, object to using the media to demean the human body for profit. "Pornography" comes from two Greek words: *Porne* meaning "harlot" and *grapho* meaning, "writing." Porne is derived from a root word which means "to sell." The emphasis of pornography, as the name indicates, is on material gain and not on relationships between people. Pornography is the antithesis of community because it promotes consumerism for individual gratification.

A pornographic home video game, "Custer's Revenge," which features the rape of an Indian woman as entertainment, was discontinued due to protest by feminists, Native Americans, and the American public. Money is clearly the key motivating force behind "Custer's Revenge." A Hispanic woman doing research on the pornography industry has observed "a hierarchy of sexual imagery. The more violent the pornography, the more images there are of racial ethnic women."

Such pornographic "entertainment" defines women of color as not worthy of being created in God's image. The church must not be silent on this issue, and by its silence seem to say "amen." The church must acknowledge the sacredness of the life of people of color. The sacred and the secular are closely related in traditional nonwestern cultures.

Our racial ethnic experience tells us that the sacred way is the will of God. But our experience also tells us every day that anger, violence, greed and every evil passion surround us. Except where lewd pictures and advertisements of pornographic entertainment are allowed to be displayed, there is little evidence of the pornography industry. Inner city dwellers find objectionable material within their home neighborhoods. Often these are racial ethnic families whose options for homes, workplaces, and schools are limited. The impact of the pornographic trade on racial ethnic communities is divisive as well as dehumanizing. Reflections voiced among Asian parents, teachers, and clergymen in Los Angeles on the prevalence of pornography in public places reveal that they feel victimized because of their helplessness to do anything of significance about these conditions.

Women of color live with the reality that the theology of the church has been better than its practice. We desire the church to be an agent of empowerment for us as we respond to the pornography which is undermining the values in our communities. The vision which begins to take form is one of mobilizing women and men who believe in wholesome sexuality, pledged to the protection of an environment that would be healthy for young people to grow up in and in which all women would be safe from oppression. The unity of church-related women committed to one such goal would be like giving each other a valuable look of sisterhood. This single agenda would be that of speaking out whenever the principles of personhood are violated. The market for pornography could decline, forcing profit losses if Christians themselves would stop purchasing and renting and selling pornographic materials.

42.651

3. Pornography and Language by Isabel Wood Rogers, Moderator, 199th General Assembly (1987)

For some time, we in the Presbyterian Church have been struggling with questions about the language we use—language used to talk about ourselves and about God. We have come to understand the power of language, how it not only reflects our picture of reality but also shapes and perpetuates that picture.

As people of faith, we have had a particular concern for the power of religious language. Our language about God affects not only the way we "image" God but also the way we think about women and men. We have tended to ascribe to men and to God language which conveys images of power, dominance and authority and to withhold these attributes from women. Furthermore, we have not historically associated femaleness with Godness. So when we speak of God only in male language, and refer to human beings corporately as "he," we are in danger of placing women outside the realm of the fully human. The images of male-exclusive language have ascribed to women a status of inferiority, weakness and "otherness."

What we now need to face is the reality that pornography is also language—language about sexuality. And like all language, it has the power to shape our perceptions and experiences. It not only reflects the historic power relationship of dominance and submission in human sexuality, but it also reinforces, shapes and perpetuates such images as normative in our minds.

All of this means that there is a disturbing link between pornography and religious language that is exclusively masculine. Pornography's images of power and dominance in sexuality are replicated and reinforced by our traditional religious language about

174

people and God. When we learn through religious imagery that "God" and "men" mean power and authority, while "women" means inferiority and invisibility, then the stage is set for accepting sexual images of dominance and submission in human relationships. Disturbing as it may be, images of power are connected throughout all of society's institutions, including the church, and they have reinforced the patterns of violence toward women that for too long have been unexamined and even condoned by Western society.

All forms of distorted power images in human relationships are a violation against the biblical image of God and God's intent for equality and mutual respect between people. We need to look carefully at the destructive impact of pornography in our society and at our own images of faith. We Presbyterians can be grateful to the Task Force on Pornography for making the reality clearer for us.

42.652

4. Freed to Be Lovers, Freed to Be Friends by Paul Spalding, Ph.D., Co-pastor, First Presbyterian Church, Elba, New York

The New Yorker magazine appeared recently with a cartoon by J. J. Sempe on its front cover.[1] It showed four long rowboats in a lake, their sterns meeting in a hub and their bows pointing out like spokes in different directions. At the hub were four vivacious women in gaily colored swimsuits, chatting happily with one another. But isolated on the far ends of the boats, facing outwards and fishing quietly, wearing drab clothes and expressionless faces, were their husbands.

I could appreciate this scene drawn by another male, for how well it depicted what it often feels like to be a man. Conditioned to act independently and competitively, we usually find it difficult to establish relationships with other people outside the world of work and its standards of performance, standards which creep even into our pastimes. It is hard enough to relate to other men with any real intimacy, let alone to women, that erotically attractive breed on the other end of the boat. So often our experience gives anything but support to the claim of Genesis 2, that God gave human beings their sexuality because "it is not good that the earthling [*adam*, a nongeneric term for "human being," from *adamah* or "earth," "soil"] should be alone" (v. 18; see vv. 20b-24; 5:2).

One still safely distant way for us men to deal with women is through pornography. As the display of one human being (usually a man) dominating another (usually a woman) sexually, pornography allows us to maintain that safe distance in the darkness and anonymity of a movie theater or the privacy of our home, to feel in control even if vicariously, to simplify another human being from being a "Thou" with all of her mysteries to being another "It" among innumerable others we act upon so self-evidently in the male world. But pornography still leaves us men as lonely as ever.

The Genesis story of Eden's fall tells us that one of the God-defying fissures in life is precisely that existing between male and female, which together were meant to be "in the image of God" (1:27; 5:1-2). The relationship of male and female is the original human one, in which all other relationships are involved.[2] Their estrangement from one another is dramatized in the shame of the primeval man and woman in Genesis, which drives them to cover themselves with aprons of fig leaves (3:7). It takes a concrete form in male dominance (3:16). It proves to be the spore of social rupture, mushrooming into stories of violence within the family (4:1-16), beyond the family (4:23-24), and throughout the world (6:11). In light of Eden's story, all biblical representations of society as hierarchical and violent (including sexual exploitation of women and violence against them) stand under a general condemnation.

Still, the damage of Eden's fall is divinely contained and circumvented. History is ruled not only by human confusion but also by God's providence.[3] God's graceful healing of the sexual rupture appears in touching accounts of mutuality and companionship between Abraham and Sarah (Gen. 23:1-2), Isaac and Rebekah (24:62-27), Jacob and Rachel (29:9-12) Moses and Zipporah (Ex 2:15-22), Ruth and Boaz (Ruth 2:1-4:12). Central for any male reader of these stories must be, in each case, how a woman has filled the void of a man's loneliness.

The Song of Songs offers the most fleshed-out biblical depiction of mutual, erotic heterosexuality. Two lovers, a man and a woman, are in sexually intimate dialogue with one another, including extensive praise of each other's bodies.[4] Along with the eroticism, the male calls the female literally, and uniquely in the Hebrew Bible, "my (female) friend" [rayah] (1:9, 15; 2:2, 10, 13; 4:1, 7; 5:2, 6:4) *She* is not a sex object, but a sex subject. She is different, wonderfully different, but also equal; a person from whom he can receive love and companionship as well as a person to whom he can give it.

The feeling is clearly mutual: Indeed, most of the lines in the song are hers rather than his. "This is my beloved" says the woman, "and this is my friend" [rea] (5;16, RSV)! She stresses the reciprocity of their love in inverted statements: "My beloved is mine and I am his" (2:16); "I am my beloved's and my beloved is mine" (6:3). Elsewhere, a chorus breaks into a shout of blessing on them as "friends" as well as "lovers" (5:1).

It is as if Eden had returned: The world is young and green again, a man related to a woman on equal terms, and neither gender rules over the other. Granted that separation, violence, and chaos exist now even in the garden of the Song (examples are 2:6, 15; 3:1-3; 4:8; 5:6-8; 6:1; 8:1-3), the mutual, heterosexual companionship shared here represents a challenge to their eventual triumph: "For Love is strong as Death; Passion fierce as Hell" (8:6).[6]

While the description of the sexes' creation for the sake of companionship gives Genesis 2 claim to being "the Old Testament Magna Carta of humanity," the Song of Songs joins it as "a second Magna Carta."[7] It models the sexual friendship God intends between man and woman, that frees males from their characteristic loneliness and the related, counterfeit sexiness of pornography, for the erotic intimacy they were made to enjoy.

Notes

[1] 62/29 (Sept. 7, 1987).

[2] Karl Barth, *Church Dogmatics* III/2:292-293.

[3] Barth, *Church Dogmatics* IV/3.2:693.

[4] A clinical translation is that by Marvin Pope: *Song of Songs: A New Translation with Introduction and Commentary, Anchor Bible* 7C (Garden City, NY: Doubleday & Company, Inc., 1977). Note, however, criticisms of it by Jack Sasson: "On Pope's Song of Songs," *Maarov* 1/2 (1979): 177-196.

[5] In the Gospel According to John, Jesus calls his disciples his "friends" [philioi] (15:13-15)—which includes women. This gospel recognized women to be "first-class' disciples" of Jesus: "In researching the evidence of the fourth Gospel, one is still surprised to see to what extent in the Johannine community women and men were already on an equal level in the fold of the Good Shepherd. This seems to have been a community where in the things that really mattered in the following of Christ there was no difference between male and female—a Pauline dream (Gal 3:28) that was not completely realized in the Pauline communities" (Ramond Brown, "Roles of Women in the 4th Gospel," *Theological Studies* 36/4 [1975]:699).

It may be noted in this connection that Jesus' famous comment on the looks men give other men's wives, in Matthew 5:28, concerns considerate treatment of one's female neighbor. Correctly translated, it demands that men resist aggressive behavior toward women beginning with the snide looks: "Whoever so looks at a married woman that she becomes desirable, has already misled her to adultery in his heart." On this, see Klaus Hacker, "Der Rechtsatz vom Jesus zum Thema Ehebruch (Mt. 5, 28)," *Biblische zeitschrift* 21/1 (1977): 113-116.

[6] The translation is that of Pope, *Song of Songs*.

[7] Barth, *Church Dogmatics* III/2:291, 293. Taken together, Genesis 2 and the Song of Songs represent for Barth "this Magna Carta in its twofold form" (p. 296).

42.653

5. Human Sexuality: Dualistic and Holistic Paradigms: A Presentation for the Task Force on Pornography by Wilson Yates, Ph.D., United Theological Seminary of the Twin Cities, New Brighton, Minnesota

Margaret Sanger, the birth control reformer of the first part of this century, began one of her books with the sentence: "Sex is the Pivot of Civilization." Perhaps she was given to hyperbole. But few of us in the latter part of this century would deny that sexuality is a central human force that can exploit and destroy or enhance and enrich personal life and the human community. We have come to appreciate Sanger's insistence that the power of sexuality is a profound and an ever-present power. As Anthony Kosnick writes:

> Sex is . . . a force that permeates, influences, and affects every act of a person's being at every moment of existence. It is not operative in one restricted area of life (that is, simply physical intercourse) but it is rather at the core and center of our total life response.[1]

Precisely because sexuality is so important a part of life, the church has been expected to deal with its morality and meaning, and this the church has done. It has given shape to sexual ethics and theologies of sexuality down through the ages. In our own day, however, the church finds itself in a quandary, for the way it has defined and interpreted sexuality in the past is being challenged by forces and groups within the church and outside of it, and it is being forced to rethink what it has said in the past, what it is saying now and what it ought to say in and for the future. In effect, when we pull the curtain on the church's own stage, we find that its actors—its theologians, its congregations, its leaders, its denominations—are very much involved with the question of sexuality. Further, they are often in sharp disagreement with one another with some busy defending old scripts, other busy revising them and still others writing new scripts. Needless to say, there is some confusion regarding the plot and message, though one could hardly say there is an absence of excitement and, I should add, anxiety about the outcome. It is these scripts of the church that I want to consider in this discussion. In so doing, I hope we will gain a better sense of where the church has been and, more importantly, where it might be going.

In undertaking this task, I want to frame my approach in terms of a paradigm analysis. I need to begin, therefore, with a note on what such an approach involves. Thomas S. Kuhn, a historian of science in his work *The Structure of Scientific Revolutions*[2] developed the idea of paradigm analysis in an effort to understand changes in scientific perspectives or theories. He maintains that a scientific theory develops out of particular historical context as a way of understanding some aspect of scientific reality. In turn, the theory or perspective or paradigm changes when it is no longer able to satisfactorily explain that reality—a situation that arises in the face of new questions or discoveries. When such a theory or paradigm is first posed with new data that the paradigm cannot respond to in an adequate fashion, there is usually an attempt to modify or revise the paradigm so that it is able to incorporate such information and answer the questions being raised—respond to the anomalies that have presented themselves. If such revisions fail, however, the anomalies precipitate a search for a new paradigm. If a new paradigm emerges then a paradigm shift has taken place—a revolution occurs. In the period when such a shift is occuring, there is often uncertainty—the old paradigm which made us comfortable in its ability to make sense out of reality is breaking down and we experience ourselves living in a period of crisis, a time between the times when a secure way of understanding that particular reality eludes us. During this period many options may present themselves before one becomes dominant and we are forced to explore a range of new possibilities whether we desire to do so or not. When a paradigm shift does take place, the new paradigm often draws on ideas and insights that existed in the past but were given little credence or significance in the old paradigm. What has gone before, therefore, is of value; indeed, often of much greater value than was recognized in the past as it is blended with fresh insight to form the new paradigm's tapestry. Using this thesis, Kuhn traces the rise and fall of scientific theories or paradigms as they have emerged to provide us a way of viewing scientific reality, have been called into question, and have finally collapsed in the face of anomalies that they could not explain.

Now what I want to suggest is that Kuhn's scheme can be helpful in making sense out of changes that are emerging in the church's understanding of sexuality. Using Kuhn's model, I want to suggest the following scenario. The church helped give rise to a major paradigm regarding the morality and meaning of sexuality which has dominated western civilization down to the twentieth century. It was not unchallenged, for different periods ranging from the Old Testament to New Testament periods, from Patristic to Medieval, from the Reformation to the eighteenth century posed new questions and issues, but the old paradigm was reshaped in such a way that it remained viable and dominant. For example, a sharp revision occured in the movement from biblical times to the neoplatonic period of the early church regarding how the body-spirit relationship was to be understood and during the Reformation regarding significance attached to celibacy, but accomodations were made without a major paradigm shift occuring. By the' nineteenth century, however, forces were taking place that began to stretch the old paradigm beyond its limits. The threat of over population, processes of urbanization, medical breakthroughs that brought down the infant mortality rate, technological developments regarding birth control, changes in our psychological understanding of the human, new views of human nature and the rise in the importance of love and sentiment in marriage and the family—all posed questions and issues that the old paradigm, while defended with great zeal by some, had broken down for others and the shaping of new theories had begun. By our own time—the end of the twentieth century—new ideas and perspectives have been set forth and the questions has become one of whether a new paradigm is emerging that shall become a new and dominant way of viewing human sexuality. My judgment is that a new paradigm is emerging and while it is radically new at points, its radicalness stems in part from seeds planted long ago. Thus, the church is not having to forsake its past so much as draw upon different strands that have been ignored or denied validity. The new, therefore, is, in part, the child of the old, as it envisions a new paradigmatic way of perceiving the purpose and meaning of human sexuality.

Given these theoretical comments, I want to focus on a description of the old paradigm, which I shall call the *dualistic paradigm*, that I am maintaining has been breaking down over this century and on the new paradigm which I shall call *a holistic paradigm* that has been emerging as a primary paradigm for the church.[3]

In speaking of the older paradigm or dualistic perspective, I am speaking of a perspective that has been dominant throughout much of western history and, while it has undergone revisions, its primary assumptions have remained basic to its life. Those assumptions include the following:

1. Sexuality is interpreted in light of a patriarchal perspective in which women are considered to be subordinate to the wisdom and authority of men.

2. Sexuality is interpreted in light of a dualistic perspective regarding body and spirit in which body and spirit are considered separate and often antagonistic realities, and in which the body is considered inferior to the spirit and subject to its domination.

3. Procreation is considered the primary moral justification for sexual relations with all other justifications considered secondary and subordinate to that of procreation.

4. Sexual intimacy is recognized, at best, as erotic love which remains unrelated to either agapaic love or to dimensions of grace or holiness.

5. Sexuality is primarily in terms of external sexual activity that must be controlled through strict rules of sexual conduct—rules that are applicable to all.

6. Homosexual relationships are judged to be morally unjustifiable.

I want to comment briefly on each of these. To begin, a consideration of *the first assumption in* which sexuality and patriarchy are linked. Patriarchal thinking is present from ancient to modern times. It does not always manifest itself in the same way but it is present in the framing of all major attempts to understand sexuality and the relationship of the sexes. The Old Testament provides us a good illustration of how patriarchal theory varied in the interpretation of the relationship of men and women yet never varied so much that the underlying presuppositon of male superiority was challenged. Phyllis Trible has observed that one can see the Old Testament images in three different bodies of material: the holiness or legal codes, the wisdom literature of Proverbs and in the historical writings.[4] Patriarchal thought is most sharply expressed in the legal codes where the woman is, in effect, owned by her father or husband. Adultery is seen as a capital offense with the woman treated more harshly than the man. Virginity is a necessity before marriage. The woman has no legal or economic rights and she is religiously of secondary importance. Sexually she is essential for procreation though she is considered to be no more than a vessel of the male sperm which is thought to be the total nucleus of life. She is considered unclean as a sexual creature with menstruation and childbirth requiring ritual purification. And, foremost, she is a symbol of temptation.

In the Wisdom literature, she is perceived in more human terms as more than a procreative instrument. Her nurturing role as well as her birthing role is recognized and relationality with her husband is valued as one who is a companion—a theme the historical writings elaborate.

But, as Trible points out, it is "only in the historical writings that women become real— a flesh and blood person with name, biography, and individual character. We met Deborah, Jezebel, the Queen of Sheba, Rachael, Rizpah, Miriam, Hannah, Rahab, and Abigail."[5] It is also in this material that we see an image of marriage developed in which genuine respect and love are affirmed as important to marriage, and we see introduced the notion that marriage is part of the covenant with God and a wife and husband called to be companions to one another.

But even in the historical writings, the patriarchal subordination of women holds firm. Men are autonomous and primary and, finally, the source of wisdom and the revealers of truth. Down through history such patriarchal thought has been modified, but never abandoned in any substantive fashion until our own time when significant inroads have been made for a more egalitarian understanding of male-female relationship—inroads, I should add, that the church has at points helped make through the use of Old Testament concepts of justice and covenant. But even with this change, biblical literalism, particular church traditions, and natural law theory are all used to legitimate patriarchal images of reality even in our own day.

The second assumption posits a dualism of body and spirit. Again, I want to draw on a single historical "frame" for appreciating what such dualism is about; namely, the Patristic period of Christianity— the period of the early church. In so doing, however, I want to add that such a dualistic view is not limited to that period. It was present in some of the New Testament writings that were influenced by Hellenistic thought and while the Patristic period gives it full theological grounding, dualism does not end with that period but continues down to the present.

The early centuries of the church constitute a period in which the treatment of sexuality accents the darker side of sexual energy and a general religious and moral devaluing of it. It is a period of history in which various religious sect groups saw sexuality as demonic and procreation as evil with still other groups advocating sexual license. Some of the church fathers sought a middle path by insisting that sexuality was good because it was a part of creation and because, as a part of creation, it served the moral end of procreation. But the middle path was marked by detours. The detours were the consequence, most of all, of a neo-platonic dualism in light of which body and soul were seen as antagonistic to each other. Following from this basic split, other aspects of life were also split along body-soul lines identified with passion, soul with reason; body with the earthly, soul with the eternal; body with unbridled energy, soul with self-control; body with eros, soul with agape; body with sexuality, soul with spirituality; and, most significantly, body with female and soul with male.

This dualistic view wrought its own havoc insofar as a positive view of sex was concerned, for it led to a suspicion, fear, and excessive need to control sexual desire and expression by that which was considered to be morally superior; namely, reason. It was argued that if control were lost and passion reigned, then evil would result and sin abound. If passion were controlled and reason reigned then sexual relations could be tamed. In this formula, the purpose of sex was that of procreation—thus sexual relations were, finally, for the purpose of procreation rather than pleasure or love. St. Clement warned couples to have sex preferably after supper since one's passions are diminished at that time. And, he argued, that a couple should use restraint of intense pleasure else the couple suffer a loss of self-control. Here, of course, is the fear that in the moment of sexual activity reason will be abandoned and passion will rule.[6]

St. Jerome much later stated this fear quite succinctly: "He who too ardently loves his wife is an adulterer."[7] And later, fearing that sexuality would taint the spiritual experience, he insisted that both prayer and communion are inappropriate immediately after sexual relationships. St. Jerome also insisted, in one of his more negative judgments regarding sexuality, that "the only good of marriage is that it produces virgins." With all the major Patristic theologians, a life of celibacy was the higher road to travel, for the road of mutual sexual relationships—even those in marriage—was, at best, a briar path filled with moral ambiguities and spiritual pitfalls.

During this period, Augustine, the greatest mind of the period and one of the greatest minds in the history of the church, struggled with the question of sexuality. Influenced by the theological battles over sexuality that were current during his time and informed by his own emotional and spiritual sexual scars, he produced a negative theology of sexuality. Most importantly, he argued that original sin was not the consequence of disobedience but concupiscence; i.e., lust or sexual desire—a notion that remained, in large part, unchallenged until the writings of John Milton. Augustine argued much as other Patristic theologians had argued, that sexual passion led to a loss of rational control and, consequently, to a state of sin. Perhaps his most extreme attempt to argue the case is found in his exegisis of the Genesis story of Adam and Eve. In his treatment he creates a way for procreation to have occured without sexual desire by maintaining that Adam could control the flexing of his muscles at will and, accordingly, "Human organs, without the need for lust could have obeyed human will for the purpose of procreation."[10]

This dualism, therefore, in which body and soul were placed over and against one another and sexual passion judged to be inferior and often dangerous passion, left little room for the positive evaluation of sexual experience as a morally justifiable experience. In our own time this dualism has been greatly eroded, and yet it is still present whenever we differentiate our sexuality from self and deem sexuality an inferior aspect of our life.

This leads to the paradigm's *third assumption*, that procreation is the primary moral justification for sexual expression. Procreation as an expression of the natural ordering of things is the one positive basis and justification for sexual expression. In appreciating this position, it must be kept in mind that through most of human history procreation has been a dominant concern in the battle for survival; the fear was not of overpopulation but underpopulation. Plague, famine, and war—the three scourges—were ever present and, therefore, the reproductive needs of the human community required that procreation be given a morally central significance. The significance is expressed by this assumption. But it is also the case that procreation was used to give validity to sexuality which otherwise had no validity for early theologians. And it was used to validate women, at times her only validity in an otherwise hostile understanding of women. Augustine observed "I do not see what other help woman would be to man if the purpose of generating was eliminated."[11] (It is of psychological interest that Augustine fathered a child by a woman he refused to marry and later left, at the insistence of another woman, his mother.)

Given this understanding of the place of procreation, it is not surprising that the church opposed contraception or birth control of all sorts. And the formal teachings of the Catholic Church still remain opposed to "artificial" birth control on grounds that it violates natural law—a position that polls have shown is not shared by the majority of North American educated Catholic laity.[12]

The fourth assumption of the dualistic paradigm has to do with the relationship of sex to love. Sexual expression is at best identified as erotic love which is inferior to both agapaic love and companionate love. Furthermore it is unrelated to expressions of agapaic love. In early Christian statements erotic love was, for the most part, denied moral legitimacy—it was nothing more than an earthly pagan form of love which we were to be ultimately freed. In later thought, allowance was given for such erotic love but it was deemed an inferior form of love unrelated to agapaic love. In effect, eros and agape do not meet; do not inform each other or empower each other. With regard to companionate or filial love, eros is also seen as inferior and unrelated to such expressions of love in early Christian thought. This however begins to change when Puritan marriage theory explores how erotic love can be related to companionate love in marriage.[13] Eros and agape, however, still remain theologically unrelated in any positive fashion. The religious implications of this are severe: Sexual love belongs to the inferior realms of life unrelated to a life of grace and holiness.

The fifth assumption is that sexuality is to be understood primarily in terms of external sexual activity that must be controlled through strict rules that define what is morally justifiable and unjustifiable sexual conduct. By the eighth century, a number of penitential books began to set forth a code of conduct as strict in its condemnation of sex as its writers were fascinated by sex.[14] The first code is an exhortation to lead a celibate life. The rules are primarily focused on the control of sexual acts—on the definition of what are right or wrong expressions of sexual desire. The second paramount rule is that sexual relations should be expressed within the bonds of marriage alone, which means by definition persons of the opposite sex. Informing this rule is the judgment that only in marriage is sex provided with the social and rational boundaries which we can hold to and control its destructive propensity. In turn, there are rules against premarital, extramarital and postmarital sex as well as masturbation—masturbation received the most extensive consideration—and most other forms of sexual pleasure other than conventional sexual intercourse between a man and a woman. Thus, rules, prohibitions, and control are of primary concern. Important to this position is the fact that rules can be created in an objective and detached manner and applied in a rather indiscriminate fashion. In effect, the rules apply to everyone regardless of circumstances or context. It is well to note that the focus is on the control of external acts with little recognition that sexuality is related to anything more than the desire to engage in certain types of sexual activity. As with other of the assumptions, sex is to be viewed with suspicion, an inferior and potentially destructive aspect of human life which is to be carefully controlled. The rules, obviously, have little concern with enhancing or enriching sexual expression or linking sexuality to the fullness of human life.

The last assumption is that homosexual relationships are immoral. This judgment has woven its way down through history leading to sharp discrimination and cruelty against persons of homosexual orientation.[15] It is important to remember when dealing with this understanding that before modern times it was assumed that homosexuals were simply heterosexuals who were distorting their own sexuality. This view underlies several biblical passages where homosexual acts are condemned. There is no understanding until the modern period that some people had a homosexual orientation—a deeply embedded natural attraction for members of the same sex rather than the opposite sex. The church developed its own perspective into a full condemnation of homosexuality contributing to the homophobic fear that exists today regarding same sex relationships. This position is changing though the change is very slow. James B. Nelson in his book, *Embodiment*, has observed that among theologians today there are four different theological stances regarding homosexuality: rejecting and punitive; rejecting and non-punitive; qualified acceptance, and full acceptance.[16] The first two reflect variations of the old paradigm's condemnation of homosexuality, the third—qualified acceptance—reflects a breaking away from the old paradigm, while the fourth is expressive of a new paradigm. In light of its condemnation, the church has joined in the creation of moral rules and laws created to control same-sex relationships.

These assumptions that are foundational to the dualistic paradigm provide a perspective, a vision, of how sexuality ought to be interpreted and expressed. It is a vision that is suspicious of sexual energy and sees no reason to integrate sexual and spiritual dimensions into a whole. It is dualistic in style: women and men; body and soul; sexuality and spirituality; eros and agape; homosexual and heterosexual are judged to be different in type and in significance from one another. In acknowledging as much, however, it is important to recognize that within the history of the church there were also present other insights regarding sexuality. There were secondary themes to ones I have sketched and they were not a part of—indeed, they were in large part condemned in light of—the old paradigm. But they were present, and in the search for a new paradigm they become significant material, ideas, elements to work with: the Old Testament emphasis on the goodness of sexuality as a part of God's creation; the New Testament value of the equality of both men and women; the Calvinist accent on the importance of companionship in marriage; and the later Puritan accent on sexual love as one means of expressing that companionship. The reclaiming of such elements from the past as elements in the creation of a new paradigm is indeed the work of our own time. It is to that work that I want now to turn, for I want to sketch the major outline of what I see emerging as a new paradigm for the church—a new theological and ethical perspective. My sketch will necessarily be brief, but hopefully adequate enough to chart some sense of the course being taken.[17]

I want to call this paradigm a holistic paradigm and I want to suggest that it has the following assumptions:

1. Sexuality should be viewed in light of an egalitarian perspective in which men and women are considered to be equal to one another.

2. The morality of homosexual expression should be judged much as we judge heterosexual expression: in light of whether it enables persons to realize wholeness.

3. Sexuality as a part of creation is good.

4. Sexuality should be understood to be related to both body and spirit.

5. Sexuality should be seen as a dimension of the self that is expressive through all forms of love—forms that together constitute holistic love.

6. Sexuality should be seen as a means through which persons can know the grace of God.

7. Rules governing sexual behavior are important to sexual health and wholeness.

As introduction to the discussion of these assumptions, it is important to define two key concepts: *wholeness* and *sexuality*. Wholeness is a word rooted linguistically in such New Testament concepts as holy, health, unity and salvation.[18] It is the experience of well-being, of health, of integration, of trust, of love, of knowing one's self to be autonomous and, as such, a significant part of a greater whole. Wholeness is not limited to peak experiences beyond the process of daily living, but rather includes experiences realized in the midst of daily existence in response to the problems and possibilities life poses. It is not a continuing state we achieve, but an experience realized in moments of an event or relationship. It is the experience of broken life made whole.

Sexuality is a concept that in religious thought has been too often limited to genital sexual experience. There is a need, however, for a more encompassing understanding, which I offer in the following terms: Sexuality is our basic identity as males and females; it expresses itself in our attraction for, our drive to know, and our way of relating to ourselves, to others, and to God.

With these definitions as a backdrop, I want now to turn to the assumptions of the holistic paradigm of sexuality that I find to be most central.

The first assumption in the new paradigm insists that we are to understand male and female—maleness and femaleness—in egalitarian terms. This egalitarianism is rooted theologically in the assumption that we are all equal in the eyes of God—we are all of equal value as persons.

It is rooted ethically in the principles of freedom, which means we have the right to choose; equality, which means we have equal opportunity to choose; and justice, which means that we create the conditions for such freedom and equality to exist.

It is rooted sociologically in the proposition that men and women are equal to each other in their opportunity to choose the roles they play. This means that they can choose their roles on the basis of ability, energy, interest, time, and place rather than simply gender. In turn, social structures should support that possibility.

It should be noted that his egalitarian position does not mean that men and women are all alike. It does mean that the differences that exist do not make one sex subordinate to the other. The realization of wholeness, then, begins with the assumption that we should realize an equality with one another.

The second assumption affirms an inclusive stance towards sexual orientations. In this perspective, both opposite, bi-sexual, and same-sex relationships should be judged on the basis of whether they enable persons to realize some degree of wholeness in their lives rather than on the grounds that a given orientation is intrinsically right or wrong, natural or unnatural. The theological issue regarding sexual orientation is whether one's orientation is moral: whether persons are able within their orientations to know that wholeness and grace is offered them, or whether they fall into sexually alienated and destructive behavior.

The third assumption is that sexuality as a part of creation is good. God created them male and female . . . they became one flesh . . . they knew one another . . . they were fruitful and multiplied . . . and it was good, so the Old Testament affirms. From the beginning we were created sexual beings, we were invited to express our sexuality in creative and procreative fashion.

The Song of Songs provides one of the most beautiful testimonies to the goodness of love between man and woman. In the story the lovers come to a garden and there amidst an Eden-like world they speak, touch, embrace with a full giving and receiving of themselves. The richness of the song's sensuality speaks for itself:

Oh that you would kiss me with the kisses of your mouth, For your love is better than wine (1.2). Oh may your breasts be like clusters of the vine, and the scent of your breath like apples, and your kisses like the best wind (7:8-9). I am my beloved's and his desire is for me. Come my beloved, let us go out into the country, Let us spend the night in the villages.

Let us rise early and go to the vineyards; Let us see whether the vine has budded and its blossoms have opened, And whether the pomegranates have bloomed.

There I will give you my love (7:10-12).

In the story, the poet expresses the way that sexuality can become a means of knowing, of loving, of realizing union with the other. It becomes a means of knowing the presence of wholeness, of being at one with another in a loving relationship. It becomes a means of discovering the goodness of creation.

Sexuality is also expressive of the goodness of creation by virtue of its procreative powers. Our reproductive capacity links us in a special way with both the natural world (for it is expressive of our organic, biological nature), and with our self-transcending world of feelings and reflection (for it is expressive of emotional, rational, and cultural aspects of our lives).

Sexuality, then, as a part of creation is good, and that goodness is expressed in terms of the purposes central to its nature—intimacy and procreation. Scripture does not deny that our sexuality and its expression can be a source of alienation. It can become the source of distrust and fear, of brokenness and manipulation. But what it can become in the interest of one's self-centeredness and what it is created to be are not the same. The creation of sexuality and the intentions of that creation are the key concerns here.

The fourth assumption is that sexuality is understood to be related to both body and spirit. The Song of Songs symbolizes this in beautiful fashion. On the one hand, it is a canticle of sensuality lifting up and celebrating the bodies of the lovers. Voices speak, eyes behold. Lips meet. Bodies join in the joy of erotic communication. It is a song of the body and the body's beauty and fullness.

However, as a song of erotic communication of the union of two bodies, it becomes a song of the spirit, of the union of two persons. The lovers in their very acts of looking, speaking, touching, and reaching out to hold one another engage in a spiritual act of togetherness in a conscious, intimate manner. Feelings yield thoughts. Touches yield words. They transcend to see themselves so that they as persons might have union with each other. They seek to know—to communicate so that they become persons bound together—not simply bodies or spirits.

The fifth assumption is that body and spirit are to be understood in holistic terms. There is no body and spirit dualism. Rather, body and spirit are essential and equal dimensions of a whole. As the ancient Old Testament story suggests, we were created from dust into which spirit was breathed so that we might become human beings.

To speak of body and spirit in dualistic terms, to speak of them in terms of one being superior to the other, is to speak of them as unrelated realities coexisting, if not struggling against one another. A dualistic approach to body and spirit distorts their relationship to each other and skews understanding of human existence as an integrated whole.

The sixth assumption is that our sexuality is seen as a dimension of the self that is expressive through all dimensions of love—dimensions that together constitute holistic love. These expressions of love have traditionally been thought of in their classical Greek formulations of *epithymia, eros, filia,* and *agape.*[19] In the old paradigm they were separated from one another and treated in hierarchical fashion. What now becomes important is that they be seen as dimensions of a whole. Epithymaic love as an inner desire for sexual pleasure, erotic love as the passion that drives us to seek union with the other, filial love as companionate or friendship love, and agapaic love as the love that is manifest in self-giving—all are dimensions of love necessary for love to be known in its fullness. I want to comment on each of these.

Epithymia is the inner desire for sexual or sensual pleasure and satisfaction. It is the experience of sexual excitement and the desire to satisfy the tension that excitement creates. It is the "spark" of attraction that we can have for other persons. It is present in the sexual feelings we have for ourselves and for others.

The most intense expression of this form of love is the desire for relations. It is wrong, however, to limit epithymia to that act. It is expressed, equally, in the pleasure experienced from looking, touching, hugging, or holding. It is felt in being physically present with another and experiencing that presence with anticipation and joy.

Epithymia is present, therefore, in my desire to each down and pick up the infant, or to reach out and hug the elderly friend, or to toss my arm around the shoulders of my son when he beats me in tennis. As such, I am not seeking or desiring to have sexual intercourse. I am desirous of making contact in a pleasurable sensual way quite removed from genital expression but no less personal and important, no less filled with anticipation and satisfaction.

This form of love contains a self-oriented need that does not necessarily take into account the other person's needs or desires. It focuses on the self and the self's desires of the moment. If that focus becomes the only grounds on which a person finally acts, then love becomes a self-centered expression of love rather than one stream that feeds a flowing body of love including but transcending the self.

Eros or erotic love drives us to seek union with that which can provide fulfillment, which can give us a sense of wholeness by reuniting us to that which we long for but are not a part of it. It is the passion to find, to experience, to know the other. Eros provides epithymia with a power of passion that drives the self towards the other, in order to experience and know the other in a meaningful way.

Thus I desire to have sexual relations with my wife, to enjoy the sensual delight of our bodies. But desire is more than simply the need to satisfy a sexual urge. I desire to be united in a meaningful way so that my satisfaction, my sense of completeness, is more than that from sexual release. My satisfaction comes from giving and being given to, from having a sense of oneness and integration.

I desire to pick up and cuddle the baby not simply out of the need to have certain sensations satisfied that come from touching an infant. I also desire to touch the baby as a meaningful interaction with another person—a person whom I once was like, who needs to be touched. In the touching, human contact occurs that is fulfilling to us both. (Women tell me that birth-giving and breast-feeding are wonderfully erotic experiences.)

Further, my sexuality as an expression of myself as a sexual person reaching out to the other is manifest through the third dimension of love, that of *filia*, Filial love is the love of friendship, of companionship. It is love in which a mutual life of giving and receiving is present in an ongoing fashion. It is or should be a strong element in sexual relationships. (Too often we ignore the importance of friendship as a necessary ingredient for the creation of a good marriage.)

Such a relationship involves a genuine interest in other persons, in what they think and feel, in what they do and believe, in how they live and why they live the way they do. This genuine interest forms the grist of friendship. But the underlying power of erotic love runs the wheels of the gristmill. That underlying power is initiatory and sustaining.

I become a person's friend because I am attracted to the possibility of knowing and becoming a part of that person's life. Whether intense or reserved, genuine companionship comes together and holds together by such attraction. Furthermore, I am attracted to this person because I am a sexual person whose sexual identity at some level is present as an energy in the dynamic of the friendship. This does not mean we will seek to have sexual relations, but this does not deny that there is the presence of a sexual energy working as a part of the excitement about that person and forming the mutual attraction we experience.

Sexuality, therefore, is a part of filial love. As the theologian Norman Pittenger states: "In human relationships as such, of whatever sort, there is a sexual element precisely because those who are party to them are sexual beings."[20]

The final dimension of love is that of *agape* or self-giving love. Agape should not be seen as one form of love alongside the other forms, but rather as a love that informs or infuses those other expressions. Paul Tillich sees it as a quality of self-giving that should ground all other forms of love. And the ethicist James B. Nelson provides a unified understanding of love in which agape "undergirds and transforms" the other modes of love. He writes:

> Agape is not another kind of love. . . . It is the transformative quality essential to any true expression of any of love's modes. If we define Christian love as agape or self-giving alone—without elements of desire, attraction, self-fulfillment, receiving—we are describing a love which is both impoverishing and impoverished. But the other elements of love without agape are ultimately self-destructive. Agape is present with sexual desire, erotic aspiration and mutuality releases these from self-centeredness and possessiveness in a relationship that is humanly enriching and creative. It does not annihilate or replace the other modes of our loving. It undergirds and transforms. And faith knows that agape is gift, and not of our own making.[21]

Agape, then, is to be seen as that form of love that should transform all our expressions of love. A few years ago a photographic essay was published under the title of *Gramp*.[21] The authors tell the story of their grandfather and the grandfather's relationship to his family. They include two photographs that, taken together, provide a powerful statement of the character of love that I have been discussing. One picture shows the grandfather as a middle-aged man holding his grandson. The other shows the grandson as a middle-aged man holding his thin and very aged grandfather.

The statement is obviously not a statement about "sex" in the narrow sense of that word. It is a statement about love—a love in which the sexuality of these persons is very much present in a rich and meaningful fashion. The grandfather and the grandson in each picture stand as persons with a physical presence to each other in their acts of touching and holding. Two persons deeply attracted to one another have reached out and have been drawn close together in a union that includes yet transcends simple holding. There is present, both physically and spiritually, the warm mutual love of camaraderie, of friendship, of familial devotion. Thus the acts of touching and holding are transformed by the inexplicable gift of self-giving that infuses the revealed love. Our sexuality and our love, from the perspective of a holistic vision, are necessarily interwoven. To deny one or the other would be to split that which creation and creativity have made into one cloth.

The sixth assumption is that sexuality should be seen as a means through which we can know the grace of God. Our sexuality is one of the pivotal dimensions of human life; it becomes one of the means through which the grace of God is expressed. For through it we encounter and participate in the creative, sustaining, and reconciling grace given to us by God.

The expression of our sexuality can become a means of experiencing creative grace insofar as it engages us in creatively using our imaginations, in responding to the self and to the other. Grace comes at that point when we are seeking to find a vital way of relating, of touching, of responding. Suddenly we find a way that "fits," that is appropriate, that moves the relationship to a new level of meaning. We experience a breakthrough to the new. It is a gift, for we do not simply bring it about, but rather, in bringing and allowing, in releasing and opening, we receive it. It is an act informed by imagination. It is a creative act.

We also participate in creative grace through the procreativity of which we can be a part. Procreation has biological, emotional, social, and moral dimensions. Finally, though, beneath these aspects we confront a mystery—a mystery of why we are created in such a fashion and how that fits into a cosmic whole. Understanding that mystery, we recognize that life has been given by the grace of God. We know this grace when we become a part of the procreative process. We do participate in a miracle of birth.

Sexual expression can also become the means of sustaining grace. As human beings we know sustaining grace in loving and being loved, in disclosing and discovering. A parent's massaging of a child's back, the holding of a friend in grief, the sexual union of partners—thousands of acts over thousands of days that are acts of physical presence become the means by which we receive the grace of sustenance and nurture.

Sexual expression can also be a means of reconciling grace. In a broken relationship sexual expression as an act of reconciliation can become a means of overcoming that brokenness. It may be the one place in a couple's life where they find some type of vital communion together. It may be the way of maintaining touch on the road back to togetherness.

In all of these forms of grace, the experience becomes that of wholeness—of integration, of love, of fulfillment. In that experience of wholeness we know God. To be sexually whole is to know divine grace.

The final assumption is that norms governing sexual behavior should exist as guides to the realization of sexual health and wholeness. Anthony Kosnick and his colleagues in their study, *Human Sexuality*, have suggested one set of norms that I find indicative of what the new paradigm seeks when they call for sexual relations to be self-liberating, other-enriching, honest, faithful, socially responsible, life-serving, and joyous.[22] It is important to note that these norms are focused on the realization of well-being for persons and community, on the realization of some experience of wholeness, rather than simply on the rightness or wrongness of a particular act. I should like to sketch certain broader norms for sexual expression in the following manner:

1. Our sexual expressions should be expressions of loving intimacy in which passion, companionship, and self-giving are all present.

2. The primary context for healthy sexual relations should be within a stable structure, such as marriage or a union or a primary commitment, in order that continuity and depth may be more nearly realized and the relationship of sexual expression to an ongoing life together may be more nearly experienced.

3. Procreative choices should be made in a deliberate and cautious manner in light of whether the best interests of the child, the parents, and the larger community will be served.

4. The expression of our own sexuality should be made in a fashion that is respectful and responsive to the needs for sexual wholeness that the self, the other, and the larger community have.

I believe a paradigm shift is taking place. What finally the new paradigm will look like remains to be seen, but I think that the directions I have charted are suggestive of the course being taken.

Endnotes

1 Anthony Kosnick, et al, *Human Sexuality, New Directions in American Catholic Thought*, (Paulist Press, 1977) p. 92.

2 Thomas Kuhn, *The Structure of Scientific Revolution*, (The University of Chicago Press, 1970).

3   The thesis of this address was first developed for lectures given at the University of St. Jerome's College, Waterloo University. See James B. Nelson, *Between Two Gardens*, (Pilgrim Press, 1983), Chapter 5 for a discussion of old and new paradigms in Protestant positions on sexuality and the shift he sees taking place.

4   Phyllis Trible, "Biblical Foundations," in *Human Sexuality, a Preliminary Study*, The United Church of Christ, (United Church Press, 1977) pp. 36-39.

5   *Ibid.*, p. 39.

6   See John Noonan, *Contraception, A History of its Treatment by the Catholic Theologians and Canonists* (Harvard University Press, 1965) chs. 4-8 for a detailed discussion of patristic and early medieval theologians' perspectives on sexuality and their fear of sexual desire. Of particular insight is Noonan's treatment of Augustine. See also G. Rattray Taylor, *Sex in History* (Harper, 1973) chs. 2-6 for a good overview of theological positions; and Roland H. Bainton, *Sex, Love and Marriage, A Christian Survey*, (Fontana books, 1958) chs. 2 and 3 for an overview of the place of sex in marriage in the history of Christianity.

7   Noonan, *ibid.*, p. 80.

8   Bainton, *ibid.*, p. 32.

9   Noonan, *op. cit.*, ch. 4.

10 Augustine, *On Genesis*.

11 Noonan, *op. cit.*, p. 129.

12 *Ibid.*

13 Wilson Yates, "Population Ethics: Religious Traditions: Protestant Perspectives," in *Encyclopedia of Bioethics*, pp. 2359-1263; and "The Protestant View of Marriage," in *Journal of Ecumenical Studies*, Vol. 22, No. 1, Winter, 1985.

14 Noonan, *op. cit.*, chs. 4-5; and Taylor, *op. cit.*, ch. III.

15 See A.L. Rowse, *Homosexuals in History*, (Macmillan, 1977).

16 James B. Nelson, *Embodiment* (Augsburg, 1978) ch. 8.

17 This treatment of the holistic paradigm drawn on material from an earlier article: Wilson Yates, "Sexuality, Love and Wholeness," in *Engage/Social Action*, November, 1982.

18 See James E. Sellers, *Theological Ethics* (Macmillan, 1966) pp. 55-6. In this study he develops an ethic of wholeness and gives attention to the theological roots of the word.

19 Several theologians have developed perspectives regarding the interdependence of the various forms of love, including Paul Tillich, *Love, Power and Justice* (Oxford, 1960) ch. II; Daniel Day Williams, *The Spirit and Forms of Love* (Seabury, 1975) chs. I, II and V; Rosemary Reuther, "Misogynism and Virginal Feminism in the Fathers of the Church," in *Religion and Sexism*, Rosemary Reuther, ed. (Simon and Schuster, 1974); and James B. Nelson, *Embodiment*, op. cit., ch. v. Nelson's study provides the most thorough understanding of the interrelatedness of the four dimensions of love and the present discussion draws on his treatment: see ch. V.

20 Norman Pittenger, *Making Sexuality Human* (Pilgrim Press, 1970), p. 30.

21 Nelson, *ibid.*, pp. 113-114.

22 Mary and Dan Jury, *Gramp* (Penguin, 1978).

23 Kosnick, *op. cit.*, pp. 92-95.

42.654

B. Process of the Study

Prior to the first meeting of the Task Force on Pornography, study coordinator Sylvia Thorson-Smith and COWAC-COWC staff, Elizabeth H. Verdesi, Carole Goodspeed, and Judith Mead-Atwell, began reading extensively on the issue of pornography, including the *Final Report of the Attorney General's Commission on Pornography*, which was released during the summer of 1986. In September, the group attended a seminar at the Interchurch Center entitled "Women's rights, the New Right, and the Religious Right," and interviewed keynote speaker Betty Friedan regarding her concerns about pornography as a women's issue. While in New York, the staff team for the study visited the 47th Street office of Women Against Pornography and viewed the film, "Not a Love Story" (a documentary about the production of pornographic films).

In October, Thorson-Smith attended the annual meeting of Iowans Concerned about Pornography in order to observe local efforts on the issue. Featured speaker for the event was Diane Cusack of Scottdale, Arizona, who had served as a member of the Attorney General's Commission on Pornography.

In November, Thorson-Smith and study committee members Anne Callison and Elizabeth McWhorter attended a meeting in Washington, D.C., of the Religious Alliance Against Pornography. This event began with a three-hour briefing at the White House, which included presentations by Attorney General Edwin Meese III and two members of his Commission on Pornography. Dr. James Dobson and Father Bruce Ritter. Speakers for the conference included representatives of many religious traditions (Catholic, Jewish, Greek Orthodox, Methodist, Episcopal, Baptist, Church of God, National Council of Churches), governmental agencies (FBI, Postal Service), law schools, other organizations (Women Against Pornography, Parents' Music Resource Center), pollster George Gallup, and another member of the Attorney General's Commission, Dr. Park Elliott Dietz.

The first meeting of the Task Force on Pornography was held in New York City in December. As part of its introduction to the issue, members viewed three films: "Killing Us Softly," "Rate It X," and "Not a Love Story." Dale Rasmussen, consultant to the Program Agency, prepared a preliminary bibliography and presented an overview of the Meese Commission Report, as well as the report of the 1970 Governmental Commission on Obscenity and Pornography. Members reviewed the actions of previous General Assemblies, studied the positions and activities of other denominations, and began to explore the issue within a biblical and theological context. In order to accurately understand the availability of pornography, the task force went to Show World, a sex shop located in the 42nd Street area. The visit was conducted by a staff member from Women Against Pornography, which regularly sponsors educational tours.

Following the December meeting, members began to read the diversity of opinion available on the issues of pornography and obscenity. Summaries of books and articles were written by members and shared with each other by mail as part of their information-gathering.

In February 1987, Thorson-Smith attended a seminar at Grinnell College, Grinnell, Iowa, on "The U.S. Constitution and First Amendment Issues." Two feminists spoke to different sides of the issue of pornography, Dr. Elizabeth Fox-Genovese, director of Women's Studies at Emory University in Atlanta, Georgia, spoke against pornography regulation in her address entitled "Pornography and Individual Right: The Issues." Catherine A. MacKinnon, an attorney who advocates for pornography regulation, spoke concerning "Sexual Politics and the First Amendment." Archibald Cox, special prosecutor for the Watergate investigation, also addressed the issues of First Amendment rights.

Also in February, Thorson-Smith had a lengthy phone conversation with Twiss Butler, Washington, D.C., coordinator of the pornography issue for the National Organization for Women (*NOW*). Subsequently, Ms. Butler provided the Task Force with numerous resources reflecting *NOW's* position on the issue.

In March, the task force met in Minneapolis, Minnesota. In 1985, the Minneapolis City

Council adopted an ordinance to regulate pornography, which was subsequently vetoed by the mayor. The task force heard from representatives of both sides of that debate: Jeanne M. Barkey, a feminist from the Pornography Resource Center, which supported the ordinance; and David M. Gross, an attorney for the City of Minneapolis, who opposed the ordinance.

During the Minneapolis meeting, the task force also heard a presentation by the Rev. Dr. Jerry R. Kirk, pastor of College Hill Presbyterian Church in Cincinnati, Ohio, and Sharlynn Stare, an elder from that congregation. Rev. Kirk is organizer and president of the National Coalition Against Pornography and chair of the Religious Alliance Against Pornography. Ms. Stare is an active member of Cincinnati Presbytery's Committee on Pornography. As part of their presentation, Mr. Kirk and Ms. Stare showed the film, "Pornography: A Winnable War."

Throughout the study, members have sought to understand the issue of pornography within a biblical and theological context. During its March meeting, the task force discussed the issue of pornography with Dr. Wilson Yates, professor of social ethics at United Theological Seminary in New Brighton, Minnesota. Dr. Yates presented a paper to the group entitled, "Human Sexuality: Dualistic and Holistic Paradigms." (Dr. Yates' paper in the Theological Perspectives section of the Background Material of this report.)

At the conclusion of the Minneapolis meeting, the task force discussed the role of pornography in the lives of women who are prison inmates with the Rev. Carrie Dorfman, a Presbyterian chaplain with the Minnesota correctional system.

In May, Thorson-Smith and study committee member Jim Spalding attended the third annual meeting of the National Coalition Against Pornography in Cincinnati. While there, they also met with members of the Cincinnati Presbytery Committee on Pornography.

Also in May, Mead-Atwell and study committee member Carol Davies attended a conference at New York University School of Law in New York City. The conference, entitled "The Sexual Liberals and the Attack on Feminism," explored the debate over pornography and sexuality issues within the feminist community with speakers including Susan Brownmiller, Phyllis Chesler, Andrea Dworkin, Sonia Johnson, Catherine MacKinnon, and Robin Morgan.

Members who were at the 1987 General Assembly for other responsibilities conducted an open hearing to which anyone was invited to speak about their concerns regarding the issue of pornography. Discussion during the hearing focused on two dimensions: the global connections, with ecumenical visitors, Dr. Marie Assad of Egypt and Prokai Nontawassee of Thailand; and the connections between pornography and prostitution with the Rev. Ann Hayman, General Assembly commissioner and director of the Mary Magdalene Project in Los Angeles, California. While at General Assembly, Thorson-Smith had an interview about the issue of pornography with Dr. Ralph Blair, a psychotherapist in New York City and speaker at the luncheon sponsored by Presbyterians for Gay and Lesbian Concerns. Mr. Keith Wulff of the Communications Unit of the Support Agency also met with task force members to begin preparation of a Presbyterian Panel survey on the issue of pornography.

Members of the task force met together in June at Ghost Ranch in Abiquiu, New Mexico. They worked to further the process of the study and attended a seminar entitled, "Female Sexuality and Bodily Functions in World Religions." led by Dr. Marie Assad of Egypt. This seminar was based on the results of a study of the connections between issues of female sexuality in the world's major religions, which was coordinated by Dr. Assad when she was Deputy Secretary of the World Council of Churches. While at Ghost Ranch, task force members held a session of open conversation around the issue of pornography with interested persons who were attending seminars at the ranch.

In August, Mead-Atwell and Thorson-Smith met in New York City with Dr. Ann Welbourne-Moglia, executive director of the Sex Information and Education Council of the United States (SIECUS). Dr. Welbourne-Moglia testified in 1985 before the Attorney General's Commission on Pornography.

The Presbyterian Panel on the issue of pornography was mailed to respondents in September. (Results of this survey of Presbyterian opinion will be available at the General Assembly.)

The task force concluded its meetings together in Atlanta, Georgia, September 20-22. During this session, members reviewed a preliminary draft of the report. The task force also heard a presentation by Dave Ely of the Georgia Coalition Against Pornography and discussed the perspectives of women of color on the issue of pornography with Dr. Beverly Guy-Sheftall, director of the Women's Resource Center at Spelman College, Atlanta. As a worship experience, the task force attended the opening service of the executive committee of the World Council of Churches which was held at Central Presbyterian Church.

Progress reports on the work of the task force were presented to the Council on Women and the Church (COWAC) and the Committee on Women's Concerns (COWC) at their meetings in March and July 1987. The report was adopted by COWC and COWAC in November 1987, and recommended to the 200th General Assembly (1988). The Advisory Council on Church and Society (ACCS) reviewed the report at its December, 1987 meeting and took action to support it.

42.655

C. Actions of Previous General Assemblies

42.656

1. *189th General Assembly (1977) IX, Action on Overtures (Minutes, UPCUSA, 1977 Part I, p. 118).*

   A. *Overture 7-77.* On opposing the Use of Pornography and Violence in the Entertainment and Marketing Media; and *Overture 48-77.* On Addressing the Destructive Nature of Violence on Television.

   The committee recommends that the 189th General Assembly (1977) take no action on these overtures and that the General Assembly adopt the following resolution:

   Whereas, it is the concern of the 189th General Assembly (1977) of The United Presbyterian Church in the United States of America, that the media is using violence and the sexual degrading of human beings for commercial purposes; and

   Whereas, this Assembly recognizes that this practice by the media, besides being morally degrading and economically wasteful, is spiritually destructive; and

   Whereas, this Assembly recognizes that in the recent filing of legal activity surrounding the use of violence and pornography in the media, Christians should make a response to such activity that will reflect their faith more than their fears; and

   Whereas, this Assembly recognizes the duty to reinforce the use of a dignified image of human beings, but in such a manner which reflects the Christian faith rather than fears and retaliatory tactics;

   Therefore, the 189th General Assembly (1977) of The United Presbyterian Church in the United States of America does hereby resolve to take a public stand against the use of pornography and violence in the media and to reinforce the dignity of human beings, and thereby strengthen the Christian faith. Specifically, this General Assembly meeting in Philadelphia, PA, June 21-29, 1977, resolves to:

   1. Urge the individual members of The United Presbyterian Church in the United States of America to act responsibly as members of Christ's body by: (a) refraining from supporting economically all motion pictures offensive to that individual's personal and moral convictions, and refraining from supporting economically companies that sponsor TV or radio programs or advertise in media in ways offensive to that individual's personal moral convictions; (b) by filing objections with the management and refusing to patronize those businesses which

they personally feel contribute to the moral decay of our homes and families; (c) writing personally to those against whom the above action has been taken, informing them of the action and the reason for it.

2. Urge individuals to participate in the week-long seminar of the Advisory Council on Church and Society, July 25-Aug. 1, 1977, at Ghost Ranch, exploring the issue of violence on television, and direct this advisory Council to make its report on the seminar and the findings of this seminar to all churches and to the 190th General Assembly (1978).

3. Call upon other Christian denominations and other religions to join with the United Presbyterian Church in the reinforcement of the dignity of human beings.

4. Direct the Stated Clerk to transmit immediately this statement opposing the use of pornography and violence in the entertainment and marketing media to all major networks and news media.

42.657

2. *196th General Assembly (1984), Resolution on Pornography (Minutes, 1984, Part I, pp. 63-64).*

Whereas, in the last few years there has been an explosive escalation of the portrayal of sexual immorality and deviation, profanity, alcoholism and other drug abuse, and demonic violence on television and radio; and

Whereas, the lifestyle that is modeled for our children on the mass media outlets, which portray these excesses without regard for time of day or age of audience, is potentially dehumanizing and morally destructive; and

Whereas, many of the ideals lifted up on mass media programming are in direct contradiction to those lifestyle ideals that are proclaimed and modeled in the gospel of Jesus Christ; and

Whereas, we are called as members of the church of Jesus Christ to name the principalities and powers that are seeking to claim our allegiance; and

Whereas, the General Assemblies of both the former UPCUSA and the PCUS have acted in response to violence, sexual exploitation for commercial purposes, and lax morality in the public media; and

Whereas, the former PCUS at its 121st General Assembly (1981) recorded its opposition to themes of violence and immorality in the public media and further called for appropriate federal agencies to employ their influence to eliminate extreme portrayals of these themes in the public media; and

Whereas, the former UPCUSA at its 189th General Assembly (1977) adopted a resolution, "to take a public stand against the use of pornography and violence in the media and to reinforce the dignity of human beings, and thereby strengthen the Christian faith," (Minutes, 1977, Part I, p. 118); and

Whereas, among the comments that have been made by past General Assemblies, the 185th General Assembly (1973) noted a concern for the following problem areas as they are portrayed in the mass media:

a. glorification of violence and its numbing effect on ethical standards;

b. commercialization and exploitation of sex;

c. overt appeals to materialism as the ideal style of life;

d. emphasis on advertising instant relief of problems through medication; and

Whereas, pastors, counselors, social agencies, and law officials are seeing families broken and lives adversely affected, as well as persons of both sexes and of all ages victimized by pornography and obscenity; and

Whereas, pornography, "kiddie porn," and materials depicting excessive violence and murder combined with sexual content are part of a growing six billion dollar industry (more than the movie and record industries combined) controlled largely by organized crime (ranked as their third largest money-maker); and

Whereas, the Supreme Court of the United States in 1973 established basic guidelines for determining "what is obscene," and

Whereas, the Supreme Court of the United States has traditionally held that obscenity is not protected by the First Amendment and that obscenity is not protected expression; and

Whereas, there are existing federal and state laws to stem the rampant flow of obscene materials and to control their availability; therefore, be it

Resolved, That the 196th General Assembly (1984) of the Presbyterian Church (U.S.A.):

1. Direct the Stated Clerk to notify the President of the United States that it is the desire of the General Assembly of the Presbyterian Church (U.S.A.) to have the laws related to obscenity enforced by the U.S. Attorney General and the U.S. attorneys, the U.S. Postal Service, the Commerce Department, and the Customs Department, and that the Presbyterian Church (U.S.A.) is supportive of current efforts to include obscenity under the R.I.C.O. Statutes. (R.I.C.O. Statutes: Racketeering Influenced and Corrupt Organizations statutes currently cover obscenity. Legislation to this effect was introduced into the House and Senate in 11-14-83.)

2. Mandate the Council on Women and the Church and the General Assembly Mission Board (Office of Women) to persevere in their work in the areas of pornography and obscenity and the education of the church and society to combat the abusive treatment of women.

3. Establish official, visible relationship with other denominations and their leaders who are taking action against obscenity and pornography.

4. Encourage every Presbyterian to:

   a. develop awareness of the depth of the problem and its implications for the church and the world;

   b. take an active supportive role in one of the organizations working to establish the enforcement of current laws;

   c. refrain from supporting economically all motion pictures offensive to the individual's personal and moral convictions, and refrain from supporting economically companies that sponsor TV or radio programs or advertise in media in ways offensive to that individual's personal moral convictions;

   d. file objections with the management or refuse to patronize those businesses that they personally feel contribute to the moral decay of our homes and families;

   e. write personally to those against whom the above action has been taken, informing them of the action and the reason for it.

5. Call on our churches to minister both to those who have been victimizers and to those who are or who have been victimized by violence, pornography, and sexual abuse, affirming the love of God and the new life in Jesus Christ that is for all persons.

6. Instruct the Stated Clerk to send a copy of this action to the appropriate executives of denominations in the United States with whom we are in correspondence, informing them of our concern and commitment and encouraging their consideration of this matter. (Minutes, 1984, Part I, pp. 63-64.)

42.658

3. *197th General Assembly (1985)*

A. *Overture 92-85*, on developing material for educational purposes concerning obscenity, pornography, sexual harassment, exploitation, etc.

    1. That the above overture be adopted as amended so that it shall read as follows:

    That the 197th General Assembly (1985) of the Presbyterian Church (U.S.A.)

        a. Appropriate $42,900 ($7,000 in 1985, $20,000 in 1986, $15,900 in 1987) to the Council on Women and the Church and the Council [sic. i.e., Committee] on Women's Concerns for research to complete the task given them by the 196th General Assembly (1984);

        b. Direct COWAC-COWC to present to the 199th General Assembly (1987) the results of such research and proposals to develop educational material and plans to distribute them to sessions and congregations;

        c. Request COWAC-COWC to develop material for educational purposes concerning obscenity, pornography, sexual harassment, and other forms of sexual exploitation of persons, appropriate for study within the sessions and congregations;

        d. Encourage all pastors and churches in the Presbyterial Church (U.S.A.) to support actively the national pornography awareness week (last week in October);

        e. Encourage COWAC-COWC to make the church aware of educational resources already in existence that cover the topics of obscenity, pornography, sexual harassment, and other forms of sexual exploitation. This should be done at the direction of the above named councils.

42.659

4. *198th General Assembly (1986)*

The General Assembly adopted *Commissioners' Resolution* 3-86, which reads:

    Whereas, the United States Attorney General's Commission on Pornography has documented that sexually explicit and violent materials are addictive and demoralizing to individuals, victimize children, women and men, and contribute to the destruction of family life . . . in essence, pornography is not a victimless crime;

    Whereas, the content of pornography is antithetical to the Judeo-Christian calling and values;

    Whereas, the 196th and 197th General Assemblies (1984, 1985) declared their awareness and growing concern for the devastating effects of pornography on the social, and moral and spiritual conditions of our nation by adopting strong overtures with definitive recommendations;

    Whereas, the 197th General Assembly (1985) mandated that a $45,000 three-year study be undertaken by the Council on Women and the Church (COWAC) to develop resources to inform and equip congregations in the battle against pornography, but the General Assembly Finance Committee has not funded this work by COWAC;

    Whereas, the proposed Mission Design specifies "pornography" as an area of concern of the Social Justice and Peacemaking Ministry Unit (second draft, p. 16. 91); therefore, be it:

    Resolved, That the 198th General Assembly (1986) of the Presbyterian Church

(U.S.A.) reaffirm the actions of the 196th and 197th General Assemblies (1984 and 1985) related to pornography; and

Mandate the appropriate agency (Advisory Council on Church and Society and the Social Justice and Peacemaking Ministry Unit) to advocate the public policy position of the General Assembly in the area of pornography and assist the church in its social witness (this includes the immediate funding of work to implement the actions of the two previous General Assemblies).

42.660

5. Guidelines from the 1973 PCUS Statement "On Pornography, Obscenity, and Censorship"

III. Guidelines for Christian Decision

Christians have no simple and easy answers to the complex legal, psychological, and sociological questions we have considered. We cannot formulate a solution to them which we could claim is the Christian solution. What we can do is to look at the various aspects of the problem of obscenity and pornography in light of the biblical and theological presuppositions of our faith and try to formulate some guidelines for Christian action which are both faithful and realistic.

1. *Human physical life.* The Christian doctrine of the creation of male and female in the image of God, the incarnation of God in a flesh and blood man, and the promise of the "resurrection of the body" all teach us that the human body and all its functions, including human sexuality, are willed and blessed by God. They are therefore to be accepted and used with thanksgiving, joy, pleasure, and responsibility as the good gifts of God. There is nothing inherently dirty, obscene, or sinful about any aspect of our physical existence and relationships.

2. *Human relatedness.* The Christian doctrine of human beings made in the image of God teaches us that they are more than just biological creatures. They are creatures to whom God has given the capacity for personal relationship with him and their fellow human beings. In relationship with each other our physical existence becomes genuinely human existence when we live together with respect for the special dignity and value God has given every human life, in mutual loving and helping, giving and receiving.

3. *A Christian view of obscenity.* The Christian view of both the physical and the distinctively human aspects of our creaturely life suggests a basis for a Christian understanding of what is pornographic or obscene. Obscenity is a way of looking at human life which makes it less than what God created, treating human beings as if they were only animals or objects. Christians regard as obscene not physicality but inhuman physicality, not our biological functions and relationships, but an impersonal treatment of them. Pornography is the intrusion of a stranger who neither knows nor cares about the people involved in intimate physical processes and thus reduces what is happening to bare physical functions without meaning or personal involvement. This understanding of the problem helps us to recognize obscenity and pornography in the two ways they most often occur.

   a. Sexual obscenity. The portrayal of nudity or sexual relations as such is not pornography but is a portrayal of sexuality in such a way that what we are invited to see is not human beings but sex organs for their own sake, and what we are invited to feel is not a sense of the wonder and excitement of human relationships but only impersonal physical excitement for its own sake.

   b. The obscenity of violence or brutality. Many Americans are very sensitive to sexual obscenity and are concerned about what their children are exposed to in this area, yet often they are indifferent to the obscenity of violence and are causal about letting their children see in TV productions or movies the most callous infliction of pain, suffering, and death of human beings. The immorality of brutality or the sheer indifference which despises and degrades the God-given value and dignity of human life is at least as serious as sexual immorality. As with sexual relationships, so in this area the mere portrayal of brutality and violence is not in itself pornographic; it becomes pornographic if it is presented in such a way that we are encouraged to regard human pain, suffering and death as humorous, unimportant, or impersonal.

These criteria do not enable us infallibly to identify any particular book, movie, or TV program as obscene, nor do they solve the problem of how such a view of obscenity could be embodied in legal formulas—or even whether or not it should be. What they may do is to help us approach the problem with a deeper understanding so that we are freed from the ancient but still popular heresy that human sexuality is dirty and should be publicly outlawed, sensitized to the obscenity of violence which is so often accepted without protest in our society, and enabled to distinguish between responsible and pornographic treatment of physical human life and sexuality.

4. *The limits of individual freedom and the need for social control.* Since human beings are created for responsible relatedness to each other and can be human only in community, the freedom and rights of the individual must be related to and limited by the welfare of the whole society in which he or she lives. This tells us something about the Christian approach to the legal questions of whether and how pornography should be censored by legislation or court action. Christians cannot support the position that every person have the freedom to do and say or hear and see anything he pleases—especially when the speaking and listening and acting are done in a way which directly or indirectly affects other people, and most especially when it adversely affects the young and those who are otherwise helpless, defenseless, or vulnerable. This recognition of the limits of individual freedom opens up the possibility that some Christians may properly support the legal censorship of pornographic material despite the ambiguities and difficulties involved in such a legal solution to the problem. But such support is legitimate only after careful consideration of the present dangers and future consequences (political and religious as well as personal) of limiting freedom of speech and communication, and after careful evaluation on the basis of all available psychological and sociological evidence of the extent to which pornography is a real and not imagined threat to public health and welfare.

5. *The limits of social control and the need for individual freedom.* As individual freedom must be limited by community welfare, so community policies must be limited by the rights of individuals and minority groups. Individuals need the protection and help of the community, and the community needs the creativity, criticism, and reformation which come from free individuals. This also has bearing on the legal question of censorship.

Christians above all recognize the vital importance of the guarantee to individuals and minority groups of freedom of expression and the right to hear and see. The freedom to proclaim the gospel in word and deed, especially in situations where the promises and demand of the gospel are unpopular, depends on this freedom. Can we justly deny to others, even those with whom we seriously disagree or those who are radically out of step with the majority of our society, the freedom of expression we demand for ourselves?

Christians above all recognize the fact that "contemporary standards" of the "average person" should not be automatically accepted and enforced. They know about the fallibility and sinfulness of human beings and societies, and are called to witness to God's judgment and renewal. Can we justly deny to others the right we demand for ourselves to disagree with, criticize, and seek to change commonly accepted moral standards—even when what others stand for seems immoral or unchristian to us?

Christians also know about their own and the church's fallibility and sinfullness and are open to God's judgment and correction of their own understanding of right personal and social relationships. Do we not need to have our own values and standards challenged and criticized to help us determine whether they are genuinely Christian or only the reflection of cultural and historical influences unrelated to the Christian faith and life?

Such questions pointing to the legitimacy of and need for individual freedom in opposition to community standards may lead some Christians to oppose all censorship of pornographic material despite the possible dangers involved in such a position. But such opposition is legitimate only after careful consideration of how social health, justice, and unity may be threatened by an irresponsible individualistic concept of freedom in moral as well as in economic and political questions.

6. *Christian action in a pluralistic society.* Whatever our individual decisions about censorship, we must resist the temptation to demand or allow political authorities or courts to enforce on everyone specifically Protestant or even generally Christian standards of belief and conduct—just as we oppose the enforcement of the standards of any church or religion. Both the democratic principles of our Constitution which prohibit the establishment of any religion and our understanding of the Christian faith speak against such a solution to the problem of pornography. The Christian church exists in the world to serve and not be served, to give itself for men and not to make itself the lord over men. It proclaims in word and deed a gospel which judges and renews individuals and the social order, but it does not force people to live as if they were Christians when in fact they are not. The Church and individual Christians may and should work through the various political and legal instruments of society for laws and policies which reflect the Christian understanding of the nature and purpose of human life. But in the political, legal, and social spheres we will not argue for such laws and policies because they are biblical and Christian, but because they are the best expression of the proper relationship between individual freedom and community responsibility, because they most adequately respect and protect the value and dignity of human life, and because they promote the most human understanding of man's physical functions and relationships. Speaking and acting in these terms in the political, legal, and social spheres, we remain faithful to our Christian presuppositions and goals, yet stand together with people of other religions or of no religion who are also concerned about human life and freedom, and work for policies which are legitimate and possible under the Constitution of our nation.

7. *The limits of legal solutions.* Whatever our individual decision about legal measures to control pornography, we cannot expect them to solve the real problems which lie behind it. Laws and rules can control external actions to some extent, but they cannot control what people desire and will and think. Christians therefore will not expect or allow legislation or court actions to become a substitute for deeper solutions to the problem—the solutions to be found in their own homes, in the church, and in public schools. The dangers of pornography or obscenity are best fought by parents, teachers and ministers who by their own lives and by instruction teach both children and adults the dignity and value of human life, the horrible obscenity of wanton infliction of pain, suffering, and death of human beings, the beauty and goodness of the human body and its functions, and the meaning of sexuality and sexual relationships

which are not mechanical or animalistic but personal and human. Pornography or obscenity then loses it power and fascination as exposed for what it really is not some tremendous and delicious evil which is secretly relished even as it is righteously opposed, but a stupid, trivial, and boring parody of the real joy, excitement, pleasure, and wonder of authentic human life as God has willed and created it.

42.661

6. *Guidelines From the 1984 UPCUSA Study "On Dignity and Exploitation"*

In dealing with legislative matters, Christians have a peculiar obligation to insure that others' freedoms are guaranteed, even when that means the freedom to make choices of which one might personally disapprove. The obligation is nowhere clearer than in the area of obscenity and pornography, where we can see it as a Christian responsibility to be sure the law allows other consenting adults to read, watch or listen to things we might find distasteful at best, disgusting at worst. John Milton's argument against censorship laws proposed to the Parliament in seventeenth century England is still a good one. He opted for a free market of ideas, tastes and concepts, saying, "I cannot praise a fugitive and cloistered virtue." For Christians, there are some criteria, born of their faith, which can be brought to bear on the development of workable local and state laws, and on the manner in which they are applied. Here are a few representative, not definitive, examples:

1. Minors deserve certain protections. When Christian parents respond to the questions put to them at the baptism of their children, they promise to bring them up in the nurture and admonition of the Lord. They undertake an obligation, therefore, to influence the spiritual and ethical environment of their children. The first level at which that influence must be exercised is through example, a language children understand more clearly than any other. A second level of influence is by showing approval or disapproval, a powerful and important contribution to the nurture of children even when they howlingly disagree with their parents' judgments. A third level of influence is through parental action to protect children from untoward and disruptive emotional experiences. While one cannot and should not try to bring up children in cotton batting, there are some aspects of human experience for which children are unprepared at certain ages. Parents are being neither deceptive nor overprotective when they try to protect their children from experiences for which they are developmentally unprepared.

2. Do not overestimate what the law can do to protect the moral climate. The cultivation of healthy attitudes toward all aspects of human experience, the sexual included, in home and church is more significant for that climate than any law. It is worth remembering that what is well done at home cannot be undone at a magazine rack. If children have been taught to enjoy, respect and understand their own sexuality, and have been taught elemental respect for the privacy and integrity of others, those things will provide them better protection that any law against the potentially destructive influence of obscenity or pornography.

3. Respect the rights of other adults. There are two sides to this criterion: (a) it supports the right to limit public display of all forms of obscenity, the violent as well as the sexual; (b) it also supports the right of consenting adults to have discrete access to publications, films, etc., which, while offensive to some, are enjoyable or even therapeutic to others.

4. Remember that law is for protection, not harassment. In the experience of Christian faith, law is the structure of freedom, not its enemy. St. Paul reminds us that freedom is God's gift in Christ, and that law is meant to serve that gift, not to deny it. We are called upon, therefore, to see to it that laws intended to protect against wanton assault on public sensitivities by material judged obscene or pornographic are not used, in

turn as an instrument to harass those whose sexual proclivities may arouse fear or anger (or even jealousy) in the majority. Nor should we drop our guard against the law being used to harass teachers through censorship of their curricula by pressure groups in the community.

5. Do not trade freedom for security. The supreme gift of the Gospel is confidence in the love and the power of God. On the basis of this gift, Christians are invited to live out the risks of this life without anxiety. While the Gospel is not a counsel of deliberate imprudence, it is an invitation to live in an open, giving, unafraid and joyous manner of life. Anything that enhances the freedom of all without destroying the rights of any deserves the support of Christians, who furthermore should not trade their essential manner of life for any illusory security offered by the power of the state.

42.662

D. Statements and Activities of Other Religious Bodies

42.663

Some of the religious institutions that have responded to the issue of pornography through statement and activities are:

42.664

The Lutherans

In 1974, the American Lutheran Church adopted a statement challenging its members to understand the complexities of the issue of pornography and the tension between human freedom and responsibility. That statement was updated with a supplement in 1985, in recognition that "both the nature of pornography and the social climate in the United States have changed." The supplement discusses the problem of defining pornography, analyzes the debate over regulating pornography, presents biblical and theological considerations. It calls on members to affirm human sexuality as a gift from God, wherein "portrayals of respectful, even erotically explicit, sexual encounters may be edifying," while advocating a range of appropriate activities that members may use to demonstrate rejection of materials which "undermine human dignity and promote hatred or violence."[1]

In 1986, the Lutheran Church-Missouri Synod adopted a "guiding statement for moral reflection," analyzing the issue of pornography within the context of Christian understanding of sexuality.[2]

In late 1986, the Lutheran Council in the U.S.A., representing five Lutheran denominations, sent all members of Lutheran congregations in the United States a letter, urging them to give serious consideration to several statements on pornography and to support "both the First Amendment and enforcement of laws against child and violent pornography."[3]

42.665

The United Church of Canada

In 1984, the United Church of Canada adopted a resolution defining pornography and urging members to become involved with the issue. Its Division of Mission in Canada prepared a "Pornography Kit," which includes information about pornography, a suggested worship service, Bible study guides, and a bibliography.

42.666

The United Methodist Church

In 1985, the United Methodist Church sponsored a conference on "Pornography, Violence and Christian Values." Judith Mead-Atwell, staff person for COWAC, attended the two-day event, which featured presentations representing a variety of viewpoints on the issue of pornography. Materials produced by the United Church of Canada and a resource entitled "Pornography Hurts," by Joanna FairHeart, were distributed. The United Methodists also published a series of articles, "Pornography: Increasing Sexual Violence," in their social action magazine.

42.667

Other Denominational Actions

Denominational resolutions have been made by the Baptist General Conference, the Southern Baptist Convention, the Church of God (Indiana), the Church of the Nazarene, the Evangelical Free Church, the Free Methodist Church of North America, the Presbyterian Church in America, the Reformed Presbyterian Church of North America, the Church of Jesus Christ of Latter-Day Saints, the Church of God (Tennessee), and the Missionary Church. Both Orthodox Archdioceses of North and South America have issued statements regarding pornography, including plans for action. The "Women's Concerns Report," a publication by women in the Mennonite Central Committee of the U.S., devoted one issue to the topic of pornography, discussing definition, effects, and First Amendment considerations.

42.668

National Council of Churches

In 1985 the National Council of Churches adopted a report produced by a study committee of its Communication Commission entitled, "Violence and Sexual Violence in Film, Television, Cable and Home Video." Included in the report are guidelines for determining a response to the increase of excessive violence in the media and recommended actions related to television, motion pictures, cable TV, videocassettes, public broadcasting.

The National Council of Churches, and other religious bodies (the American Jewish Committee, the National Council of Jewish Women, the Unitarian Universalist Fellowship, the United Church of Christ, and the Communications Division of the United Methodist Church) are participating organizations of the National Coalition Against Censorship. Some leaders of the National Council of Churches are also participating individuals in the Religious Alliance Against Pornography.

42.669

Religious Alliance Against Pornography

In July of 1986, in response to the initiative of Rev. Jerry R. Kirk, Presbyterian minister from Cincinnati, Ohio, leaders from Protestant, Roman Catholic, Greek Orthodox, Jewish and Mormon religious bodies formed the Religious Alliance Against Pornography. Its foundational document is in the Background Materials of this report. In November of 1986, the Religious Alliance Against Pornography held a two-day strategy conference in Washington, D.C., which included a briefing at the White House and a meeting with President Ronald Reagan. In the Presbyterian news release following the session with the President, Kirk stated: "We asked him and he was in total agreement that the battle against child pornography, pornography involving children sexually with one another and with adults, and hard-core obscenity, which is illegal and against the law, would be a new priority for this administration."[4]

42.670

The National Council of Jewish Women

The National Council of Jewish Women, in keeping with a long history of Jewish opposition to censorship and governmental regulation of printed materials, produced a resource in 1983 entitled, "Endangered: The Right to Read as We Choose." Subsequently, NCJW has produced workshop materials to address the difficult issues of censorship and pornography. An article in a 1986 journal entitled "Censorship, Sex and the First Amendment" concludes: "With the exception of child pornography, NCJW has historically been opposed to any regulation which would limit the publication or sale of any materials, even if that material might be offensive. However, there is considerable debate as to how pornographic materials should be displayed and whether restraints placed on the exhibit of such material constitute censorship.''[5]

Notes

[1] "The Victims of Pornography," Analysis by the American Lutheran Church, Office of Church and Society, 1985, p. 1.

[2] Resolution 2-08, "To Intensify Efforts to Curb Pornography, Violence, Obscenity, and Indecency," Adopted by the Lutheran Church-Missouri Synod, July, 1986.

[3] Letter from the Lutheran Council in the U.S.A., 1986.

[4] Presbyterian News Report, P-86219, November 21, 1986, p. 11.

[5] Censorship, Sex and the First Amendment,'' NCJW Journal, Winter, 1986, Vol. IX, No. 4, p. 13.

42.671

E. Religious Alliance Against Pornography

(Foundational Statement)

As religious leaders, we believe in the inherent dignity of each human being. Created in God's image and likeness, the human person is the clearest reflection of God's presence among us. Because human life is sacred, we all have a duty to develop the kind of societal environment that protects and fosters its development. This is why we address a broad range of life threatening and life diminishing issues. These assaults on human life and dignity are all distinct, each requiring its own moral analysis and solution. But they must be confronted as elements of a larger picture.

The purpose of RAAP is to bring into clear focus a major factor in the assault on human dignity and the consequent dehumanization that it promotes: hard core and child pornography. This concern brought us together following the release of the Report of the Attorney General's Commission on Pornography. We are in unanimous agreement that hard core and child pornography, which are not protected by the Constitution, are evils which must be eliminated.

As religious leaders, our primary responsibility is to teach and motivate. We can and must help people understand the moral dimensions of the problem of hard core and child pornography and what their responsibility is in this regard, while fully respecting freedom of expression guaranteed by the First Amendment. In particular, we wish to make it clear that we do not and will not advocate censorship. Our understanding of censorship implies actions being taken against materials which are protected by the First Amendment.

As teachers, we will do all in our power to proclaim the truth of human dignity and freedom, and to promote the God-given human values needed for the moral health of our society. Given the information and motivation, people will do what is necessary to affect public policy.

The membership of RAAP, representing a broad spectrum of America's religious community, is an indication of the seriousness of the problem and our commitment to addressing it. This represents the beginning of an ongoing process which will facilitate greater cooperation on this vital issue among religious bodies.

42.672

F. Examples of Social Science Research on Pornography

42.673

Following are brief summaries of a few of the studies that have been conducted to determine the effects of exposure to pornography:

42.674

1. Dr. Edward Donnerstein, Professor of Communication Studies at the University of California, Santa Barbara, has spent considerable effort investigating the effects of sexually explicit material on attitudes. In one study, Donnerstein used X-rated movies where violence, rape and assault against women are themes, but there are no explicit acts of intercourse. Testing 156 male college students, he followed the showing of films with the reenactment of a rape trial. Students who had viewed the violent films regarded the rape victim as more worthless and rape as a more trivial offense than did students in a control group who had not seen the films. Donnerstein concluded that ''there is a definite pattern of desensitization to violence against women and, in particular, a trivialization of the crime of sex.''[1]

   In a recent book entitled, *The Question of Pornography*, Donnerstein cites other research in drawing his fundamental conclusion that ''violence against women need not occur in a pornographic or sexually explicit context to have a negative effect upon viewer attitudes and behavior. But even more importantly, it must be concluded that violent images, rather than sexual ones, are most responsible for people's attitudes about women and rape.''[2]

42.675

2. Dr. Victor B. Cline, a clinical psychologist at the University of Utah, has found that men who use pornography mixing sex and violence are ''(1) aroused sexually and aggressively, (2) tend to increase their aggressive attitudes and behavior, (3) have an increased production of aggressive rape fantasies, (4) are more accepting of such rape myths as 'women ask for it,' (5) have a lessened sensitivity about rape and an increased callousness toward women, (6) admit an increased possibility of themselves raping someone, especially if they think they can get away with it.''[3] Cline cites a study by Seymour Feshback at UCLA where, following exposure to violent pornography, 51 percent of male students who were tested indicated the likelihood of raping a woman if assured they would not get caught.

42.676

3. Dorf Zillmann of Indiana University and Jennings Bryant of the University of Houston selected average male and female students from four universities. They also selected a male and female population from a midwestern city. One group saw six sexually explicit films that were non-violent and non-degrading, once a week for six weeks. Another group saw three films of the same type, once a week for six weeks. A third group saw six innocuous films at the same intervals. One week after the film series ended, the groups were brought back together and viewed three more films. The first was non-violent and non-degrading; the second was sensuous but not graphic; the third was degrading and violent. Since the subjects demonstrated increased disinterest in the milder films and increased interest in the more violent films, Zillman and Bryant concluded that people become bored by mild forms of pornography and develop an appetite for stronger forms of it.[4]

42.677

4. In 1977, researchers R.A. Baron and P.A. Bell ''exposed male students to stimuli that included semi-nude females, nudes, heterosexual intercourse and some explicit erotic passages. The mild erotic stimuli (semi-nudes and nudes) inhibited aggression levels whereas the 'stronger' stimuli had no effects. A follow-up study (Baron, 1979), this time on female subjects, using the same stimulus materials found mild stimuli inhibiting aggressive behavior while the stronger stimuli increased aggression. Both these studies measured aggressive behavior via 'shocks' delivered on an aggression machine.''[5]

Notes

[1] Minnery, Tom, ed., *Pornography: A Human Tragedy*, 1986, p. 132.

[2] Donnerstein, Edward I. and Daniel G. Linz, "The Question of Pornography," *Psychology Today*, December, 1986, p. 59.

[3] Cline, Victor, "The Effects of Pornography on Behavior," Resource Booklet, Third Annual Conference of the National Coalition Against Pornography, September, 1985, p. 31.

[4] Minnery, *op. cit*, pp. 118-125.

[5] *Final Report of the Attorney General's Commission on Pornography*, Rutledge-Hill Press edition, 1986, p. 276.

42.678

G. Testimonies

42.679

1. *Interview with "Fantasy Girl" by Judith D. Atwell*

Penny Jones (not her real name) is an intelligent and vivacious 30-year old Black woman with a vibrant and infectious sense of humor. Penny agreed to talk about her experience as a "Fantasy Girl" because she believes that her story may help others understand the economic realities of some working-poor women and the choices they make.

Penny worked in the national church headquarters as a "Secretary B" with a gross salary of $285 a week, $210 net. The rent on her apartment was $210, utilities $45, telephone $30, and transportation approximately $100. Adding in food, clothing, and occasional entertainment, Penny "sort of broke even." Complicating her financial situation were two additional factors: she had just moved into an apartment and had to furnish it, and her daughter, who was living with Penny's parents in New Jersey, would soon be coming to live with her. She had been helping to support her daughter financially and frequently visited her on weekends.

It became apparent to Penny that she would have to get a second job. She was no stranger to hard work. In the past she had held down two full-time jobs and had a job while attending college full-time. When she considered what was available to her, she realized that the options were extremely limited. Her word processing skills were not sufficient to enable her to work "temp," and after working full-time during the day, she did not want a job that would necessitate travel on the subway, which was stressful and dangerous at night, especially for a woman. So when she saw the ad in the *Village Voice* for telephone work at home, she called the number listed.

She was invited to attend an "orientation" meeting at the Barbizon Hotel in mid-Manhattan where two men oriented the prospective employees and current employees talked about their work. Penny was told she would need a telephone capable of three-way-calling and that for tax purposes she should register as an "independent contractor." The company would furnish her with a Sprint number and would assume the cost for all long distance calls. For legal purposes, the company was a mail order business and Penny was "consumer services personnel." The company was very scrupulous in its record keeping; at the end of the year it assisted Penny to complete her special tax form. It encouraged employees to give customer satisfaction and provided motivational inducements including an annual Christmas party.

At the orientation Penny was given a portfolio containing several "scripts." During the training period she practiced with a tape recorder or with another woman, and her performance was critiqued. Because she is Black, and most clients prefer white women, she was coached to sound "white."

203

The operation worked in the following way: At the company offices in mid-Manhattan a receptionist received calls and quickly screened out children and callers who sounded inebriated or "high". The clients (almost all of whom were men) were then asked their phone numbers, preference of Fantasy Girl, and credit card number. After checking the client's credit, the receptionist would call Penny, or another woman, and tell her the phone number and client's fantasy if he had one.

Penny would call the client. She received $5 per call, or $7 if the client specifically requested her Fantasy Girl persona. (Each employee had several personas that they developed; in addition, each employee was assigned the persona of one of the models advertising the service whose picture appeared in *Playboy* and *Penthouse*. Penny's was "Sheri.")

The company received a minimum of $49 per call and the average phone call was $85. The caller was told he had 30 minutes, but the employees developed tactics to get the caller off the phone in less time—usually only five to ten minutes was required. After the call was completed, Penny called the receptionist to tell her the phone line was open.

Penny usually worked four nights a week, 10 PM-4 AM or 12 AM-6 AM. She made approximately $300 a week, but often much more, especially when she worked 24 hour shifts on the weekends. She averaged ten calls a night, and some nights took up to thirty calls, especially during football season. Half-time during the Super Bowl was the highest volume night. Her calls came from all over—Australia, Hawaii, Alaska, Texas. Some callers became regulars and conversation covered many areas including family concerns, sports, and business. In between calls she would sleep or do housework.

A camaraderie developed between her and the other women who worked on the service and they often called each other to gossip or to exchange tips. Some of the women were actors or models between jobs, some were students, some were in relationships with pimps and drug users, some women had no marketable skills. Some, like Penny, needed extra money because their full time employment did not pay enough to make ends meet.

At first the job seemed easy and the money good, but as time went on, it became intolerable. Penny functioned on the edge of exhaustion and found it difficult to stay awake at her secretarial job. It got to the point where she thought "one more phone call and I'll break into tears." The bizarre nature of the work, the fantasies that she had to fulfill or create, took its toll. "What kind of men are these?" she wondered. Some seemed like "regular guys." But what kind of man would call, begging to be beaten or tied up?" (Her neighbors, unable to subdue their curiosity, would ask what was going on in her apartment; they could hear banging all hours of the night as she was beating on books.) "These men were so submissive that the most active thing they did was place the initial call—after that they became merely passive participants in the fantasy. They wanted to be dominated, yet did not want a 'live' partner—not even a paid prostitute. When they knew what they wanted, it was easy. But often they just said, 'Turn me on,' and it was up to me to create the fantasy. It took a lot of imagination and energy to come up with something. Even though it was a sleazy job, part of me still wanted to do it well. Often there would be no response, and I'd say, 'Are you still with me? Stay with me now.' I'd keep talking, spinning out the fantasy, until we were on the same wavelength. Then I'd get a grunt or a groan, sometimes a thank you, often the phone would just click off." To Penny it was the "ultimate oral sex—no body, no brain—just my voice."

Penny started going to basketball games, she needed a crowd situation, normal people, something to be grounded in. In her exhausted state Penny's world was blurring, fantasy and reality were coming together. One night a regular customer with whom she had developed a rapport, called all excited because "now he knew her." He said that he had seen her picture in *Playboy*. He was ecstatic. Penny felt violated. "Did he know me? If he saw me on the street would he say hello?" She knew that was impossible—"Sheri" was one of her personas. That was whom he was talking about. Not her, not Penny. But she had shared with him, and liked him. It was getting all mixed up.

She started to cut back on the hours she worked as a Fantasy Girl and began reading the training manuals for the word processor. She taught herself all the functions, including the most advanced. After she became accomplished on the word processor, she quit both her Fantasy Girl job and her secretarial job preferring to work as a temporary word processor. At first it was hard going, but now she commands an excellent salary and works the hours she chooses at companies she likes.

When asked what sustained her through those six months as a Fantasy Girl, she replied, "the acceptance and emotional support of me by my family." Her mother was a domestic and her father a laborer, so both knew the hazards of working in occupations where one is dependent upon the good will of others.

When she was just beginning as a "temp" and times were tough, had she considered working again as a Fantasy Girl? "It crossed my mind—I know it is always there and the customers will always be there. But I stuck it out and found a good temp agency. Now I have the skills and the experience to make a decent salary for my daughter and myself and I never have to go that route again."

42.680

2. *Testimony of Linda Marchiano at the Public Hearings on the Minneapolis Pornography Ordinance*

Ms. Marchiano: I feel I should introduce myself and tell you why I feel I am qualified to speak out against pornography. My name today is Linda Marchiano. Linda Lovelace was the name I bore during a two and a half year period of imprisonment. (For those of you who don't know the name, Linda Lovelace was the victim of this so-called victimless crime. Used and abused by Mr. Traynor, her captor, she was forced through physical, mental, and sexual abuse and often at gunpoint and threats of her life to be involved in pornography. Linda Lovelace was not a willing participant but became the sex freak of the '70s.)

It all began in 1971. I was recuperating from a near fatal car accident at my parents' home in Florida. A girlfriend of mine came to visit me with a person by the name of Mr. Charles Traynor. He came off as a considerate gentleman, asking us what we would like to do and how we would like to spend the afternoon and opening doors and lighting cigarettes and all so-called manners of society.

Needless to say I was impressed, and started to date him. I was not getting along with my own parents. I was twenty-one and resented being told to be home at 11:00 o'clock and to call and say where I was and to call and give the phone number and address where I would be.

Here comes the biggest mistake of my life. Seeing how upset I was with my home life, Mr. Traynor offered me his assistance. He said I could come and live at his home in Miami. The relationship was platonic, which was fine with me. My plan was to recuperate and then go back to New York and live. I thought then he was being kind and a nice friend. Today I know why the relationship was platonic. He was incapable of a sexual act without inflicting some type of pain or degradation upon a human being.

When I decided to head back north and informed Mr. Traynor of my intention, that was when I met the real Mr. Traynor and my two and half years of imprisonment began. He began a complete turnaround and beat me up physically and began the mental abuse, from that day forward my hell began.

I literally became a prisoner. I was not allowed out of his sight not even to use the bathroom. Why, you may ask, because there was a window in the bathroom. When speaking to either of my friends or my parents, he was on the extension with a .45

automatic 8 shot pointed at me. I was beaten physically and suffered mental abuse each and every day thereafter.

In my book, *Ordeal, An Autobiography*, I go into greater detail of the monstrosity I was put through. From prostitution to porno films to celebrity satisfier. The things that he used to get me involved in pornography went from .45 automatic 8 shot and M-16 semi-automatic machine gun to threats on the lives of my family. I have seen the kind of people involved in pornography and how they will use anyone to get what they want.

So many people ask me why didn't you escape? Well, I did, I'm here today. I did try during the two and a half years to escape on three separate occasions. The first and second time I was caught and suffered a brutal bearing and an awful sexual abuse as punishment. The third time I was at my parents' home and Mr. Traynor threatened to kill my parents. I said, "No, you won't, my father is here in the other room" and he said, "I will kill him and each and every member of your family." Just then my nephew came in through the kitchen door to the living room, he pulled out the .45 and said he would shoot him if I didn't leave immediately. I did.

Some of you might say I was foolish but I'm not the kind of person who could live the rest of my life knowing that another human being had died because of me.

The name, Linda Lovelace, gave me a great deal of courage and notoriety. Had Linda Borman been shot dead in a hotel room, no questions would be asked. If Linda Lovelace was shot dead in Los Angeles, questions would have been asked. After three unsuccessful attempts at escaping, I realized I had to take my time and plan it well. It took six months of preparation to convince Mr. Traynor to allow me out of his sight for fifteen minutes. I had to tell him he was right, woman's body was to be used to make money, that porno was great, that beating people was the right thing to do. Fortunately for me, after I acquired my 15 minutes out of his presence, I also had someone that wanted to help me.

I tried to tell my story several times. Once to a reporter, Vernon Scott, who worked for the UPI. He said he couldn't print it. Again on the Regis Philbin Show and when I started to explain what happened to me, that I was beaten and forced into it, he laughed. Also at a grand jury hearing in California after they had watched a porno film, they asked me why I did it. I said, "Because a gun was being pointed at me" and they just said "Oh," but no charges were ever filed.

I also called the Beverly Hills Police Department on my final escape and I told them that Mr. Traynor was walking around looking for me with an M-16. When they first told me that the couldn't become involved in domestic affairs, I accepted that and asked them and told them that he was illegally possessing these weapons and they simply told me to call back when he was in the room.

During the filming of Deep Throat, actually after the first day. I suffered a brutal beating in my room for smiling on the set. It was a hotel room and the whole crew was in one room; there was at least twenty people partying, music going, laughing, and having a good time. Mr. Traynor started to bounce me off the walls. I figured out of twenty people, there might be one human being that would do something to help me and I was screaming for help, I was being beaten, I was kicked around and again bounced off of walls. And all of a sudden the room next door became very quiet. Nobody, not one person come to help me.

The greatest complaint the next day is the fact that there was bruises on my body. So many people say that in *Deep Throat* I have a smile on my face and I look as though I am really enjoying myself. No one ever asked me how those bruises got on my body.

Mr. Traynor stopped searching for me because he acquired Marilyn Chambers who I believe is also being held against her will.

A reporter from the Philadelphia newspaper did an interview, his name is Larry Fields.

During the course of the interview, Ms. Chambers asked for permission to go to the bathroom and he refused it. Mr. Fields objected and said, why don't you let the poor girl go to the bathroom, she is about to go on stage and he came back with, I don't tell you how to write your newspaper, don't tell me how to treat my broads.

I have also been in touch with a girl who was with Mr. Traynor two months prior to getting me, who was put through a similar situation but not as strong. And as it stands today, she still fears for her life and the life of her family. Personally, I think it is time that the legal system in this country realize that one, you can't be held prisoner for two and a half years and the next day trust the society which has caused your pain and resume the life you once called yours. It takes time to overcome the total dehumanization which you have been through. It is time for something to be done about the civil rights of the victims and not criminals. The victims being women. But realize, please, it is not just the women who are victims but also children, men, and our society.

42.681

H. Civil Legislation

42.682

1. Pornography Victims Protection Act (H.R.1213) To amend chapter 110 of title 18, United States Code, to create remedies for children and other victims of pornography and for other purposes.

In the House of Representatives
February 24, 1987

Mr. Green (for himself, Mr. Bryant, Mr. Crockett, Mr. Dannemeyer, and Mr. Fish) introduced the following bill; which was referred to the Committee on the Judiciary

A Bill

To amend chapter 110 of title 18, United States Code to create remedies for children and other victims of pornography and for other purposes. Be it enacted by the Senate and House of Representatives of the United States of America in Congress assembled, Section I. Short Title. This Act may be cited as the Pornography Victims Protection Act of 1987.

Section 2. Section 2251 Amendments

Section 2251 of Title 18, United States Code is amended:

(1) in subsection (a), by striking out "subsection (c)" and inserting in lieu thereof "subsection (d)" and by inserting before the period at the end thereof the following: "or if such person knows or has reason to know that the minor was transported in interstate or foreign commerce for the purpose of producing any such visual depiction of such conduct";

(2) in subsection (b), by striking out "subsection (c)" and inserting in lieu thereof "subsection (d)" and by inserting before the period at the end thereof the following: "or if such person knows or has reason to know that the minor was transported in interstate or foreign commerce for the purpose of producing any such visual depiction of such conduct";

(3) by inserting immediately after subsection (b) the following: (c)(1) Any person who coerces, intimidates, or fraudulently induces an individual 18 years or older to engage in any sexually explicit conduct for the purpose of producing any visual depiction of such conduct shall be punished as provided under subsection (d), if such person knows or has reason to know that such visual depiction will be transported in interstate or foreign commerce or mailed, if such visual depiction has actually been transported in interstate or foreign commerce of mailed, or if such person knows or has reason to know that the individual 18 years or older was transported interstate or foreign commerce for the purpose of producing any such visual depiction of such conduct.

(2) Proof of one or more of the following facts of conditions shall not, without more, negate a finding of coercion under this subsection

(A) that the person is or has been a prostitute;

(B) that the person is connected by blood or marriage to anyone involved in or related to the making of pornography;

(C) that the person has previously had, or been thought to have had, sexual relations with anyone, including anyone involved in or related to the making of the pornography;

(D) that the person has previously posed for sexually explicit pictures for or with anyone, including anyone involved in or related to the making of the pornography at issue;

(E) that anyone else, including a spouse or other relative, has given permission on the person's behalf;

(F) that the person actually consented to a use of the performance that is changed into pornography;

(G) that the person knew that the purpose of the acts or events in question was to make pornography;

(H) that the person signed a contract to produce pornography; or

(I) that the person was paid or otherwise compensated.;

(4) in subsection (c), by striking out "(c)" and inserting in lieu thereof "d"; and

(5) by amending the heading to read as follows: 2251. Sexual exploitation."

Section 3. Section 2252 Amendments.

(a) Subsection (a)(1) Offense—Section

2252 (a)(1)(A) of title 18, United States Code, is amended by inserting after "conduct" the following: "or the use of an adult who was coerced, intimidated, or fraudulently induced to engage in sexually explicit conduct and the person knows or has reason to know that the adult was coerced, intimidated, or fraudulently induced."

(b) Subsection (a)(2) Offense—Section

2252 (a)(2)(A) is amended by inserting after "conduct" the following: "or the use of an adult who was coerced, intimidated, or fraudulently induced to engage in sexually explicit conduct and the person knows or has reason to know that the adult was coerced, intimidated, or fraudulently induced."

(b) Subsection (a)(2) Offense—Section

(c) Conforming Amendment—The heading for section 2252 is amended to read as follows:

2252. Certain activities relating to material involving sexual exploitation.

Section 4. Civil Remedies.

(a) redesignation.—Chapter 110 of part 1 of title 18, United States Code, is amended by redesignating section 2255 as section 2261.

(b) Creation of Remedies—Chapter 110 of part J of title 18, United States Code, is amended by inserting after section 2254 the following:

2255. Civil remedies.

(a) The district courts of the United States shall have jurisdiction to prevent and restrain violations of section 2251 or 2252 by issuing appropriate orders, including—

(1) ordering any person to divest himself of any interest, direct or indirect, in any legal or business entity;

(2) imposing reasonable restrictions on the future activities or investments of any person including prohibiting such person from engaging in the same type of legal or business endeavor; or

(3) ordering dissolution or reorganization of any legal or business entity after making due provision for the rights of innocent persons.

(b) The Attorney General or any person threatened with losses or damage by reason of a violation of section 2251 or 2252 of this title may institute proceedings under subsection (a) of this section and, in the event that the party bringing suit prevails, such party shall recover the cost of the suit, including a reasonable attorney's fee. Pending final determination, the court may at any time enter such restraining orders or prohibitions, or take such other actions, including the acceptance of satisfactory performance bonds, as it shall deem proper. For purposes of this section, a violation of section 2251 or 2252 of this title shall be determined by a preponderance of the evidence.

(c) Any victim of a violation of section 2251 or 2252 of this title who suffers physical injury, emotional distress, or property damage as a result of such violation may sue to recover damages in any appropriate United States district court and shall recover threefold the damages such person sustains as a result of such violation and the cost of the suit, including a reasonable attorney's fee. For purposes of this section, violation of section 2251 or 2252 of this title shall be determined by a preponderance of the evidence.

(d) A final judgment or decree rendered in favor of the United States in any criminal proceeding brought by the United States under this chapter shall stop the defendant from denying the essential allegations of the criminal offense in any subsequent civil proceeding.

(e) Nothing in this section shall be construed to authorize any order restraining the exhibition, distribution or semination of any visual material without a full adversary proceeding and a final judicial determination that such material contains a visual depiction of sexually explicit conduct, as defined by section 2261 of this title, engaged in by a minor or by a person who was coerced, intimidated, or fraudulently induced to engage in such sexual explicit conduct.

2256. Civil penalties.

(a) Any person found to violate section 2251 or 2252 of this title by preponderance of the evidence shall be liable to the United States Government for a civil penalty of $100,000 and forfeiture of any interest in property described in section 2254. The Attorney General may bring an action for recovery of any such civil penalty or forfeiture against any such person. If the Attorney General prevails he may also recover the cost of the suit, including a reasonable attorney's fee.

(b) If the identity of any victim of an offense provided in section 2251 or 2252 of this title is established before an award of a civil penalty made to the United States under this section, the victim shall be entitled to the award. If there is more than one victim, the court shall apportion the award among the victims on an equitable basis after considering the harm suffered by each such victim.

2257. Venue and process.

(a) Any civil action or proceeding brought under this chapter may be instituted in the district court of the United States for any district in which the defendant resides, is found, has an agent, or transacts his affairs.

(b) In any action under section 2255 or 2256 or this title in any district court of the United States in which it is shown that the ends of justice require that other parties residing in any other district be brought before the court, the court may cause such parties to be summoned, and process for that purpose may be served in any judicial district of the United States by the marshall of such judicial district.

(c) In any civil or criminal action or proceeding under this chapter in the district, a subpoena issued by such court to compel the attendance of witnesses may be served in any other judicial district except that no subpoena shall be issued for service upon any individual who resides in another district at a place more than one hundred miles from the place at which such court is held without approval given by a judge of such court upon a showing of good cause.

(d) All other process in any action or proceeding under this chapter may be served on any person in any judicial district in which such person resides, is found, has an agent, or transacts his affairs.

2258. Expedition of actions

In any civil action instituted under this chapter by the United States in any district court of the United States, the Attorney General may file with the clerk of such court a certificate stating that in his opinion the case is of general public importance. A copy of that certificate shall be furnished immediately by such clerk to the chief judge or in his absence to the presiding district judge of the district in which such action is pending. Upon receipt of such copy, such judge shall designate immediately a judge of that district to hear and determine the action, shall assign the action for hearing as soon as practicable and hold hearings and make a determination as expeditiously as possible.

2259. Evidence

In any proceeding ancillary to or in any civil action instituted under this chapter the proceedings may be opened or closed to the public at the discretion of the court after consideration of the rights of affected persons.

2260. Limitations

A civil action under section 2255 or 2256 of this title must be brought within six years from the date the violation is committed. In any such action brought by or on behalf of a person who was a minor at the date the violation was committed, the running of such six-year period shall be deemed to have been tolled during the period of such person's minority.

Section 5. Clerical Amendment

(a) Table of Sections.—The table of sections for chapter 110 of Part I of title 18, United States Code, is amended to read as follows:

Chapter 110-Sexual Exploitation

Sections

2251. Sexual exploitation.
2252. Certain activities relating to material involving sexual exploitation.
2253. Criminal forfeiture.
2254. Civil forfeiture.
2255. Civil remedies.
2256. Civil penalties.
2257. Venue and process.
2258. Expedition of actions.
2259. Evidence.
2260. Limitations.
2261. Definitions for chapter.
2262. Severability.

(b.) Table of Chapters—The table of chapters for part I of title 18, United States Code, is amended by striking the item relating to chapter 110 and inserting in lieu thereof the following:

110. Sexual Exploitation, 2251.

Section 6. Severability.

Chapter 110 of title 18, United States Code, is amended by inserting after section 2261 the following:

2262. Severability.

If any part of this chapter, or the application thereof, to any person or circumstances is held invalid, the other parts of this chapter and their application to other persons or circumstances shall not be affected.

42.683

Ordinance of the City of Minneapolis

The City Council of the City of Minneapolis do ordain as follows:

Special findings on pornography: The Council finds that pornography is central in creating and maintaining the civil inequality of the sexes. Pornography is a systematic practice of exploitation and subordination based on sex which differentially harms women. The bigotry and contempt it promotes, with the acts of aggression it fosters, harm women's opportunities for equality of rights in employment, education, property rights, public accomodations and public services; create public harassment and private denigration; promote injury and degradation such as rape, battery and prostitution and inhibit just enforcement of laws against these acts; contribute significantly to restricting women from full exercise of citizenship and participation in public life, including in neighborhoods; damage relations between the sexes; and undermine women's equal exercise of rights to speech and action guaranteed to all citizens under the constitutions and laws of the United States and the state of Minnesota.

[The ordinance further delineates what falls within its definition, as follows:]

1. Pornography is the sexually explicit subordination of women, graphically depicted, whether in pictures or in words, that also includes one or more of the following:

   • women are presented dehumanized as sexual objects, things or commodities; or

   • women are presented as sexual objects who enjoy pain or humiliation; or

   • women are presented as sexual objects who experience sexual pleasure in being raped; or

   • women are presented as sexual objects tied up or cut up or mutilated or bruised or physically hurt; or

   • women are presented in postures of sexual submission; or

   • women's body parts—including but not limited to vaginas, breasts, and buttocks—are exhibited, such that women are reduced to those parts; or

   • women are presented as whores by nature; or

   • women are presented being penetrated by objects or animals; or

   • women are presented in scenarios of degradation, injury, abasement, torture, shown as filthy or inferior, bleeding, bruised, or hurt in a context that makes these conditions sexual.

2. The use of men, children, or transsexuals in the place of women is pornography. . . .

[The ordinance defines its violation as:]

Discrimination by trafficking in pornography. The production, sale, exhibition, or distribution of pornography is discrimination against women by means of trafficking in pornography;

   • City, state, and federally funded public libraries or private and public university and college libraries in which pornography is available for study, including open shelves, shall not be construed to be trafficking in pornography but special display presentations of pornography in said places is sex discrimination.

   • The formation of private clubs or associations for purposes of trafficking in pornography is illegal and will be considered a conspiracy to violate the civil rights of women.

● Any woman has a cause of action hereunder as a woman acting against the subordination of women. Any man or transsexual who alleges injury by pornography in the way women are injured by it will also have a cause of action.

Coercion into pornographic performances. Any person, including transsexual, who is coerced, intimidated, or fraudulently induced (hereafter, ''coerced'') into performing for pornography shall have a cause of action against the maker(s), seller(s), exhibitor(s) or distributor(s) of said pornography for damages and for the elimination of the products of the performance(s) from the public view. [*Actionable for five years after last sale or performance.*]

[*The following conditions do not negate a finding of coercion;*]

● that the person is a woman; or

● that the person is or has been a prostitute; or

● that the person has attained the age of majority; or

● that the person is connected by blood or marriage to anyone involved in or related to the making of the pornography; or

● that the person has previously had, or been thought to have had, sexual relations with anyone, including anyone involved in or related to the making of the pornography; or

● that the person has previously posed for sexually explicit pictures for or with anyone, including anyone involved in or related to the making of the pornography at issue; or

● that anyone else, including a spouse or other relative, has given permission on the person's behalf; or

● that the person actually consented to a use of the performance that is changed into pornography; or that the person knew that the purpose of the acts or events in question was to make pornography; or

● that the person showed no resistance or appeared to cooperate actively in the photographic sessions or in the sexual events that produced the pornography; or

● that the person signed the contract, or made statements affirming a willingness to cooperate in the production of pornography; or

● that no physical force, threats, or weapons were used in the making of the pornography; or

● that the person was paid or otherwise compensated.

Forcing pornography on a person. Any woman, man, child, or transsexual who has pornography forced on him/her in any place of employment, in education, in a home, or in any public place has a cause of action against the perpetrator and or institution.

Assault or physical attack due to pornography. Any woman, man, child, or transsexual who is assaulted, physically attacked or injured in a way that is directly caused by specific pornography has a claim for damages against the perpetrator, the maker(s), distributor(s), seller(s), and/or exhibitor(s), and for an injunction against the specific pornography's further exhibition, distribution, or sale. . . [Not applicable to material antedating the ordinance.]

Defenses. It shall not be a defense that the defendant did not know or intend that the materials were pornography or sex discrimination.

Notes: *The Presbyterian Church (U.S.A.) was formed through the 1983 merger of the United Presbyterian Church in the U.S.A. (UPCUSA) and the Presbyterian Church in the United States (PCUS). This report is the culmination of the three-year study mandated by the Presbyterian Church (U.S.A.) in 1985, and was prepared jointly by the Council on*

Women and the Church and the Committee on Women's Concerns. It is interesting to note that the study of this issue was given exclusively to these women's groups and not to a committee on ethics, family life, or other general topics. This indicates that the problem of pornography is seen not in terms of explicit sexuality per se, or a general breakdown of morality, but in terms of its portrayal of women. This report, indeed, views sexism as a fundamental cause of pornography, a sexism in which the church itself has participated.

Pornography is defined by the council as "graphic displays of sexual behavior . . . that eroticize . . . through the exploitation of power over another person." Material that is merely sexually explicit and intended for sexual arousal, then, is not necessarily pornographic. Child pornography is basically defined as a separate issue. The report states that control of pornography should not rely primarily on the regulation of law, since present law involves a paralyzing ambiguity of interpretation, and further control would lead to the more dangerous situation of moralistic censorship. Pornography is not identified as a major cause of violent behavior, though it may be a "contributing catalyst." The major cause of abusive behavior is a personal history of having been abused. The council urges passage of the Equal Rights Amendment as an aid to combatting an atmosphere which permits the degradation of women.

REFORMED CHURCH IN AMERICA
STATEMENT ON PORNOGRAPHY (1972)

The General Synod of 1971 instructed the Christian Action Commission to report to the 1972 General Synod on the subect of pornography. The following study has been prepared in compliance with that request.

The Report of the Commission on Obscenity and Pornography concludes that there is no measurable correlation of anti-social behavior and the use of explicit sexual materials (hereinafter called pornography). This was offensive to many churchmen who sought to cast doubt on the conclusions or to rebut them with new data or new interpretations of the Commission data. The supporters of the Commission Report met this act with more data and more interpretation.

The question asked by critics of the Report "Is the Commission Report truth?" may be the wrong question. Probably the report is no more the full truth than any other conclusion at any given time is the full truth for all times and spaces (or even for a particular time and space). Rather, for the church the question which needs asking is: Does the Report indicate any individual or group behavior which should be taken regarding pornography? The answer to this question would only be "yes" if pornography caused some changes in behavior or attitudes which were at a variance with a widely held belief of the church.

There are several levels at which one could deal with cause and effect relationships of pornographic material and behavior, and it is the way one would define the problem as to whether he might see pornographic material as producing behavior which was in conflict with the values which he held. Perhaps two major distinctions with illustrations from the Commission Report will point up this definition problem. One definition of the bad effects which one might expect to result from the widespread use of pornographic material would be definite sexual behaviors and sexual attitudes. A second major definition of bad effects which might result from widespread use of pornography is that this type of material is part of a wide variety of stimuli which combine to change the way that a person is viewed, particularly viewing a person as a sum of parts rather than as a totality.

The Commission Report has measured and reports on the following effects from pornographic material: It does arouse sexually; although there is not much effect on sexual behavior there is an increase in sexual fantasies; the only seeming effect on a person's code of morality is an increase in toleration of those who view pornographic material; and there is conflicting data on delinquent behavior, with some types increasing and some forms decreasing. This will be examined in more detail below. That there is an increase in a dehumanized view of people, the Commission Report says very little. It does report that about one-half of the U.S. male population could be called exploitative and that this exploitative male felt more aroused sexually after viewing erotic films. However, their exploitative attitudes were at a lower level 24 hours after viewing the film.

It should be noted that the Commission Report deals with only one aspect of the complex twentieth century man. This is accepted technique because of the intricate problems (both conceptual and mathematical) involved in dealing with a large number of variables which affect behavior in interdependent ways. This partial view of man ignores the reality, and helps to suggest answers to questions as to why there was a dramatic decrease in sex crimes in Denmark following the laws which allowed a wider availability of pornography while in the U.S. the number of forceable rapes has increased and the total number of juvenile arrests for all crimes has increased 100 percent during the period of increased availability of pornography. This Report does not contain information correlating pornography with the increase in venereal disease (300 percent to 500 percent in the past 15 years). The point is that there is evidence on the Commission's own definition of the problem to raise questions on their recommendations which concern the behavior of certain deviants and potential deviants.

On an intermediate level, between the behavior and the wholistic definition of the problem, is the question of attitudinal changes which might be commented on from a value orientation. One of the major contributors in terms of studies was T.R. Mosher. One interesting study on attitudes was made using pornographic films. Mosher's conclusions were that the attitudes which were increased from viewing these films were disgust, depression, and a loss of peacefulness and serenity. Increases were also noted in attitudes of impulsiveness, feeling pepped-up, being "driven" and anxiousness. If an individual felt that these attitudinal changes were wrong from his value situation, he would surely conclude that showing these films was bad.

Dealing with the problem of pornography on the level of dealing with a person as a totality rather than as a collection of subsets of behavior—the sexual man, the working man, the playing man, etc.—the Christian view of a person is that an individual is a human reflecting God. A person is a whole and cannot be considered as body without mind and soul. While the Christian views man in this way, art, literature, businesses, unions, churches, schools, governments, movies, or any individual or institution has the power to treat or depict a person as less than the totality that the Christian believes that person is.

It is rather well accepted that the attitudes of individuals are affected (if not formed) by the system which surrounds the individual. Thus, a society which is constantly reinforcing the members of the society with a view of the individual which is partial rather than wholistic represents a viewpoint which a Christian cannot support and would attempt to change. It is this aspect of the problem, which is the aspect which is of most concern to the church, which is really not dealt with in the Commission Report. One can speculate that there is some interplay between pornography and violence as both tend to treat the individual as of little worth, but no real in-depth study from the behaviorial increase or decrease of "humanity" as discussed has been undertaken. In the absence of this type of study, the church will have to act or not act on the basis of its interpretation of whether other social institutions are dealing with the individuals in less than wholistic ways which are acceptable to the church.

It would seem logical from the Commission Report that a Christian encourage sex education classes. In light of both the report and the church's attitude toward the person, it would be imperative that the course deal with a great deal more than sex "techniques." In reality all such courses in our schools do. The concerned Christian might well request that the main part of the course should develop the attitude that the individual is more than a sexual plaything. He might further insist that students achieve at an exceptional level in their understanding and observable behavior in this area before they are allowed to discuss "technical" aspects of sex. While this undeniably is interference with the teacher's right to teach, it seems justifiable as a political move to present the philosophy of the Christian segment of the community (after all the schools are, among other things, a reflection of the community).

In the area of literature and art, action quickly involves itself into judgment. Judgment is not a dirty word; people do have to make judgments. The Christian should be encouraged to judge s acceptable those materials which, though sexy in tone and description, do in the main try to picture most of the individuals as total beings. He would judge other materials as unacceptable. This approach would tend to rule out the numerous "Positions of Lovemaking" as mechanistic but rule in "Fanny Hill" as dealing with real persons. It would also tend to rule our "James Bond" and rule in "The Naked and the Dead" and so on. A system of judgment will always be frail enough to be attacked by those who hold different values. But, from a Christian viewpoint of the individual, it would be better than no system at all or a vague system of judgment which relies on "appeals to the prurient" senses as the Supreme Court of the U.S. now uses to judge. Perhaps someone could come up with the aspects of the individual which must be treated in art: greed, compassion, humor, fraility, love, and so on. In any case, the thrust of the Christian action is not censoring "dirty words and filthy pictures" but offering their voices to the criteria by which art and literature could be judged.

Finally, other institutions and individuals should be judged by the same standard. A business or other employer who terminates employment without regard to the impact on the total individual is worthy of censure (boycott?) also. An institution which deals with so many people that they are identifiable only by numbers (Social Security, insurance, Student I.D., Army Serial, etc.) is also worthy of censure. Particular strategies are appropriate for different situations and do not have a place in this paper. These further problems are suggested only to alert the Christian to the degree to which society has allowed the individual to be atomized and to suggest that these institutions with their approaches to the person as less than a whole, may have to share the responsibility for the present popularity of the atomized sexual attitudes which make up the approach of the Commission Report.

The Christian Action Commission continues to study the influences on human character development and on attitudes, including sexuality, which may lead to recommendations to future Synods.

Notes: *This report of the Reformed Church in America (approximately 350,000 members) reacts to the 1970 report of its Commission on Obscenity and Pornography, which surprised many with its liberal response to pornography. The commission report is criticized mainly as conforming to the notion of the "atomized" person whose sexual behavior is related to his/her overall unity of body and soul.*

REFORMED CHURCH IN AMERICA

HUMAN SEXUALITY: SEXISM AND PORNOGRAPHY (1978)

One medical doctor defines pornography as "a daydream in which activities are projected into written or pictorial material to induce genital excitement in an observer."[1] These depictions, he adds, are not pornographic in themselves—they become so when the observer's fantasies are added. No fantasy, no pornography.

He goes onto say that pornography is also dependent upon the existence of a victim. No matter how disguised, pornography always has a victim or object. No fantasy, no victim, no pornography.

A further peculiarity of pornography is that it is generally produced and used by men. It has been speculated that if pornography depended upon female consumers, the industry would quickly die. On the other hand, pornography depends heavily on women, for "no victim, no pornography" is synonymous with "no women, no pornography." Women are the primary victims of pornography.

The word "victim" implies a condition of directed, intentional hostility. To be victimized means to be in some way the object of someone's aggression. Indeed, sociologists and psychologists assert that pornography is a means by which men express fantasied thoughts or actions of sexual aggression or revenge toward women. Rollo May points out that it is no accident that the most common expletive in our contemporary language to express latent hostility is a colloquilism for sexual intercourse.[2]

Accepting the premise that pornography is an expression of latent male hostility, then our task is to examine some of the reasons why this might be so. What is it about the "sexual politics" between men and women which gives rise to unnatural and non-biblical perversions of human sexuality? Why are women the pornographically exploited sex?

It is our intent here to relate the phenomenon of pornography to sexism. Although sexism certainly is not the single cause for the popularity of pornography, it does play a major role in any attempt to discover the reason for the exploitation of women in pornography.

The words "sexist" and "sexism" have come to be used rather loosely in the past several years. Specifically they refer to "all the beliefs, values, attitudes and practices which create and maintain an environment in which one sex . . . is conceptually and behaviorally favored over the other. Sexism divides all human qualities into two sharply delineated and incompatible categories, one a power configuration, the other a caring-serving configuration, and through profound sanctions and reinforcing institutions, provides for the internalization of these configurations by men and women respectively."[3]

In our culture, sexism sets forth maleness as humanness, normal standard. To womanhood are ascribed the qualities of not-manhood. In other words, all the things men aren't *supposed* to be, women are: nurturing, chaste, loyal, receptive, impulsive, dependent, naive, virginal. Conversely, men are all the things women aren't supposed to be: strong, aggressive, self-assured, independent, organized, emotionally cool, knowing, sexual. Man is the seed-producer, woman the seed-bearer. As exemplified in this poetic perception, "she is the mysterious keeper of all the gentler dreams and colors of life; through her men may safely enjoy what they dare not harbor in themselves."[4]

Because of these traditional and formidable sexist delineations, men ascribe certain qualities or powers to women and vice versa. These ascriptions and their manifestations are comprised in the term "sexual politics." This phrase seeks to describe the overt and covert dynamics of power in male-female relationships. "Sexual politics" encompasses the powers which men and women perceive each other as having, and the way those perceptions (or misperceptions) affect relationships.

It should be understood that "sexual politics" does not necessarily suggest a negative condition. Men and women do indeed have varied characteristics and powers, and these can be a positive aspect of the gift of sexuality. Their expression is both desirable and natural. Power is not an inherently negative word—it becomes so only when it is misperceived and abused. Sexual power is abused when it is based on sexism: when the powers and needs of men are perceived to be more important than those of women and vice versa.

There are two powers which men may perceive women as having over them. The first is expressive power—the ability to express emotions. Since men are "not supposed" to express emotions, many experience them vicariously through women. They may depend on women simply for help in expressing themselves, or to fully express their emotions for them. One clinical psychologist says that at the ultimate level, many men are unable to feel emotionally alive except through relationships with women.[5]

A second form of power which men attribute to women is the power to validate their masculinity. There are certain prescribed attitudes or actions which women perform for men in order to affirm and strengthen their masculinity. This power is best exercised by women acting as "feminine" as possible—that is, by not exhibiting any of the characteristics which sexist society has reserved for men only. Above all, women are not to initiate leadership in any male realms, including sex. They should not ask questions, make plans, offer opinions. They are to remain willing and accessible only, if they want to validate masculinity. They should simply *be there* as symbols of non-threatening refuge.

These traditionally sexist attitudes regarding women place heavy burdens on them. "By and large, these are not powers over men that women have wanted to hold. These are powers that men have handed over to women, by defining the male role as being emotionally cool and inexpressive, and as being ultimately validated by heterosexual success."[6] These are powers which men do not wish to have, but insist that women exercise.

There are, however, many women who view themselves in the same ways that men view them. They have no internalized masculine perspectives that they cannot see, or do not object to, such strict role delineations. They accept their "place" as naturally inherited and therefore valid. As sexist men need women for masculine validation, sexist women accept that "assignment" and view it as the proper female role. Thus the circle closes—women feel feminine when they make men feel masculine.

In summary: sexist men attribute to women the powers of vicarious emotional expression and affirmation of masculinity. Both are powers which serve men. Sexist women accept these powers as being naturally feminine, thereby depending on men's needs for their own sense of femininity. In serving men, they feel like women.

If we follow these orientations to their negative extreme, the relationship between sexism and pornography becomes apparent. For if men do indeed depend on women to fulfill such basic needs as the ones described above, alteration or withholding of these powers for any length of time could have only negative consequences. Women who are viewed as the preservers of potency inflict serious damage to the male psyche if those powers are denied. Women who cannot or refuse to perform their "duties" in the manner prescribed by society suddenly become threatening and dangerous. The power to validate masculinity carries with it the power to emasculate. The hostility toward the feminist movement reveals the nature of the threat: "Women's Libbers want to reject their true feminity . . . make men impotent . . . castrate men . . . dominate men, etc. etc."[8]

The hostility which such a view of women engenders in men finds expression in pornography. It provides the means by which men can consciously or unconsciously retaliate toward women in their personal histories who have failed to affirm their sexuality. Pornography "condenses in itself the subject's sexual life history—his memories and fantasies, traumas, frustrations and joys. Pornography is for restitution."[9]

The appeal of pornography is that sexual gratification does not have to be offered; a depersonalized commodity, it is simply taken. Pornography is a nonviolent form of rape which disregards the personhood of women in favor of the sexual gratification they provide. "One easily sees therein a power struggle disguised as sexuality: the dangerous woman who is reduced to a victim and the boy, who, by means of pornography becomes a man."[10]

Pornography then, may be viewed as a means by which men attempt to reassert masculine power over women who withhold their supposed ability to make men feel like real men. The easiest way to assert power over women is to strip them not only of their clothing, but of their strength, assertiveness, their sense of self. In such a condition, women are conveniently exploitable and sexually exciting—stripped of the privacy of their own sexuality, they reinforce male sexuality by default.

(Here an important distinction must be made. Sexist society has determined that "proper" women should not need or enjoy sex. Double standards have not allowed women to seek sexual fulfillment in the same ways that men do. Women who make overt sexual remarks or admit to being excited by nudity are labelled as "fast", "loose," "promiscuous" or "unlady-like". However, such comments made by men are often dismissed with a "men will be men" smile.

The need for emotional intimacy and affection is thought to be a feminine desire, whereas it is assumed that men are aroused simply by sweating anatomy, nudity or tales of bizarre sexual encounters. Sexist society has wrongly assigned sexual fulfillment through romance and emotional intimacy to women,[11] and sexual fulfillment through pornographic stimuli to men.

It is evident then that pornography is based in sexist traditions and serves sexist people. It affirms the notion that men need women most for sexual fulfillment and that women need to serve men in this way. Pornography illustrates the consequences when such an arrangement does not exist.

The man who receives sexual satisfaction by the stimulus of pornography has found a way to possess what women symbolize to him without having to deal with the realities of an intimate relationship. He victimizes women by taking from them that which is not given. There is no threat because there is no need to reciprocate. There is no concern over feelings or future. Pornography offers to men to powers of women for free: convenient sexual gratification without inconvenient relationships.

Quotations:

[1] Robert J. Stroller. "Pornography and Perversion" in *The Case Against Pornography*, David Holbrook, editor. La Salle, Illinois, Open Court, 1973, p. 111.

[2] Rollo May. "Paradoxes of Sex and Love in Modern Society" in Holbrook, p. 22.

[3] Sheila Ruth. "Sexism, Patriarchy, and Feminism" in *Women & Men: The Consequences of Power*, D. Hiller and R.A. Sheets, editors. Cincinnati, University of Cincinnati, 1976, p. 50.

[4] *Ibid.*, p. 15.

[5] Joseph H. Pleck. "Men's Power with Women, Other Men, and Society: A Men's Movement Analysis" in Hiller and Sheets, p. 14.

[6] *Ibid.*, p. 15.

[7] Joyce J. Walstedt. "An Exploration of Female Powerlessness: The Altruistic Other Orientation" in Hiller and Sheets, p. 153.

[8] Sheila Ruth in Hiller and Sheets, p. 47.

[9] Robert J. Stoller in Holbrook, p. 111.

[10] *Ibid.*, p. 125.

[11] *Ibid.*, p. 127.

Additional Resources:

Susan Brownmiller. *Against Our Will: Men, Women and Rape.* New York, Simon and Schuster, 1975.

Harvey Cox. "Playboy's Doctrine of the Male" in *Christianity and Crisis*, April 17, 1961.

Human Sexuality: Pornography in U.S. Culture

The issue of pornography is one which challenges the Christian community in a number of ways, we believe that our religious convictions commit us to a clear perception about human sexuality. As such we must be assertive in our affirmation of sexuality and a sexual expression which is consistent within the context of respect for wholeness of personhood. We are bound, by our religious affirmations, to take strong positions against any violations and perversions of this kind of sexual expression. We engage in this study by using the following definitions of pornography:

1. Pornography is a form of violence which removes us from a healthy conception of our sexuality. It represents an assault on the natural development of sexuality which we

believe to be within the context of mutuality and respect for humans as expressed in loving, caring relationships.

2. Pornography is the objectification of women, children and men as sources for sexual gratification.

3. Pornography is the victimization of women through many forms of physical and psychological rape. Women experience this oppression as nothing short of physical humiliation and a form of psychological terrorism. A result of the aggression of male sexuality, it is typical of the kind of intimidation used to maintain patriarchal forms of dominance in our society.

4. Pornography is the systemic trivialization of sexual relationships by the stripping away of their human substance and content. This includes both our over-romantization of love and sexuality and a false sense of reality as it is portrayed in male dominated family movies, hard-core porno movies, and daytime TV.

5. Pornography is the commodification of sexuality for the purposes of economic profit and a false sense of sexual gratification. Profiteering off the bodies of women and the false needs of blocked and deflected male sexuality is both manipulative of personal lives and helps to sustain distorted views of sexual relatedness. It adds to the attitude people have that erotic sexual expression is somehow evil but available for a price.

6. Pornography is the exploitation of victims by a sexually sublimated (deflected) and repressed (blocked) culture, one which prevents the attainment of the natural goal of sexuality. The socialization process conducted by all institutions of the society (including many times the family, schools, churches, workplaces, marriages, and so forth) work within the particular cultural context in which they exist, to remove people from a sense of their own sexual identity and from affirming assertively their own sexuality.

7. Pornography is any attempt to equate greater sexual license with what is necessary to bring about greater sexual liberation. To equate real sexual freedom with apparent sexual freedom.

Cultural Background

We come from a historical tradition which does as much damage to our understanding of sexuality as it does to provide us with ethical guidelines to take a firm stand in favor of its healthy expression. On the one hand, we have affirmed a conservative sexual ethic based on the principles that looseness and irresponsibility in sexual behavior causes a breakdown in the reverence we have for loving and structured relationships. On the other hand, such a sexual ethic sometimes causes fear, guilt, inhibition, manipulation and perversion in the natural expression of sexuality as it has been socialized throughout the development of persons. This morality makes us shy and ignorant in our talking about sexuality. There is an entire vocabulary of legitimate words and expressions that we are uncomfortable with because they relate to sex. Our jokes reveal the level at which we are comfortable talking about sexuality.

Double Standards of Sexual Practice

1. Men are allowed considerable latitude in their independent expression of their sexuality. Men are allowed to make mistakes for which they will be socially forgiven. Such male mistakes do not generally affect their standing in the community and in the eyes of other men and they are, of course, at the expense of women. Women are much more restricted and oppressed in their sexual expression. Women suffer alienation when caught in violation of the same sexual mores.

2. Social class is another variable in how we understand types of sexual repression and expression. We are sharply critical of hard-core movies and *Hustler Magazine* and less critical of sexually suggestive advertising and *Playboy Magazine*. We attack the blatant use of sex-peep shows for sexual gratification while we are less critical of the more

fashionable construction of sexual fantasies which exists for the upper classes—the focus of the media on cheerleaders attire (or lack of it) during the Superbowl, hot-pants stewardesses and cocktail waitresses and TV soap operas. Classes of people in this society not only experience radically different material existences but are correspondingly socialized with value structures which legitimize these material conditions, and different concepts about social relations. The variety of types of sexual repression and pornography will vary correspondingly. We too often fail to see that causes of this repression grow from a cultural sense of relational logic as well as a sexist one. We judge lower income and working class distortion of sexual expression as porno and moral decay without seeing the relationship of sexual gratification in their everyday life as often frustrated by images through the media which are aimed at a group of people that don't in reality exist. People frustrated by what is not attainable, at any level in society, will develop all kinds of perversions as a way of adapting their personal needs to the real environment. We condone indirectly upper class porno, which is just as inhuman and degrading, because it has been legitimized and masked to fit into the sexual mores with which we are more familiar. We are correct and quick to judge with condemnation the outrageous forms of pornography (child exploitation as a good example) but we are too slow to notice subtle pornographic ads on our nation's billboards.

Pornography: Symptom of Society

Our analysis of pornography and its social manifestations is limited by the way in which we often approach the topic. We accept the fact that pornography is not simply another issue which is separate and unrelated to the totality of our cultural order. We reject such a liberal tendency in our study. If we understand it to be simply sin, perversion, decadence, filth and moral decay then we will arrive at limited solutions. We will end up affirming human decency, sexual wholeness and ethical purity, which is all well and good—but not sufficient.

1) Our analysis of pornography must also include the responses to some very clear questions. To say only that pornography exists because people are weak by nature will not suffice by itself as an explanation to this complex phenomenon. What is the role of societal structures and socialization processes which encourage a deflected and distorted sexuality? How does this form of sexuality evolve into pornographic expressions? 2) Pornography causes violence because it destroys our ability to attain lasting and authentic forms of interpersonal sexual relationships. Rather, it exists to perpetuate an outlet for the immediate sexual gratification of people which rests on a false sense of intimacy and the construction of fantasies. How does our economic orientation feed a pornographic industry based on quick profits, exploited labor and commodity marketing? How does our sexist culture produce and encourage by its very logic of social relations, a pornographic conception of sexual relationship? 3) We refuse to accept the naive position that because sexuality is private that it is not political. Pornography is political because it claims power over the sexual identities of people. For example, it is political because it perpetuates a false sense of male identity, superiority and security in a patriarchal order. It is political because it creates a form of consciousness which violates the sensibilities we have as Christian people proclaiming wholeness and mutuality in human relationships.

Pornography and Civil Liberties

It is widely understood that the dilemma regarding pornography and its social implications has to do with the tensions between one's civil liberties to distribute material, print material and make movies or to read material and look at movies; and what should legally be imposed on one's personal business. People who argue the liberal postion of civil liberties ask for a politic which is based on the presupposition that if no one is done bodily harm and if sexuality is expressed privately or between consenting adults, that it should be legally permissable— as a matter of rights. We are suspicious about the use of the conception of "rights" when they are made to include forms of justifying violence against women, children and men (violence in the deeper sense of the term), repression of the healthy sexual development of persons and a manipulation of our sex lives to serve the broader interests of reinforcing cultural social relations. We realize that taking an anti-civil libertarian viewpoint has dangerous implications for our future political freedom. Nonetheless, we find a curious blend of conservative and radical analysis which leads us to challenge civil liberties that violate our clearest religious convictions about a social issue.

1) We call attention to another concept of "rights" which affirms the dignity of all people—men, women and children, and one which necessitates the creation of a cultural order which produces a healthier view of sexual wholeness; civil rights which emphasize, uncompromisingly, the mutual self-empowerment of all people to a non-repressed personal development and to a non-manipulated sexual growth. While they have been held as an ideal for everyone, civil liberties have too often been used in our nation's history by those who have the actual class, sex and racial privileges to attain them. We affirm our national ideals but we call them into question when they are interpreted in such a way as to deny the fundamental necessity of creating a social order which is not exploitive. 2) We therefore call for a re-examination of such fundamentals as "freedom of the press". Not that we will tolerate a society which destroys our ability to get information and investigate openly and to exchange freely new and creative ideas, stories and forms of entertainment, but that we will not tolerate violence to women, men and children and repression of our sexuality through degradation and oppression in the media. We want these principles of our faith to be held as non-negotiables in the construction of our society and we want our civil liberties to be developed within the allegiances to these principles. 3) We believe that in such a society, a logic of social relations will arise which will have in it, little space for the generation of sexual perversion and pornography. We believe that people are heavily influenced by the culture (and its values) in which they grow up: the dictatorship of the unconscious. We must meet such a challenge by active involvement in criticism of our culture and its systems—both political and economic as well as ideological. We must be clear about the role of caring, human relationships in a society which minimizes such relatedness in its everyday life bureaucracies. Pornography is interrelated and interconnected with the totality of our experience; within our religious and social ethics as well as within the relationships that we engage in every day.

Pornography and Therapy

Pornography as we have defined it, could never be used to 'solve' a sexual problem. It may relieve a particular sexual dilemma and relational block of some sort, but it will inevitably continue to perpetuate (at some level) the deeper problematics of distorted sexual attitudes. We may be able to measure the immediate success of such a solution but will be unable to gauge the consequences of the deeper attitudes legitimized in the process and we will not have recognized the wider cultural reality which makes such a solution workable in the first place.

On the other hand, we recognize the contradictions of living in a society such as ours and the need to help people with specific and immediate solutions to their sexual problems. We therefore believe that sexual therapies can and should be developed which increase people's sensitivity to their bodies, to the sexual needs of their partners, to people's erotic nature and to a creative awareness of sensuality. We think that this can be done through nonpornographic methods and strategies, Porno has no good use except as a way to expose and understand the negative realities of human sexual expression. Sexual therapy is something we affirm in its most creative and venturesome forms. But sexual liberation is its goal, not the continuance of illusory forms of sexual freedom.

Affirmation on Human Sexuality

First: Our human sexuality is a gift from God. Our sexuality is given to facilitate our exit from a pre-occupation with self into that community of relationships which God intends for us. Our sexuality is that mysterious bond which grants us entry into the life of others and eventually is the link which binds us to the mystery of the life of God himself, as we become collaboraters with him, in the continuing work of creation.

Second: Our human sexuality is not to be seen exclusively as a matter of personal preference, for this very personal reality has social, economic, moral and religious considerations of which we must always be aware. We make our decisions not in solitude, but in solidarity with the Covenant community.

Third: Our human sexuality is not synonymous with external conformity expressed, but is preeminently concerned with the motive and intention of the individual as we increasingly discover that the real issues of morality and immorality are waged within the deepest recesses of the human spirit.

Fourth: Our human sexuality must reflect a social ethic which encompasses sexual expression, practice and attitude. This ethic presupposes a critique of the social realities which assault (by any and all means) the mental conception and actual practice of such an ethic.

Fifth: Our human sexuality becomes idolatrous and inhumane when it permits us to debase and depersonalize our fellow human beings. Our human sexuality is to mirror the very nature of our gracious God himself. Our sexuality is given to be exercised within the context of loving, supportive and caring mutuality, for in this we discover what it is to be fashioned in the "image of God".

Sixth: Our outward expression of human sexuality is derived from the nature of people as culturally shaped (specifically with respect to sex and social class). Human sexuality is both deflected from its natural development and repressed by the very logic of our cultural understanding of social relations. People's sexuality is objectified, exploited and commodified. Sexual relationships are trivialized. Sexual license and freedom is systemically confused with sexual liberation. We affirm a theology about the nature of people and a culture which influences people's lives which can be genuinely liberating. Ways must be explored to construct an image of sexual expression which is both biblically responsive and honestly sensitive and critical to the realities in which we live.

Films

History has shown us that films known as or carrying the rating "X" or beyond have been the product of exploitative profiteering people. We deplore their making and distribution and call for legal action to stop this.

THEREFORE, the Christian Action Commission RECOMMENDS:

R-1. THAT General Synod urge the members of the RCA to call upon their legislators to enact legislation to control pornographic film-making, and further,

THAT the *Church Herald* be encouraged to print a review of current films. (ADOPTED)

Television

WHEREAS,

the media of television has shown itself as a major propagator of material which is not reflective of human sexuality in the light of God's love for the individual, and since the television medium too often objectifies and perverts the human sexual being, and we believe that the members of Christ's Church should take positive action towards becoming more aware of the adverse effects of this medium to our sexual attitudes:

THEREFORE, the Christian Action Commission RECOMMENDS:

R-2. THAT General Synod call upon the churches, and therefore church members, to make known objections to such television programming to their families, friends and to those who more directly control the media when television portrays an image of human sexuality abhorrent to the biblical images of persons. (ADOPTED)

Advertising

WHEREAS

pornography is increasingly evident in more and more aspects of American life and,

WHEREAS

it is becoming more and more evident in the advertising which we experience and,

WHEREAS

there is no such thing as objectionable material—UNLESS SOMEONE OBJECTS.

THEREFORE, the Christian Action Commission RECOMMENDS:

R-3.THAT the General Synod call upon the membership of the Reformed Church in America to respond to this desensitizing "spillage" from blatant pornography to subtle pornography, from the advertising of pornography to pornographic advertising as we personally determine and boycott those who indulge in these advertising techniques and inform them of our decisions and actions born our of our commitment to be good stewards of God's precious gifts. (ADOPTED)

WHEREAS

in the light of the foregoing resolutions, it becomes obvious that it is not only necessary for Christians to make their negative opinions known in the area of films, advertising, TV programming, etc., but also necessary to voice our affirmation of materials which we find worthwhile and wholesome:

THEREFORE, the Christian Action Commission RECOMMENDS:

R-4.That General Synod call upon the people of the church to exercise their individual responsibility to respond positively to television programs, advertisements, films, etc. which sustain the level of human worth we feel is God's will for his people. (ADOPTED)

Children

WHEREAS,

there is no question that children are exploited in the production of pornographically printed material and films and are in no way protected by the First Amendment, and

WHEREAS,

child abuse in any form, but particularly in this sexual form, together with its attendant permanent damage, is abhorrent to Christians:

THEREFORE, the Christian Action Commission RECOMMENDS:

R-5.That General Synod, recognizing that sexual exploitation is child abuse, call upon the churches, and therefore, church members, to support legislation at all levels of government making child abuse a crime, and actively use those means to bring the offenders to justice. (ADOPTED)

Education

WHEREAS,

pornography is a plague which is increasing in scope; and

WHEREAS,

the growth of pornography is tied to a lack of knowledge regarding human sexuality; and

WHEREAS,

the educative means are available to the body of Christ:

THEREFORE, the Christian Action Commission RECOMMENDS:

R-6. That the General Synod urge the churches of the RCA to avail themselves of the various types of Christian sex education materials, marriage enrichment, preparation and growth seminars, and those groups involved in halting the spread of pornography, and that as much as is possible the education process occur at the family and church level. Resources are available through the Office of Family Life. (ADOPTED)

The Commission additionally RECOMMENDS:

R-7. That our seminaries provide training for ministerial candidates in the field of sex education counseling and that as a part of their continuing education, all RCA ministers seek to prepare themselves to serve their local families as a resource in human sexuality. (ADOPTED)

Notes: *This statement from the Reformed Church in America connects pornography with sexism and reflects on the political and socialization processes in society. Sexuality is portrayed as good, but not if it is viewed as an object or a commodity. Members are urged to make their objections to pornography known and to increase the levels of sex education.*

REFORMED CHURCH IN AMERICA

RESOLUTION ON PORNOGRAPHY (1987)

The 1986 General Synod instructed this commission to study the issue of pornography, giving special attention to child pornography, the new behavioral evidence on the effects of pornography, and conditions within which pornography flourishes (*MGS 1986*, pp. 104-105).

Pornography is of ongoing concern. The General Synod received reports from this commission in 1972 (*MGS 1972* pp. 203-206) and again in 1978 (*MGS 1978*, pp. 185-199). These reports concluded that pornography represents the dehumanization of the person and perverts the nature of sexuality as a way of expressing humanness.

The 1978 study expanded the definition of pornography to include violence against the person, most specifically against those used as objects for sexual gratification, especially women and children. The 1978 study concluded with a series of recommendations that called on the church to affirm the positive nature of sexuality through education, and to support images in our culture that reinforce the biblical view of person. That Synod also urged the churches to oppose the production of pornographic materials and especially the violence done to children in the production of such material.

When talking about pornography, one must be careful to deliniate just what is meant. Although pornography is generally understood to be that which simply offends, and thus what counts as pornography tends to be highly subjective, the commission offers some definitional clarity. Pornography is that material which promises to fulfill the quest for human sexuality by dehumanizing either other persons, the person offered the promise, or both. While pornography is usually associated with the perversion of sexuality, and while that use of the term is now under consideration by the Synod, the commission reminds the church that pornography has a much wider scope. In our society, sexual pornography most often results in the dehumanization of women and children by portraying these persons as objects for sexual fulfillment. This in turn leads us to the suggestion that pornography sets the stage for a violent sort of dehumanization.

Since 1978 there has been much study aimed at discovering a link between pornography and violence. Recent conclusions from the social scientific community tend to lend credence to the intuitive sense that pornography leads to aberrant sexual behavior or to violence. A gathering of researchers called together by the US Surgeon General offered the following statements of consensus from their study:

1. Children and adolescents who participate in the production of pornography experience adverse, enduring effects.
2. Prolonged use of pornography increases beliefs that less common sexual practices are more common.
3. Pornography that portrays sexual aggression as pleasurable for the victim increases the acceptance of the use of coercion in sexual relations.
4. Acceptance of coercive sexuality appears to be related to sexual aggression.
5. In laboratory studies measuring short-term effects, exposure to violent pornography increases punitive behavior toward women. (*Reprot of the Surgeon General's Workshop on Pornography and Public Health,* pp. 13-39.)

The commission is cautious in its use of these conclusions, for the researchers themselves state:

> Pornography has been consistently linked to changes in some perceptions, attitudes, and behaviors. These links, however, are circumscribed, few in number, and generally laboratory-based. To say that this means any observed effects are antifactual, however, would be in error. Pornography does have effects; it is just not yet known how widespread or powerful they really are. There is a clear lack of extensive knowledge or unifying theory, and global statements about the effects of exposure to pornography have not yet been substantiated. (Ibid., p. 35)

However, the commission does note that the conclusion of these studies support the position previously taken by the General Synod.

The research since 1978 offers further reason for concern, especially for children. This Commission is especially troubled by the abuse of children and the images of sexuality transmitted to all children through pronography. In the first instance, children themselves are made direct victims of violence against their person. In the second instance, children are raised in a culture that condones the victimization of others. The producers of pornographic material defend their action by claiming the right to a free spread of ideas, including, one presumes, the idea that the sexual use of children is a healthy and proper expression of sexuality. While sensitive to the notion of the right to free expression as a means by which truth can emerge into the public domain, we reject the use of rights as a legitimate defense. Scripture offers a picture of an "inequality of rights." The God revealed in history is a God of the widow and the orphan; that is, a God of the powerless, the victim. Jesus himself was Victim, standing in for all the world's victims as evil did its worst. Thus, also, the church must stand on the side of children, vigorously supporting efforts to eradicate child pronography through the enforcement of labor laws, laws against child abuse, and the like.

The second abuse to children is the evergrowing availability of pornographic material to children. This is especially evident in the "video revolution" whereby young persons can enter video outlets to rent pornographic tapes for viewing on home video equipment.

The church's response to this reality is of a different order than its response to the use of children themselves in pornography. We have often far too quickly responded negatively to any explicit sexual portrayal. Human sexuality is a gift to our nature. To call for the banning of all sexually explicit material would not be coherent with a Christian affirmation of our sexual nature. It would, in fact, be a denial of our human nature, the very humanness that God so fully and finally affirms in the Incarnation of his Son.

Thus congregations should support sexual education in the home, in the school, and most especially in the church. It is from within the community of faith that we can educate our children to choices made within the values that come to us as a people shaped by the God who is Lord of all of life. The General Program Council's Office of Education and Faith Development can provide materials.

Congregations should also support those laws that require store owners to display the fact that they sell pronographic materials, and that such materials be made separate and off limits to minors.

The effects of pornography on children is not the only concern. Since pornography by definition dehumanizes the persons portrayed in its materials, we resist its presence. Pornography distorts not only the humanness of women, but perverts the nature of male-female relation, the very image of God (Genesis I:27). The church cannot in the name of "rights," defend those who produce that which engenders violence against persons, being careful to remember that the violence in question is not the offense caused the viewer or reader or listener. At the same time, pornography must be recognized as a symptom of a societal sickness, a phenomenon that cannot be eliminated simply by sophisticated laws or rigorous prosecution. Until the alienation between persons—the loss of the God-given intimacy in which we are made to be human—is overcome, pornography will find fertile soil in which to take root.

The church's response must be twofold. First, the church is to conserve and proclaim the message that our true humanness is granted us in the community God makes with us. We place sexuality in the context of God's community with his people. Second, the church continues its proclamation of the kingdom of God, a society aborning in Jesus Christ, a kingdom not yet fully present. Because we hope to image this new society in the midst of the old, we participate in public discussions of how we best shape our present society to reflect this kingdom. The new order will be one where we need not engage in violence to attain our aims. It will include a profound respect for persons. Thus it will presume, through gospel proclaimed and enacted, to eliminate the roots pornography. And because we envision this kingdom as taking societal shape, the church can urge the encodement of kingdom possibilities in those laws that can, consistent with the protection of the human person, restrict the production and display of pornography.

The commission recognizes that there is no quick nor morally easy solution to the availability of pornography. We urge that our churches and their members enter the public discussion concerning the sorts of values we desire our culture to bear. We do so boldly, exposing those forces that make for victims even as we support a culture in which healthy sexual expression can be enjoyed fully within the covenant of persons given us by God.

R-7.

To reissue the 1972 and 1978 reports entitled "Pornography," "Human Sexuality: Biblical Perspectives," and "Human Sexuality: Pornography in US Culture" for distribution to RCA congregations. (ADOPTED)

R-8.

To instruct the General Program Council to prepare an education packet for distribution to the churches that will include: (1) resources for education in human sexuality for adults and children, (2) resources on the nature of sexual pornography, and (3) resources that offer possibilities for local action. (ADOPTED)

R-9.

To encourage RCA congregations to educate their members on the topic of sexuality from a Christian perspective. (ADOPTED)

R-10.

To urge RCA congregations to express their disapproval of the production and distribution of pornography as defined in this statement, through the support of local laws that will curtail its presence. (ADOPTED)

R-11.

To urge RCA congregations to engage in local public discussion on the presence and nature of pornography, affirming the value of persons, and promoting an understanding of sexuality consistent with the Christian faith.(ADOPTED)

R-12.

To urge RCA congregations to express pastoral care to victims of pornography. (ADOPTED)

R-13.

To distribute this statement to RCA congregations. (ADOPTED)

Notes: *It this 1987 statement, the Reformed Church in America defines pornography as that which sexually dehumanizes other persons. It points to the evidence documenting the harm caused by pornography, particularly as it relates to children. The church supports stricter laws against pornography.*

SALVATION ARMY

THE SALVATION ARMY'S POSITION ON PORNOGRAPHY (1983)

The Salvation Army, concerned that the diginity of mankind should be preserved, deplores the increasing pornography and blasphemy infecting books, magazines and newspapers, featured in the theatre, at the movies, and in radio and television.

The Salvation Army believes that its position reflects widespread feeling against blasphemy and the commercialization of sex in ways which ensure financial gain for the exploiters and the creation of distorted values in the lives of the exploited, including children.

The Salvation Army maintains its stand against evils which threaten the quality of personal and national character and seeks to arouse public conscience against such evils.

The Salvation Army wholeheartedly supports the proper education of people on matters relating to the sanctity of right sexual relationships based on the teaching of the New Testament.

Above all, The Salvation Army believes that the wholesomeness of society depends upon the conversion of men and women everywhere to a new life in Christ Jesus, in which high standards of morality are established.

Notes: *The Salvation Army (approximately 433,000 members) links pornography with blasphemy as evils in the media to be deplored. It supports wholesome relationships and education (based on New Testament teaching) on "right" sexual relationships.*

SEVENTH-DAY ADVENTIST CHURCH

STANDARDS OF CHRISTIAN LIVING (1986)

Reading

The mind is the measure of the man. Food for the mind is therefore of the utmost importance in developing character and in carrying out our life's purposes. For this reason our mental habits should be carefully checked. There is no better index to character than what we choose to read and hear. Books and other literature are among the most valuable means of education and culture, but these must be well chosen and rightly used. There is a wealth of good literature, both books and periodicals; but equally there is a flood of evil literature, often in most attractive guise but damaging to mind and morals. The tales of wild adventure and of moral laxness, whether fact or fiction, which are presented in many magazines and over the radio are unfit for the youth or adult.

"Those who indulge the habit of racing through an exciting story are simply crippling their mental strength, and disqualifying their minds for vigorous thought and research."— *Counsels to Parents, Teachers, and Students*, p. 135.

Along with other evil results from the habit of reading fiction, we are told that "it unfits the soul to contemplate the great problems of duty and destiny," and "creates a distaste for life's practical duties" (*ibid.*, p. 383).

Radio and Television

Radio and television have changed the whole atmosphere of our modern world and have brought us within easy contact with the life, thought, and activities of the entire globe. Radio and television are great educational agencies. By these means we can greatly enlarge our knowledge of world events, and enjoy important discussions and the best in music.

Unfortunately, however, radio and television also bring to their audiences almost continuous theatrical performances and many influences that are neither wholesome nor uplifting. If we are not discriminating and decisive, radio and television will turn our homes into theaters and minstrel shows of a cheap and sordid kind.

Safety for ourselves and our children is found in a determination, by God's help, to follow the admonition of the apostle Paul: "Finally, brethren, whatsoever things are true, whatsoever things are honest, whatsoever things are just, whatsoever things are pure, whatsoever things are lovely, whatsoever things are of good report; if there be any virtue, and if there be any praise, think on these things" (Phil 4:8).

Recreation and Entertainment

Recreation is a purposeful refreshing of the powers of body and mind. A vigorous, wholesome mind will not require worldly amusement, but will find a renewal of strength in good recreation.

"Many of the amusements popular in the world today, even with those who claim to be Christians, tend to the same end as did those of the heathen. There are indeed few among them that Satan does not turn to account in destroying souls. Through the drama he has worked for ages to excite passion and glorify vice. The opera, with its fascinating display and bewildering music, the masquerade, the dance, the card table, Satan employs to break down the barriers of principle, and open the door to sensual indulgence. In every gathering for pleasure where pride is fostered or appetite indulged, where one is led to forget God and lose sight of eternal interests, there Satan is binding his chains about the soul."— *Patriarchs and Prophets*, pp. 459, 460. (See also p. 192.)

We earnestly warn against the subtle and sinister influence of the moving-picture theater, which is no place for the Christian. Dramatized films that graphically present by portrayal and by suggestion the sins and crimes of humanity—murder, adultery, robbery, and kindred evils—are in no small degree responsible for the present breakdown of morality. We appeal to parents, children, and youth to shun those places of amusement and those theatrical films that glorify professional acting and actors. If we will find delight in God's great world of nature and in the romance of human agencies and divine workings, we shall not be attracted by the puerile portrayals of the theater.

Another form of amusement that has an evil influence is social dancing. "The amusement of dancing, as conducted at the present day, is a school of depravity, a fearful curse to society.''—*Messages to Young People,* p. 399 (see also p. 192). (See 2 Cor. 6:15-18; 1 John 2:15-17; James 4:4; 2 Tim. 2:19-22; Eph. 5:8-11; Col. 3:5-10.)

Let us not patronize the commercialized amusements, joining with the worldly, careless, pleasure-loving multitudes who are "lovers of pleasures more than lovers of God."

Recreation is essential. We should endeavor to make the friendships and recreations of our people church centered. We recommend that in every home where there are children, materials be provided which will afford an outlet for the creative energies of youth. Wholesome association and recreation may be provided through music organizations, AJY class projects, and missionary service bands.

Music

"Music was made to serve a holy purpose, to lift the thoughts to that which is pure, noble, and elevating, and to awaken in the soul devotion and gratitude to God."—*Patriarchs and Prophets,* p. 594. Jesus "held communion with heaven in song" (*The Desire of Ages,* p. 73).

Music is one of the highest arts. Good music not only gives pleasure but elevates the mind and cultivates the finest qualities. Spiritual songs have often been used of God to touch the hearts of sinners and lead to repentance. Debased music, on the contrary, destroys the rhythm of the soul and breaks down morality.

Great care should be exercised in the choice of music. Any melody partaking of the nature of jazz, rock, or related hybrid forms, or any language expressing foolish or trivial sentiments, will be shunned by persons of true culture. Let us use only good music in the home, in the social gathering, in the school, and in the church.

Social Relationships

The social instinct is given us of God, for our pleasure and benefit. "By mutual contact minds receive polish and refinement; by social intercourse, acquaintances are formed and friendships contracted which result in a unity of heart and an atmosphere of love which is pleasing in the sight of heaven."—*Testimonies,* vol. 6, p. 172. Proper association of the sexes is beneficial to both. Such associations should be conducted upon a high plane and with due regard to the conventions and restrictions which, for the protection of society and the individual, have been prescribed. It is the purpose of Satan, of course, to pervert every good thing; and the perversion of the best often leads to that which is worst. So it is highly important that Christians should adhere to very definite standards of social life.

Today the ideals that make these social relationships safe and happy are breaking down to an alarming degree. Under the influence of passion unrestrained by moral and religious principle, the association of the sexes has to an alarming extent degenerated into freedom and license. Sexual perversions, incest, and sexual abuse of children prevail to an alarming degree. Millions have abandoned Christian standards of conduct and are bartering the sweet and sacred experiences of marriage and parenthood for the bitter, remorseful fruits of lust. Not only are these evils damaging the familial structure of society, but the breakdown of the family in turn fosters and breeds these and other evils. The results in distorted lives of children and youth are distressing and evoke our pity, while the effects on society are not only disastrous but cumulative.

These evils have become more open and threatening to the ideals and purposes of the Christian home. Adultery, sexual abuse of spouses, incest, sexual abuse of children, homosexual practices, and lesbian practices are among the obvious perversions of God's original plan. As the intent of clear passages of Scripture (see Ex. 20:14; Lev. 18:22, 29 and 20:13; 1 Cor. 6:9; 1 Tim. 1:10; Rom. 1:20-32) is denied and as their warnings are rejected in exchange for human opinions, much uncertainty and confusion prevail. This is what Satan desires. It has always been his plan to cause people to forget that God is their Creator and that when He "created man in His own image" He created them "male and female" (Gen. 1:27). The world is witnessing today a resurgence of the perversions of ancient civilizations.

The degrading results of the world's obsession with sex and the love and pursuit of sensual pleasure are clearly delineated in the Word of God. But Christ came to destroy the works of the devil and reestablish the relationship of human beings with their Creator. Thus, though fallen in Adam and captive to sin, those who are in Christ receive full pardon and the right to choose anew the better way, the way to complete renewal. By means of the cross and the power of the Holy Spirit, all may be freed from the grip of sinful practices as they are restored to the image of their Creator.

It is incumbent upon the parents and the spiritual guides of the youth to face with no false modesty the facts of social conditions, to gain more fully a sympathetic understanding of the problems of this generation of young people, to seek most earnestly to provide for them the best environment, and to draw so near to them in spirit as to be able to impart the ideals of life and the inspiration and power of Christian religion, that they may be saved from the evil that is in the world through lust.

But to our young men and young women we say, The responsibility is yours. Whatever may be the mistakes of parents, it is your privilege to know and to hold the highest ideals of Christian manhood and womanhood. Reverent Bible study, a deep acquaintance with the works of nature, stern guarding of the sacred powers of the body, earnest purpose, constancy in prayer, and sincere, unselfish ministry to others' needs will build a character that is proof against evil and that will make you an uplifting influence in society.

Social gatherings for old and young should be made occasions, not for light and trifling amusement, but for happy fellowship and improvement of the powers of mind and soul. Good music, elevating conversation, good recitations, suitable still or motion pictures, games carefully selected for their educational value, and, above all, the making and using of plans for missionary effort can provide programs for social gatherings that will bless and strengthen the lives of all. The Youth Department of the General Conference has published helpful information and practical suggestions for the conduct of social gatherings and for guidance in other social relations.

The homes of the church are by far the best places for social gatherings. In large centers where it is impossible to hold them there, and where there is no social center of our own, a proper place free from influences destructive to Christian standards should be secured rather than a place that is ordinarily used for commercial amusements and sports, such as social halls and skating rinks, which suggest an atmosphere contrary to Christian standards.

Notes: *This statement by the Seventh-day Adventist Church (approximately 667,000 members) warns of unwholesome influences in the media, including fiction novels, movie theaters, and any presentation which focuses on the pursuit of sensual pleasure. The church holds dramatized sins responsible for much of the breakdown of morality.*

SOUTHERN BAPTIST CONVENTION

ON BEVERAGED ALCOHOL AND PORNOGRAPHY (1976)

WHEREAS, Beveraged alcohol and pornography are two dehumanizing and devastatingly destructive problems of our nation as we celebrate our Bicentennial, and

WHEREAS, The Bible teaches the worth of each individual, while beveraged alcohol destroys individuals and pornography degrades and corrupts individuals.

Be it therefore *Resolved,* that this 1976 Southern Baptist Convention reaffirm its historic stance of pointing out the corruption and dehumanizing nature of ponography in all of its forms, and

Be it further *Resolved*, that we reaffirm our historic stance of pointing out the deceptive and destructive nature of beveraged alcohol, and

Be it finally *Resolved*, that we ask all of our people to work for corrective laws at all levels to specifically work for legislation that prohibits the advertising of beveraged alcohol and the portrayal of pornography in all public media. Further, that we ask our people to express their opposition to these menacing evils in every possible and appropriate way. Further that we ask our people to personally express their concern for the victims of these evils as we point all peoples to Jesus Christ as "the way, the truth and the life."

Notes: *This 1976 resolution by the Southern Baptist Convention (about 14,000,000 members) connects pornography with beveraged alcohol as corrupting influences which are supported by positive portrayals in the media. The Southern Baptists passed similar resolutions against pornography in 1953, 1959, 1968, and 1974.*

SOUTHERN BAPTIST CONVENTION
ON CHRISTIAN MORALITY (1977)

WHEREAS, We are surrounded by many indications of declining moral, ethical, and spiritual standards in our nation, and,

WHEREAS, This lowering of such standards has resulted in the portrayal in mass media of immoral and questionable practices as normal lifestyles, and,

WHEREAS, There is an urgent need for Baptist and other concerned citizens to stand for high moral principles.

Be it therefore *Resolved*, that the Southern Baptist Convention in Kansas City in June 1977 urge our churches and their members to give strong support to our Christian Life Commission's leadership in protesting television's use of illicit sex, casual violence, alcoholic promotion, materialism, vulgarity, and profanity.

Be it finally *Resolved*, that we reaffirm our continuing opposition to such immoral practices as pornography, obscenity, child abuse, and the exploitation of children in pornography, and that we express vigorous opposition to gambling in all its forms, and especially to the efforts of the gambling industry to legalize gambling by state and national laws; and that we commend members of our legislatures and of Congress who take a stand against the evils of legalized gambling and support them in their defense of public morality.

Notes: *The 1977 Southern Baptist Convention resolution on morality connects pornography with gambling, vulgarity, materialism, and other issues as symptoms of "declining moral, ethical, and spiritual standards in our nation."*

SOUTHERN BAPTIST CONVENTION
ON PORNOGRAPHY (1978)

WHEREAS, We are created in the image of God and our body is the temple of the Holy Spirit, and

WHEREAS, The body is to be used in every way to bring glory to God, and

WHEREAS, Pornography seeks to exploit the body and desecrate the mind of both young and old, and

WHEREAS, Pornography is a tool of Satan and a growing detriment to the moral climate of our nation and world,

Therefore be it *Resolved*, that the messengers to the Southern Baptist Convention in regular session in Atlanta, Georgia, go on record as being diametrically opposed to pornography in any form, and

Be it further *Resolved,* that we support and commend citizen's group and law enforcement agencies who openly and courageously oppose pornography, and

Be it further *Resolved,* that we encourage our churches to become involved in the fight against pornography.

Notes: *The 1978 Southern Baptist Convention resolution portrays pornography as a "tool of Satan" which is used to exploit the body and desecrate the mind. The convention urged its members to oppose all forms of pornography.*

SOUTHERN BAPTIST CONVENTION

ON TELEVISION MORALITY (1981)

WHEREAS, Television is a valuable resource available to citizens of our land; and

WHEREAS, Television provides some programming that is morally and intellectually helpful; and

WHEREAS, There is a proliferation of profanity, violence, sex, alcohol, drug abuse, and marital infidelity that portrays an unacceptable life-style, and

WHEREAS, Much leisure time of adults, youth, and children is spent watching television;

Be it therefore *Resolved,* That we urge the proper use of this medium by encouraging higher quality programming in commercial television and by supporting the efforts of our own Radio and Television Commission; and

Be it further *Resolved,* That we appeal to television viewers to be more selective in their viewing; and

Be it further *Resolved,* That we affirm the strong stand taken by the Christian Life Commission concerning television morality; and

Be it further *Resolved,* That southern Baptists vigorously oppose any attempt to remove the public interest standard as the basis for television regulation and communicate such opposition to the Federal Communications Commission and Congress; and

Be it further *Resolved,* That the Southern Baptist Convention, meeting in Los Angeles, June 9-11, 1981, call on churches and individuals to share with networks, local stations, and sponsors concerns about the quality of programming.

Notes: *The 1981 Southern Baptist Convention resolution on television morality condemned television's portrayal of unacceptable lifestyles. The convention urged its members to be selective in their viewing and to communicate their interest in higher programming quality to government officials.*

SOUTHERN BAPTIST CONVENTION

ON PORNOGRAPHY (1985)

WHEREAS, The messengers to the Southern Baptist Conventions in 1978, 1979, 1980, 1981, and 1983 resolved their opposition to pornography in general and child pornography in particular; and

WHEREAS, There is an increasing availability of pornographic video tapes, pornographic cable television channels, and pornographic telephone messages; and

WHEREAS, These are particularly insidious forms of pornography because of their availability directly into the home, thus becoming accessible to children without parental awareness.

Be it therefore *Resolved,* That we, the messengers of the Southern Baptist Convention, meeting in Dallas, June 11-13, 1985, affirm our opposition to all forms of pornography and encourage all Southern Baptist churches to influence public policy to eliminate the availability of all forms of pornography; and

Be it further, *Resolved,* That we strongly urge the Christian Life Commission to continue to develop and disseminate helpful materials opposing pornography; and

Be it further *Resolved,* That we urge the Christian Life Commission and local churches to foster the initiation and passage of legislation to eliminate this parasite on our society.

Notes: *This resolution of the 1985 Southern Baptist Convention reaffirmed opposition to all forms of pornography, especially child pronography.*

SOUTHERN BAPTIST CONVENTION

ON PORNOGRAPHY (1986)

WHEREAS, The Southern Baptist Convention has frequently expressed alarm about the consequences of pornography upon the moral, family, and social life of our nation and the dramatic rise in the availability of pornography; and

WHEREAS, New applications of media technology have produced new opportunities for obscene communication through media such as "Dial-A-Porn", cable television and various obscene video cassettes; and

WHEREAS, Pornographers lure or kidnap many women and children annually for the purpose of being forced into a life of prostitution and sexual abuse; and

WHEREAS, Legal opinion has long held that obscenity is not protected by the First Amendment to the Constitution; and

WHEREAS, The Supreme Court of the United States has set forth clear and precise standards which allow for a determination of obscenity applying the local community standards; and

WHEREAS, There is growing concern about the relationship between pornography and anti-social effects such as sexual violence, child abuse, and dehumanizing attitudes toward men, women and children.

Be it therefore *Resolved,* That we, the messengers of the Southern Baptist Convention meeting in Atlanta, Georgia, June 10-12, 1986, call upon Southern Baptist churches to intensify moral education of church and other community members about the harmful effects of pornography; and

Be it further *Resolved,* That we encourage Southern Baptists to vigorously urge law enforcement officers, prosecutors, and judges to enforce laws which in many states are adequate to restrict the dissemination of obscene materials and the related sexual and other exploitation of men, women, and children; and

Be it further *Resolved,* That we encourage Southern Baptists to participate actively in legally permissible means of protest to dissuade retail outlets from selling pornographic materials; and

Be it further *Resolved,* That the messengers of this Convention commend President Ronald Reagan and Attorney General Edward Meese, III for appointing the Attorney General's Commission on Pornography and urge every Southern Baptist to write to the President and Attorney General thanking them for their past efforts and requesting them to enforce the existing federal laws concerning pornography; and

Be it further *Resolved*, That we urgently plead with the Christian Life Commission to prepare and distribute materials and methods that will assist local churches, associations, or groups in the battle against pornography, especially cable pornography which promotes homosexuality, nudism, incest, bestiality, sadomasochism, rape, abortion, and infidelity right in the living rooms of our nation; and

Be it finally *Resolved*, That we call upon the Christian Life Commission to communicate our gratitude to those retail corporations which recently have voluntarily discontinued the sale of sexually-explicit magazines, and also communicate our gratitude to the National Federation for Decency for their courageous and effective leadership in the battle against pornography.

Notes: *This resolution by the Southern Baptist Convention responded positively to the 1986 Meese Commission on Pornography and encouraged members to fight actively against pornography, especially cable pornography.*

SOUTHERN BAPTIST CONVENTION

ON PORNOGRAPHY (1987)

WHEREAS, The Southern Baptist Convention has spoken on numerous occasions about the harmful effects of pornography; and

WHEREAS, The pornography industry is a multi-billion dollar industry which contributes to many harmful effects in society; and

WHEREAS, New technologies have made possible obscene communications such as "Dial-A-Porn," a sexually-explicit telephone conversation conducted for commercial gain; and

WHEREAS, The primary users of such obscene communication appear to be America's teenagers; and

WHEREAS, Pornographic and sexually explicit films are offered for viewing in hotels and motels, of which the Holiday Inn chain is the largest offender; and

WHEREAS, Obscene communication has never been protected under our Constitution.

Be it therefore *Resolved*, That we, the messengers to the Southern Baptist Convention, meeting in St. Louis, Missouri, June 16-18, 1987, call upon Southern Baptist churches to lead out in opposition to the spread of obscenity, whether by print or electronic media; and

Be it further *Resolved*, That we encourage Southern Baptists to work actively for the passage of federal legislation, now pending in Congress, which would prohibit the use of telephone services as a means of obscene communication which appeals primarily to America's teenagers; and

Be it further *Resolved*, That we call upon the Christian Life Commission to communicate support for this legislation to the appropriate members and committees of Congress; and

Be it finally *Resolved*, That we encourage local congregations to join with similiar effective local and national organizations in active involvement through boycotts, letter writing to advertisers, and selective purchasing-fighting the many dimensions of the pornographic blight.

Notes: *This 1987 resolution by the Southern Baptist Convention emphasized the new reach of "Dial-A-Porn" services and their influence on teenagers, who appear to be "the primary users of such obscene communication." The convention urged its members to actively work for the passage of federal legislation against such use of the phones.*

UNITED CHURCH OF CANADA

CONTROL OF INDECENT LITERATURE (1962)

WHEREAS The United Church of Canada, through its Commission on Christian Marriage and Divorce, has encouraged frank discussion of such subjects as sex, marriage and relationships between men and women, on a high level of respect for the dignity of these relationships as given of God to mankind, and particularly in order that youth may be properly instructed in such matters; and

WHEREAS there is a marked decline in standards of decency in literary works such as novels, picture magazines and pocket books, so that references to sexual and other physical details of life are often made in terms of coarse vulgarity, obscenity and sensuality; and

WHEREAS the Criminal Code of Canada prohibits the dissemination of obscene literature:

THEREFORE BE IT RESOLVED THAT this General Council:

1. Urge the government of Canada to enforce the provisions of the Criminal Code in this matter;

2. Urge our church members, working through our church courts, to exercise vigilance and lay complaints against distributors of literature which they believe to be obscene.

Criminal Code of Canada, Section 150

1. Everyone commits an offence who

   a. (*Obscene matter*) makes, prints, publishes, distributes, circulates or has in his possession for the purpose of publishing, distributing or circulating, any obscene written matter, picture, model, phonograph record or other thing whatsoever.

2. Everyone commits an offence who knowingly, without lawful justification or excuse

   a. (*Selling obscene matter*) sells, exposes to public view or has in his possession for such a purpose any obscene written matter, picture, model, phonograph record or other thing whatsoever.

Notes: *This 1962 resolution by the 20th General Council of the United Church of Canada (approximately 2,186,000 members) notes a "marked decline in standards of decency" in the media and urges enforcement of obscenity laws. The resolution is similar to a statement of the 18th General Council in 1958, which remarked on "a new tide of filth in the form of sex exciting novels and fifty-cent picture magazines of a revolting kind."*

UNITED CHURCH OF CANADA

STATEMENT ON PORNOGRAPHY (1984)

BE IT RESOLVED that The United Church of Canada accept the following as a working definition of pornography; and that this definition be understood to apply in all the following recommendations:

Pornography is material that represents or describes degrading, abusive and/or violent behaviour for sexual gratification so as to imply and/or give endorsement or recommendation to the behaviour as depicted.

BE IT RESOLVED that the 30th General Council authorize the Division of Mission in Canada to undertake the following action on its behalf:

1. WHEREAS pornography is a ten billion dollar industry in North America; and

WHEREAS it exploits, degrades and violates the image of God in all persons, particularly women; and

WHEREAS Christians believe the Word became flesh in Jesus and are called to reverence the body:

THEREFORE BE IT RESOLVED that all United Church people be urged to:

a. Study the issue using this report as an initial step;

b. Speak to friends and families about it;

c. Express opposition to pornography anywhere it is found - stores, family and social settings;

d. Become involved in a church or community group working against pornography;

e. Encourage study on the impact of pornography on men, women and children, on the organizations and institutions to which they relate, and on society as a whole.

2. WHEREAS a critique of pornography on a theological basis and relating to the Canadian context is not readily available; and

WHEREAS United Church members have expressed a desire for such a critique:

THEREFORE BE IT RESOLVED that the Division of Mission in Canada be asked to make this report, together with any appropriate additional material, available throughout the church.

3. WHEREAS more and more pornography shows the torture of women in particular; and

WHEREAS workers at rape crisis centres report pornography is increasingly found in the possession of rapists:

THEREFORE BE IT RESOLVED that all congregations be urged to:

a. Set up a group to take action, which may include holding vigils in front of stores selling pornography, writing letters to politicians, holding worship services around this theme;

b. Work with anti-pornography community groups which need support;

c. Help young people gain a solid understanding and respect for mutually-affirming sexuality;

d. Work toward a positive, life-affirming view of human sexuality.

4. WHEREAS in the past our church in its preaching and teaching office has been remiss in not affirming the divine gift of human embodiment and sexuality:

THEREFORE BE IT RESOLVED that the preachers and teachers of the church be urged to undertake forthright affirmation of the goodness of these gifts.

5. WHEREAS the Obscenity section of the Criminal Code, Section 159(8), is not precise enough to prevent violent and degrading pornographic images, especially of women and children:

THEREFORE BE IT RESOLVED that The United Church of Canada through the Division of Mission in Canada urge the Federal Minister of Justice to draft amendments to the Criminal Code that would include the following:

a. Concise and complete definition of the term "pornography";

b. The phrase "degrading representation of a male or female person" so as to endorse/recommend the behaviour as depicted as a characteristic to be regulated;

c. Prohibition of the undue exploitation of violence, as well as, but distinct from, the undue exploitation of sex;

d. Provision that would no longer permit as a defence in court the argument that the violence in pornography is merely simulated;

e. Legislation prohibiting the use of children in pornography (where "children" means persons under the age of 18 or depicted as being under the age of 18);

f. Broadening of the definition of "material" to "any matter or thing" in order to regulate video material and television programming;

g. Provision that production, distribution, rental or leasing of any pornographic material be included as an offence.

WHEREAS the struggle against pornography is a human rights issue; and

WHEREAS the Hate Literature Section of the Criminal Code, Section 281(2), now reads that hate propaganda must specifically attack an identifiable group, by virtue of "colour, race, religion or ethnic origin":

THEREFORE BE IT RESOLVED that The United Church of Canada through the Division of Mission in Canada urge the Federal Minister of Justice to include addition of the words "gender or sexual orientation."

7. WHEREAS other acts of Parliament pertain to pornography:

THEREFORE BE IT RESOLVED that The United Church of Canada through the Division of Mission in Canada urge the federal government to amend the Customs Tariff Act and the Post Office Act to reflect the proposed changes to the Criminal Code.

8. WHEREAS the introduction of pay TV has made pornographic programming increasingly available; and

WHEREAS this pressures public channels and cable companies to provide similar programming and advertising:

THEREFORE BE IT RESOLVED that The United Church of Canada through the Division of Mission in Canada urge the federal government to amend the Broadcasting Act to include the words "gender or sexual orientation" in the section that now reads, "No station, network operator or pay television licensee shall broadcast any abusive comment or abusive pictorial representation of any race, religion or creed."

FURTHER BE IT RESOLVED that United Church members be urged to become aware of pornographic advertisements and programs, boycott them, and write letters of protest about them.

9. WHEREAS Provincial Censor Boards are established to delete offensive material before films are publicly viewed; and

WHEREAS a system of prior regulation is necessary to prevent pornographic material proliferating without restraint until charges are laid under the provisions of the Criminal Code; and

WHEREAS not all provinces have established Censor Boards:

THEREFORE BE IT RESOLVED that United Church members be urged to become aware of their province's policy and lobby for the establishing of a censor board under strict control of a legal definition of pornography; and if a censor board exists, that videotapes should be included in its jurisdiction.

10. WHEREAS provincial and municipal laws concerning pornography vary across the country:

THEREFORE BE IT RESOLVED that members of congregations be urged to study these laws, lobby for appropriate change and urge governments at all levels to work together on this issue.

Notes: *The United Church of Canada's 30th General Council resolution defined pornography as presentations of degrading or abusive behavior for sexual gratification. Members are urged to show their support for restrictions on pornography, which is described as particularly evocative of violence against women. An impetus behind this report is the February 1982 entrance of pay television, including the "Playboy" channel, into Canada.*

UNITED CHURCH OF CHRIST

RECOMMENDATIONS IN REGARD TO THE HUMAN SEXUALITY STUDY (1977)

RESOLVED, That the 11th General Synod of the United Church of Christ:

1. Receives the report, "Human Sexuality: A Preliminary Study" with appreciation, and commends it to the congregations, associations, conferences, and instrumentalities of the United Church of Christ for study and response.

2. Reaffirms the present important ministries throughout the United Church of Christ and recommends the development of new liturgies, theology, and counseling services which enable the full participation and sharing of gifts of all persons: children, youth, older persons, nuclear families, those who live alone, or choose other lifestyles.

3. Calls upon the United Church Board for Homeland Ministries to continue to provide leadership in developing resources concerning human sexuality for appropriate use by various age groups in local churches and to provide consultative services and training for conferences, associations and congregations who wish to sponsor programs concerned with human sexuality and family life.

4. Requests the UCC-related seminaries, conferences, and instrumentalities to continue developing courses and resources through which clergy, seminary students, and laity may be prepared to minister in the area of human sexuality and to address related public policy issues.

5. Urges pastors, members, congregations, conferences and instrumentalities to support programs in which information about human sexuality can be made available through such major American institutions as elementary and secondary education, adult education, social welfare agencies, medical services, and the communication media.

6. Encourages the congregations of the United Church of Christ, assisted by conferences and instrumentalities, to study and experiment with liturgical rites to celebrate important events and passages in human experience (transitions, anniversaries, separations, and reunions) and relationships of commitment between persons. The Office for Church Life and Leadership and the Board for Homeland Ministries are asked to facilitate the sharing of such liturgical experience.

7. Calls upon the Board for Homeland Ministries, the Commission for Racial Justice, the Office of Communication, and the conferences to develop and share model programs that can help local churches minister to and educate their communities about the components of sexual violence, including rape, marital violence, child abuse, abusive medical practices, and domination and submission images in the media of relationships between women and men portrayed as exclusive expressions of human interaction.

8. Calls upon pastors, congregations, conferences and instrumentalities to address, in their own programs and in those of public and private agencies, the concerns for sexuality and lifestyle of persons who have physical or emotional handicaps, or who are retarded, elderly, or terminally ill. Because of its faithful ministry through care of the young, handicapped, retarded and aged, we urge the council for Health and

Welfare Services to encourage administrators and staff of member institutions to respect the needs for intimacy of adult persons served, and protect the right of sexual expression as important to self-worth, affirmation of life, and avoidance of isolation.

9. Urges the Board for Homeland Ministries, the Commission for Racial Justice, and the Office for Church in Society to work for the protection of persons threatened by coercive use of sterilization, medical treatment, experimental research, or the withholding of medical information, and to fully inform these persons of their rights under the law.

10. Calls upon pastors, members, congregations, conferences and instrumentalities to encourage the extension of contraceptive information and services by both public and private agencies for all youth and adults as instrumental to preventing undesirable pregnancies and fostering responsible family planning.

11. Affirms the right of women to freedom of choice with regard to pregnancy expressed by the Eighth General Synod and interpreted as a constitutional right in the January 22, 1973 decisions of the Supreme Court which remove the legal restrictions on medical termination of pregnancy through the second trimester. Pastors, members, congregations, conferences, instrumentalities and agencies are urged to resist in local communities or in legislative halls attempts to erode or negate the 1973 decisions of the court and to respect and protect the First Amendment rights to differences of opinion and freedom from intimidation concerning the issue of abortion.

Deplores the June 20, 1977 decision of the U.S. Supreme Court and recent actions of the U.S. Congress that effactually deprive the poor of their Constitutional rights of choice to end or complete a pregnancy, while leaving the well-to-do in the full enjoyment of such rights.

Calls upon UCC members, congregations, associations, conferences and instrumentalities to assure that publicly supported hospitals provide medical services to women within their usual service area to exercise their Constitutional right to end or complete pregnancies; and to petition their State legislatures and the U.S. Congress to assure that poor will be provided with medical services to exercise their Constitutional rights to end or complete pregnancies.

12. Calls upon instrumentalities to address the economic structures which victimize women (and men) and explore such strategies as compensation for housework and child care, Social Security for homemakers, programs for displaced homemakers, insurance benefits for pregnancies, and quality day care.

13. Affirms the wide public attention being given to issues related to sexuality and sex roles, particularly as they affect women, but expresses concern regarding the need to explore such issues as they affect men. The 11th General Synod urges the Board for Homeland Ministries, the Office for Church Life and Leadership, conferences, associations, and congregations to develop programs which take into account the needs, experiences and viewpoints of both males and females, and which encourage further understanding of sexual identity; the effects of sex role sterotyping and present economic, legal, political and other societal conditions based upon gender.

14. Recommends to all instrumentalities, agencies, conferences, associations, and congregations that language they use reflect both feminine and masculine metaphor about God, and draw upon the diverse metaphor of God represented in the Bible, in the Christian tradition and in contemporary experience.

15. Recognizes that diversity exists within the UCC about the meaning of ordination, the criteria for effective ministry, and the relevance of marital status, affectional or sexual preference or lifestyle to ordination and performance of minstry. It requests the congregations, associations, and conferences to address these issues seeking more full

and common understanding of their implications. It requests the Office for Church Life and Leadership to develop resources to facilitate such understanding.

16. Urges congregations, associations, conferences, and instrumentalities to work for the decriminalization of private sexual acts between consenting adults.

17. Urges that States legislatively recognize that traditional marriage is not the only stable living unit which is entitled to legal protection in regards to socio-economic rights and responsibilities.

18. Deplores and condemns the dehumanizing portrayals of women and men, the abuse of children, and the exploitation of sex in printed and electronic media of communication, recognizes the rights of adults to access to sexually explicit materials, and affirms that efforts toward change must recognize First Amendment principle.

Moderator Nace declared that 409 votes represents 66 percent of the delegates and that the 210 votes against the motion was 34 per cent. This would enable those delegates to submit a minority statement. The delegates wishing to participate in the minority report were asked to meet after the recess.

Notes: *The statement of the 11th General Synod of the United Church of Christ (approximately 1,676,000 members) responds to a major study completed on human sexuality. It relates to the issue of pornography particularly in paragraphs 7 and 18, where the exploitation of sex and dehumanizing portrayals of persons are rejected. The church also prepared a minority, dissenting resolution from this study, but it does not appear that the dissent was related to the statements on sex in the media.*

UNITED CHURCH OF CHRIST

RESOLUTION ON PORNOGRAPHY (1987)

INASMUCH as the United Church of Christ is concerned with the moral and ethical atmosphere of our communities; and

WHEREAS human sexuality and the human body are gifts of God's good creation; and

WHEREAS pornography which depicts violence and abuse of children, women, and men in sexually explicit situations degrades all people, exploits children, and assaults human dignity; and

WHEREAS such pornography undermines the family structure as well as church and community values; and

WHEREAS the use of children in pornographic materials is growing at an alarming rate and that "kiddie porn" is apart of a growing eight billion dollar industry;

THEREFORE BE IT RESOLVED, the Sixteenth General Synod:

1. Strives clearly to articulate its abhorrence of pornography which demeans and victimizes children, women, and men, takes sex out of the context of God's gift to humankind and makes sordid that which is holy;

2. Communicates that position to its members, its associates in the Christian community and to the general public;

3. Urges all its constitutents, pastors and lay persons, to take an active role to develop an awareness of the depth of the problem and the implications for the church and community and to take appropriate action.

4. Urges that each local congregation strive to minister to both those who have become

victimizers and those who are or who have been victimized by violence, pornography and sexual abuse, affirming the love of God that is for all persons.

BE IT FINALLY RESOLVED that the Sixteenth General Synod adopts this Resolution as a church-wide concern, calls upon the support of every local United Church of Christ church in this matter, and urges the United Church Board for Homeland Ministries to develop strategies and programs to implement this Resolution.

Notes: *This United Church of Christ resolution urges action against pornography which "depicts violence and abuse of children, women, and men in sexually explicit situations."*

UNITED METHODIST CHURCH

THE CHURCH IN A MASS MEDIA CULTURE (1984)

The world is moving from an agricultural and industrial dominance into the information and communication age. In the United States, more persons are employed in information-related industries than in all other types of work combined. Public governments and private industries control the technology and flow of information, wielding great power over the lives of billions of people.

All people are affected by the information revolution. Persons in developing countries may receive most of their news from First World news services while their crop development and natural resources may be surveyed by foreign satellite. Some Third World nations are leapfrogging past the wired nation into the satellite era.

In First World countries such as the United States, persons are spending more and more time in communication activities: viewing more television programming as cable and direct signals from satellites increase, using the home computer and playing video games.

This new development in world history is driven by quantum leaps in basic information management technology and can be described as a revolution because of its pervasive effects at several levels:

- The centralization of control and ownership of information in First World countries.

- The socializing acculturating effects of world media bringing the same messages and information to diverse audiences.

- The increasing amounts of time persons are interacting with media rather than with other persons and the passive nature of much media viewing.

- The incentive for a mass audience leads to dominant content of the entertainment and information media categorized by escapism, consumerism, violence and exclusion of minorities.

- The increasing involvement of the work force and capital investment in information technolgy-related endeavors in the developed and developing world.

As United Methodists, we have "emphasized God's endowment of each person with dignity and moral responsibility" (¶69, page 76, 1980 *Book of Discipline*). We recognize that "faith and good works belong together" (¶69, p. 77). We have a long history of concern for social justice, so it is within both a biblical and historical context that we as United Methodists speak to the communication and information revolution.

The goals of The United Methodist Church, based on our understanding of the gospel, are clear.

- Persons everywhere must be free in their efforts to live meaningful lives.

- Channels of communication must operate in open, authentic and humanizing ways.

241

- Christians should be involved seriously and continuously in the communication systems of their societies.

In the implementation of these goals, we must be aware of the power of the mass media. All media are educational. The mass media—especially radio, television, cable TV, motion pictures, newspapers, books and magazines—are pervasive and influential forces in our culture. The new media of video games, direct broadcast satellite, video recordings for home use and computers are increasing. Whether they deal with information, opinion, entertainment, escape, explicit behavioral models or subtle suggestion, the mass media always are involved, directly or indirectly, in values. Furthermore, all media messages speak from some theological assumptions. Therefore, we as Christians must ask such major questions as:

- Who controls the media in a country? Who determines the structures of and the public's access to the mass media? Will deregulation of radio, television and cable in the United States result in greater diversity, freedom and justice, or less? Who controls international technologies of communication?

- Who determines message content and within what guidelines of responsibility?

- Who uses the media and for what purposes?

- What rights do users have in determining media structure and content? What is the user's responsibility in bringing critical appraisal and judgment to the messages received?

- What is the appropriate response to the growing demands of developing countries that there be new and more just world information systems which meet their needs?

As Christians, we affirm the principle of freedom of expression as both an individual and corporate right. We oppose any laws or structures which attempt to abridge freedom of expression and we state our concern about the numerous incidents of repression of freedom of expression occurring in the United States and around the world. We believe:

- Freedom of expression—whether by spoken or printed work, or any visual or artistic medium—should be exercised within a framework of social responsibility. The church is opposed to censorship.

- The principle of freedom of the press must be maintained and must receive full support from the church and its constituents, even when the cost is high.

- The electronic spectrum is a limited natural resource. The airwaves should be held in trust for the public by radio and television broadcasters and regulated in behalf of the public by government. While the broadcaster has great discretion for the program content this does not abridge the public's "right to know," to be fairly represented and to have access to the media.

- Public broadcasting as it continues to develop should be supported by both public and private sectors of the society to help further the diversity of programming and information sources.

- All persons of every nation should have equal access to channels of communication so they can participate fully in the life of the world. We encourage United Methodist members and agencies to participate in the study and continuing dialogue across national boundaries concerning the development of fair and just communication and information systems within nations and between nations.

- No medium can be truly neutral. Each brings its own values, limitations, criteria, authoritarian or democratic structures and selection processes with it.

- Appropriate agencies of The United Methodist Church should keep abreast of new communication technologies and structures, helping the church to stay informed so it may respond to developments which affect the human condition.

While we acknowledge the practicality of the necessity of media professionals to determine the societal and moral content of mass media, we must continue to oppose the practices of those persons and systems which use media for purposes of exploitation. Exploitation comes in many forms:

- Emphasizing violence.
- Showing pornography.
- Appealing to self-indulgence.
- Presenting consumerism as a way of life.
- Offering easy solutions to complex problems.
- Favoring the mass audience to the exclusion of individual and minority needs.
- Withholding significant information.
- Treating news as entertainment.
- Presenting events in isolation from the larger social context.
- Stereotyping characters in terms of sex roles, ethnic or racial background, occupation, age, religion and economic status.
- Failing to deal with significant political and social issues objectively and in depth.
- Exhibiting an overriding concern for maximizing profit.
- Discriminating in employment practices.
- Presenting misleading or dangerous product information or omitting essential information.
- Failing to educate adequately and inform the public about the nature and processes of these media themselves.

We call upon the mass media industries and their leaders to recognize their power and to use this power responsibly in enabling persons to achieve their fullest potential as members of the family of God. We urge Christians and church members involved in the media industries to utilize their faith in their decision-making and in their work place, to find others with moral and ethical commitment, and to discuss ways of enabling their industries to exercise their power for the good of humankind.

We urge the church to devise ways of responding to the mass media, including the following:

- Participating in research on the effects of media and information technologies.
- Developing criteria and resources by which church members can evaluate and interpret what is being communicated to them through the mass media.
- Recognizing that all information and entertainment programs can be used for learning, thereby making use of mass media programming in the church's ministry.
- Recognizing that communication professions offer opportunities for ministry and service.
- Working with the mass media at local and national levels, linking the life of the church with the life of the community.
- Participating in the development of the regulatory requirements of media.

We urge our churches to communicate, minister, and serve their communities through the public media. This will require them to:

- Discover the needs of persons in the community and determine how the church can minister to those needs through the media.
- Work with other churches in an ecumenical spirit of service and ministry.

- Commit time, budget, and talent to ministry through the media.

- Recognize the variety of purposes the church can fulfill in communicating through mass media, such as education, witness, evangelism, information, social service, and ministry.

- Be advocates for those shut out of the media; the poor, less powerful, and those on the margins of society.

In our own communication structures and processes within the church, we need to establish models of communication which are freeing, which respect the dignity of the recipient, and which are participating and non-manipulative. We need to democratize our own media to allow access and open dialogue. As a major institution within our society, we can demonstrate to other institutions the power of a connectional church which structures its communication patterns not by concentrating media power but by emphasizing the values of the gospel which recognize the sanctity of every individual.

Notes: *The United Methodist Church (approximately 9,400,000 members) places the problem of pornography in the context of living in a mass media culture. The church holds the media accountable for exploitation through its portrayals of pornography, violence, and stereotyping.*

UNITED METHODIST CHURCH

SEXUAL VIOLENCE AND PORNOGRAPHY (1988)

"So God created humankind in God's own image, in the image of God was the human created; male and female God created them. . . . And God saw everything that was made, and behold, it was very good. . . ." (Genesis 1:27; 31, RSV-AILL). Human sexuality is a sacred gift of God. It "is crucial to God's design that creatures not dwell in isolation and loneliness, but in communion and community . . . sexual sins lie not in being too sexual, but in not being sexual enough in the way God has intended us to be." ("Reuniting Sexuality and Spirituality" by James B. Nelson, *The Christian Century*, Feb. 25, 1987.)

God created human beings with an ability to make a choice for good or evil. This divinely created freedom is one to be cherished as are all gifts from God.

We face a massive public health problem based on people's choosing violence. In 1977, the Centers for Disease Control initiated a program to study the nature of violence in our society. In 1985, violence was declared a major health problem.

Violence takes many forms and many different weapons are being used. Many people use their bodies as weapons to abuse children, their spouses and the elderly or to commit rape and other forms of violent battery. Deprivation of many kinds are forms of violence. Discrimination and poverty are forms of social violence. Indeed, Ghandi once said that poverty is the worst form of violence.

And the threat of nuclear war constitutes a violent cloud over all of us.

The causes of violence and the escalation of violence in the U.S. are varied. However, public attitudes toward violence play a major factor in the cause and acceptance of violence in our society. In the United States is a large-scale tolerance of interpersonal violence. This society is permeated with images and myths about violence from the old cowboy movies where justice and violence became synonymous, to the new type of stalk and slash movies which combine sexual exploitation with violence.

New technology has made sexually violent and pronographic films more available to more people regardless of age, location, or level of moral understanding. Now persons of all ages can go to their own video stores and secure a wide variety of tapes for play on their videotape recorders or telephone-dial-a-porn from the privacy of their own homes.

These new phenomena are especially dangerous for several reasons:

1. A wide variety of videos are easily available at low cost.

2. Violent or sexually explicit scenes can be played over and over again, teaching through powerful visual images and repetition.

3. The highly erotic stimulation of dial-a-porn is particularly damaging to children and youth.

4. Videos and dial-a-porn are used without parental knowledge, consent or interaction.

As a result, the sex education of our children is shifting dramatically from parents and the responsible institutions of our society to the powerful mass media of film, television, cable TV and video cassettes.

Carefully documented research has found false messages that predominate in many media images of sexuality:

● Violence is a normal part of sexual relationships;

● Women "enjoy" being forced into sex;

● Women "invite" men to violate them;

● Sex is something you "do to" rather than share with someone else.

The repeated viewing of sexually violent material by men:

● Desensitizes men to violence on the screen;

● Decreases their empathy with victims of sexual violence;

● Increases their belief in the "rape myths" that women ultimately enjoy being raped, that "no" doesn't mean no, that women are responsible for their own rape.

As Christians and as citizens, we recognize the need to differentiate between sex education materials, erotica, sexually explicit material and obscenity. The lines are neither self-evident nor clear and will differ among persons and groups. The Supreme Court has not defined pornography while finding "obscenity" not protected under the free speech provisions of the First Amendment.

We affirm the need for sex education in our schools, community youth organizations and churches. Our young people need to know the biological facts, the health risks, the emotional impact and consequences of their choices, and the moral basis of their faith. We recognize the appropriateness and need for explicit sexual information both verbally and visually. In all instances, information should be used with restraint and a clear attempt should be made to minimize erotic qualities.

Child pornography uses children alone, in sexual relationships with other children, or in sexual relationships with adults. Children are psychologically or physically coerced into participation by older children, or adults. Child pornography victimizes children and harms them physically, emotionally and spiritually. Child pornographers and distributors should be prosecuted to the full extent of the law.

The Supreme Court declared that obscenity is not protected by the free speech provisions of the First Amendment. Material to be judged illegal must be offensive to community standards and appeal to prurient interests, lack serious scientific, educational, literary, political or artistic value. We believe that sexually violent material should be judged "obscene" within the context of the Supreme Court decision.

In order to discuss issues related to sexually explicit material more clearly and precisely, we propose the following definitions:

Erotic material is sexually explicit and arousing but does not use coercion, inflict pain, use violence in any way, and rarely depicts sexual intercourse. Some of the world's greatest masterpieces are erotic.

Soft pornography may show persons in sexual intercourse, but does not use coercion, inflict pain or use violence. However, we believe that soft-core pornography usually is harmful and erotica may be harmful to disturbed or immature persons.

Hard core pornography may show persons in intercourse using coercion, or using violence and inflicting pain. It generally presents women in subordinate situations and degrades both men and women.

Sexual exploitation is a form of social violence that, when communicated to a large number of people, can create both tolerance of sexual violence and increase the incidence of such violence. The national Council of Churches conducted a study of ''Violence and Sexual Violence in Film, Television, Cable and Home Video.'' Some key points that are relevant to this issue include: violence in all of its forms—whether social as in the cases of discrimination and sexual exploitation or physical as in the cases of battery or sexual abuse—is a major public health problem in this nation. Therefore, a combined Christian and public health approach to resolving the problem needs to be applied.

As Christians, we need to examine those materials with which we interact to determine their social or physical violence characteristics. We must insure that we do not communicate myths that perpetuate violence or allow images of violence, victimization, or exploitation to become a part of institutional communications.

A public health approach instructs our secular institutions to imitate educational and communication strategies that enable people to learn alternatives to violence, as well as other violence prevention measures. People must be encouraged to seek help when victimized.

Institutions such as family counseling centers, drop-in crisis nurseries, battered women shelters, runaway shelters need to be provided by both church and community.

In examining our own and secular media the following points adopted by the National Council of Churches are helpful:

1. Our media environment is more complex than ever before. As entertainment forms increasingly include excessive portrayals of violence, parents and other concerned citizens often feel helpless before a media system that is seemingly our of control.

2. Christians are called to a ministry of concern and constructive response so that moral values which have emanated from families of faith can be preserved, perpetuated and shared with others in our society. Christians also are called upon to bring prophetic judgement to bear on threats to public welfare through what is seen as a moral pollution of our media environment.

3. Only a genuinely open marketplace of ideas can guarantee the search for truth. For this reason we are determined to defend the First Amendment guarantees of freedom of religion, of speech and of the press. Society should seek to maximize the diversity of sources and ideas, and to minimize the power of government or individuals to block or constrict this diversity of sources.

4. However, prior control of the content of media does exist in our society exercised by the government, by business, by education, by the power of money and monopoly. With respect to any program, someone must decide what shall be included or what is left out. The issue is not whether there should be prior control, but who should exercise it, and how it should be exercised.

5. As Christians we affirm our adherence to the principles of freedom of expression as a right of every person, both individually and corporately. We oppose any law which attempts to abridge the freedom of expression guaranteed by the First Amendment. At

the same time, as Christians we affirm that the exercise of this freedom must take place within a framework of social responsibility.

6. Children are especially threatened by the pervasiveness of violence and sexual violence in media. Both ethically and constitutionally it is the responsibility of the entire society to protect the interests of children and to provide for their education and welfare. We support the 1968 Supreme Court ruling that children may legally be barred from theatre showings of films deemed unsuitable for them. Parents should be helped to avoid the showing of that same material in their homes via television, cable and videocassette.

7. The airwaves are held in trust for the public by radio and television broadcasters with licenses regulated by the government. The broadcaster is therefore responsible for the content of programming. However, this right does not abridge the public's "right to know" and to be fairly represented.

8. Federal regulations should require broadcast licensees and cable operators to make available regularly scheduled constructive programming to enlighten and entertain children.

9. We support criminal obscenity laws which do not embody prior restraint but which punish after the fact certain kinds of speech which the Supreme Court had determined are not protected by the First Amendment.

10. In any competitive business environment, some rules are necessary to bring about positive change. Laws and governmental regulation are essential in dealing with reform in the communication industry, because they can place all competitors on an equal basis and thus not disturb the working of the economic marketplace.

11. All mass media are educational. Whether they deal with information, opinion, entertainment, escape, explicit behavior models or subtle suggestion, the mass media always, directly or indirectly, shape values.

12. In all broadcast and film media, advance information about the products offered should be made available by the industry to parents so they can guide their children's viewing.

13. It is important for research into the effect of media to continue, under a variety of auspices, so society will have increasingly accurate information as the basis for remedial action to the problems presented by violence and sexual violence in the media. The Church has a special role for congregational education and public policy relative to pornography, violence and sex exploitation. The NCCC developed action strategies for churches on local, annual conference and national levels.

   a. Communication agencies within the denominations and through the National Council of Churches' Communication Commission should monitor programs in order to assess danger levels of violence and sexual violence. Findings should be published for the guidance of parents, educators and others.

   b. Theologians should examine the moral and spiritual implications of the violence phenomenon in media.

   c. Clergy, parents and teachers within Christian communions should be trained and equipped to prepare children and youth to survive with integrity in a complex media environment.

   d. Churches and their agencies should join forces with other groups in society who share the same concern over the extent of violence in media, in order to plan concerted counteraction.

   e. Religious communities should establish dialogue with creative media professionals. Their objective should be to support and encourage those producers, directors, writers, and actors who are willing to seek ways within the industry to provide viable alternatives to programming that exploits violence and sexual violence.

f. Churches and church agencies should assist in funding and promoting general distribution programming which presents positive messages and does not contain exploitative sex and gratuitous violence.

g. Opinions, both positive and negative, should be solicited from members of Christian churches and their leaders, to be presented to those responsible for media productions. Affirmation and encouragement should be sent to those responsible for quality presentations that lift the human spirit while complaints and protests should go to those responsible for programs that exploit, demean or desensitize audiences through excessive applications of violence and sexual violence.

Since United Methodists represent a broad spectrum of American society, and since pornography is no respecter of age, social, economic or even religious condition, there are undoubtedly those among our constituency who are afflicted and dependent on the habit of sexually violent material. There are persons within our congregations who need help. There are young people who need guidance. There are children who are being sexually abused, and women who are being physically abused.

Therefore, we encourage our congregations to:

a. Use United Methodist sex education curriculum.

b. Study the issues surrounding pornography.

c. Undertake training programs to learn to hear the "cries of help" from abused children and women and develop a plan of referral of these persons to appropriate community service organizations.

d. Support shelters for battered women and children.

e. Join with other community groups in taking appropriate steps to curb distribution of sexually violent material and child pornography in our communities.

Further, we request that the United Methodist Church should, through all its agencies which manage investments, monitor such investments to assure that no church funds are invested in companies which are involved in the production, distribution or sale of pornographic material, and further, if such investments are found, should move to divest holdings in such companies.

The misuse of our human sexuality through violence and coercion separates us from one another by making women and children fearful of men and separates us from our creator God.

ADOPTED 1988

Notes: *The United Methodist Church differentiates between erotic material (which is not offensive), soft core pornography (which is borderline), and hard core pornography (which is offensive in that it depicts violence and coercion and places women in subordinate roles). Children especially are considered prone to damage from pornography. The church encourages members to take actions to counter the proliferation of pornography.*

WESLEYAN CHURCH

PORNOGRAPHY AND OBSCENITY (1984)

The 1984 General Conference of The Wesleyan Church adopted this anti-pornography and anti-obscenity resolution:

Whereas, The six-billion-dollar pornographic industry in America has grown to epidemic proportions and invaded every segment of society;

Whereas, The public media is being exploited by pornographic and obscene content;

Whereas, The lifestyle propagated by the pornographic industry is contrary to biblical teachings;

Whereas, Family, church, and community values are being seriously threatened;

Whereas, The Supreme Court in 1973 reaffirmed the right of the community to protect its standards; and

Whereas, The lowering of standards has resulted in increasing teenage pregnancies, child prostitution, and other sexual abuses;

Resolved, That this General Conference declare its support for the following goals:

1. To create awareness of the serious effects of pornography and obscenity in our society.
2. To inform concerned citizens what they can do to reduce this blight locally and nationally.
3. To provide an arena where concerned citizens can begin to formulate specific actions that they can take individually and in concert with others.

Resolved, That we observe a special Morals Awareness Sunday on October 28, 1984, to inform our congregations about the seriousness of the problem;

Resolved, That we ask the Task Force on Public Morals to provide materials for our congregations so that they will be equipped to take positive action in a continuing manner;

Resolved, That we encourage our congregations to become involved in a plan of action in their own communities as well as using their voice as a positive influence for the media and law;

Resolved, That we urge our people to write the president of the United States:

1. Asking him to make a public announcement that enforcement of the four federal obscenity laws is a matter of importance to him.
2. Requesting him to order the Justice Department to enforce the obscenity laws which are now on the books.
3. Pledging him our prayers and support in his effort to exercise increased vigilance through

   —the Attorney General

   —the Federal Bureau of Investigation

   —the Postmaster General

   —the United States Customs Commissioner

Resolved, That we also urge our people in Canada and the British Isles to contact the appropriate governmental persons and departments with positive encouragement toward curbing the blight of pornography and obscenity in their respective countries.

Notes: *The Wesleyan Church (approximately 111,000 members) says that pornography is threatening family and community values and has resulted in "teenage pregnancies, child prostitution, and other sexual abuses." The church urges members to show support for stricter enforcement of existing laws.*

Jewish Groups

Organized Jewish religious communities in the United States involve approximately half of the six million Jewish citizens. They are generally divided into three main branches—Orthodox, Conservative, and Reform. Each branch has approximately one million adherents. Additionally, the Reconstructionist Movement claims about 40,000 members. The Jewish tradition recognizes the abuses of pornography, as indicated by the statement from the National Federation of Temple Sisterhoods, and at the same time is sensitive to the issues of government censorship and repression.

NATIONAL FEDERATION OF TEMPLE SISTERHOODS

CHILDREN AND THE FAMILY (1983)

Issue

I.   The Breakdown of the Family

    a. Domestic Violence

    b. Child Abuse and Pornography, Missing Children

    c. Spouse Abuse

    d. Child Support

II. Day Care

III. Public Education

Background

Our Jewish family, once the model of stability, respect and devotion, is falling victim to the forces in modern life which brought about the breakdown of the family generally. Changing social patterns of increased divorce, domestic violence, child abuse, drugs, alcoholism, pressures and tensions fragment and severely challenge family life. Single parent families or the decision not to marry and have children especially affect the Jewish family. (Excerpted from NFTS 70th Anniversary press release).

Domestic violence is not new. It has always happened. Battered children and battered wives have suffered in silence while doctors and authorities often looked the other way. Society is beginning to attempt to come to the assistance of these helpless victims with shelters and counseling services.

The abused child is not only a physically battered child; the child may be the victim of sexual abuse by a member of the family. Those who photograph children nude or engaged in sexually explicit activities are not always strangers. The victims of child abuse bear the scars for the rest of their lives, but the perpetrators often go free.

With more frequent divorce many homes are single parent homes. Too frequently, the father not only physically and emotionally absents himself from the home but also forfeits his obligations to his children through non-payment of child support.

The increasing number of working mothers as well as the increasing number of single parent homes make it imperative that responsible child care centers be available. Ten years ago as the number of mothers with full time jobs began to increase, it was assumed that industry would move to provide on-site day care for its workers. This has not been the case although in 1982 more than 7 million women with children under six years of age were employed in full time positions. ("Corporate Ambivalence on Day Care," Ardee Brooks.) Women now comprise nearly 43% of the work force and are the sole support of nine million families.

Resolution

1. We urge Sisterhoods to work in concert with other organizations to provide a variety of services such as shelters, counseling, food, clothing and jobs for the victims of spouse, child or family abuse. We especially urge Sisterhoods to undertake programs and projects in specific relationship to the Jewish community and where appropriate establish or support programs that will deal especially with Jewish victims.

2. We abhor child pornography and deplore it as a form of entertainment. We urge recognition that the production and distribution of pornographic material featuring children is not a right guaranteed by either the US or Canadian Constitutions, but a violation of the child's freedom and dignity. We urge legislation which will guarantee that convicted pornographers, producers and sellers of such pornography and child abusers will be prevented from repeating their crimes.

3. In affirmation of the efforts already enacted on behalf of missing children, we urge Sisterhoods to participate in or initiate local and statewide programs that will secure the safety of our children including such appropriate security measures as voluntary fingerprinting, educational programs for children and adequate supervision of playgrounds, nursery schools and public schools.

4. We urge that spouse, child and family abuse not be viewed as merely social ills by the police, the courts and others but as criminal acts.

5. We urge Sisterhoods to support passage and enforcement of legislation that ensures payment of child support.

6. We encourage Sisterhoods to continue their support of the establishment and mainte- nance of community day care centers which would provide appropriate environments for young children of working mothers. In addition we urge Sisterhoods to establish day care centers within their congregations to handle pre-school children of their own members, recognizing that these particular day care centers should provide an atmos- phere of Jewish learning in addition to that which would normally be expected in the home.

7. We reaffirm our commitment to the public school system and to the doctrine of separation of church and state in the education of our children. We believe that while the public school system must exemplify moral and ethical standards the primary responsi- bility for teaching these values is within the family and home.

Notes: *The National Federation of Temple Sisterhoods is an independent organization composed of about 100,000 women primarily from the Reformed and Conservative branches of Judaism. This statement condemns child pornography and urges legislation that would eliminate it.*

UNION OF AMERICAN HEBREW CONGREGATIONS

CENSORSHIP OF BOOKS (1981)

Across our nation there is a growing effort to ban books from schools and public libraries.

THEREFORE, BE IT RESOLVED:

1. The UAHC affirms its support for First Amendment guarantees of free speech.
2. The UAHC calls on public school boards and library boards across our country to resist these pressures.
3. The UAHC asks its congregations and their memberships to urge public school boards and public library boards to support these First Amendment rights and to give support, as necessary, to those that do.

Notes: *Reform Judaism is represented by the Union of American Hebrew Congregations (approximately 1,200,000 members). While this statement does not specifically mention pornography, it does present a general condemnation of literary censorship.*

Other Religious Bodies

America is now home to many groups which are neither Christian in the traditional sense (i.e. Catholic, Protestant, or Eastern Orthodox) nor Jewish. Other groups include Hinduism and Buddhism from Asia, Islam from the Middle East and elsewhere, the Latter-day Saint tradition native to the United States, and those that follow other traditions, both ancient and modern. Only a few of these groups have issued formal statements on social issues like pornography.

SHI'A ISLAM

ISLAM AND THE POSITION OF WOMEN (1977)

The West's vociferous partisans of Women's Lib. have no idea of the revolutionary leap forward in women's position which Islam brought about. In the days of Islam's first appearance the position of women was that of chattels of the men—little above the domesticated animals. Yet the West, for all their vaunted freedom, have added nothing to what Islam gave to women, except liberty for increased corruption and licentiousness. Islam prohibits debauchery, laxity, vulgarity, debasement and demoralisation. Is that to hinder women's upward advance?

Islam regards both man and woman as created by God to rise to the full stature of the perfect human. This is in stern contrast with those versions of the Heavenly Book which Jews and Christians have tampered with and published as reading: "Amongst every thousand men appears one beloved of God: but amongst all the women in the world there is not to be found one who is included in God's grace and favour." (My quotation is from page 519 of "Islamic and Arab Civilisation", an authoritative work to which due respect must be paid.)

Islam proclaims that in God's eyes there is no difference between man and woman. Each is a precious soul. In His eyes all that makes people stand out from one another is their excelling in virtue, piety, reverence, spiritual and ethical qualities. It is open to both men and women to achieve that type of excellence. At Doomsday each soul will be judged, regardless of sex, according to the fruits of their actions, by the above criteria. As it is written in Sura XXVII: Nahl—"Bee": "Whosoever hath faith and performs decorous actions, man or woman, I decree as their destiny a life that will be satisfied and will win that soul a reward better than the good deeds they have done." Compare Sura XXVIII: Qasās—"The Narration" (verse 84): "To whosoever does good, the reward is better than the deed."

Islam regards men and women as complementary to each other. As it is written in Sura III: Aal-i-Imran—"Imran's Family" (verse 195): "Their Lord hath accepted their prayer and

255

answered: 'Never will I suffer the work of any one of you, male or female, to be lost. Ye are complementary to each other'.''

Many women possess such personal excellences and intelligence that they attain great heights of true humanity and happiness. Many men, alas, fall to the lowest depths because they flout reason and abandon themselves to their passions.

It is related that on one occasion the Second Caliph, Omar, said from the pulpit in the presence of a large crowd: ''I will fine any man who gives his bride 500 darhams or more as dowry. He shall be made to give the same amount as that by which his dowry exceeds the Mahr-as-Sunna (traditional dowry) to the public treasury.'' At this a woman who was at the foot of the pulpit cried out in a loud voice her objection to Omar's statement saying: ''Your proclamation contradicts God's law: for does not the Sura IV: Nisa'a—'The Women', say (verse 20): 'But if you decide to take one wife in place of another, even if you have given the wife you put away a talent of gold as her marriage portion, take not the least bit of it back'? How can you, then, in contradiction of the Divine Law which has stated that it is permissible to give more than the legal minimum marriage portion, make your proclamation?'' Omar could not deny the impeachment and withdrew his proposition saying: ''It was a man who erred and a woman who uttered the truth.''

Contrast with this the tragic depression of women in pre-Islamic Arabia. What a height of dignity has been conferred by Islam on the female sex to enable one of them to lift up her voice in public rebuke to a Caliph and cause him to reverse his own public utterance! Islam took from men the right to own women. It instituted equality of human souls, with due regard to differences of male and female constitutions.

In the 19th century religious leaders of France, after long discussions, decided: ''Woman is a human being, but made to serve man.'' It was not until recent years that women in European lands had any rights to own property. In England it was not till about AD 1850 that women were counted in the national population census. It was in 1882 that a British law, unprecedented in the country's history, for the first time granted women the right to decide how their own earnings should be spent, instead of handing them over direct to their husbands immediately. Until then, even the clothes on their back had been their husband's property. Henry VIII had in his day even forbidden women to study the Bible when the first English translations began to appear.

Fourteen centuries ago Islam had decreed women's total financial independence, their right to own and dispose of property without the surveillance or control of any man, to conduct business, trade and all the transactions concerning their profit and loss, including the execution of deeds of gift, without having to check with anyone. As it is written in the Sura IV: Nisa'a—''The Women'', verse 33: ''In no wise covet gifts bestowed by God seemingly more freely on some than on others. Whatsoever a man earns is his own. Whatsoever a woman earns is her own. Pray to God for the bounty of His Providence for He knows all things.''

Besides property rights Islam bestowed dignity, liberty and freedom on women. This is not least true in the matter of marriage. Marriage is the most important and sensitive step in a woman's life. Islam did everything to secure her in it, and to enable her to consider the financial as well as all the other matters concerning the situation before she accepted him in wedlock.

Thus the rights and privileges which European women extorted after bringing forceful pressure to bear on the societies in which they lived, and only recently achieved, Islam bestowed upon all women voluntarily without any form of revolt or pressure many centuries back. Indeed there is no moment of a woman's life, and no problem she is likely to face, for which Islam has not made beneficent and wise provision.

It is true that today far too many women are condemned in the East to an unsatisfactory way of life. But this is not due to Islam's regulations. It is due to the neglect of religious precept in political, social and financial institutions.

Poverty is one important reason for the bad conditions under which Eastern women have to live. A few are too rich; but the majority far too poor, victims of hunger and wretchedness. The resultant weakness has deprived people of the strength to rise up and insist on a change in their environment, for the sake of their families and children. Nor have the women the power in such a situation to make use of their legal rights and to take the men to court for the violence and tyranny of their behaviour. Women fear the difficulties of having to live without a male companion in a man's world.

The same economic needs cause a diminution in morals and in human affections. Violence and injustice replace moral values.

Although Islamic lands are amongst the worst sufferers from these modern disasters, it is not Islam itself, but the deliberate neglect and abandonment of Islamic principles by Muslims and their leaders which has brought these tragedies upon us. For Islam is the very acme of the counterforces to poverty and injustice, and insists that wealth must be fairly divided amongst people of all classes, declaring that it is wrong for people to have to live under the torture of indigence and its pressure on hearts and souls, not least those of women and children.

Have we not men wise and just enough to eradicate these wrongs? To cure the bitterness which they produce? To re-enact sound Islamic measures? To restore respect for the dictates of piety and reverence for God and men? Should not that same Islam which once rescued woman from degrading depression, now raise her again by instituting a new society?

What is the situation in the West? Women have fallen victims to the bestial passions to which men have abandoned themselves under the influence of subversive propaganda of all kinds, in which the mass-media, particularly cinema and TV, and the advertisements that disgrace the hoardings of our great cities, play so tragically fateful a part.

Nowadays a woman's good reputation and dignity does not come, as it used to, from her possession of moral excellences, education and knowledge. Too often women of piety and learning are left in obscurity. Respect, reputation go too much with the name of "artiste" which some women arrogate to themselves. They perform no useful function in society. They do not help the men forward. The name "artiste" seems to cover a multitude of sins of incontinence and debauchery, which are the very opposite of that virtue and chastity in which the honour of women once resided. How many earn a shameful living as "models"?

An American sociologist writes that the modern stripteaser can earn a million dollars a year: a fellow who is able to knock out another man with one blow of his fist gets half a million: a man who has spent a lifetime in the service of his fellows, in his white hairs finds hardly enough to live on.

Professor Albert Connolly writes: "In 1919 England's women fought for the right to be elected to Parliament, and in their battle went to prison and suffered physically in fearless vindication of their sex. What use are their grandchildren making of the privileges gained for them by these courageous women pioneers? And what would their grandmothers think of them? Maybe they are actually turning in their graves at seeing the liberties they fought for perverted to shameless license. This last half century has taught us that the liberation of women is not enough. Besides all their other sacrifices for their cause, women seem also to have connived at the sacrifice of the respect and the ancient realities, the moral dignity and the devotion to mankind's uplift which in former days brought honour to the name of 'woman' and 'mother'." (Quoted from "The Enlightened Thinkers' Magazine", No. 829).

Notes: *This statement is an excerpt from the book* Western Civilization Through Muslim Eyes *(1977) by Sayid Mujtaba and Rukni Musawi Lari, and represents a Shi'a Islam* *perspective (which has an unknown number of adherents in the United States). Both men and women are condemned for being "victims to the bestial passions" supported by the mass media. The "honour of women" should reside in "virtue and chastity" and "education and knowledge."*

SUNNI ISLAM

TOWARDS UNDERSTANDING ISLAM (1963)

The Shari'ah has formulated certain rules of behaviour for wider fraternity as well. These rules oblige the Muslims to help each other, to bid the good and forbid the evil and to see that no wrong creeps into their society. Some of the injunctions of the law of Islam, in this respect, are as follows:

1. To preserve the moral life of the nation and to safeguard the evolution of society on healthy lines, free mingling of both the sexes has been prohibited. Islam affects a functional distribution between the sexes and sets different spheres of activity for both of them. Women should in the main devote to the household duties in their homes and men should attend to their jobs in the socio-economic spheres. Outside the pale of the nearest relations between whom marriage is forbidden, men and women have been asked not to mix freely with each other and even if they have to contact each other they should do so with **purdah.** When women have to go out of their homes, they should use simple dress and go out properly veiled. They should also cover their faces and hands as a normal course. Only in genuine necessity they can be unveiled, and there too they must re-cover when the necessity has expired. Along with this, men have been asked to keep down their eyes and not to look upon women. And if some one accidentally happens to look upon some woman, he should turn away the eye. To try to see them is wrong and to try to seek their acquaintance is worse. It is the duty of every man and woman to look after their personal morality and purge their souls of all impurities. Marriage is the proper form of sexual relationship and no one should attempt to overstep this limit or even think of any sexual license; the very thought and imagination of man should be purified from such perverse ideas.

2. For the same purpose it has been enjoined that proper dress should always be worn and no man should expose his body from the knees to the navel, nor should a woman expose any part of her body except the face and hand to any person other than her husband, however closely related to her he might be. This is technically called **satr** (cover) and to keep these parts covered is the religious duty of every man and woman. Through this directive Islam wants to cultivate in its followers a deep sense of modesty and purity and to suppress all forms and manifestations of immodesty and moral deviation.

3. Islam does not approve of such pastimes, entertainments and recreations as tend to stimulate sensual passions and vitiate the canons of morality. Such pastimes are sheer waste of time, money and energy and destroy the moral fibre of the society. Recreation in itself is no doubt a necessity. It acts as a spur to activity and quickens the spirit of life and adventure. It is as important to life as water and air and particularly after hard work one does require rest and recreation. But the recreations must be such that refresh the mind and enliven the spirit; and not of a type that depress the spirit and deprave the passions. The absurd and wasteful entertainments wherein thousands of people witness depraving scenes of crime and immorality, are the very antithesis of healthy recreation. Although they may be gratifying to the senses, but their effect upon the minds and morals of the people is horrifying. They spoil their habits and morality and can have no place in the Islamic society and culture.

4. To safeguard the unity and solidarity of the nation and to achieve the welfare and well-being of the Muslim community, the believers have been enjoined to avoid mutual hostility, social dissensions and sectarianism of all hue and colour. They have been exhorted to settle their differences and disputes in accordance with the principles laid down in the Qur'an and Sunnah. And if the parties fail to reach any settlement, instead of fighting and quarrelling amongst themselves they should bury the differences in the name of Allah and leave the decision unto Him. In matters of common national welfare they should help each other, keep away from quarrel-mongering, obey their leaders and avoid wasting their energies in bickerings over trivial things. Such feuds and schisms are a disgrace to a Muslim community and a potential source of national weakness and must be shunned at all costs.

Notes: *This statement is an excerpt from the book* Towards Understanding Islam *(1963) by Sayyed Abul A'La Maudoodi, and represents a Sunni Muslim perspective (which has perhaps 3,000,000 followers in the United States). Men and women are advised to always be modestly dressed and to avoid "entertainments and recreations as tend to stimulate sensual passions." Such activities are harmful to good morals and "can have no place in Islamic society and culture."*

UNITARIAN UNIVERSALIST ASSOCIATION

CENSORSHIP AND OBSCENITY LAWS (1974)

WHEREAS, US Supreme Court decisions announced on June 24, 1974 have returned the Supreme Court to a case-by-case determination of what is deemed obscene and have thereby reinstated a process which inevitably results in great uncertainty in that area; and

WHEREAS, the Supreme Court on June 24 sanctioned the application by federal jurors of their own view of what the average person in the community deems to be obscene, with the result that written and visual material must now be tailored to the standard of the most repressive locality or run the risk of being banned or confiscated; and

WHEREAS, in numerous states during the past three months there have been widespread introduction and consideration of repressive obscenity laws;

BE IT RESOLVED: That the 1974 General Assembly of the Unitarian Universalist Association:

1. Expresses deep concern at the trend of the recent decisions of the US Supreme Court toward case-by-case determination;

2. Opposes the repressive trend in recent state censorship legislation; and

3. Strongly affirms the right of adults to decide what they should read, hear, and see free from official censorship, as has been recommended by the President's Commission on Obscenity and Pornography.

Notes: *The cases referred to in this 1974 resolution by the Unitarian Universalist Association (approximately 174,000 members) are* Hamling et al. vs. United States, *in which the petitioners were convicted of mailing an obscene brochure, and* Jenkins vs. Georgia, *in which Jenkins was charged with obscenity for showing "Carnal Knowledge" in a movie theater. Jenkins was cleared when the Court ruled the film was not obscene, but the Court also ruled that "community standards" for judging obscenity need not be derived from a specified size of community." The Unitarian Universalist Association supports the recommendation of the 1970 Commission on Obscenity and Pornography that adults should be free to decide "what they should read, hear and see."*

Acknowledgments

"A Statement on Censorship." Reprinted with permission of the U.S. Catholic Conference. (copyright © 1957 by the United States Catholic Conference; Washington, D.C.).

"Resolution on Indecent Literature." Reprinted with permission of the U.S. Catholic Conference. (copyright © 1932 by the United States Catholic Conference; Washington, D.C.).

"Statement on the Introduction of the Family Viewing Period During Prime Time by the Television Networks." Reprinted with permission of the U.S. Catholic Conference. (copyright © 1975 by the United States Catholic Conference; Washington, D.C.).

"Towards Understanding Islam." Reprinted with permission of Idara Tarjuman-ul-Quran (Pvt.) Ltd., from *Towards Understanding Islam*, pp. 182-184.

Index to Organizations, Statements, and Subjects

Citations in this index refer to page numbers; page numbers rendered in boldface after an organization name indicate the location of that organization's statement(s) within the main text.

Index to Organizations, Statements, and Subjects